EMPLOYMENT LAW

An Introduction

AUSTRALIA
Law Book Co.
Sydney

CANADA and USA
Carswell
Toronto

HONG KONG
Sweet & Maxwell Asia

NEW ZEALAND
Brookers
Wellington

SINGAPORE and MALAYSIA
Sweet & Maxwell Asia
Singapore and Kuala Lumpur

EMPLOYMENT LAW

An Introduction

By

Victor Craig

Professor of Employment Law and Head of Division of Management, Heriot Watt University

and

Susan Walker

Lecturer in Law, Heriot Watt University

THOMSON

W. GREEN

First edition published in 2001
Second edition published in 2005

W. Green & Son Ltd
21 Alva Street
Edinburgh EH2 4PS

www.wgreen.thomson.com

Typeset by YHT Ltd., London
Printed and bound in Great Britain by MPG Books, Bodmin

No natural forests were destroyed to make this product;
only farmed timber was used and replanted

A CIP catalogue record for this book is available from
the British Library.

ISBN 978-0-414-01701-6

PREFACE

This brief guide to employment law is intended for students of law and other disciplines but may also be useful for lawyers and HR practitioners seeking an introduction to this complex area. It tries to cover the elements of modern employment law but it is not intended to be a comprehensive statement of employment law. By incorporating details of some cases it is hoped that the reader will develop a better understanding of the subject area and be able to apply the principles to such practical situations as are described in the sample questions at the end of each chapter. It is expected that the reader will attempt an answer and then compare that answer with the suggested answers in the Appendix.

This third edition adheres to the format of the previous editions but reflects the continued developments in this rapidly changing area. The new Transfer of Undertakings (Protection of Employment) Regulations 2006 and the Employment Equality (Age) Regulations 2006 are covered in some detail although the latter has not, as yet, given rise to the avalanche of case law that was predicted. Conversely the Employment Act 2002 (Dispute Resolution) Regulations 2004, which were about to come into force at the date of the second edition, have generated a considerable amount of case law. This, of course, is quite contrary to the intention behind the Regulations, namely to reduce the number of claims proceeding to employment tribunals. Such has been the criticism of these Regulations that the Government commissioned a wide-ranging review of Dispute Resolution in the Workplace which was carried out by Michael Gibbons and reported in March 2007. In light of his report, the Government is now consulting on whether the 2004 Regulations should be amended or repealed and change is likely to take place soon. Nonetheless, important cases regarding these Regulations have been included in this edition

The authors are grateful to Karen Fullerton and Bronwyn Spicer of W.Green & Son Ltd for their help in the production and the format of the text, but the authors alone are responsible for its content. The law is stated as at 1 September 2007.

CONTENTS

	Page
Preface	v
Table of Abbreviations	xiii
Table of Cases	xv
Table of Statutes	xxxiii
Table of Statutory Instruments	xxxvii
Table of Treaties Conventions	xli
Table of European Secondary Legislation	xliii

1. THE CONTRACT OF EMPLOYMENT

Introduction to Contract and Employment Law	1
Common Law and Statute	1
European Law	3
The Courts and Employment Tribunals	7
Why is Employment Law Important Today?	9
Legal Abstentionism	10
Practical Results for Employers and Workers	11
Why do we Need to Identify the Contract of Employment and other Contracts	12
The Employment Contract—Control and other Tests	13
Multiple and Variable Test	15
Casual and Atypical Workers	17
Personal Service	21
Name of Contract	22
The Worker and the Agency Worker	23
Agency Workers	25
Law or Fact	31
Employment Pr *Pro Hac Viceo Hac Vice*	32
Special Working Relationships	33
Apprenticeship Contracts	33
Company Directors	35
Public Employment	38
European Directives and Employees of the State	39
Civil Servants and Office Holders	40
Formation of the Contract of Employment	43
Exceptions and Special Cases	43
Implied Contracts	44
Written Statement of Particulars	45
The Terms of the Statement	45
The Employee's Remedy	47

Legal Status of Written Statement 47
Written Contracts of Employment 49
Collective Agreements 50
Legal Effect of Collective Agreements 52
Incorporation of Collective Agreements 53
Mechanics of Incorporation 53
Incorporation and Union Membership 56
Collective Agreements and Rules 59
Agency 60

2. TERMS AND CONDITIONS OF EMPLOYMENT

Contract or Statute 66
Express and Implied Contractual Terms 67
Wages 68
The Wages Act 1986 72
Excluded Deductions 74
Pay in Lieu of Notice 75
Recovering Unlawful Deductions 78
National Minimum Wage 79
Enforcement 81
Hours of Work and Time Off 81
Working Time 82
Time Off Rights 89
Other Contractual Terms and Duties 91
Obedience 95
Employer's Duty of Safety 99
Employee's Duty of Careful Performance 101
Employee's Duty of Fidelity 102
Restrictive Covenants 105

3. TERMINATION OF THE CONTRACT AND WRONGFUL DISMISSAL

Termination by Notice 114
The Employment Rights Act 1996 115
Partnership Dissolution 116
Winding Up, Receiverships and Administration Orders 117
Frustration 118
Rescission 121
Termination by Performance and Passage of Time ... 122
Agreement 122
Wrongful Dismissal 123
Remedies 124
Damages 128

4. UNFAIR DISMISSAL

Introduction 139
Wrongful Dismissal and Unfair Dismissal 139
Who is Protected against Unfair Dismissal? 140

Continuous Employment 143
What is Dismissal? 144
Termination of Contract by Employer with or without Notice 144
Expiry of Limited Term Contract without Renewal 146
Constructive Dismissal 147
Resignation which is Genuine and Intended 149
Operation of Law (Frustration) 149
Statutory Procedures 150
The Reason for Dismissal 152
The Fair Reasons 152
Retirement Dismissals 157
Admissible Evidence 160
What is the Effect of Polkey Now? 162
Appeals 165
Redundancy 166
Special Situations 168
Industrial Action and Lock-Outs 168
Union Membership and Activities 170
Union Recognition Dismissals 174
Health and Safety Dismissals 174
Asserting a Statutory Right 176
Pregnancy and Family Leave 177
Whistle-Blowing 178
Jury Service 180
Other Special Cases 180
Remedies for Unfair Dismissal 181
Interim Relief 185

5. REDUNDANCY PAYMENTS AND TRANSFERS OF UNDERTAKINGS

Introduction 195
General Principles 196
Dismissal 197
Volunteers for Redundancy 198
Redundancy 199
Hours of Work 202
Bumping 204
Renewal and Re-engagement 206
Misconduct and Strikes 208
The Onus of Proof 208
Making the Claim 208
Exclusions 209
Payments 209
Transfer of an Undertaking 210
Introduction 210
Relevant Transfer 211
Is There an Undertaking? 213
Is There a Transfer? 213

The Effect of the Regulations 214
Economic, Technical or Organisational Reasons .. 215
Who are Protected against Unfair Dismissal? 215
What is the Reason for the Dismissal? 216
Changing the Terms of Employees 216
Dismissal and Re-engagement by the Transferee .. 217
Pension Rights 218

6. DISCRIMINATION

Sex, Pregnancy and Marital Status 222
Genuine Occupational Qualifications and Positive Discrimination 227
Indirect Discrimination 231
Victimisation 233
Employment Discrimination 234
Dress Codes and Sexual Harassment 235
Gender Re-assignment 237
Race Discrimination 239
Racial Grounds 241
Indirect Discrimination 243
Genuine Occupational Qualifications and Positive Discrimination 244
Sexual Orientation 245
Genuine Occupational Requirements and Positive Action 246
Religion or Belief 247
Genuine Occupational Requirements and Positive Action 250
Disability 251
Definition of Disability 252
Employment Discrimination 254
Disability Discrimination Act in Action 257
Enforcement and Remedies 260
Onus of Proof 262
Vicarious Liability 262
Part-time Workers 264
Fixed Term Contracts 268
Age Discrimination 269
Discrimination in Employment and Vocational Training 270
Retirement 271
Miscellaneous other Exceptions 272
Equal Pay 272
The Three Entitlements 273
Like Work 273
Work Rated Equivalent 274
Equal Value 274
Genuine Material Factor 275
Time Limits 278

Same Employment 279
Remedies 280
European Community Law 281
Scope of Art.141 281
Statutory Rights for Working Parents 283
Pregnant Workers 283

7. INSTITUTIONS OF EMPLOYMENT LAW

Introduction 292
Employment Tribunals 293
Procedure 293
Composition of Tribunal 296
Dispute Resolution Procedure 298
Appeal against Tribunal Decisions 302
Advisory Conciliation and Arbitration Service (ACAS) 303

Appendix A (ET1) 306
Appendix B (ET3) 315

Index 321

TABLE OF ABRREVIATIONS

Acts

DDA	Disability Discrimination Act 1995
Employment Rights Act	Employment Rights Act 1996
EPA	Equal Pay Act 1970
NMWA	National Minimum Wage Act 1998
RRA	Race Relations Act 1976
SDA	Sex Discrimination Act 1975
TUL(C)A	Trade Union and Labour Relations (Consolidation) Act 1992

Regulations

NMWR	National Minimum Wage Regulations 1999 (SI 1999/584)
TUPE	Transfer of Undertakings (Protection of Employment) Regulations 1981 (SI 1981/1794)
WTR	Working Time Regulations 1998 (SI 1998/1833)

Courts and Tribunals

CA	Court of Appeal
EAT	Employment Appeal Tribunal
ECHR	European Court of Human Rights
ECJ	European Court of Justice
ET	Employment Tribunal
HL	House of Lords
IH	Inner House of the Court of Session
OH	Outer House of the Court of Session

Case Reports

A.C.	Appeal Cases (Law Reports-House of Lords and Privy Council)
All E.R.	All England Law Reports
I.C.R.	Industrial Cases Reports
I.R.L.R.	Industrial Relations Law Reports
I.T.R.	Industrial Tribunal Reports
S.C.	Session Cases (Court of Session Reports)
S.L.T.	Scots Law Times
W.L.R.	Weekly Law Reports

General

ACAS	Advisory Conciliation and Arbitration Service
CRE	Commission for Racial Equality
DRC	Disability Rights Commission
EDT	Effective Date of Termination
EOC	Equal Opportunities Commission
ITU	Independent Trade Union
SMP	Statutory Maternity Pay
SSP	Statutory Sick Pay

TABLE OF CASES

A v Chief Constable of West Yorkshire. *See* Chief Constable of West Yorkshire v A

A Links & Co Ltd v Rose, 1993 S.L.T. 209; [1991] I.R.L.R. 353, IH (1 Div) 4–15, 4–27

A&D Bedrooms Ltd v Michael 1984 S.L.T. 297, OH 2–41

Abrahams v Performing Right Society [1995] I.C.R. 1028; [1995] I.R.L.R. 486, CA (Civ Div) 3–16

Addis v Gramophone Co Ltd [1909] A.C. 488, HL 3–14

Adin v Sedco Forex International Resources Ltd [1997] I.R.L.R. 280; 1997 G.W.D. 6-223, OH 2–1

Advocate General for Scotland v MacDonald; Pearce v Mayfield Secondary School Governing Body; sub nom. MacDonald v Ministry of Defence; Secretary of State for Defence v MacDonald; MacDonald v Advocate General for Scotland [2003] UKHL 34; [2004] 1 All E.R. 339; 2003 S.C. (H.L.) 35; 2003 S.L.T. 1158; 2003 S.C.L.R. 814; [2003] I.C.R. 937; [2003] I.R.L.R. 512; [2003] E.L.R. 655; (2003) 100(29) L.S.G. 36; (2003) 147 S.J.L.B. 782; 2003 G.W.D. 23-677, HL 6–9, 6–18

Agma Chemical Co Ltd v Hart, 1984 S.L.T. 246, IH (1 Div) 2–42

Ahmad v United Kingdom (8160/78) (1982) 4 E.H.R.R. 126, Eur Comm HR 6–20

Alcan Extrusions v Yates [1996] I.R.L.R. 327, EAT 4–7

Alexander v Standard Telephones & Cables Ltd (No.1); Wall v Standard Telephones & Cables Ltd (No.1) [1990] I.C.R. 291; [1990] I.R.L.R. 55, Ch D 1–40, 1–42

Alexander v Standard Telephones & Cables Ltd (No.2); Wall v Standard Telephones & Cables Ltd (No.2) [1991] I.R.L.R. 286, Ch D 1–40

Ali v Southwark LBC [1988] I.C.R. 567; [1988] I.R.L.R. 100, Ch D 3–11

Allen v Thomas Scott & Sons Bakers Ltd; sub nom. Thomas Scott & Sons Bakers Ltd v Allen [1983] I.R.L.R. 329, CA (Civ Div) 2–23

Allinson v Drew Simmons Engineering [1985] I.C.R. 488, EAT 5–4

Allonby v Accrington and Rossendale College (C256/01) [2005] All E.R. (EC) 289; [2004] E.C.R. I-873; [2004] 1 C.M.L.R. 35; [2004] I.C.R. 1328; [2004] I.R.L.R. 224; [2004] O.P.L.R. 83; [2004] Pens. L.R. 199, ECJ ... 1–03, 6–52

Anderson v Pringle of Scotland Ltd, 1998 S.L.T. 754; [1998] I.R.L.R. 64; 1997 G.W.D. 40-2033, OH 3–12

Aramark Plc v Sommerville 1995 S.L.T. 749, OH 2–42

Archibald v Fife Council [2004] UKHL 32; [2004] 4 All E.R. 303; 2004 S.C. (H.L.) 117; 2004 S.L.T. 942; 2004 S.C.L.R. 971; [2004] I.C.R. 954; [2004] I.R.L.R. 651; (2005) 82 B.M.L.R. 185; (2004) 101(31) L.S.G. 25; (2004) 148 S.J.L.B. 826; 2004 G.W.D. 23-505, HL 6–28

Archibald v Rossleigh Commercials [1975] I.R.L.R. 231, IT 5–7

Armstrong v Newcastle upon Tyne NHS Hospital Trust [2005] EWCA Civ 1608; [2006] I.R.L.R. 124, CA (Civ Div) 6–50

Associated Newspapers Ltd v Wilson; Associated British Ports v Palmer; sub nom. Wilson v Associated Newspapers Ltd [1995] 2 A.C. 454; [1995] 2 W.L.R. 354; [1995] 2 All E.R. 100; [1995] I.C.R. 406; [1995] I.R.L.R. 258; (1995) 92(17) L.S.G. 48; (1995) 145 N.L.J. 417; (1995) 139 S.J.L.B. 110, HL 4–37

Associated Tunnelling Co v Wasilewski [1973] I.R.L.R. 346; [1973] I.T.R. 651, NIRC ... 2–35
Atbury v Gist Ltd (EAT 0619/06) ... 1–18
Attridge Law (A Firm) v Coleman [2007] I.C.R. 654; [2007] I.R.L.R. 88; [2007] 2 C.M.L.R. 24, EAT ... 6–23
Azmi v Kirklees MBC [2007] I.R.L.R. 484, EAT ... 6–21

BBC v BECKETT [1983] I.R.L.R. 43, EAT ... 4–9
BBC v Farnworth [1998] I.C.R. 1116, EAT ... 5–7
BBC Scotland v Souster, 2001 S.C. 458; [2001] I.R.L.R. 150; 2000 G.W.D. 40-1490, IH (Ex Div) ... 6–15
BSM (1257) Ltd v Secretary of State for Social Services [1978] I.C.R. 894, QBD ... 1–16
Banks v Viroy Cleaning Services Ltd (ET Case No.17934/84, unreported) ... 6–4
Barber v Guardian Royal Exchange Assurance Group (C262/88) [1991] 1 Q.B. 344; [1991] 2 W.L.R. 72; [1990] 2 All E.R. 660; [1990] E.C.R. I-1889; [1990] 2 C.M.L.R. 513; [1990] I.C.R. 616; [1990] I.R.L.R. 240; [1990] 1 P.L.R. 103; (1990) 140 N.L.J. 925, ECJ ... 5–2
Barber v Guardian Royal Exchange Assurance Group; Roberts v Tate & Lyle Food and Distribution Ltd [1983] I.C.R. 521; [1983] I.R.L.R. 240, EAT ... 6–55
Barber v Somerset CC Baker Refractories Ltd v Bishop; Sutherland v Hatton; Sandwell MBC v Jones; sub nom:. Jones v Sandwell MBC; Hatton v Sutherland; Bishop v Baker Refractories Ltd; Somerset CC v Barber [2004] UKHL 13; [2004] 1 W.L.R. 1089; [2004] 2 All E.R. 385; [2004] I.C.R. 457; [2004] I.R.L.R. 475; [2004] E.L.R. 199; [2004] P.I.Q.R. P31; (2004) 77 B.M.L.R. 219; (2004) 101(18) L.S.G. 34; (2004) 148 S.J.L.B. 419, HL ... 30–36
Barber v Staffordshire CC [1996] I.C.R. 379; [1996] I.R.L.R. 209; (1996) 140 S.J.L.B. 43, CA (Civ Div) ... 6–55
Barclay v Glasgow City Council [1983] I.R.L.R. 313, EAT ... 4–7
Bashir v Brillo Manufacturing Co [1979] I.R.L.R. 295, EAT ... 3–7
Bass Leisure Ltd v Thomas [1994] I.R.L.R. 104, EAT ... 5–6
Bateman v British Leyland (UK) [1974] I.C.R. 403; [1974] I.R.L.R. 101; 16 K.I.R. 284; [1974] I.T.R. 266, NIRC ... 4–50
Beedell v West Ferry Printers Ltd [2001] EWCA Civ 400; [2001] C.P. Rep. 83; [2001] I.C.R. 962, CA (Civ Div) ... 4–23
Berlitz Schools of Languages Ltd v Duchene (1903) 11 S.L.T. 491, IH (1 Div) ... 3–3
Berriman v Delabole Slate Ltd; sub nom. Delabole Slate Ltd v Berriman [1985] I.C.R. 546; [1985] I.R.L.R. 305, CA (Civ Div) ... 5–21, 5–24
Bilka-Kaufhaus GmbH v Weber von Hartz (170/84) [1986] E.C.R. 1607; [1986] 2 C.M.L.R. 701; [1987] I.C.R. 110; [1986] I.R.L.R. 317, ECJ ... 6–6
Birch v University of Liverpool. *See* University of Liverpool v Humber and Birch
Bisset v Martins, UKEATS/0022/06/RN, UKEATS/0023/06/RN, EAT (SC) ... 7–11
Bladon v ALM Medical Services Ltd; sub nom. ALM Medical Services Ltd v Bladon [2002] EWCA Civ 1085; [2002] I.C.R. 1444; [2002] I.R.L.R. 807; [2002] Emp. L.R. 1054; (2002) 99(38) L.S.G. 33; (2002) 146 S.J.L.B. 199, CA (Civ Div) ... 4–43
Bluebell Apparel Ltd v Dickinson, 1978 S.C. 16; 1980 S.L.T. 157, IH (1 Div) ... 2–41
Borders RC v Maule [1993] I.R.L.R. 199, EAT ... 2–24
Bouchaala v Trusthouse Forte Hotels Ltd [1980] I.C.R. 721; [1980] I.R.L.R. 382, EAT ... 4–19
Bowden v Tuffnells Parcels Express Ltd (C133/00); sub nom. Bowden v Tufnells Parcels Express Ltd (C133/00) [2001] All E.R. (EC) 865; [2001] E.C.R. I-7031; [2001] 3 C.M.L.R. 52; [2001] I.R.L.R. 838; [2002] Emp. L.R. 1, ECJ (1st Chamber) ... 2–15

British Airways Plc v Boyce, 2001 S.C. 510; [2001] I.R.L.R. 157; 2000 G.W.D. 40-1489, IH (Ex Div) 6–15
British Home Stores Ltd v Burchell [1980] I.C.R. 303; [1978] I.R.L.R. 379; (1978) 13 I.T.R. 560, EAT 4–28
British Steel Corporation v Dingwall, 1976 S.L.T. 230 1–31
Brookes v Borough Care Services [1998] I.C.R. 1198; [1998] I.R.L.R. 636, EAT 5–17
Brown v Knowsley BC [1986] I.R.L.R. 102, EAT 3–8
Brown v Southall & Knight [1980] I.C.R. 617; [1980] I.R.L.R. 130, EAT ... 4–7
Bruce v National Coal Board [1967] I.T.R. 159 5–9
Bruce v Wiggins Teape (Stationery) Ltd [1994] I.R.L.R. 536, EAT 2–7
Brunnhofer v Bank der Osterreichischen Postsparkasse AG (C381/99) [2001] All E.R. (EC) 693; [2001] E.C.R. I-4961; [2001] 3 C.M.L.R. 9; [2001] I.R.L.R. 571; [2001] Emp. L.R. 1176, ECJ (6th Chamber) 6–50
Buchan v Secretary of State for Employment; Ivey v Secretary of State for Employment [1997] B.C.C. 145; [1997] I.R.L.R. 80, EAT 1–24
Bull v Pitney Bowes Ltd [1967] 1 W.L.R. 273; [1966] 3 All E.R. 384; 1 K.I.R. 342; (1967) 111 S.J. 32, QBD 2–41
Burton v Pinkerton (1866-67) L.R. 2 Ex. 340, Ex Ct 2–35
Bushaway v R.N.L.I.. *See* Royal National Lifeboat Institution v Bushaway
Butler v Dillon, 87 I.L.T. 95 1–22
Byrne Bros (Formwork) Ltd v Baird; sub nom. Baird v Byrne Bros (Formwork) Ltd [2002] I.C.R. 667; [2002] I.R.L.R. 96; [2002] Emp. L.R. 567, EAT 1–17

CRE v Precision Manufacturing Services Ltd (ET Case No.4106/91, unreported 6–14
Cable & Wireless Plc v Muscat; sub nom. Muscat v Cable & Wireless Plc [2006] EWCA Civ 220; [2006] I.C.R. 975; [2006] I.R.L.R. 354; (2006) 103(12) L.S.G. 30; (2006) 150 S.J.L.B. 362, CA (Civ Div) 1–19
Cadman v Health and Safety Executive (C17/05) [2007] All E.R. (EC) 1; [2006] E.C.R. I-9583; [2007] 1 C.M.L.R. 16; [2007] C.E.C. 318; [2006] I.C.R. 1623; [2006] I.R.L.R. 969, ECJ 6–41
Cadoux v Central RC, 1986 S.L.T. 117; [1986] I.R.L.R. 131, OH 1–43
Cahuc, Johnson & Crouch v Amery (Allen), 1 K.I.R. 254; [1966] I.T.R. 313, IT 5–9
Cairns v Visteon UK Ltd [2007] I.C.R. 616; [2007] I.R.L.R. 175, EAT 1–02
Caledonian Mining Co v Bassett [1987] I.C.R. 425; [1987] I.R.L.R. 165, EAT 4–7, 5–4
Cameron v Gibb, 1967 3 S.L.R. 282 2–39
Carmichael v National Power Plc [1999] 1 W.L.R. 2042; [1999] 4 All E.R. 897; [1999] I.C.R. 1226; [2000] I.R.L.R. 43; (1999) 96(46) L.S.G. 38; (1999) 143 S.J.L.B. 281, HL 1–14, 1–20
Cartin v Botley Garages [1973] I.C.R. 144; (1972) 14 K.I.R. 203; [1973] I.T.R. 150, NIRC 5–11
Cassidy v Ministry of Health [1951] 2 K.B. 343; [1951] 1 All E.R. 574; [1951] 1 T.L.R. 539; (1952) 96 S.J. 253; (1951) 95 S.J. 253, CA 1–11
Cerberus Software Ltd v Rowley; sub nom. Rowley v Cerberus Software Ltd [2001] EWCA Civ 78; [2001] I.C.R. 376; [2001] I.R.L.R. 160; [2001] Emp. L.R. 173, CA (Civ Div) 3–16
Cheesman v R Brewer Contracts Ltd [2001] I.R.L.R. 144; [2001] Emp. L.R. 143, EAT 5–17
Chief Constable of Lincolnshire v Stubbs [1999] I.C.R. 547; [1999] I.R.L.R. 81, EAT 6–32
Chief Constable of West Yorkshire v A; sub nom. A v Chief Constable of West Yorkshire [2004] UKHL 21; [2005] 1 A.C. 51; [2004] 2 W.L.R. 1209; [2004] 3 All E.R. 145; [2004] 2 C.M.L.R. 37; [2004] Eu. L.R. 841; [2004] I.C.R. 806; [2004] I.R.L.R. 573; [2004] 2 F.C.R. 160; [2004] H.R.L.R. 25; [2004] U.K.H.R.R. 694; 17 B.H.R.C. 585; (2004) 101(20) L.S.G. 34; (2004) 154 N.L.J. 734; (2004) 148 S.J.L.B. 572, HL 6–11

Chief Constable of West Yorkshire v Khan; sub nom. Khan v Chief Constable of West Yorkshire [2001] UKHL 48; [2001] 1 W.L.R. 1947; [2001] 4 All E.R. 834; [2001] I.C.R. 1065; [2001] I.R.L.R. 830; [2001] Emp. L.R. 1399; (2001) 98(42) L.S.G. 37; (2001) 145 S.J.L.B. 230, HL 6–3
Clark v Oxfordshire HA [1998] I.R.L.R. 125; (1998) 41 B.M.L.R. 18, CA (Civ Div) 1–13, 1–4
Clark v TDG Ltd (t/a Novacold Ltd); sub nom. Clark v Novacold Ltd [1999] 2 All E.R. 977; [1999] I.C.R. 951; [1999] I.R.L.R. 318; [1999] Disc. L.R. 240; (1999) 48 B.M.L.R. 1, CA (Civ Div) 6–27, 6–28
Clydesdale Bank Beatson (1882) 10 R 88 2–37
Commission for Racial Equality v Dutton [1989] Q.B. 783; [1989] 2 W.L.R. 17; [1989] 1 All E.R. 306; [1989] I.R.L.R. 8; (1989) 133 S.J. 19, CA (Civ Div) 6–14
Commotion Ltd v Rutty [2006] I.C.R. 290; [2006] I.R.L.R. 171, EAT 7–11
Condor v The Barron Knights Ltd [1966] 1 W.L.R. 87; (1966) 110 S.J. 71, Assizes (Bedford) 3–5
Coopsey v WWB Devon Clays Ltd [2003] IDS Brief 767 6–20
Coors Brewers Ltd v Adcock [2007] EWCA Civ 19; [2007] I.R.L.R. 440; (2007) 151 S.J.L.B. 160, CA (Civ Div) 2–11
Craigie v Haringey LBC, UKEAT/0556/06/JOJ, EAT 1–02, 1–19
Crawford v Swinton Insurance Brokers Ltd [1990] I.C.R. 85; [1990] I.R.L.R. 42, EAT 5–21
Croft v Royal Mail Group Plc (formerly Consignia Plc) [2003] EWCA Civ 1045; [2003] I.C.R. 1425; [2003] I.R.L.R. 592; [2003] H.R.L.R. 34; (2003) 147 S.J.L.B. 904, CA (Civ Div) 6–11
Crown Suppliers (PSA) v Dawkins. *See* Dawkins v Crown Suppliers (PSA)
Currie v Glasgow Central Stores Ltd (1905) 13 S.L.T. 88, IH (2 Div) 2–39

DACAS V BROOK STREET BUREAU (UK) LTD; SUB NOM. BROOK STREET BUREAU (UK) LTD V DACAS [2004] EWCA Civ 217; [2004] I.C.R. 1437; [2004] I.R.L.R. 358, CA (Civ Div) 1–02, 1–19, 1–30
Davies v Presbyterian Church of Wales [1986] 1 W.L.R. 323; [1986] 1 All E.R. 705; [1986] I.C.R. 280; [1986] I.R.L.R. 194; (1986) 83 L.S.G. 968; (1986) 130 S.J. 203, HL 1–20
Dawkins v Crown Suppliers (PSA); sub nom. Crown Suppliers (PSA) v Dawkins [1993] I.C.R. 517; [1993] I.R.L.R. 284, CA (Civ Div) 6–14
Day v Tait (Liquidators of Pattisons Ltd.) (1900) 8 S.L.T. 40, OH 3–4
De Grasse v Stockwell Tools [1992] I.R.L.R. 269, EAT 4–31
Degnan v Redcar and Cleveland BC. *See* Redcar and Cleveland BC v Degnan
Dekker v Stichting Vormingscentrum voor Jonge Volwassenen Plus (177/88) [1990] E.C.R. I-3941; [1992] I.C.R. 325; [1991] I.R.L.R. 27, ECJ 6–2
Delaney v Staples (t/a De Montfort Recruitment) [1992] 1 A.C. 687; [1992] 2 W.L.R. 451; [1992] 1 All E.R. 944; [1992] I.C.R. 483; [1992] I.R.L.R. 191; (1992) 142 N.L.J. 384, HL 2–10, 3–2
Dellas v Premier Ministre (C14/04); sub nom. Dellas v Secretariat General du Gouvernement (C14/04) [2005] E.C.R. I-10253; [2006] 2 C.M.L.R. 2; [2006] C.E.C. 328; [2006] I.R.L.R. 225, ECJ (2nd Chamber) 2–16
Department for Work and Pensions v Thompson [2004] I.R.L.R. 348, EAT . 6–9
Devonald v Rosser & Sons [1906] 2 K.B. 728 2–3
Discount Tobacco & Confectionery Ltd v Armitage [1995] I.C.R. 431; [1990] I.R.L.R. 15, EAT 4–37
Distillers Co (Bottling Services) v Gardner [1982] I.R.L.R. 47, EAT 4–28
Dixon v BBC; BBC v Constanti; Throsby v Imperial College of Science and Technology; Gwent CC v Lane; sub nom. BBC v Dixon [1979] Q.B. 546; [1979] 2 W.L.R. 647; [1979] 2 All E.R. 112; [1979] I.C.R. 281; [1979] I.R.L.R. 114; (1978) 122 S.J. 713, CA (Civ Div) 4–8, 5–11
Draper v Mears Ltd [2006] I.R.L.R. 869, EAT 7–11
Duke v GEC Reliance Ltd; sub nom. Duke v Reliance Systems Ltd [1988] A.C. 618; [1988] 2 W.L.R. 359; [1988] 1 All E.R. 626; [1988] 1 C.M.L.R.

719; [1988] I.C.R. 339; [1988] I.R.L.R. 118; [1988] 1 F.T.L.R. 398; (1988) 85(11) L.S.G. 42; (1988) 132 S.J. 226, HL 1–03
Duke v Reliance Systems Ltd. *See* Duke v GEC Reliance Ltd
Dunbar v Baillie Brothers, 1990 G.W.D. 26-1487 3–6
Dundon v GPT Ltd [1995] I.R.L.R. 403, EAT 4–38
Dunk v George Waller & Son [1970] 2 Q.B. 163; [1970] 2 W.L.R. 1241; [1970] 2 All E.R. 630; (1970) 114 S.J. 356, CA (Civ Div) 1–23
Dunlop RSA (IT Case No. S/3696/76), unreported 6–3

East Lindsey DC v Daubney [1977] I.C.R. 566; [1977] I.R.L.R. 181; (1977) 12 I.T.R. 359, EAT 4–27
East Riding of Yorkshire Council v Gibson; sub nom. Gibson v East Riding of Yorkshire DC [2000] 3 C.M.L.R. 329; [2000] I.C.R. 890; [2000] I.R.L.R. 598, CA (Civ Div) 1–03, 1–26
Eclipse Blinds Ltd v Wright [1992] I.R.L.R. 133 4–27
Edinburgh City Council v Brown [1999] I.R.L.R. 208, EAT 1–37, 1–40
Edmonds v Lawson; Edmunds v Lawson [2000] Q.B. 501; [2000] 2 W.L.R. 1091; [2000] I.C.R. 567; [2000] I.R.L.R. 391; (2000) 97(14) L.S.G. 42; (2000) 144 S.J.L.B. 151, CA (Civ Div) 1–23
Edwards v Skyways [1964] 1 W.L.R. 349; [1964] 1 All E.R. 494; (1964) 108 S.J. 279, QBD 1–44
Edwards v Surrey Police [1999] I.R.L.R. 456, EAT 3–7
Enessy Co SA (t/a Tulchan Estate) v Minoprio [1978] I.R.L.R. 489, EAT ... 4–47
Equal Opportunities Commission v Secretary of State for Trade and Industry [2007] EWHC 483 (Admin); [2007] I.R.L.R. 327; (2007) 104(13) L.S.G. 25, QBD (Admin) 6–10
Etam v Rowan [1989] I.R.L.R. 150, EAT 6–4
Express & Echo Publications Ltd v Tanton [1999] I.C.R. 693; [1999] I.R.L.R. 367; (1999) 96(14) L.S.G. 31, CA (Civ Div) 1–15

FC Shepherd & Co v Jerrom [1987] Q.B. 301; [1986] 3 W.L.R. 801; [1986] 3 All E.R. 589; [1986] I.C.R. 802; [1986] I.R.L.R. 358; (1986) 130 S.J. 665, CA (Civ Div) 3–5, 4–11
Faccenda Chicken Ltd v Fowler; Fowler v Faccenda Chicken Ltd [1987] Ch. 117; [1986] 3 W.L.R. 288; [1986] 1 All E.R. 617; [1986] I.C.R. 297; [1986] I.R.L.R. 69; [1986] F.S.R. 291; (1986) 83 L.S.G. 288; (1986) 136 N.L.J. 71; (1986) 130 S.J. 573, CA (Civ Div) 2–38, 2–40
Farrell Matthews & Weir v [2005] I.C.R. 509; [2005] I.R.L.R. 160, EAT ... 2–9
Federatie Nederlandse Vakbeweging (FNV) v Netherlands (C124/05) [2006] All E.R. (EC) 913; [2006] E.C.R. I-3423; [2006] 2 C.M.L.R. 46; [2006] C.E.C. 797; [2006] I.C.R. 962; [2006] I.R.L.R. 561, ECJ (1st Chamber) 2–20
Ferguson v Prestwick Circuits [1992] I.R.L.R. 266, EAT 4–31
Ferguson v Telford, Grier & McKay & Co [1967] I.T.R. 387 3–4
Fernandes v Netcom Consultants (UK) Ltd, Case No.648, unreported 4–43
Ferrie v Western DC [1973] I.R.L.R. 162 2–35
Financial Techniques (Planning Services) v Hughes [1981] I.R.L.R. 32, CA (Civ Div) 4–9
Fleming v Xaniar Ltd (In Liquidation), 1998 S.C. 8; 1998 S.L.T. 703; [1997] I.R.L.R. 682; 1997 G.W.D. 31-1582, IH (1 Div) 1–24
Forsyth v Heathery Knowe Coal Company (1880) 7 R 887 3–1
Foster v British Gas Plc (C188/89) [1991] 1 Q.B. 405; [1991] 2 W.L.R. 258; [1990] 3 All E.R. 897; [1990] E.C.R. I-3313; [1990] 2 C.M.L.R. 833; [1991] I.C.R. 84; [1990] I.R.L.R. 353, ECJ 1–26
Foster Bryant Surveying Ltd v Bryant [2007] EWCA Civ 200; [2007] I.R.L.R. 425; [2007] 12 E.G. 154 (C.S.); (2007) 104(13) L.S.G. 24, CA (Civ Div) ... 2–40, 2–41
Founders v St Mary's Convent Preparatory School, unreported, EAT 6–4
Four Seasons Healthcare Ltd (formerly Cotswold Spa Retirement Hotels Ltd) v Maughan [2005] I.R.L.R. 324, EAT 3–6

Francovich v Italy (C6/90); Bonifacti v Italy (C9/90) [1991] E.C.R. I-5357; [1993] 2 C.M.L.R. 66; [1995] I.C.R. 722; [1992] I.R.L.R. 84, ECJ 1–03
Franks v Reuters Ltd [2003] EWCA Civ 417; [2003] I.C.R. 1166; [2003] I.R.L.R. 423; (2003) 100(25) L.S.G. 45; (2003) 147 S.J.L.B. 474, CA (Civ Div) 1–19
Fuller v Lloyds Bank Plc [1991] I.R.L.R. 336, EAT 4–29

GF Sharp & Co Ltd v McMillan [1998] I.R.L.R. 632, EAT 3–2, 3–5
Garland v British Rail Engineering Ltd (12/81) [1982] 2 All E.R. 402; [1982] E.C.R. 359; [1982] 1 C.M.L.R. 696; [1982] I.R.L.R. 111, ECJ 6–55
Gascol Conversions v Mercer [1974] I.C.R. 420; [1974] I.R.L.R. 155; [1975] K.I.R. 149; [1974] I.T.R. 282; (1974) 118 S.J. 219, CA (Civ Div) ... 1–34, 1–35
Gibbons v Associated British Ports [1985] I.R.L.R. 376, QBD 1–42
Gibson v Scottish Ambulance Service, EATS/0052/04, EAT (SC) 6–33
Gill v Ford Motor Co Ltd; Wong v BAE Systems Operations Ltd; sub nom. Ford Motor Co Ltd v Singh [2004] I.R.L.R. 840; (2004) 101(33) L.S.G. 34, EAT 2–8
Gillespie v Northern Health and Social Services Board (C342/93) [1996] All E.R. (EC) 284; [1996] E.C.R. I-475; [1996] 2 C.M.L.R. 969; [1996] I.C.R. 498; [1996] I.R.L.R. 214; (1996) 31 B.M.L.R. 65, ECJ 6–55
Gillick v BP Chemicals Ltd [1993] I.R.L.R. 437, EAT 6–8
Glasgow City Council v Marshall [2000] 1 W.L.R. 333; [2000] 1 All E.R. 641; 2000 S.C. (H.L.) 67; 2000 S.L.T. 429; 2000 S.C.L.R. 889; [2000] I.C.R. 196; [2000] I.R.L.R. 272; (2000) 2 L.G.L.R. 679; [2000] B.L.G.R. 229; (2000) 97(7) L.S.G. 39; (2000) 144 S.J.L.B. 101, HL 6–49, 6–50
Glenboig Union Fireclay Co v Stewart, 1971 S.L.T. (Notes) 27; [1971] I.T.R. 14, IH (1 Div) 5–5
Glendale Managed Services Ltd v Graham; sub nom. Graham v Glendale Managed Services Ltd [2003] EWCA Civ 773; [2003] I.R.L.R. 465, CA (Civ Div) 1–40
Gogay v Hertfordshire CC [2000] I.R.L.R. 703; [2001] 1 F.L.R. 280; [2001] 1 F.C.R. 455; (2001) 3 L.G.L.R. 14; [2000] Fam. Law 883; (2000) 97(37) L.S.G. 40, CA (Civ Div) 3–14
Goodwin v United Kingdom (28957/95) [2002] I.R.L.R. 664; [2002] 2 F.L.R. 487; [2002] 2 F.C.R. 577; (2002) 35 E.H.R.R. 18; 13 B.H.R.C. 120; (2002) 67 B.M.L.R. 199; [2002] Fam. Law 738; (2002) 152 N.L.J. 1171, ECHR 6–12
Graham v R&S Paton Ltd, 1917 S.C. 203; 1917 1 S.L.T. 66, IH (1 Div) 2–38, 2–39
Grant v South West Trains Ltd (C249/96) [1998] All E.R. (EC) 193; [1998] E.C.R. I-621; [1998] 1 C.M.L.R. 993; [1998] C.E.C. 263; [1998] I.C.R. 449; [1998] I.R.L.R. 206; [1998] 1 F.L.R. 839; [1998] 1 F.C.R. 377; 3 B.H.R.C. 578; [1999] Pens. L.R. 69; [1998] Fam. Law 392; (1998) 162 J.P.N. 266, ECJ 6–18
Griffiths v Secretary of State for Social Services [1974] Q.B. 468; [1973] 3 W.L.R. 831; [1973] 3 All E.R. 1184; (1973) 117 S.J. 873, QBD 3–4
Gryf-Lowczowski v Hinchingbrooke Healthcare NHS Trust [2005] EWHC 2407; [2006] I.C.R. 425; [2006] I.R.L.R. 100; [2006] Lloyd's Rep. Med. 199; (2006) 87 B.M.L.R. 46, QBD 3–12

HJ Heinz Co Ltd v Kenrick [2000] I.C.R. 491; [2000] I.R.L.R. 144, EAT . 6–28
HSBC Bank Plc (formerly Midland Bank Plc) v Madden; Foley v Post Office; sub nom. Post Office v Foley; Midland Bank Plc v Madden [2001] 1 All E.R. 550; [2000] I.C.R. 1283; [2000] I.R.L.R. 827, CA (Civ Div) ... 4–23, 4–28
Habib v Elkington & Co [1981] I.R.L.R. 344 7–5
Haden Carrier Ltd v Cowen; sub nom. Cowen v Haden Carrier Ltd [1983] I.C.R. 1; [1982] I.R.L.R. 314; (1982) 126 S.J. 725, CA (Civ Div) 5–5
Hall v Woolston Hall Leisure Ltd [2001] 1 W.L.R. 225; [2000] 4 All E.R. 787; [2001] I.C.R. 99; [2000] I.R.L.R. 578; (2000) 97(24) L.S.G. 39; (2000) 150 N.L.J. 833, CA (Civ Div) 6–8

Hamilton v Futura Ltd [1990] I.R.L.R. 478 1–41
Hampson v Department of Education and Science [1991] 1 A.C. 171; [1990] 3 W.L.R. 42; [1990] 2 All E.R. 513; [1990] I.C.R. 511; [1990] I.R.L.R. 302; (1990) 154 L.G. Rev. 811; (1990) 140 N.L.J. 853; (1990) 134 S.J. 1123, HL 6–6
Hanlon v Allied Breweries (UK) [1975] I.R.L.R. 321, IT 2–4
Harper v Tayside University Hospitals NHS Trust, 2001 G.W.D. 1-50, OH ... 3–12
Harper v Virgin Net Ltd [2004] EWCA Civ 271; [2005] I.C.R. 921; [2004] I.R.L.R. 390; (2004) 101(14) L.S.G. 25; (2004) 148 S.J.L.B. 353, CA (Civ Div) 3–13
Harris v Richard Lawson Autologistics Ltd [2002] EWCA Civ 442; [2002] I.C.R. 765; [2002] I.R.L.R. 476; (2002) 99(18) L.S.G. 36; (2002) 146 S.J.L.B. 99, CA (Civ Div) 1–44
Harris v Towergate London Market Ltd, March 21, 2007, unreported, EAT 7–11
Harrison Bowden Ltd v Bowden [1994] I.C.R. 186, EAT 5–23
Harrods Ltd v Remick; Harrods Ltd v Seely; Elmi v Harrods Ltd [1998] 1 All E.R. 52; [1998] I.C.R. 156; [1997] I.R.L.R. 583, CA (Civ Div) 1–18
Harvest Press Ltd v McCaffrey [1999] I.R.L.R. 778, EAT 4–40
Haseltine Lake & Co v Dowler [1981] I.C.R. 222; [1981] I.R.L.R. 25, EAT . 4–7
Hayward v Cammell Laird Shipbuilders Ltd (No.2) [1988] A.C. 894; [1988] 2 W.L.R. 1134; [1988] 2 All E.R. 257; [1988] 2 C.M.L.R. 528; [1988] I.C.R. 464; [1988] I.R.L.R. 257; (1988) 152 L.G. Rev. 501; (1988) 138 N.L.J. Rep. 133, HL 6–45
Heatherwood and Wexham Park Hospitals NHS Trust v Kulubowila, UKEAT/0633/06/LA, EAT 1–19
Hellyer Bros Ltd v Atkinson [1994] I.R.L.R. 88, CA (Civ Div) 3–9
Helmet Integrated Systems Ltd v Tunnard [2006] EWCA Civ 1735; [2007] I.R.L.R. 126; [2007] F.S.R. 16, CA (Civ Div) 2–40
Hermolle v GCHQ, unreported, EAT 6–4
High Quality Lifestyles Ltd v Watts [2006] I.R.L.R. 850, EAT 6–27
High Table Ltd v Horst [1998] I.C.R. 409; [1997] I.R.L.R. 513; (1997) 94(28) L.S.G. 25; (1997) 141 S.J.L.B. 161, CA (Civ Div) 5–6
Hill v CA Parsons & Co [1972] Ch. 305; [1971] 3 W.L.R. 995; [1971] 3 All E.R. 1345; (1971) 115 S.J. 868, CA (Civ Div) 3–1
Hillingdon LBC v Morgan, unreported, 1998, EAT 6–28
Hinton & Higgs Ltd v Murphy [1989] I.R.L.R. 519 2–41
Hivac Ltd v Park Royal Scientific Instruments Ltd [1946] Ch. 169, CA 2–39
Hoey v McEwan & Auld (1867) 5 M 814 .... 3–3, 3–5
Holc-Gale v Makers UK Ltd [2006] I.C.R. 462; [2006] I.R.L.R. 178, EAT ... 7–11
Hollister v National Farmers Union [1979] I.C.R. 542; [1979] I.R.L.R. 238, CA (Civ Div) 4–20
Hone v Six Continents Retail Ltd [2005] EWCA Civ 922; [2006] I.R.L.R. 49, CA (Civ Div) 2–21, 2–36
Hugh-Jones v St John's College (Cambridge) [1979] I.C.R. 848; (1979) 123 S.J. 603, EAT 6–8
Hulse v G Embey Ltd (EAT 400/77) 1–40
Hussman Manufacturing Ltd v Weir [1998] I.R.L.R. 288; (1998) 95(31) L.S.G. 34, EAT 2–7

Ibex Trading Co Ltd v Walton [1994] B.C.C. 982; [1994] I.C.R. 907; [1994] I.R.L.R. 564, EAT 5–23
Iceland Frozen Foods Ltd v Jones [1983] I.C.R. 17; [1982] I.R.L.R. 439; (1982) 79 L.S.G. 1257, EAT 4–23
Initial Services v Putterill [1968] 1 Q.B. 396; [1967] 3 W.L.R. 1032; [1967] 3 All E.R. 145; 2 K.I.R. 863; (1967) 111 S.J. 541, CA (Civ Div) 2–41
Inland Revenue Commissioners v Ainsworth; Inland Revenue Commissioners v Kilic; Inland Revenue Commissioners v Stringer; Inland Revenue Commissioners v Thwaites; sub nom. Ainsworth v Inland

Revenue Commissioners [2005] EWCA Civ 441; [2005] I.C.R. 1149; [2005] I.R.L.R. 465, CA (Civ Div) 2–9, 2–21
Inner London Education Authority v Gravett [1988] I.R.L.R. 497, EAT ... 4–28
Irani v Southampton and South West Hampshire HA [1985] I.C.R. 590; [1985] I.R.L.R. 203; (1985) 82 L.S.G. 1167, Ch D 3–11, 3–12
Ironmonger v Movefield Ltd (t/a Deering Appointments) [1988] I.R.L.R. 461, EAT 3–8

James v Eastleigh BC [1990] 2 A.C. 751; [1990] 3 W.L.R. 55; [1990] 2 All E.R. 607; [1990] I.C.R. 554; [1990] I.R.L.R. 288; (1991) 155 L.G. Rev. 205; (1990) 140 N.L.J. 926, HL 6–3
James v Great North Eastern Railways, UKEAT/0496/04/SM, EAT 6–35
James v Greenwich LBC [2007] I.R.L.R. 168; [2007] I.C.R. 577, EAT . 1–02, 1–19
James v Redcats (Brands) Ltd [2007] I.R.L.R. 296, EAT 1–10, 1–15
Janata Bank v Ahmed [1981] I.C.R. 791; [1981] I.R.L.R. 457, CA (Civ Div) ... 2–37
John Brown Engineering Ltd v Brown [1997] I.R.L.R. 90, EAT 4–31
Johnson v Nottinghamshire Combined Police Authority; Dutton v Nottinghamshire Combined Police Authority [1974] 1 W.L.R. 358; [1974] 1 All E.R. 1082; [1974] I.C.R. 170; [1974] I.R.L.R. 20; (1974) 9 I.T.R. 164; (1974) 118 S.J. 166, CA (Civ Div) 5–7
Johnson v Unisys Ltd [2001] UKHL 13; [2003] 1 A.C. 518; [2001] 2 W.L.R. 1076; [2001] 2 All E.R. 801; [2001] I.C.R. 480; [2001] I.R.L.R. 279; [2001] Emp. L.R. 469, HL 3–14
Johnstone v Bloomsbury HA [1992] Q.B. 333; [1991] 2 W.L.R. 1362; [1991] 2 All E.R. 293; [1991] I.C.R. 269; [1991] I.R.L.R. 118; [1991] 2 Med. L.R. 139; (1991) 141 N.L.J. 271, CA (Civ Div) 2–34
Jones v Friends Provident Life Office [2004] N.I. 125; [2004] I.R.L.R. 783, CA (NI) 1–18
Jones v Governing Body of Burdett Coutts School [1999] I.C.R. 38; [1998] I.R.L.R. 521; (1998) 95(18) L.S.G. 32; (1998) 142 S.J.L.B. 142, CA (Civ Div) 5–9
Jones v Tower Boot Co Ltd. *See* Tower Boot Co Ltd v Jones

KB v NHS Pensions Agency (C117/01) [2004] All E.R. (EC) 1089; [2004] E.C.R. I-541; [2004] 1 C.M.L.R. 28; [2004] I.C.R. 781; [2004] I.R.L.R. 240; [2004] 1 F.L.R. 683; [2004] O.P.L.R. 145; [2004] Pens. L.R. 191; [2004] Fam. Law 249, ECJ 6–12
Kalanke v Freie und Hansestadt Bremen (C450/93) 1996] All E.R. (E.C.) 66; [1995] E.C.R. I-3051; [1996] 1 C.M.L.R. 175; [1996] C.E.C. 208; [1996] I.C.R. 314; [1995] I.R.L.R. 660, ECJ 6–4
Kaur v MG Rover Group Ltd [2004] EWCA Civ 1507; [2005] I.C.R. 625; [2005] I.R.L.R. 40, CA (Civ Div) 1–42
Keeley v Fosroc International Ltd [2006] EWCA Civ 1277; [2006] I.R.L.R. 961; (2006) 103(40) L.S.G. 33; (2006) 150 S.J.L.B. 1328, CA (Civ Div) 1–42
Kelly v Northern Ireland Housing Executive; Loughran v Northern Ireland Housing Executive [1999] 1 A.C. 428; [1998] 3 W.L.R. 735; [1998] N.I. 240; [1998] I.C.R. 828; [1998] I.R.L.R. 593; (1998) 95(36) L.S.G. 31; (1998) 142 S.J.L.B. 254, HL (NI) 6–8
Kennell v Sanders & Sanders, 13 K.I.R. 198; [1972] I.T.R. 399, IT 2–34
Kent CC v Mingo [2000] I.R.L.R. 90, EAT 6–28
Kerry Foods Ltd v Creber [2000] I.C.R. 556; [2000] I.R.L.R. 10, EAT 5–22
Khan v Chief Constable of West Yorkshire. *See* Chief Constable of West Yorkshire v Khan
Khan v G and J Spencer Group plc v NIC Hygiene Ltd (Case No.1893250/04), unreported 6–21
King v Eaton Ltd (No.1) 1996 S.C. 74; 1997 S.L.T. 654; 1996 S.C.L.R. 232; [1996] I.R.L.R. 199, IH (2 Div) 4–31
King v Eaton Ltd (No.2); sub nom. Eaton Ltd v King, 1999 S.L.T. 656; 1998 S.C.L.R. 1017; [1998] I.R.L.R. 686; 1998 G.W.D. 27-1381, IH (2 Div) ... 4–50
King v Fife Council, 2004 Rep. L.R. 33; 2003 G.W.D. 39-1063, OH 1–21

Kingston and Richmond AHA v Kaur [1981] I.C.R. 631; [1981] I.R.L.R. 337, EAT 6–16
Knight v Barra Shipping (Case No.187/92), unreported 2–35
Kodees Waaran v Attorney General of Ceylon [1972] W.L.R. 456 1–27
Kraus v Penna Plc [2004] I.R.L.R. 260, EAT 4–43
Kwik-Fit (GB) Ltd v Lineham [1992] I.C.R. 183; [1992] I.R.L.R. 156; (1992) 89(5) L.S.G. 31, EAT 4–7

LAMBETH LBC v COMMISSION FOR RACIAL EQUALITY [1990] I.C.R. 768; [1990] I.R.L.R. 231, CA (Civ Div) 6–4
Lambeth LBC v Corlett [2007] I.C.R. 88, EAT 7–11
Landeshauptstadt Kiel v Jaeger (C151/02) [2004] All E.R. (EC) 604; [2003] E.C.R. I-8389; [2003] 3 C.M.L.R. 16; [2004] I.C.R. 1528; [2003] I.R.L.R. 804; (2004) 75 B.M.L.R. 201, ECJ 2–16
Langston v Cranfield University [1998] I.R.L.R. 172, EAT 4–31
Lanton Leisure v White and Gibson [1987] I.R.L.R. 119, EAT 3–2
Lawrence v Regent Office Care Ltd (C320/00) [2002] E.C.R. I-7325; [2002] 3 C.M.L.R. 27; [2003] I.C.R. 1092; [2002] I.R.L.R. 822; [2002] Emp. L.R. 1248, ECJ 6–52
Lawrie-Blum v Land Baden-Wurttemberg (C66/85) [1986] E.C.R. 2121; [1987] 3 C.M.L.R. 389; [1987] I.C.R. 483, ECJ 1–03
Lawson v Serco Ltd; Crofts v Veta Ltd; Botham v Ministry of Defence; sub nom. Serco Ltd v Lawson [2006] UKHL 3; [2006] 1 All E.R. 823; [2006] I.C.R. 250; [2006] I.R.L.R. 289; (2006) 103(6) L.S.G. 36; (2006) 156 N.L.J. 184; (2006) 150 S.J.L.B. 131, HL 4–4
Lee v GEC Plessey Telecommunications [1993] I.R.L.R. 383 1–29
Lee Ting Sang v Chung Chi-Keung [1990] 2 A.C. 374; [1990] 2 W.L.R. 1173; [1990] I.C.R. 409; [1990] I.R.L.R. 236; (1990) 87(13) L.S.G. 43; (1990) 134 S.J. 909, PC (HK) 1–20
Lennox v Allan & Sons (1880) 3 R 38 3–8
Leonard v Southern Derbyshire Chamber of Commerce [2001] I.R.L.R. 19, EAT 6–25
Leverton v Clwyd CC; sub nom. Clwyd CC v Leverton [1989] A.C. 706; [1989] 2 W.L.R. 47; [1989] 1 All E.R. 78; [1989] 1 C.M.L.R. 574; [1989] I.C.R. 33; [1989] I.R.L.R. 28; (1988) 138 N.L.J. Rep. 366; (1989) 133 S.J. 45, HL 6–45
Levez v TH Jennings (Harlow Pools) Ltd (C326/96) [1999] All E.R. (EC) 1; [1998] E.C.R. I-7835; [1999] 2 C.M.L.R. 363; [1999] C.E.C. 3; [1999] I.C.R. 521; [1999] I.R.L.R. 36, ECJ (1st Chamber) 6–53
Lignacite Products v Krollman [1979] I.R.L.R. 22, EAT 5–10
Lister v Romford Ice and Cold Storage Co Ltd; sub nom. Romford Ice & Cold Storage Co v Lister [1957] A.C. 555; [1957] 2 W.L.R. 158; [1957] 1 All E.R. 125; [1956] 2 Lloyd's Rep. 505; (1957) 121 J.P. 98; (1957) 101 S.J. 106, HL 2–37
Litster v Forth Dry Dock & Engineering Co Ltd; sub nom. Forth Estuary Engineering Ltd v Litster [1990] 1 A.C. 546; [1989] 2 W.L.R. 634; [1989] 1 All E.R. 1134; 1989 S.C. (H.L.) 96; 1989 S.L.T. 540; [1989] 2 C.M.L.R. 194; [1989] I.C.R. 341; [1989] I.R.L.R. 161; (1989) 86(23) L.S.G. 18; (1989) 139 N.L.J. 400; (1989) 133 S.J. 455, HL 1–03, 1–04, 5–22
Lloyd-Briden v Worthing College, UKEAT/0065/07/RN, EAT 5–2
London Underground Ltd v Edwards (No.2) [1999] I.C.R. 494; [1998] I.R.L.R. 364; (1998) 95(26) L.S.G. 32; (1998) 148 N.L.J. 905; (1998) 142 S.J.L.B. 182, CA (Civ Div) 6–6
Loughran v Northern Ireland Housing Executive. *See* Kelly v Northern Ireland Housing Executive
Louies v Coventry Hood & Seating Co [1990] I.C.R. 54; [1990] I.R.L.R. 324, EAT 4–29
Lyon v St James Press Ltd [1976] I.C.R. 413; [1976] I.R.L.R. 215, EAT 4–37

MacCartney v Oversley House Management [2006] I.C.R. 510; [2006] I.R.L.R. 514, EAT 2–16
McClaren v Home Office; sub nom. McLaren v Secretary of State for the Home Department [1990] I.C.R. 824; [1990] I.R.L.R. 338; (1990) 2 Admin. L.R. 652; [1990] C.O.D. 257; (1990) 87(17) L.S.G. 31; (1990) 134 S.J. 908, CA (Civ Div) 1–27
McDermid v Nash Dredging & Reclamation Co Ltd [1987] A.C. 906; [1987] 3 W.L.R. 212; [1987] 2 All E.R. 878; [1987] 2 Lloyd's Rep. 201; [1987] I.C.R. 917; [1987] I.R.L.R. 334; [1987] 2 F.T.L.R. 357; (1987) 84 L.S.G. 2458; (1987) 131 S.J. 973, HL 2–36
MacDonald v Ministry of Defence. *See* Advocate General for Scotland v MacDonald
MacFarlane v Glasgow City Council [2001] I.R.L.R. 7, EAT 1–15
McLory v Post Office [1993] 1 All E.R. 457; [1992] I.C.R. 758; [1993] I.R.L.R. 159, Ch D 4–9
McMeechan v Secretary of State for Employment [1997] I.C.R. 549; [1997] I.R.L.R. 353, CA (Civ Div 1–18, 1–19
McMenemy v Capita Business Services Ltd, 2007 S.L.T. 428; [2007] I.R.L.R. 400; 2007 G.W.D. 13-267, IH (Ex Div) 6–35
Main v Ministry of Defence (ET Case No.3101031/97) 6–4
Malik v Bank of Credit and Commerce International SA (In Liquidation); sub nom. Mahmud v Bank of Credit and Commerce International SA (In Liquidation); BCCI SA, Re [1998] A.C. 20; [1997] 3 W.L.R. 95; [1997] 3 All E.R. 1; [1997] I.C.R. 606; [1997] I.R.L.R. 462; (1997) 94(25) L.S.G. 33; (1997) 147 N.L.J. 917, HL 2–32, 3–14
Malik v Bertram Personnel Group Ltd, 1979, unreported, ET 6–16
Mandla (Sewa Singh) v Dowell Lee [1983] 2 A.C. 548; [1983] 2 W.L.R. 620; [1983] 1 All E.R. 1062; [1983] I.C.R. 385; [1983] I.R.L.R. 209; (1983) 127 S.J. 242, HL 6–5, 6–14, 6–15, 6–16
Mangold v Helm (C144/04) [2006] All E.R. (EC) 383; [2005] E.C.R. I-9981; [2006] 1 C.M.L.R. 43; [2006] C.E.C. 372; [2006] I.R.L.R. 143, ECJ 5–2
Market Investigations Ltd v Minister of Social Security [1969] 2 Q.B. 173; [1969] 2 W.L.R. 1; [1968] 3 All E.R. 732; (1968) 112 S.J. 905, QBD 1–12
Marley v Forward Trust Group [1986] I.C.R. 891; [1986] I.R.L.R. 369, CA (Civ Div) 1–42
Marschall v Land Nordrhein-Westfalen (C409/95) 1997] All E.R. (EC) 865; [1997] E.C.R. I-6363; [1998] 1 C.M.L.R. 547; [1998] C.E.C. 152; [2001] I.C.R. 45; [1998] I.R.L.R. 39, ECJ 6–4
Marshall v Harland & Wolff Ltd [1972] 1 W.L.R. 899; [1972] 2 All E.R. 715; [1972] 1 R.L.R. 90; [1972] I.C.R. 101; [1972] I.R.L.R. 90; (1972) 7 I.T.R. 150; (1972) 116 S.J. 484, NIRC 3–5, 4–11
Marshall v Southampton and South West Hampshire AHA (152/84) [1986] Q.B. 401; [1986] 2 W.L.R. 780; [1986] 2 All E.R. 584; [1986] E.C.R. 723; [1986] 1 C.M.L.R. 688; [1986] I.C.R. 335; [1986] I.R.L.R. 140; (1986) 83 L.S.G. 1720; (1986) 130 S.J. 340, ECJ 1–03, 1–26, 6–30
Martin v Glynwed Distribution (t/a MBS Fastenings) [1983] I.C.R. 511; [1983] I.R.L.R. 198, CA (Civ Div) 5–4
Martin v Yeomen Aggregates [1983] I.C.R. 314; [1983] I.R.L.R. 49, EAT ... 4–7
Massey v Crown Life Insurance Co [1978] 1 W.L.R. 676; [1978] 2 All E.R. 576; [1978] I.C.R. 590; [1978] I.R.L.R. 31; (1978) 13 I.T.R. 5; (1978) 122 S.J. 791, CA (Civ Div) 1–16
Matthews v Kent and Medway Towns Fire Authority; sub nom. Mathews v Kent and Medway Towns Fire Authority [2006] UKHL 8; [2006] 2 All E.R. 171; [2006] I.C.R. 365; [2006] I.R.L.R. 367; [2006] Pens. L.R. 61, HL 6–34
Mears v Inland Revenue Commissioners; Mears v Safecar Security [1983] Q.B. 54; [1982] 3 W.L.R. 366; [1982] 2 All E.R. 865; [1982] I.C.R. 626; [1982] I.R.L.R. 183; (1982) 79 L.S.G. 921, CA (Civ Div) 2–5
Mears v Safecar Security. *See* Mears v Inland Revenue Commissioners
Melon v Hector Powe Ltd; sub nom. Hector Powe Ltd v Melon [1981] 1 All

E.R. 313; 1981 S.C. (H.L.) 1; 1981 S.L.T. 74; [1981] I.C.R. 43; [1980] I.R.L.R. 477; (1980) 124 S.J. 827, HL 5–5
Mennell v Newell & Wright (Transport Contractors) Ltd [1997] I.C.R. 1039; [1997] I.R.L.R. 519; (1997) 94(33) L.S.G. 26; (1997) 141 S.J.L.B. 185, CA (Civ Div) 4–41
Mersey Docks and Harbour Board v Coggins & Griffith (Liverpool) Ltd; sub nom. McFarlane v Coggins & Griffiths (Liverpool) Ltd [1947] A.C. 1; [1946] 2 All E.R. 345; (1946) 79 Ll. L. Rep. 569; 62 T.L.R. 533; 115 L.J. K.B. 465; 175 L.T. 270, HL 1–21
Merton LBC v Gardiner; sub nom. Gardiner v Merton LBC [1981] Q.B. 269; [1981] 2 W.L.R. 232; [1981] I.C.R. 186; [1980] I.R.L.R. 472; 79 L.G.R. 374; (1981) 125 S.J. 97, CA (Civ Div) 4–5
Midland Counties District Bank Ltd v Attwood [1905] 1 Ch. 357, Ch D ... 3–4
Migrant Advisory Service v Chaudri, July 28, 1998, unreported, EAT 1–29
Ministry of Defence v Jeremiah; sub nom. Jeremiah v Ministry of Defence [1980] Q.B. 87; [1979] 3 W.L.R. 857; [1979] 3 All E.R. 833; [1980] I.C.R. 13; [1979] I.R.L.R. 436; (1979) 123 S.J. 735, CA (Civ Div) 6–6
Ministry of Defence HQ Defence Dental Service v Kettle, UKEAT/0308/06/LA, EAT 1–15, 1–20
Moffat v Boothby (1884) 11 R 501 2–33
Monaghan v Leicester Young Men's Christian Association (Case No.1901830/04), unreported 6–21
Moore v C&A Modes [1981] I.R.L.R. 71, EAT 4–16
Morganite Crucible Ltd v Street [1972] 1 W.L.R. 918; [1972] 2 All E.R. 411; [1972] I.C.R. 110; (1972) 7 I.T.R. 182; (1972) 116 S.J. 484, NIRC 5–9
Morran v Glasgow Council of Tenants Associations, 1997 S.C. 279; 1997 S.L.T. 1133; 1997 S.C.L.R. 841; [1998] I.R.L.R. 67; 1997 G.W.D. 20-977, IH (1 Div) 3–13
Morris v Ford Motor Co [1973] Q.B. 792; [1973] 2 W.L.R. 843; [1973] 2 All E.R. 1084; [1973] 2 Lloyd's Rep. 27; (1973) 117 S.J. 393, CA (Civ Div) 2–37
Morris v John Grose Group Ltd [1998] I.C.R. 655; [1998] I.R.L.R. 499, EAT 5–23
Morrish v Henlys (Folkestone) [1973] 2 All E.R. 137; [1973] I.C.R. 482; [1973] I.T.R. 167, NIRC 2–33
Moyhing v Barts & London NHS Trust [2006] I.R.L.R. 860, EAT 6–3
Mugford v Midland Bank Plc [1997] I.C.R. 399; [1997] I.R.L.R. 208, EAT ... 4–31
Murray v Dumbarton CC (Interdict), 1935 S.L.T. 239, OH 3–11
Murray v Foyle Meats Ltd [2000] 1 A.C. 51; [1999] 3 W.L.R. 356; [1999] 3 All E.R. 769; [1999] N.I. 291; [1999] I.C.R. 827; [1999] I.R.L.R. 562; (1999) 96(31) L.S.G. 36; (1999) 143 S.J.L.B. 214, HL (NI) 5–8

National Coal Board v Galley [1958] 1 W.L.R. 16; [1958] 1 All E.R. 91; (1958) 102 S.J. 31, CA 1–40
National Heart and Chest Hospitals Board of Governors v Nambiar; sub nom. Board of Governors National Heart and Chest Hospitals v Nambiar [1981] I.C.R. 441; [1981] I.R.L.R. 196; (1988) 132 S.J. 9, EAT 4–24
Neary v Dean of Westminster [1999] I.R.L.R. 288, Visitor (Westminster) ... 4–16
Nelson v BBC (No.1) [1977] I.C.R. 649; [1977] I.R.L.R. 148; [1977] T.R. 273, CA (Civ Div) 5–8
Nethermere (St Neots) Ltd v Gardiner; sub nom. Nethermere (St Neots) Ltd v Taverna [1984] I.C.R. 612; [1984] I.R.L.R. 240; (1984) 81 L.S.G. 2147; (1984) 134 N.L.J. 544, CA (Civ Div) 1–13, 1–14
New Century Cleaning Co v Church [2000] I.R.L.R. 27, CA (Civ Div) 2–9
Norfolk CC v Bernard [1979] I.R.L.R. 220, EAT 4–16
Northern Joint Police Board v Power [1997] I.R.L.R. 610, EAT 6–15
Norton Tool Co Ltd v Tewson [1973] 1 W.L.R. 45; [1973] 1 All E.R. 183; [1972] I.C.R. 501; [1972] I.R.L.R. 86; (1972) 13 K.I.R. 328; [1973] I.T.R. 23; (1973) 117 S.J. 33, NIRC 4–50
Norwest Holst Group Administration Ltd v Harrison; sub nom. Harrison v

Norwest Holst Group Administration Ltd [1985] I.C.R. 668; [1985] I.R.L.R. 240; (1985) 82 L.S.G. 1410, CA (Civ Div) ... 3–1

Notcutt v Universal Equipment Co (London) [1986] 1 W.L.R. 641; [1986] 3 All E.R. 582; [1986] I.C.R. 414; [1986] I.R.L.R. 218; (1986) 83 L.S.G. 1314; (1986) 136 N.L.J. 393; (1986) 130 S.J. 392, CA (Civ Div) ... 3–6

O'Brien v Associated Fire Alarms [1968] 1 W.L.R. 1916; [1969] 1 All E.R. 93; 3 K.I.R. 223; (1968) 112 S.J. 232, CA (Civ Div) ... 2–34

O'Dea v ISC Chemicals Ltd [1996] I.C.R. 222; [1995] I.R.L.R. 799, CA (Civ Div) ... 4–38

O'Hanlon v Revenue and Customs Commissioners [2007] EWCA Civ 283; [2007] I.R.L.R. 404, CA (Civ Div) ... 6–28

Ojutiku v Manpower Services Commission [1982] I.C.R. 661; [1982] I.R.L.R. 418; (1982) 79 L.S.G. 920, CA (Civ Div) ... 6–16

O'Kelly v Trusthouse Forte Plc [1984] Q.B. 90; [1983] 3 W.L.R. 605; [1983] 3 All E.R. 456; [1983] I.C.R. 728; [1983] I.R.L.R. 369, CA (Civ Div) ... 1–13

Orphanos v Queen Mary College [1985] A.C. 761; [1985] 2 W.L.R. 703; [1985] 2 All E.R. 233; [1986] 2 C.M.L.R. 73; [1985] I.R.L.R. 349; (1985) 82 L.S.G. 1787; (1985) 129 S.J. 284, HL ... 6–16

Ottoman Bank v Chakarian [1930] A.C. 277; [1930] 2 W.W.R. 82, PC (Cy) ... 2–35

P v S and Cornwall CC (C13/94); sub nom. P v S (Sex Discrimination) (C13/94) [1996] All E.R. (EC) 397; [1996] E.C.R. I-2143; [1996] 2 C.M.L.R. 247; [1996] C.E.C. 574; [1996] I.C.R. 795; [1996] I.R.L.R. 347; [1996] 2 F.L.R. 347; [1997] 2 F.C.R. 180; [1996] Fam. Law 609, ECJ 6–11, 6–18

Pagano v HGS [1976] I.R.L.R. 9, IT ... 2–33

Page One Records, Ltd v Britton [1968] 1 W.L.R. 157; [1967] 3 All E.R. 822; (1967) 111 S.J. 944, Ch D ... 3–11

Peace v Edinburgh City Council, 1999 S.L.T. 712; 1999 S.C.L.R. 593; [1999] I.R.L.R. 417; 1999 G.W.D. 8-394, OH ... 3–12

Pearson v Jones (William); sub nom. Pearson and Workman v Jones (William) [1967] 1 W.L.R. 1140; [1967] 2 All E.R. 1062; 3 K.I.R. 49; (1967) 111 S.J. 603, DC ... 1–40

Perceval-Price v Department of Economic Development [2000] N.I. 141; [2000] I.R.L.R. 380, CA (NI) ... 1–03, 1–27, 6–8

Percy v Church of Scotland Board of National Mission [2005] UKHL 73; [2006] 2 A.C. 28; [2006] 2 W.L.R. 353; [2006] 4 All E.R. 1354; 2006 S.C. (H.L.) 1; 2006 S.L.T. 11; [2006] I.C.R. 134; [2006] I.R.L.R. 195; (2006) 150 S.J.L.B. 30, HL ... 1–27

Performing Rights Society v Mitchell and Booker [1924] 1 K.B. 762 ... 1–11

Polkey v AE Dayton Services Ltd; sub nom. Polkey v Edmund Walker (Holdings) Ltd [1988] A.C. 344; [1987] 3 W.L.R. 1153; [1987] 3 All E.R. 974; [1988] I.C.R. 142; [1987] I.R.L.R. 503; (1987) 137 N.L.J. 1109; (1988) 138 N.L.J. Rep. 33; (1987) 131 S.J. 1624, HL ... 4–25, 4–26, 4–27, 4–28, 4–29, 4–31

Porcelli v Strathclyde RC; sub nom. Strathclyde RC v Porcelli, 1986 S.C. 137; [1986] I.C.R. 564, IH (1 Div) ... 6–9

Post Office v Foley. *See* HSBC Bank Plc (formerly Midland Bank Plc) v Madden

Powdrill v Watson; Ferranti International Plc, Re; sub nom. Paramount Airways Ltd (No.3), Re; Talbot v Cadge; Talbot v Grundy; Leyland DAF Ltd (No.2), Re [1995] 2 A.C. 394; [1995] 2 W.L.R. 312; [1995] 2 All E.R. 65; [1995] B.C.C. 319; [1994] 1 B.C.L.C. 386; [1995] I.C.R. 1100; [1995] I.R.L.R. 269; (1995) 92(17) L.S.G. 47; (1995) 145 N.L.J. 449; (1995) 139 S.J.L.B. 110, HL ... 3–4

Power Packing Casemakers Ltd v Faust [1983] Q.B. 471; [1983] 2 W.L.R. 439; [1983] 2 All E.R. 166; [1983] I.C.R. 292; [1983] I.R.L.R. 117, CA (Civ Div) ... 4–35

Prescription Pricing Authority v Ferguson, 2005 1 S.C. 171; 2005 S.L.T. 63; 2006 S.C.L.R. 1; 2005 G.W.D. 1-11, IH (1 Div) ... 7–6

Preston v Wolverhampton Healthcare NHS Trust (C78/98); Fletcher v Midland Bank Plc (C78/98) [2001] 2 A.C. 415; [2001] 2 W.L.R. 408; [2000] All E.R. (EC) 714; [2000] E.C.R. I-3201; [2000] 2 C.M.L.R. 837; [2000] C.E.C. 587; [2000] I.C.R. 961; [2000] I.R.L.R. 506; [2000] O.P.L.R. 115; [2000] Pens. L.R. 171, ECJ 6–51, 6–53

Preston v Wolverhampton Healthcare NHS Trust (No.2); Fletcher v Midland Bank Plc (No.2) [2001] UKHL 5; [2001] 2 A.C. 455; [2001] 2 W.L.R. 448; [2001] 3 All E.R. 947; [2001] 1 C.M.L.R. 46; [2001] I.C.R. 217; [2001] I.R.L.R. 237; [2001] Emp. L.R. 256; [2001] O.P.L.R. 1; [2001] Pens. L.R. 39; (2001) 98(10) L.S.G. 41; (2001) 145 S.J.L.B. 55, HL 6–51, 6–53, 6–55

Prestwick Circuits Ltd v McAndrew 1990 S.L.T. 654, IH (Ex Div) 2–34

Price v Civil Service Commission (No.1) [1977] 1 W.L.R. 1417; [1978] 1 All E.R. 1228; [1978] I.C.R. 27; [1977] I.R.L.R. 291; (1977) 12 I.T.R. 482; (1977) 121 S.J. 558, EAT 6–5, 6–37

Print Factory (London) 1991 Ltd v Millam [2007] EWCA Civ 322; [2007] I.R.L.R. 526; (2007) 104(18) L.S.G. 28, CA (Civ Div) 3–4, 5–17

Qua v John Ford Morrison Solicitors [2003] I.C.R. 482; [2003] I.R.L.R. 184; (2003) 153 N.L.J. 95, EAT 2–27

R. v Secretary of State for Employment Ex p. Equal Opportunities Commission [1995] 1 A.C. 1; [1994] 2 W.L.R. 409; [1994] 1 All E.R. 910; [1995] 1 C.M.L.R. 391; [1994] I.C.R. 317; [1994] I.R.L.R. 176; 92 L.G.R. 360; [1994] C.O.D. 301; (1994) 91(18) L.S.G. 43; (1994) 144 N.L.J. 358; (1994) 138 S.J.L.B. 84, HL 4–5, 6–55

R. v Secretary of State for Employment Ex p. Seymour-Smith (C167/97) [1999] 2 A.C. 554; [1999] 3 W.L.R. 460; [1999] All E.R. (E.C.) 97; [1999] E.C.R. I-623; [1999] 2 C.M.L.R. 273; [1999] C.E.C. 79; [1999] I.C.R. 447; [1999] I.R.L.R. 253, ECJ 4–3, 5–2, 6–55

R. v Secretary of State for Employment Ex p. Seymour-Smith (No.1) [1997] 1 W.L.R. 473; [1997] 2 All E.R. 273; [1997] 2 C.M.L.R. 904; [1997] I.C.R. 371; [1997] I.R.L.R. 315; (1997) 147 N.L.J. 414, HL 5–2

R. v Secretary of State for Employment Ex p. Seymour-Smith (No.2) [2000] 1 W.L.R. 435; [2000] 1 All E.R. 857; [2000] 1 C.M.L.R. 770; [2000] I.C.R. 244; [2000] I.R.L.R. 263; (2000) 97(9) L.S.G. 40, HL 5–2

Rainey v Greater Glasgow Health Board [1987] A.C. 224; [1986] 3 W.L.R. 1017; [1987] 1 All E.R. 65; 1987 S.C. (H.L.) 1; 1987 S.L.T. 146; [1987] 2 C.M.L.R. 11; [1987] I.C.R. 129; [1987] I.R.L.R. 26; (1987) 84 L.S.G. 188; (1986) 136 N.L.J. 1161; (1986) 130 S.J. 954, HL 6–49

Rankin v British Coal [1995] I.C.R. 774; [1993] I.R.L.R. 69, EAT 1–03, 5–2, 6–55

Rask v ISS Kantineservice A/S (C209/91) [1992] E.C.R. I-5755; [1993] I.R.L.R. 133, ECJ 5–17

Redcar and Cleveland BC v Degnan; sub nom. Degnan v Redcar and Cleveland BC [2005] EWCA Civ 726; [2005] I.R.L.R. 615; [2005] E.L.R. 475, CA (Civ Div) 6–45

Redfearn v Serco Ltd (t/a West Yorkshire Transport Service); sub nom. Serco Ltd v Redfearn [2006] EWCA Civ 659; [2006] I.C.R. 1367; [2006] I.R.L.R. 623; (2006) 150 S.J.L.B. 703, CA (Civ Div) 6–13

Reigate v Union Manufacturing Co (Ramsbottom) Ltd [1918] 1 K.B. 592, CA 3–4

Rigby v Ferodo Ltd [1988] I.C.R. 29; [1987] I.R.L.R. 516, HL 2–4, 3–7

Riordan v War Office [1961] 1 W.L.R. 210; [1960] 3 All E.R. 774 (Note), CA 3–1

Robertson v British Gas Corp [1983] I.C.R. 351; [1983] I.R.L.R. 302, CA (Civ Div) 1–34

Robertson v Department for the Environment, Food and Rural Affairs; sub nom. Department for the Environment, Food and Rural Affairs v

Robertson [2005] EWCA Civ 138; [2005] I.C.R. 750; [2005] I.R.L.R. 363; (2005) 102(15) L.S.G. 33, CA (Civ Div) 6–52
Robinson-Steele v RD Retail Services Ltd (C131/04) Clarke v Frank Staddon Ltd (C257/04); Caulfield v Hanson Clay Products Ltd (C257/04) [2006] All E.R. (EC) 749; [2006] E.C.R. I-2531; [2006] 2 C.M.L.R. 34; [2006] C.E.C. 771; [2006] I.C.R. 932; [2006] I.R.L.R. 386, ECJ (1st Chamber 2–20
Royal National Lifeboat Institution v Bushaway [2005] I.R.L.R. 675, EAT ... 1–35
Royce v John Greig & Sons, 1909 2 S.L.T. 298, OH 1–22
Rutherford v Secretary of State for Trade and Industry; Bentley v Secretary of State for Trade and Industry; sub nom. Rutherford v Harvest Towncircle Ltd (In Liquidation); Secretary of State for Trade and Industry v Rutherford [2006] UKHL 19; [2006] 4 All E.R. 577; [2006] I.C.R. 785; [2006] I.R.L.R. 551; (2006) 103(20) L.S.G. 24; (2006) 150 S.J.L.B. 604, HL 5–2

Safeway Stores Plc v Burrell [1997] I.C.R. 523; [1997] I.R.L.R. 200, EAT . 5–8
Sanders v Parry [1967] 1 W.L.R. 753; [1967] 2 All E.R. 803; (1967) 111 S.J. 296, Assizes 2–38
Sartin v Co–operative Retail services Ltd (1969) 7 K.I.R. 382 5–7
Saunders v Scottish National Camps Association [1981] I.R.L.R. 277, IH ... 4–20
Sayers v Cambridgeshire CC [2006] EWHC 2029; [2007] I.R.L.R. 29, QBD ... 2–21
Schmidt v Spar- und Leihkasse der Fruheren Amter Bordesholm, Keil und Cronshagen (C392/92) [1994] E.C.R. I-1311; [1995] 2 C.M.L.R. 331; [1995] I.C.R. 237; [1994] I.R.L.R. 302, ECJ (5th Chamber) 5–17
Scotch Premier Meat Ltd v Burns [2000] I.R.L.R. 639, EAT 5–4
Scott Packing & Warehousing Co v Paterson [1978] I.R.L.R. 166, EAT 4–20
Scottish Daily Record & Sunday Mail (1986) Ltd v Laird 1996 S.C. 401; 1997 S.L.T. 345; [1996] I.R.L.R. 665, IH (1 Div) 4–28
Scottish Midland Cooperative Society v Cullion [1991] I.R.L.R. 261, SC ... 4–23
Scullard v Knowles and Southern Regional Council for Education and Training [1996] I.C.R. 399; [1996] I.R.L.R. 344, EAT 6–52
Secretary of State for Employment v Atkins Auto Laundries [1972] 1 W.L.R. 507; [1972] 1 All E.R. 987; [1972] I.C.R. 76; [1972] I.T.R. 59; (1971) 116 S.J. 238, NIRC 5–12
Secretary of State for Trade and Industry v Bottrill; sub nom. Bottrill v Secretary of State for Trade and Industry [2000] 1 All E.R. 915; [1999] B.C.C. 177; [2000] 2 B.C.L.C. 448; [1999] I.C.R. 592; [1999] I.R.L.R. 326; (1999) 96(10) L.S.G. 30; (1999) 143 S.J.L.B. 73, CA (Civ Div) 1–24
Seide v Gillette Industries [1980] I.R.L.R. 427, EAT 6–14
Selfridges Ltd v Malik [1998] I.C.R. 268; [1997] I.R.L.R. 577, EAT 4–20
Serco Ltd v Lawson. *See* Lawson v Serco Ltd; Crofts v Veta Ltd
Shamoon v Chief Constable of the Royal Ulster Constabulary [2003] UKHL 11; [2003] 2 All E.R. 26; [2003] N.I. 174; [2003] I.C.R. 337; [2003] I.R.L.R. 285; (2003) 147 S.J.L.B. 268, HL (NI) 6–3
Sharp v Caledonia Group Services Ltd [2006] I.C.R. 218; [2006] I.R.L.R. 4, EAT 6–50
Sheffield v Oxford Controls Co Ltd [1979] I.C.R. 396; [1979] I.R.L.R. 133, EAT 4–7
Shepherds Investments Ltd v Walters [2006] EWHC 836 (Ch); [2007] I.R.L.R. 110; (2006) 150 S.J.L.B. 536; [2007] F.S.R. 15, Ch D 2–40
Shergold v Fieldway Medical Centre [2006] I.C.R. 304; [2006] I.R.L.R. 76, EAT 7–11
Shook v Ealing LBC [1986] I.C.R. 314; [1986] I.R.L.R. 46, EAT 4–15
Shove v Downs Surgical Plc [1984] 1 All E.R. 7; [1984] I.C.R. 532; [1984] I.R.L.R. 17; (1984) 81 L.S.G. 893; (1983) 133 N.L.J. 938; (1984) 128 S.J. 221, QBD 3–13
Showboat Entertainment Centre Ltd v Owens [1984] 1 W.L.R. 384; [1984] 1 All E.R. 836; [1984] I.C.R. 65; [1984] I.R.L.R. 7; (1983) 80 L.S.G. 3002; (1984) 134 N.L.J. 37; (1984) 128 S.J. 152, EAT 6–13

Silva v The Vidyodaya University of Ceylon. *See* University Council of the Vidyodaya University of Ceylon v Silva
Sim v Rotherham MBC; Townend v Doncaster MBC; Barnfield v Solihull MBC; Rathbone v Croydon LBC [1987] Ch. 216; [1986] 3 W.L.R. 851; [1986] 3 All E.R. 387; [1986] I.C.R. 897; [1986] I.R.L.R. 391; 85 L.G.R. 128; (1986) 83 L.S.G. 3746; (1986) 130 S.J. 839, Ch D 2–33
Simmons v Hoover [1977] Q.B. 284; [1976] 3 W.L.R. 901; [1977] 1 All E.R. 775; [1977] I.C.R. 61; [1976] I.R.L.R. 266; [1976] I.T.R. 234; (1976) 120 S.J. 540, EAT 5–10
Sindicato de Medicos de Asistencia Publica (SIMAP) v Conselleria de Sanidad y Consumo de la Generalidad Valenciana (C303/98) [2001] All E.R. (EC) 609; [2000] E.C.R. I-7963; [2001] 3 C.M.L.R. 42; [2001] I.C.R. 1116; [2000] I.R.L.R. 845, ECJ 2–16
Singh v British Steel Corp [1974] I.R.L.R. 131, IT 1–40
Singh v London Country Bus Services [1976] I.R.L.R. 176, EAT 4–20
Singh v Rowntree MacKintosh Ltd [1979] I.C.R. 554, EAT 6–16
Skerret v Oliver (No.3); sub nom. Skerret v Oliver (1896) 23 R. 468; (1896) 3 S.L.T. 257, IH (1 Div) 3–11
Smith v Gardner Merchant Ltd [1998] 3 All E.R. 852; [1999] I.C.R. 134; [1998] I.R.L.R. 510; (1998) 95(32) L.S.G. 29; (1998) 142 S.J.L.B. 244, CA (Civ Div) 6–18
Smith v Safeway Plc [1996] I.C.R. 868; [1996] I.R.L.R. 456, CA (Civ Div) ... 6–9
Smith v St Andrew Ambulance, unreported, July 12, 1973, NIRC 2–33
Smith v United Kingdom (33985/96); Grady v United Kingdom (33986/96) [1999] I.R.L.R. 734; (2000) 29 E.H.R.R. 493; (1999) 11 Admin. L.R. 879, ECHR 6–18
Snell v Exclusive Cleaning and Maintenance (Northern) Ltd (ET Case No.1298/123), unreported 6–4
Sogbetun v Hackney LBC [1998] I.C.R. 1264; [1998] I.R.L.R. 676, EAT ... 1–05
South Ayrshire Council v Morton; sub nom. Morton v South Ayrshire Council, 2002 S.L.T. 656; [2002] 2 C.M.L.R. 8; [2002] I.C.R. 956; [2002] I.R.L.R. 256; 2002 G.W.D. 7-236, IH (2 Div) 6–52
Speciality Care Plc v Pachela [1996] I.C.R. 633; [1996] I.R.L.R. 248, EAT ... 4–37
Spencer v Marchington [1988] I.R.L.R. 392, Ch D 2–41
Spink v Express Foods Group [1990] I.R.L.R. 320, EAT 4–29
Staffordshire Sentinel Newspapers Ltd v Potter [2004] I.R.L.R. 752, EAT ... 1–15
Stagecraft Ltd v Minister of National Insurance, 1952 S.C. 288; 1952 S.L.T. 309, IH (2 Div) 1–11
Standard Telephones and Cables v Yates [1981] I.R.L.R. 21, EAT 5–9
Stanton Woolfendens Cranes [1972] I.R.L.R. 82 1–23
Stephens v Hall, unreported 4–43
Strathclyde RC v Wallace; sub nom. West Dunbartonshire Council v Wallace [1998] 1 W.L.R. 259; [1998] 1 All E.R. 394; 1998 S.C. (H.L.) 72; 1998 S.L.T. 421; 1998 S.C.L.R. 340; [1998] I.C.R. 205; [1998] I.R.L.R. 146; (1998) 95(7) L.S.G. 31; (1998) 142 S.J.L.B. 83; 1998 G.W.D. 4-181, HL 6–49, 6–50
Street v Derbyshire Unemployed Workers Centre [2004] EWCA Civ 964; [2004] 4 All E.R. 839; [2005] I.C.R. 97; [2004] I.R.L.R. 687, CA (Civ Div) 4–43
Sutherland v Hatton. *See* Barber v Somerset CC Baker Refractories Ltd v Bishop
Sutton & Gates (Luton) Ltd v Boxall [1979] I.C.R. 67; [1978] I.R.L.R. 486, EAT 4–15
Suzen v Zehnacker Gebaudereinigung GmbH Krankenhausservice (C13/95) [1997] All E.R. (EC) 289; [1997] E.C.R. I-1259; [1997] 1 C.M.L.R. 768; [1997] I.C.R. 662; [1997] I.R.L.R. 255; (1997) 16 Tr. L.R. 365, ECJ 5–17
System Floors (UK) Ltd v Daniel [1982] I.C.R. 54; [1981] I.R.L.R. 475, EAT 1–34

TSB Bank Plc v Harris [2000] I.R.L.R. 157, EAT 2–32

Tarnesby v Kensington, Chelsea and Westminster AHA (Teaching) [1981] I.C.R. 615; [1981] I.R.L.R. 369; (1981) 125 S.J. 464, HL 3–6, 4–11
Taylor v Furness Withy & Co Ltd [1969] 1 Lloyd's Rep. 324; (1969) 0 K.I.R. 488, QBD 1–30
Taylor Gordon & Co Ltd (t/a Plan Personnel) v Timmons [2004] I.R.L.R. 180; (2003) 100(44) L.S.G. 32, EAT 2–5
Taylorplan Catering (Scotland) v McInally [1980] I.R.L.R. 53, EAT 4–15
Tayside RC v McIntosh [1982] I.R.L.R. 272, EAT 4–15
Tele Danmark A/S v Handels- og Kontorfunktionaerernes Forbund i Danmark (C109/00) [2001] All E.R. (EC) 941; [2001] E.C.R. I-6993; [2002] 1 C.M.L.R. 5; [2004] I.C.R. 610; [2001] I.R.L.R. 853; [2001] Emp. L.R. 1389, ECJ (5th Chamber) 6–2
Therm-a-Stor Ltd v Atkins [1983] I.R.L.R. 78; (1982) 126 S.J. 856, CA (Civ Div) 4–37
Thomas v Farr Plc [2007] EWCA Civ 118; [2007] I.R.L.R. 419; [2007] I.C.R. 932, CA (Civ Div) 2–41
Thomson v Alloa Motor Co [1983] I.R.L.R. 403, EAT 4–16
Thomson v Thomson's Tr, 1889 16R 333 .... 1–29, 2–3
Tower Boot Co Ltd v Jones; sub nom. Jones v Tower Boot Co Ltd [1997] 2 All E.R. 406; [1997] I.C.R. 254; [1997] I.R.L.R. 168; (1997) 147 N.L.J. 60, CA (Civ Div) 6–32
Treganowan v Robert Knee & Co Ltd [1975] I.C.R. 405; [1975] I.R.L.R. 247; [1975] I.T.R. 121; (1975) 119 S.J. 490, DC 4–20
Trotter v Forth Ports Authority [1991] I.R.L.R. 419 3–2
Truelove v Safeway Stores Plc [2005] I.C.R. 589, EAT 2–27

United Bank v Akhtar [1989] I.R.L.R. 507, EAT 1–02, 2–35
United Sterling Corp Ltd v Felton and Mannion [1974] I.R.L.R. 314; [1973] F.S.R. 409; [1974] R.P.C. 162, Ch D 2–40
University Council of the Vidyodaya University of Ceylon v Silva; sub nom. Vidyodaya University of Ceylon v Silva [1965] 1 W.L.R. 77; [1964] 3 All E.R. 865; (1964) 108 S.J. 896, PC (Cey) 1–25
University of Liverpool v Humber and Birch; sub nom. Birch v University of Liverpool [1985] I.C.R. 470; [1985] I.R.L.R. 165; (1985) 82 L.S.G. 1250; (1985) 129 S.J. 245, CA (Civ Div) 4–10, 5–4

Vaux and Associated Breweries v Ward; sub nom. Vaux v Ward, 7 K.I.R. 309; (1969) 113 S.J. 920, DC 5–7
Villalba v Merrill Lynch & Co Inc [2006] I.R.L.R. 437; (2006) 150 S.J.L.B. 742; [2007] I.C.R. 469, EAT 6–50
Vine v National Dock Labour Board [1957] A.C. 488; [1957] 2 W.L.R. 106; [1956] 3 All E.R. 939; [1956] 2 Lloyd's Rep. 567; (1957) 101 S.J. 86, HL 1–25
Virgin Net Ltd v Harper. *See* Harper v Virgin Net Ltd

W Devis & Sons Ltd v Atkins [1977] A.C. 931; [1977] 3 W.L.R. 214; [1977] 3 All E.R. 40; 8 B.L.R. 57; [1977] I.C.R. 662; [1977] I.R.L.R. 314; (1978) 13 I.T.R. 71; (1977) 121 S.J. 512, HL 4–24
WA Goold (Pearmak) Ltd v McConnell [1995] I.R.L.R. 516, EAT 4–9
Walmsley v C&R Ferguson Ltd, 1989 S.C. 46; 1989 S.L.T. 258, IH (2 Div) . 3–1
Waltons & Morse v Dorrington [1997] I.R.L.R. 488, EAT 4–9
Wasileski v Associated Tunnels [1973] I.R.L.R. 346 2–35
Weathersfield Ltd (t/a Van & Truck Rentals) v Sargent [1999] I.C.R. 425; [1999] I.R.L.R. 94; [1999] Disc. L.R. 290; (1999) 96(5) L.S.G. 35; (1999) 143 S.J.L.B. 39, CA (Civ Div) 6–13
Webb v EMO Air Cargo (UK) Ltd (C32/93) [1994] Q.B. 718; [1994] 3 W.L.R. 941; [1994] 4 All E.R. 115; [1994] E.C.R. I-3567; [1994] 2 C.M.L.R. 729; [1994] I.C.R. 770; [1994] I.R.L.R. 482; (1994) 144 N.L.J. 1278, ECJ (5th Chamber) 6–2
Webley v Department for Work and Pensions; sub nom. Department for

Work and Pensions v Webley [2004] EWCA Civ 1745; [2005] I.C.R. 577; [2005] I.R.L.R. 288; (2005) 102(8) L.S.G. 30, CA (Civ Div) 6–36
West Midlands Cooperative Society v Tipton [1986] A.C. 536; [1986] 2 W.L.R. 306; [1986] 1 All E.R. 513; [1986] I.C.R. 192; [1986] I.R.L.R. 112; (1986) 83 L.S.G. 780; (1986) 136 N.L.J. 163; (1986) 130 S.J. 143, HL 4–24, 4–30
West v Kneels [1987] I.C.R. 146; [1986] I.R.L.R. 430; (1986) 83 L.S.G. 2488, EAT 3–1
Western Excavating (ECC) Ltd v Sharp [1978] Q.B. 761; [1978] 2 W.L.R. 344; [1978] 1 All E.R. 713; [1978] I.C.R. 221; (1978) 13 I.T.R. 132; (1987) 121 S.J. 814, CA (Civ Div) 4.9
Westminster City Council v Cabaj [1996] I.C.R. 960; [1996] I.R.L.R. 399, CA (Civ Div) 4–30
Westwood v Secretary of State for Employment [1985] A.C. 20; [1984] 2 W.L.R. 418; [1984] 1 All E.R. 874; [1985] I.C.R. 209; [1984] I.R.L.R. 209; (1984) 81 L.S.G. 1443; (1984) 134 N.L.J. 359; (1984) 128 S.J. 221, HL 3–2
Whitbread plc (t/a Thresher) v Gullyes (Case No.478/92), unreported, EAT 4–9
Whitbread v Mills [1988] I.C.R. 776; [1988] I.R.L.R. 501, EAT 4–30
White v Bristol Rugby Ltd [2002] I.R.L.R. 204, QBD (Merc) 1–35
Whitely v Marton Electrical Ltd [2003] I.C.R. 495; [2003] I.R.L.R. 197, EAT 1–23
Whittaker v Minister of Pensions and National Insurance [1967] 1 Q.B. 156; [1966] 3 W.L.R. 1090; [1966] 3 All E.R. 531; 1 K.I.R. 669; (1966) 110 S.J. 924, QBD 1–11
Williams v South Central (Case No.2306989/03), unreported 6–20
Williams v Watson Luxury Coaches [1990] I.C.R. 536; [1990] I.R.L.R. 164, EAT 3–6
Williams-Drabble v Pathway Care Solutions Ltd [2005] I.D.A. Brief 776 ... 6–21
Wilson v Racher [1974] I.C.R. 428; [1974] I.R.L.R. 114; (1974) 16 K.I.R. 212, CA (Civ Div) 2–35

TABLE OF STATUTES

1707 Act of Union (6 Ann c.11) 6–15
1831–1896 Truck Acts
  2–6 ....
1890 Partnership Act (53 & 54 Vict. c.39) 3–3
  s.4(2) 3–3
1944 Disabled Persons (Employment) Act (7 & 8 Geo.6 c.10) 6–23
1949 Juries Act (12, 13 & 14 Geo.6 c.27)
  s.24 2–24
1958 Disabled Persons (Employment) Act (6 & 7 Eliz.2 c.33) 6–23
1960 Payment of Wages Act (8 & 9 Eliz.2 c.37) 2–6
1963 Contracts of Employment Act (c.49) 5–1
1964 Continental Shelf Act
  s.1(7) 2–15
1965 Redundancy Payments Act (c.62) 1–07, 5–1
1970 Equal Pay Act (c.41) 1–10, 1–17, 2–1, 5–7, 6–2, 6–33, 6–44, 6–49, 6–55
  s.1(1) 6–44
  (2) 6–45, 6–52, 6–53
  (a) 6–45
  (b) 6–45
  (3) 6–49, 6–49, 6–50
  (6) 6–52
  s.2(1) 6–53
  (1A) 6–53
  (2) 6–53
  (3) 6–53
  (4) 6–51
  (5) 6–53
1974 Health and Safety at Work etc. Act (c.37) 2–21
  s.24 7–2
1975 Sex Discrimination Act (c.65) 1–10, 1–17, 5–1, 6–2, 6–7, 6–8, 6–9, 6–10, 6–11, 6–12, 6–13, 6–17, 6–18, 6–19, 6–27, 6–33, 6–55
1975 Sex Discrimination Act—*cont.*
  s.1 6–3
  (2)(b) 6–5
  s.2A 6–11
  s.3 6–3
  s.3A 6–2
  s.3B 6–2
  s.4A 6–10
  (a) 6–10
  (3) 6–12
  s.5(3) 6–3
  s.6 6–8
  (4) 1–03
  s.7 6–4
  (4) 6–4
  s.7B(2) 6–11
  s.9 .... 1–18, 6–8
  s.10A 1–27
  s.10B 1–27
  s.20A 6–7
  s.39 1–08
  s.42 1–08
  s.47 6–4
  s.48 6–4
  s.65 6–30
  s.76 1–05
  s.82(1) 6–8
  Employment Protection Act (c.71) 1–07, 2–1
1976 Race Relations Act (c.74) 1–10, 1–17, 6–13, 6–14, 6–15, 6–17,6–19, 6–20, 6–27
  s.1(1)(a) 6–13
  s.3 6–14
  s.3A 6–15
  s.5 6–17
  s.7 1–18
  s.34 6–17
  s.35 6–17
  s.36 6–17
  s.37 6–17
  s.38 6–17
  s.56 6–30
  s.78(1) 6–14
1978 Employment Protection (Consolidation) Act (c.44) 1–03, 6–55

1982 Social Security and Housing Benefits Act (c.24) 2–5
1985 Companies Act (c.6)
s.318 .... 1–24, 1–29
s.319 1–29
(1) 1–24
1986 Insolvency Act (c.45)
s.57(3) 3–4
(4) 3–4
(5) 3–4
s.386 1–24
Wages Act (c.48) 2–6, 2–7, 2–13
1988 Income and Corporation Taxes Act
s.148 3–15
1989 Employment Act (c.38)
s.12 6–16
1992 Social Security Contributions and Benefits Act (c.4) 2–5
Trade Union and Labour Relations (Consolidation) Act (c.52) 2–23, 4–2
s.68 4–41
s.86 4–41
s.146 4–41
s.152 .... 4–3, 4–37, 4–38
(1)(b) 4–38
s.153 .... 4–37, 4–38
s.168 .... 2–23, 4–41
s.168A 4–41
s.169 4–41
s.170 .... 2–23, 4–41
s.178 1–37
s.179 1–38
s.180 1–29
s.188 .... 5–1, 5–5
s.236 3–11
s.237 4–36
s.238 .... 4–33, 4–35
s.238A 4–34
s.273(1) 1–27
Sch.A1 4–39
para.161 4–39
para.162 4–39
1993 Trade Union Reform and Employment Rights Act (c.19) ... 4–40
1994 Insolvency Act (c.7) 3–4
s.19 3–4
s.44 3–4
Race Relations (Remedies) Act (c.10) 6–30
1995 Merchant Shipping Act (c.21) 1–29
Criminal Procedure (Scotland) Act (c.46)
s.85 2–24
Disability Discrimination Act (c.50) 1–10, 1–17, 4–15, 5–1, 6–23, 6–24, 6–26, 6–27, 6–28, 7–4
s.1 6–24
s.3A(1) 6–26, 6–27
(2) 6–26
(4) 6–26
(5) 6–27
s.4A 6–23, 6–26
(3) 6–26
s.4B 1–18
s.55 6–23
Sch.1 6–24
1996 Employment Tribunals Act (c.17) 7–3, 7–5
s.21 7–12
s.22 7–12
Employment Rights Act (c.18) 1–09, 1–14, 1–32, 1–40, 2–1, 2–10, 2–11, 3–1, 3–2, 3–9, 4–2, 4–8, 4–41, 4–41, 5–1, 7–1
Pt I 1–31, 1–33
Pt II 1–17, 2–5, 2–7, 2–11, 2–14, 7–10
Pt IVA 4–43
Pt XI 5–2
Pt XII 5–15
s.1 7–9
s.4 7–9
s.8 2–12
s.9 2–12
s.13 2–7
s.14 2–7
s.18 .... 2–7, 7–13
(2) 7–13
s.22(2) 2–7
s.23 4–3
s.27 2–9
(1) 2–10
(3) 2–9
ss.43C–43F 4–43
s.43G 4–43
s.43H 4–43
s.43J(2) 2–41
s.43M 2–24
s.50 2–24
s.52 2–25
s.56 2–26
s.57A 2–27, 4–42, 6–63
s.61 2–28
s.63A(1) 2–30
ss.71–80 6–57

1996 Employment Rights Act—*cont.*
s.80F 7–11
s.86 4–41
(3) 3–2
(6) 3–2
s.94(1) 4–4
s.95 4–6
(1) 5–3
(2) 4–9
s.98 4–17
(1)(b) 4–20
(2) 4–14
(a) 4–15
(b) 4–15
(c) 4–15, 5–1
(d) 4–15
(4) 4–23
s.98A 4–12
(2) 4–25, 4–31
s.98B 4–44
s.98ZA–98ZF 4–17, 6–42
s.99 .... 4–3, 4–42, 6–57
s.100 .... 4–3, 4–4, 4–40
(1)(d) 4–40
(2) 4–40
(3) 4–40
s.103A 4–4, 4–43
s.104 .... 2–26, 4–41
(4) 4–41
s.104A 2–14
s.105 4–18
s.106 4–20
s.108 4–3
s.109 5–2
s.111 1–05
ss.111–132 4–46
s.114(1) 4–47
s.115(1) 4–47
s.116(1) 4–47
s.117(2) 4–47
(4)(a) 4–47
s.119(2) 4–49
s.120(1) 4–49
s.122(1) 4–49
(2) 4–49
(4) 4–49
s.123(1) 4–50
(2) 4–50
(4) 4–50
(5) 4–50
(6) 4–50
s.131(1)(b) 5–8
s.135 .... 5–2, 5–4
(1)(b) 5–4
s.136 .... 5–3, 5–11
(2) 5–3
(3) 5–3
(5) 5–3
s.137 5–3

1996 Employment Rights Act—*cont.*
s.138(2) 5–8
s.139 5–5
(1) 4–18, 5.6
s.140 5–10
s.141 5–9
(2) 5–10
(4)(d) 5–9
s.143 5–10
(3) 5–10
(4) 5–10
(5) 5–10
s.147 5–4
s.155 5–2
s.156 .... 5–1, 5–2, 5–14
s.161(1) 5–13
s.162(1) 5–14
(2) 5–14
(4) 5–1
(5) 5–1
(8) 5–1
s.163 .... 5–12, 5–12
(1) 5–11
s.164(1) 5–12
(2) 5–12
s.165 5–12
(1) 5–13
s.166 5–15
s.188 5–15
s.191 .... 1–27, 4–4
s.192 4–4
s.193 4–4
s.196 4–4
s.200 4–4
s.203 .... 3–9, 4–4, 7–13
(2) 3–9
s.210(5) 5–11
ss.210–219 4–5
s.211(2) 5–13
s.218(5) 3–3
s.230 .... 1–10, 1–14
(2) 1–22
1997 Contract (Scotland) Act (c.34) 1–35
1998 Employment Rights (Dispute Resolution) Act (c.8)
s.11 5–12
Public Interest Disclosure Act (c.23) 2–41, 4–43
National Minimum Wage Act (c.39) 1–17, 1–23, 2–1, 2–13, 4–45
s.6 2–13
s.10 2–14
s.11 2–14
ss.17—24 2–14
s.24 2–14

1998 National Minimum Wage Act—*cont.*
s.28 2–14
s.31 2–14
s.34 1–18
Human Rights Act (c.42) 6–1, 6–18
1999 Disability Rights Commission Act (c.17) ... 6–23
Employment Relations Act (c.26) 4–34, 4–37, 4–39
s.18(1) 4–4
s.32(3) 4–4
2000 Limited Liability Partnerships Act (c.12) 3–3
2002 Employment Act (c.22) 1–33, 4–8, 4–12, 4–25, 5–12
Pt 3 7–8
s.31 7–10
s.32 2–11
2002 Employment Act—*cont.*
ss.35—38 1–32
s.37 1–32
s.38 .... 1–33, 7–9, 7–10
Sch.2 Pt 2 4–12
Sch.5 .... 1–33, 7–9
2004 Gender Recognition Act (c.7) 6–11, 6–12
Sch.6 6–12
Employment Relations Act (c.24) 4–39
s.31 7–10
s.32 7–10
Sch.2 7–10
Sch.4 7–10
Civil Partnership Act (c.33) 6–18
Pensions Act (c.35) 5–26
2005 Disability Discrimination Act (c.13) 6–24
2006 Equality Act (c.3) 6–20
Work and Families Act (c.18) 6–57

TABLE OF STATUTORY INSTRUMENTS

1977 Safety Representatives and Safety Committee Regulations (SI 1977/500) 2–29

1981 Transfer of Undertakings (Protection of Employment) Regulations (SI 1981/1794) 1–04, 2–23, 5–16, 5–17, 5–22, 5–26
- reg.5 1–24
  - (3) 1–04
- reg.8(1) 1–04

1985 Unfair Dismissal (Variation of Qualifying Period) Order (SI 1985/782) 4–3

1993 Sex Discrimination and Equal Pay (Remedies) Regulations (SI 1993/2798) 6–30

1994 Employment Tribunals (Extension of Jurisdiction) (England and Wales) Order (SI 1994/1623) 1–05, 3–16

Employment Tribunals (Extension of Jurisdiction) (Scotland) Order (SI 1994/1624) 1–05, 3–2, 3–16, 4–2, 7–2

1995 Employment Protection (Part-time Employees) Regulations (SI 1995/31) 4–5

1996 Sex Discrimination and Equal Pay (Miscellaneous Amendments) Regulations (SI 1996/438) ... 6–30, 6–48

Disability Discrimination (Meaning of Disability) Regulations (SI 1996/1455) 6–24

Health and Safety (Consultation with Employees) Regulations (SI 1996/1513) 2–29

1998 Working Time Regulations (SI 1998/1833) 1–01, 1–17, 1–29, 2–21, 2–39, 4–18, 4–41, 4–45, 4–49
- reg.2 2–15
- reg.4 2–17
  - (1) 2–21
- reg.6 2–18
- reg.7 2–18
- reg.9 .... 2–18, 2–19
- reg.11 2–19
- reg.12 2–19
- reg.13 2–20
- reg.14 2–20
- reg.15 2–20
- reg.18 2–15
- reg.19 2–17
- reg.20 2–17
- reg.21 .... 2–15, 2–16, 2–18
- reg.22 2–19
- reg.23 .... 2–15, 2–18
- reg.24A 2–15
- reg.25A 2–15
- reg.25B 2–15
- reg.29 2–21
- reg.30 2–21
- reg.31 2–21
- reg.32 2–21
- reg.36 1–18

1999 National Minimum Wage Regulations (SI 1999/584) 2–3, 2–13
- reg.3 2–13
- regs 3–6 2–13
- reg.9 2–13
- reg.10 2–13
- reg.30(b) 2–13
- reg.36 2–13

Sex Discrimination (Gender Reassignment) Regulations (SI 1999/1102) 6–11
- reg.9 6–11

Public Interest (Prescribed Persons) Order (SI 1999/1549) 4–43

1999 Maternity and Parental Leave etc. Regulations (SI 1999/3312) 6–57
reg.10 4–42
reg.20 4–42
(3) 4–42
Management of Health and Safety at Work Regulations (SI 1999/3242) 6–56
reg.16 6–56
2000 Part-time Workers (Prevention of Less Favourable Treatment) Regulations (SI 2000/1551) 6–33, 6–35
reg.2 6–34
reg.3 6–34
reg.4 6–34
reg.5 6–34
(4) 6–35
reg.7 6–35
2002 Fixed-term Employees (Prevention of Less Favourable Treatment) Regulations (SI 2002/2034) 5–13, 6–36
Paternity and Adoption Leave Regulations (SI 2002/2788) 6–57
Flexible Working (Procedural Requirements) Regulations (SI 2002/3207) 6–64
Flexible Working (Eligibility, Complaints and Remedies) Regulations (SI 2002/3236) 6–64
2003 Race Relations Act 1976 (Amendment) Regulations (SI 2003/1626) 6–13, 6–15, 6–16, 6–17
Employment Equality (Religion or Belief) Regulations (SI 2003/1660) 1–10, 1–17, 6–20, 6–26
reg.9 1–18
Employment Equality (Sexual Orientation) Regulations (SI 2003/1661) 1–10, 1–17, 6–18, 6–40
reg.9 1–18
2003 Working Time (Amendment) Regulations (SI 2003/1684) 2–15
2004 Employment Act 2002 (Dispute Resolution) Regulations (SI 2004/752) 2–11, 4–12, 5–12, 7–8
reg.7 4–12
reg.14 7–11
reg.15 .... 5–12, 7–11
Employment Tribunals (Constitution and Rules of Procedure) Regulations (SI 2004/1861) 6–48, 7–3, 7–4, 7–6
reg.8 7–5
reg.10 7–3
reg.19 r.1 7–6
Sch.1 7–6
r.8 7–4
r.10 .... 7–4, 7–7
(2) 7–7
r.14 7–3
r.18 7–7
(7) 7–7
r.26 7–7
r.27 7–7
r.28 7–4
r.29 7–4
r.30 7–4
r.33 7–7
r.34 7–7
Sch.2 7–6
Sch.3 7–6
Sch.5 7–6
Sch.6 7–6
Employment Tribunals (Constitution and Rules of Procedure) (Amendment) Regulations (SI 2004/2351) 7–6
Equal Pay Act 1970 (Amendment) Regulations (SI 2004/2352) 6–48
2005 Transfer of Undertakings (Pension Protection) Regulations (SI 2005/649) 5–26
2006 Transfer of Undertakings (Protection of Employment) Regulations (SI 2006/246) 4–41, 5–16, 5–19, 5–26
reg.3 5–17

2006 Transfer of Undertakings (Protection of Employment) Regulations—*cont.*
(4) 5–19
(5) 5–19
reg.4 5–20
(3) 5–22
(4) 5–24
(9) 4–9
reg.7 5–22
(1) 5–20, 5–21, 5–22
(2) 5–21
(3) 5–21
Employment Equality (Age) Regulations (SI 2006/1031) 1–10, 1–17, 4–3, 4–17, 5–1, 5–2, 5–14, 6–37, 6–42
reg.3(1) 6–37
reg.6 6–38
reg.7 6–39
(4) 6–39
(6) 6–39
reg.8 6–40
reg.9 1–18
reg.27 6–43

2006 Employment Equality (Age) Regulations—*cont.*
reg.28 6–43
reg.29 6–43
reg.30 6–42
reg.31 6–43
reg.32 6–41
(7) 6–41
reg.33 6–43
reg.34 6–43
Sch.2 6–43
Sch.6 .... 4–17, 4–21, 4–22, 6–42
Sch.8 6–42
Working Time (Amendment) (No.2) Regulations (SI 2006/2389) 2–15

Scotland

2001 Advice and Assistance (Advice by Way of Representation) (Scotland) Amendment Regulations (SSI 2001/2) 1–05, 7–3

TABLE OF EUROPEAN TREATIES AND CONVENTIONS

1950 Convention for the Protection of Human Rights and Fundamental Freedoms, Rome 1–05, 6–12
Art.8 6–18
Art.9 6–20
1957 EC Treaty (Treaty of Rome) establishing the European Community, March 25, 1957, Rome, 298 U.N.T.S. 11 .... 1–03, 1–05, 1–07, 6–55
Art.141 .... 1–03, 1–27, 5–2, 6–2, 6–4, 6–12, 6–33, 6–54, 6–55
Art.249 1–03

TABLE OF EUROPEAN SECONDARY LEGISLATION

Directives

1975 Dir.75/117 (Equal Pay Directive) [1975] O.J. L45/19 .... 6–2, 6–54

1976 Dir.76/207 (Equal Treatment Directive) [1976] O.J. L39/40 ...... 1–03, 4–3, 5–2, 6–2, 6–4, 6–8, 6–11, 6–18, 6–54
- Art.2(1) 6–2
- Art.5 1–03
  - (1) 1–03, 6–2

1977 Dir.77/187 (Acquired Rights Directive) [1977] O.J. L61/26 .... 1–04, 5–16
- Art.4 1–04

1980 Dir.80/987 (relating to the protection of employees in the event of the insolvency of their employer) [1980] O.J. 283/23 5–15

1991 Dir.91/533 (proof of the employment relationship) [1991] O.J. L288/32 1–31

1992 Dir.92/85 (Pregnant Workers Directive) 6–2

1993 Dir.93/104 (Working Time Directive) [1993] O.J. L307/18 .... 1–26, 2–15, 2–16, 2–17
- Art.7 .... 1–03, 1–26, 2–20
  - (1) 2–20
  - (2) 2–20
- Art.18 2–16
- Art.22 2–17

1994 Dir.93/104 (Young Workers Directive) [1993] O.J. L216/12 .... 2–15, 2–16

1996 Dir.96/34 (Parental Leave Directive) [1996] O.J. L145/4 2–27

1997 Dir.97/81 (Part-time Work Directive) [1997] O.J. L14/9 .. 6–34

2000 Dir.2000/34 (Amendments to Working Time Directive) [2000] O.J. L195/41 2–15

Dir.2000/43 (Race Directive) [2000] O.J. L180/22 6–13

Dir.2000/78 (Employment Framework Directive) [2000] O.J. L303/16 .... 6–18, 6–20, 6–23, 6–37, 6–43

Dir.2000/790 2–15

2001 Dir.2001/23 (on the safeguarding of employees' rights) [2001] O.J. L82/16 5–16

2002 Dir.2002/15 (on the organisation of the working time of persons performing mobile road transport activities) [2002] O.J. L80/35 2–15

Dir.2002/73 (on equal treatment) [2002] O.J. L269/15 6–2

2004 Dir.2004/113 (Gender Directive) [2004] O.J. L373/37 6–12

CHAPTER ONE

THE CONTRACT OF EMPLOYMENT

INTRODUCTION TO CONTRACT AND EMPLOYMENT LAW

An understanding of employment law requires a general awareness **1–01** of (a) the basic legal principles of contract and Scots law of delict (in England known as the law of torts); (b) the law made by Parliament (statute law); (c) the law made and developed by the courts (the common law); and how they relate to each other. The law of contract and delict (or torts) is the province of the common law and generally the subject of adjudication by the ordinary courts (in Scotland, the Sheriff Court and the Court of Session; and in England, the County Court and the High Court) whereas employment rights which are created by statute are the subject of adjudication in the employment tribunals. The relationship of employment is regulated by both statute and common law, which operate in parallel, and only very occasionally is the relationship regulated by criminal law. Thus the employer of an employee whose work or shift patterns cause the employee to become mentally ill may (a) break the contract of employment; (b) commit the delictual wrong (tort of negligence) of failing to take reasonable care for the employee's safety; and (c) violate the Working Time Regulations 1998 (SI 1998/1833). The first two may result in common law claims for personal injury brought by the employee and are heard by the ordinary courts; while violation of the Regulations may give rise to criminal prosecutions in the ordinary courts with regard to the length of the maximum working week or health assessments for night workers, and complaints to employment tribunals with regard to rest periods and holiday entitlement.

COMMON LAW AND STATUTE

Generally the common law develops incrementally, while more **1–02** radical policy changes in the law regulating the employment relationship are the result of parliamentary intervention in the form of statutes or regulations. It should not be thought, however, that the common law plays only a minor role because although many employment rights are created by statute, particularly so during the last 20 years, the common law has continued to develop the contract of employment by the importation or implication of important terms. The most significant common law development has been implying into the contract of employment the duty of mutual trust and confidence which allows the contract of employment to reflect contemporary values in human resource management.

Examples of the development of the contract of employment may be seen in the following decision.

United Bank v Akhtar

[1989] I.R.L.R. 507, EAT

A term in Mr Akhtar's contract of employment stated: "The bank may from time to time require an employee to be transferred temporarily or permanently to any place of business which the bank may have in the United Kingdom for which a relocation or other allowances may be payable at the discretion of the bank", and relying on that clause the bank proposed to transfer Mr Akhtar from its branch in Leeds to its branch in Birmingham at short notice and without indicating whether he would receive a relocation allowance. Although the contract did not expressly require that the bank would give notice of a transfer and gave it a discretion to pay a relocation allowance, the Employment Appeal Tribunal held that the bank had a duty to give reasonable notice and that unless the bank implemented its discretion to pay relocation allowances, its actions would require Mr Akhtar to attempt to perform something which was impossible. It was necessary therefore to imply into the contract a term that the employer's discretion under the mobility clause had to be exercised so as not to render it impossible for Mr Akhtar to comply with his contractual obligation.

By contrast statute law was required to introduce policy shifts dealing with: (1) equal pay between men and women; (2) protection against unfair dismissal; and (3) the elimination of discrimination by employers on various grounds. Without legislation, employment law in the United Kingdom would not have been able to deal effectively with contemporary problems of discrimination, unfair dismissal, redundancy compensation, entitlement to time-off for childbirth, paid maternity leave, limits on the working week and parental leave rights. These are essentially complicated, rule-based systems, which can impose costs on employers while creating benefits for employees and are best dealt with by legislation passed by Parliament. The ordinary courts would not have been able to develop such systems of protection from common law principles and to require them to do so would run the risk of undermining the independence of the judiciary. (Judicial attempts to grapple with the undoubted problems of agency workers are well illustrated in the different policy approaches adopted in *Dacas v Brook Street Bureau (UK) Ltd* [2004] I.R.L.R. 358, CA; and *James v London Borough of Greenwich Council* [2007] I.R.L.R. 168, EAT on the one hand; and *Cairns v Visteon UK Ltd* [2007] I.R.L.R. 175, AET; and *Craigie v London Borough of Haringey* (EAT 0556/06)—discussed later–on the other. In *Craigie*, Justice Bean remarked that while the law regarding the status of long-term agency workers is unsatisfactory it will need legislation to change it.)

The effect of this hybrid or dual approach to employment law in the United Kingdom is to require at least an understanding of the principles of contract law and the legislative rules created by Parliament which have, over recent years, attempted to counter employer power by creating basic or minimum rights for employees. These rights are often referred to as "a floor of rights" in the expectation that progressive and enlightened employers will seek to offer more advantageous or sophisticated provisions or do so as a result of collective bargaining. Unlike in continental legal systems the collective agreement in the United Kingdom does not create rights and duties for employers and employees throughout an industry or sector of an industry. Collective agreements therefore do not have any binding industry-wide or normative effect; in the United Kingdom such a role is played by statute.

EUROPEAN LAW

However, like in many areas of industry and society, the law of the **1–03**
European Community plays an important part in shaping employment law rights. Some articles of the European Economic Treaty create directly enforceable rights—without the need for domestic legislation—for all citizens of the European Union. In the field of employment law, the most notable example is Art.141 which provides for equal pay for men and women. Article 141 is of direct legal effect and must be applied by UK courts and tribunals, and takes priority over UK statutes. An example of the direct effect of Art.141 is seen in the following decisions.

Rankin v British Coal

[1993] I.R.L.R. 69, EAT

When Mrs Rankin, who was over 60 years of age, was dismissed on the grounds of redundancy in March 31, 1987 she was excluded from entitlement to a redundancy payment because at that time the Employment Protection (Consolidation) Act 1978 excluded women over 60 but men over

65 years from receiving a redundancy payment. Clearly that was direct sexual discrimination. That legislation was not repealed until January 16, 1990 but since redundancy payments were "pay" for the purposes of Art.141, Mrs Rankin was able to rely on Art.141 to become entitled to a redundancy payment when she was made redundant in 1987 in spite of the terms of the UK statute. The employment tribunal was bound to disapply the domestic law and give effect to the right to equal pay as enshrined in Art.141.

Perceval-Price v Department of Economic Development

[2000] I.R.L.R. 380, NICA

Perceval-Price and others were female chairpersons of tribunals in Northern Ireland who brought equal pay claims. Although the claimants were office-holders and as a result their claims were excluded by the domestic legislation, the employment tribunal was required to disapply those provisions of domestic law which were inconsistent with Art.141 which extends to anyone who is a "worker" which has a particular meaning in European Community law (see *Lawrie-Blum v Baden Wurtemberg* [1987] I.C.R. 483; and *Allonby v Accrington and Rossendale College* [2004] I.R.L.R. 224, ECJ). The claimants fell within that meaning and once the domestic provisions which were inconsistent with that meaning were disapplied the claimants were included within the domestic definition and were entitled to advance their claims of equal pay.

Also European Community law (EC Treaty, Art.249) requires Member States to give effect to the aims of a directive and this is usually done by passing national legislation. If a Member State has not implemented a directive an employee of the State (or an organisation acting on behalf of the State described as "an emanation of the State"), for example a civil servant, an employee of a health authority, a local government employee or an employee of a privatised utility, may rely on the directive which is clear, precise and unconditional in its terms in a dispute with his employer in the national courts.

Marshall v Southampton and South West Hampshire Area Health Authority

[1986] I.C.R. 335, ECJ

Mrs Marshall was employed by the Health Authority whose policy was to require employees to retire when they reached State pension age which for women was 60 and for men 65. However, because Mrs Marshall did not wish to retire when she reached 60 the Health Authority permitted her to continue working but shortly after Mrs Marshall became 62 the Authority insisted that she retire. Had Mrs Marshall been a man she would not have been required to retire at 62. At the time of her enforced retirement, UK law against sexual discrimination (Sex Discrimination Act 1975 s.6(4)) did not apply to retirement with the result that Mrs Marshall could not claim under domestic law.

However since 1976 the United Kingdom has been bound to implement the provisions of the European Equal Treatment Directive (Directive 76/207) which prohibits discrimination in employment between men and women. In particular Art.5(1) of the Directive provides that

> "[a]pplication of the principle of equal treatment with regard to working conditions, including the conditions governing dismissal, means that men and women shall be guaranteed the same conditions without discrimination on the grounds of sex".

The European Court of Justice held that "dismissal" included compulsory retirement and that, although Mrs Marshall was not protected by the domestic law, she was entitled to rely on the Equal Treatment Directive against the Health Authority which was an emanation of the State because Art.5 was clear and unconditional in its terms.

In practice the wording of the directive must be clear enough to allow a domestic court or tribunal to apply it to the facts of the case and an example of a directive not being sufficiently clear, precise and unconditional to allow it to do so is seen in *Gibson v East Riding of Yorkshire Council* [2000] I.R.L.R. 598, CA in which Gibson sought to rely on Art.7 of the Directive on Working Time Council dealing with entitlement to annual paid holidays. However where a directive is clear and precise in its terms an employee of the State (or an emanation of the State) is able to enforce the rights conferred by the directive even if, as in the case of Mrs Marshall, domestic law had not implemented the directive by enacting appropriate legislation. However, if Mrs Marshall had been employed by a private organisation she would not have been able to rely on the Directive. This distinction between the rights of those who are in a relationship with the State (or one its emanations) was upheld by the House of Lords in *Duke v Reliance Systems Ltd* [1988] I.R.L.R. 118 so that—subject to what is said below in relation to *Litster v Forth and Dry Dock Engineering Company Ltd*—the only remedy for an employee of a private organisation who is denied rights conferred by a directive is to sue the Member State government concerned for its failure to implement the directive. This is referred to as the "Francovich doctrine" and derives from the decision of the European Court of Justice in *Francovich v Italian Republic* [1991] E.C.R. I-5357; [1992] I.R.L.R. 84, ECJ.

1–04 However, even if a directive is not precise enough to be relied on by an employee of an emanation of the State it is the rule that when interpreting legislation passed to give effect to a directive a national court or tribunal must have regard to the directive and its purpose in applying and interpreting national law. Perhaps the most striking illustration of a UK court interpreting domestic law to give effect to a directive is seen in the following case.

Litster v Forth Dry Dock and Engineering Company Ltd

[1989] I.R.L.R. 161, HL

The UK Government had passed the Transfer of Undertakings (Protection of Employment) Regulations 1981 (SI 1981/1794) (TUPE) to give effect to the Acquired Rights Directive (77/187). The Directive provides that where a business or an undertaking is transferred from one employer (the transferor) to another (the transferee) the transferor's rights and duties arising from a contract of employment existing on the date of the transfer shall be transferred to the transferee and that the transfer of an undertaking or business shall not in itself constitute grounds for dismissal by the transferor or the transferee unless the dismissal was for an economic, technical or organisational reason entailing changes in the workforce. TUPE made similar provisions but added that a "reference to a person employed in an undertaking or business ... transferred is a reference to a person so employed immediately before the transfer" (reg.5(3)). Litster and other employees were employed by Forth Dry Dock and Engineering Co Ltd, which went into receivership. The receivers proposed to sell the business to a company, Forth Estuary Engineering Ltd, and an hour before the transfer was to take place, told Litster and his fellow employees that the business was to close and that they were dismissed. The question that arose was whether Litster and others could claim the benefit of having their contract of employment transferred to Forth Estuary and thereby have their employment continued. Clearly they were not employed in the business "immediately before the transfer"—they had been dismissed an hour before the transfer—but the House of Lords held that the UK Regulations had to be given a purposive interpretation consistent with the meaning and purpose of the Directive to which they were designed to give effect. This could be done if reg.5(3) was to be applied not just to persons who were employed immediately before the transfer but also to those who would have been employed at that time if they had not previously been dismissed because of the transfer.

According to Lord Oliver of Aylmerton the "provision in reg.8(1) that a dismissal by reason of a transfer is to be treated as unfair is merely a different way of saying that the transfer is not to 'constitute a ground for dismissal' as contemplated by Article 4 of the Directive and there is no good reason for denying it the same effect as in that attributed to that Article. In effect this involves reading reg.5(3) as if there were inserted after the words 'immediately before the transfer' the words 'or would have been so employed if he had not been unfairly dismissed in the circumstances described in reg.8(1)'. For my part, I would make such an implication which is entirely in keeping with the scheme of the regulations and which is necessary if they are effectively to fulfil the purpose for which they were made of giving effect to the Directive".

THE COURTS AND EMPLOYMENT TRIBUNALS

Another result of the hybrid system is that some employment law **1–05** disputes are dealt with by the ordinary courts—the same courts in England and Scotland which deal with disputes about other types of business contracts, like contracts of sale, building contracts and contracts about partnerships and franchises or dealerships, etc. For example, if an employee acts in breach of his contract by disclosing confidential information about his employer's business his employer may raise an action in the ordinary court asking the court to grant an interdict or injunction to restrain the employee from making further disclosures. Or if an employer terminates an employee's contract without giving proper notice, the employee may sue for his wrongful dismissal in the ordinary court which can order the employer to pay damages to compensate the employee for the loss he has suffered by his contract being broken. Generally, actions for breach of the contract of employment (or a contact connected with employment) whether brought by the employer or the employee must be brought in the ordinary courts and not the specialist employment tribunals, although there is an exception created by the employment tribunals (Extension of Jurisdiction) (Scotland) Order 1994 and its English counterpart (Statutory Instruments 1994/1624 and 1994/1623 respectively). The exception applies only where the contract of employment has been brought to an end and the employee's claim arises or is outstanding on the termination of the employee's employment This limited exception permits an employee who is dismissed in breach of his contract of employment without notice and without wages in lieu of notice to raise an action for breach of contract in the employment tribunal.

On the other hand, employment rights which have been created by legislation are capable of being enforced only through the employment tribunals which are given an exclusive jurisdiction (and see Ch.7 above). Frequently the disputes which come before these tribunals require a tribunal to have regard to what is reasonable conduct by an employer or good employment practice and tribunals which, unlike the ordinary courts, generally consist of a legally qualified Chairman and two other members, one from the employers' side and one from the employees' side of industry, are seen to be in a better position to assess such issues and to be less open to allegations of bias. (For some types of case the tribunal may consist of the legally qualified Chairman sitting without members, although this practice has been criticised because it deprives the Chairman of the valuable assistance and advice of "lay" colleagues: *Sogbetun v London Borough of Hackney* [1998] I.R.L.R. 676.) Also, unlike the ordinary courts, employment tribunals deal with disputes without the parties requiring to be legally represented and in that respect are able to operate less expensively and more quickly than normal court procedures. There are no complicated procedural rules and an unrepresented party will be given fair assistance from the tribunal Chairman or members where matters are complicated although the extent to which tribunals may do so has been questioned by the Employment Appeal Tribunal (see *Edinburgh Pharmaceutical Processes Ltd v Lothian* (EAT No 0085/05) and the extent to which a tribunal should adopt an inquisitorial role has been the subject of comment by the Employment Appeal Tribunal: *Beales v Secretary of State for Work and Pensions* (EAT No.0602/05); *Whyte v First Capital East Ltd* (EAT No.0686/04).

A claim may be presented by a party (employee or worker), the "claimant" completing a form (sample forms are included in the Appendices) setting out the essence of his or her case to which the other party, the "respondent", is required to respond. Frequently no other formalities occur before the tribunal hears the claim which is usually within a few weeks of the claim being presented, with the judgment of the tribunal being issued soon thereafter. However, in many cases the parties are represented by qualified lawyers or consultants specialising in employment law and it may be that they have brought to tribunal practice the formalities associated more with court procedure where professional legal representation is the norm. In addition some cases may involve consideration of complex issues of European law in the form of directives, Articles of the European Treaty or the European Convention on Human Rights and will benefit from representation by experienced practitioners. In Scotland where a case is complicated, a party may receive legal aid to assist in presenting his or her case (Advice and Assistance (Advice by Way of Representation) (Scotland) Amendment Regulations 2001 (SSI 2001/2)) and in England the Legal Aid Act 1988 (c.34). Claims usually have to be presented to an Employment Tribunals Office within three months of the right being infringed, although this can be extended if it was not reasonably practicable to do so, for example, as a result of illness of the claimant (see the Employment Rights Act 1996 s.111) or if it would generally be just and equitable to allow a late claim (see the Sex Discrimination Act 1975 s.76). The three months' time limit is generally strictly enforced by the tribunal so that claims can be dealt with while recollections are fresh, without the need for detailed documentation, thereby allowing the system to operate as speedily as possible. Disputes about the following statutory rights are capable of being heard only by the employment tribunals:

- National Minimum Wage claims and access to records;
- maternity, paternity, parental leave and adoption leave and the right to return to work;
- redundancy payments;
- discrimination by an employer;
- time-off rights and holiday pay;
- unfair dismissal;
- unlawful deductions from wages;
- equal pay (strictly such claims may also be raised in the ordinary courts but seldom, if ever, are);
- appeals against health and safety improvement, prohibition and non-discrimination notices;
- failure to consult employee representatives on business transfers;
- action short of dismissal on grounds of union membership or non-membership;
- refusal of employment on grounds of union membership;
- exclusion from trade union;
- written particulars of terms of employment;
- written statement of reasons for dismissal; and
- payment by Secretary of State where employer is insolvent.

WHY IS EMPLOYMENT LAW IMPORTANT TODAY?

Certainly until the 1950s, the relations between employees and **1–06**
employers were not the subject of regulation by Parliament. The legal relation of employment was contained within the terms of the contract of employment—frequently entered in a very informal way

with little in writing being exchanged between the employer and the employee—and in theory only, representing the freely negotiated terms of the employment. In practice, the terms of the contract were either determined by the customs and practices of the particular trade, imported from collective agreements or by the employer who would draw up such contractual documentation as he might require. Even today the law does not require that *the contract* between employer and employee be in writing, although *information* about the terms of employment must be given to employees. The period until the 1950s is often referred to as the "era of legal abstentionism" and was founded on the belief that industry could best manage its affairs without the interference of Parliament and the courts.

Legal Abstentionism

1–07 However, that era has now come to an end for a variety of reasons. Post-war governments have used employment law as an instrument of economic and social policy. A good example of this is the Redundancy Payments Act 1965 which, by offering financial compensation to employees whose jobs were disappearing through the introduction of new technology, assisted businesses in becoming more efficient and responding to new economic circumstances and the requirement for new skills. The 1965 Act ensured that employees whose jobs were disappearing received lump sum compensation. Another reason is found in the legal nature and effect of collective agreements in the United Kingdom legal system. Unlike some continental systems, collective agreements in the United Kingdom do not have any normative effect, that is to say they do not have to be observed by all employers in a particular industry, the result being that employees in an industry in the United Kingdom doing similar jobs are not required to be paid in accordance with collectively agreed norms or standards. Frequently the terms and conditions of employees reflected the degree to which their industry was unionised and there were many areas, for example where women had been traditionally employed, that unionisation was low. That the system of industrial relations which until only very recently did not require employers to negotiate with trade unions, the absence—again until very recently—of general legislation to set a national minimum wage and the fact that collective agreements lacked any normative legal effect, resulted in great inequalities in the labour market and these could be addressed only by parliamentary intervention. Furthermore, post-war Labour governments have in accordance with their own political and philosophical ideals created rights for workers, an example of which can be seen in the Employment Protection Act 1975. However, perhaps the most important reason for legislative intervention in the employment relationship has been the United Kingdom's membership of the European Community. Compliance with the

Social Policy chapter of the European Economic Treaty required that Parliament enact legislation to give effect to the rights European law has created for employees and workers. Membership of the European Community has required the United Kingdom Parliament to adopt legislation to deal with equal pay, discrimination, and leave for having and bringing up children. Other European directives are concerned with working conditions more generally and include the protection of employment and the rights of employees who work in businesses which are sold or transferred, the duty of employers to consult with workers' representatives and the right of workers to have limited working hours and paid holidays. Other directives are more concerned with employee health, safety and welfare and have required domestic legislation requiring employers to carry out risk assessments, consult workers' representatives about safety matters, rest breaks and time off. More recently still domestic legislation rendering unlawful discrimination on the grounds of sexual orientation, religion and belief and age has been enacted to give effect to European directives. The result of this is that the relations between employer and employee or worker are now heavily regulated by legislation which, if not observed, can lead to awards of compensation and, mainly in the field of health and safety, imposing criminal penalties on the employer.

Practical Results for Employers and Workers

However, it would be wrong to leave this topic without stressing **1–08**
some points. First, as employment law is now developed by legislation, it follows that managers and trade unionists need to be aware of the legislative proposals and to seek to influence these at their formative stages. Secondly, business strategy has to take place within the confines of the legal rules; a payment scheme to reward the loyalty of staff who have worked full time for at least two years may well reduce staff turnover and training costs but it may also operate to indirectly discriminate against female employees, leaving them the opportunity of bringing equal pay claims. Similarly reorganising the workforce might result in economies in the wage cost, but equally it may result in expensive claims for redundancy payments and unfair dismissal. The modern manager must be aware of these additional factors when planning his or her strategy. Other, less strategic but important matters will occur too and these may require instant decision-making. Is an employee entitled to time off to pick up a child who has become ill at school? If so, on what conditions? Is an employer required to take any special steps to allow a disabled applicant to attend an interview or take a selection test? Can an employee suspected of stealing be dismissed without notice and without a hearing? Finally, while in most cases a manager will not be personally liable for breach of an employee's rights, occasionally the law may attach responsibility to him as well as to the organisation. Thus, a manager who instructs an employee

to commit an unlawful act of discrimination, or who aids and abets an employer in committing an act of unlawful sex discrimination, will be personally liable (see for example the Sex Discrimination Act ss.39 and 42).

Equally in an environment more regulated by law than before an employee needs to be aware of his rights and duties. Must he raise his grievance with his employer before he can lodge a claim in the Employment Tribunal? Does a failure to do so mean that his access to the tribunal is blocked or does it merely affect any award the tribunal may make?

Why do we Need to Identify the Contract of Employment and other Contracts

1–09 For many years the most important distinction in employment law was the contract of employment at one end of the spectrum and the contract for services at the other—essentially the distinction between the paid servant or employee on the one hand and the independent businessman/woman on the other hand. Unlike today there were few employment relationships between the employee and the independent contractor. The distinction was important for a variety of reasons, perhaps the most important being that nearly all employment statutes conferred rights only on those who had a contract of employment or a contract of apprenticeship. Thus many of the important legal rights contained in the Employment Rights Act 1996—the main source of individual employment rights—are given only to those who have a contract of employment or a contract of apprenticeship. It is important to note precisely the terminology used. The older terminology for the contract of employment is "contract of service" but this must not be confused with the contract under which an independent contractor is engaged, namely the "contract for services". In the statutes and the common law people who have contracts of employment are referred to as "employees" (or in some older texts "servants"). Under the Employment Rights Act 1996 only employees and apprentices are entitled to (a) protection against unfair dismissal; (b) compensation if made redundant; (c) minimum notice of termination; (d) maternity, paternity and adoption leave; (e) time off for public duties; and (f) medical suspension pay. Individuals who provide their services under contracts for services or other types of contract are generally not given these rights.

1–10 Only relatively recently have other types of contracts under which work is done become significant for employment law. The most obvious examples are the rights conferred under the laws dealing with discrimination. Statutes such as the Equal Pay Act 1970, the Sex Discrimination Act 1975, the Race Relations Act 1976 and the Disability Discrimination Act 1995 and the regulations rendering unlawful discrimination by employers on the grounds of sexual orientation, religion and belief and age (Employment Equality

(Sexual Orientation) Regulations 2003, Employment Equality (Religion or Belief) Regulations 2003, Employment Equality (Age) Regulations 2006) confer protection not just on employees but on the ever increasing group of economically active persons known as "workers". The legal concept of "worker" is wider than the concept of "employee". The definition of a "worker" includes an individual who has entered into a contract of employment and "any other contract ... whereby the individual undertakes to perform personally any work or services for another party to the contract" who is not a client or customer of any profession or business carried on by the individual (Employment Rights Act 1996 s.230). In effect what the concepts of "employee" and "worker" seek to do is to describe those individuals who earn a living by performing services personally for another person, in return for a regular income. Others are regarded as independent businessmen/women or "self-employed" and provide their services as a business or undertaking to whoever may wish to purchase them, usually, but not necessarily, by a single ad hoc contract for a particular purpose. However while these terms of "independent businessman" and "self-employed" may be convenient shorthand they are over simplistic and must not take the place of the statutory language and the fact that a person is self-employed does not necessarily mean that he is engaged in a business undertaking.

In *James v Redcats (Brands) Ltd* [2007] I.R.L.R. 296 the EAT (President Elias) held that whether a courier was a "worker" might be better answered by having regard to what was the "dominant purpose" of the contractual arrangements rather than accepting that all non-employees must be in business on their own account. Is the obligation of personal service the dominant feature or is it in essence a contract between two independent business undertakings? Given the nature of modern employment whether one is seeking to identify the contract of employment or the worker's contract attributing more significance to economic dependency (or independency) may now be appropriate although it should not be regarded as the most important factor.

THE EMPLOYMENT CONTRACT—CONTROL AND OTHER TESTS

It is still the case that important rights like unfair dismissal, **1–11**
redundancy pay, maternity, paternity and adoption leave, and notice of termination are restricted to those who have contracts of employment and for that reason it is still necessary to be able to identify that contract and to distinguish it from others. Although the identification task has become more difficult of late, courts and tribunals have for many years been required to decide whether or not a contractual relationship is one of employment. In the earlier days the test to be applied to decide whether or not there was a

contract of employment was relatively simple, reflecting the essentially simple tasks carried out by employees. Frequently these tasks would be agricultural or domestic which an individual employer would be able to do himself in many cases. The result was that in the early stages, the test applied by the courts to identify the contract of employment, was simply to ask whether the person for whom the work was done, had the right to determine not just *what* had to be done but *how* it was to be done. Alternatively, the court asked whether the employer could direct not just the *ends* of the worker's labours but also the *means* that the individual would adopt. Generally, if the employer could tell the individual what to do and how to do it there would be a contract of employment. This was sometimes referred to as the "control test", an early example of which is seen in the following case.

Performing Rights Society v Mitchell and Booker

[1924] 1 K.B. 762

The Performing Rights Society, which protects copyright in music on behalf of its composers, sued Mitchell and Booker who owned a dance hall. The Society argued that the band which played in the dance hall had played music without receiving the composer's or the Society's permission. If the band were employed under contracts of employment then Mitchell and Booker would be vicariously liable for their breach of the composer's right. On the other hand if they were independent musicians they themselves could be liable for breaching the composer's right in his music. In the event, having examined the degree to which the members of the band were under the control of the dance hall owners, the court came to the conclusion that they were indeed employed under contracts of employment by the owners of the dance hall. The dance hall owners could specify the type of music to be played at particular times so that it was fair to conclude they directed not just the ends but also the means of performing the contract.

However, the simple control test was not suitable for more developed and sophisticated types of employment of skilled professionals who frequently would carry out types of work which were so technical that their employer would not be able to give them instructions as to how they should carry out the work. As a result the courts began to relax the control test so that it was sufficient if an employer could merely direct a person's individual skill. An example of this can be seen in the case of *Stagecraft v Minister of Pensions*, 1952 S.C. 288. The issue in this case was whether the company Stagecraft, which engaged circus and theatrical personnel, should be required to pay National Insurance Contributions in respect of these artistes or whether the artistes were truly independent and self-employed acrobats in which case only they would require to make contributions to the National Insurance Fund. Although the court accepted that the company Stagecraft could not interfere once an artiste's act had begun, and in that respect could not control the means, the court accepted that it was sufficient if the court could direct the end to which the artiste's individual skills were put.

Similar difficulties were experienced with the advent of professionally qualified staff in, for example, the Health Service in the case of *Cassidy v Ministry of Health* [1951] 2 K.B. 343. The issue here was whether the Minister of Health was liable for the injuries sustained by a patient in a National Health Service hospital. He would only be liable if the doctor or nurse who was negligent was an "employee" of the Minister of Health. It was argued that the Minister could not exercise control over a health professional who would make matters of judgment with regard to the patient's treatment and how it should be carried out but the Court concluded that if the Minister of Health could exercise *potential* control through the sanction of dismissal, that would be sufficient to establish the contract of employment.

In other circumstances the courts have adopted what has become known as the "organisation test" or "integration test" which allows the courts to look at whether the services or work done under the contract is done as an integral part of the employer's activities or organisation. If the work done was truly an integral part of the employer's business then the court would be prepared to conclude there was a contract of employment between the employer and the person who does the work. An excellent example of this is seen in the case of *Whittaker v Minister of Pensions* [1967] 1 Q.B. 156. The issue again concerned contributions to the National Insurance Fund and concerned a trapeze artiste in a circus. The evidence showed that the artiste did not just perform as a trapeze artiste, she was also required to undertake more mundane tasks of selling tickets at the admissions kiosk, act as an usherette and help move the circus from one location to another. Having regard to the way in which her activities had been integrated into the circus's activities, the court concluded there was a contract of employment between the trapeze artiste and the circus.

Multiple and Variable Test

In the 1960s it had become apparent that none of these tests was **1–12**
suitable in all circumstances and the courts have since developed a more flexible test that can be used to deal with many sorts of employment. This test is frequently described as the "multiple and variable" test and essentially seeks to consider, taking into account a variety of factors, the reality of the relationship between the

individual and the person or organisation for whom the work is done. In essence, the court or tribunal is concerned with the substance of the relationship and not merely its form. It permits the court to take into account a multiplicity of different factors or criteria and give a particular factor or criterion emphasis or weight according to the circumstances before the court. The test may have the advantage of being universal and flexible but it does have the disadvantage of making it difficult to predict in advance of a court decision what is the type of relationship in marginal cases. An example of the test can be seen in the case of *Market Investigations v Minister of Social Security* [1968] 3 All E.R. 732 in which market researchers for the company Market Investigations were regarded as having contracts of employment with the company for the purposes of making contributions to the National Insurance Fund. The investigators were provided with carefully worded questionnaire sheets and were required to follow a particular routine when asking questions of respondents. The court concluded that the researchers had contracts of employment with the company but the case is important for giving guidance regarding how the contract of employment should be identified and distinguished from the contract under which self-employed businessman/woman or independent contractor undertakes work, namely the contract for services.

As a result of that decision, and other decisions since then, the following may be regarded as factors which are relevant in determining whether or not there is a contract of employment.

Control: The criterion of control is clearly still an important one although it is no longer the decisive criterion.

Provision of equipment: The extent to which the person doing the work has to provide equipment at his or her own expense is significant. Generally incurring a large capital outlay to acquire equipment to perform a task is more readily associated with a contract for services—the kind of investment a business might make–rather than a contract of employment.

Hire of helpers: If the task cannot be done by the individual but requires the individual worker to hire additional helpers, that would also suggest it is not a contract of employment; a contract of employment is a contract under which there is to a large extent personal performance by the worker so that if it requires the assistance of others that would militate against it being a contract of employment.

Financial risk: If the contract involves a degree of financial risk and requires exercising responsibility for the management of the work of the contract it might suggest it is not a contract of employment but more likely to be a contract for services.

Opportunity to profit: An opportunity to profit from the sound management of the contract—as distinct from merely receiving payment for the services—will more readily be associated with a contract for services.

Label or name of contract: Frequently the parties to a contract, in an attempt to remove doubt as to the type of contract, will give the contract a particular name. However, the name the parties give a contract will not be conclusive because the existence of a contract of employment is a question of law and a matter for a court or tribunal to decide and cannot be determined by the name or "label" the parties give to the contract.

Change of status: On the other hand where the parties have genuinely intended to change the status of the contract and have applied an appropriate name or label to it the courts will bear this in mind in determining the relationship between the two parties.

Income Tax and National Insurance: Seldom will the fact that the employer does or does not deduct Income Tax or pay National Insurance Contributions as if the person was an employee be of much significance. In many cases whether such Income Tax or National Insurance Contributions should be deducted at source is the issue which has raised the question of the status of the individual. How Income Tax is paid is of little significance.

Mutuality of obligation: Is the employer required to provide work when it is available and is the individual required to do it when it is provided?

CASUAL AND ATYPICAL WORKERS

The status of such workers is frequently resolved by having regard **1–13**
to the last factor referred to above, "mutuality of obligation".

O'Kelly v Trusthouse Forte plc

[1983] I.C.R. 728

O'Kelly and others worked as casual waiters on a regular basis for banquets contracted to Trusthouse Forte. In many cases the banquets would take place in the same venues and when banquets were to be held preference would be given to staff like O'Kelly and work allocated to them. However, there was no obligation on Trusthouse Forte to give work to staff like O'Kelly when the work was available nor was there any obligation on staff like O'Kelly to do the work when it was offered to them. For that reason the court concluded there was insufficient mutuality of obligation for there to be a contract of employment. As a result O'Kelly was not able to establish that he had a contract of employment for the purposes of claiming protection against unfair dismissal or receiving a redundancy payment.

Nethermere (St Neots) Ltd v Taverna

[1984] I.C.R. 612

Nethermere St Neots manufactured trousers in a factory where they employed about 70 operatives who were undoubtedly employees and from whose wages they deducted Income Tax and National Insurance Contributions. The appellants also made use of the services of a number of home-workers from whose remuneration such deductions were not made. Mrs Taverna started as a home-worker in January 1978; her work consisted of putting pockets into trousers for which she used a machine provided by the appellants. She worked about five hours each day and in that time she put in about 100 pockets. Later her work changed and she put artificial flaps into trousers. She then worked for about seven hours per day. She had no fixed hours of work. The garments were delivered to her daily and sometimes twice a day. In the year 1979–1980 she did not work for 12 weeks; in the year 1980–1981 she did not work for nine weeks. The arrangement came to an end in July 1981. During the period she worked in 1981 she worked in every week of the year. She was paid weekly according to the garments that she completed. The court accepted that there was a regular course of dealing between parties for years under which the garments were supplied daily to the home-workers, worked on, collected and paid for. The mere fact that the home-workers could fix their own hours of work, take holidays and time off when they wished and vary how many garments they were willing to take on or sometimes to take none on a particular day, were factors for consideration in deciding whether or not there was a contract of service. Although the home-workers could decide how much work to do in fact they tended to do enough to make it worthwhile for the van driver's time in collecting it, and this could be read as an obligation on operatives like Mrs Taverna to take a reasonable amount of work. Conversely there was an obligation on the company to provide a reasonable share of work for each home worker.

Thus the expectations of continuing home-work meant that Mrs Taverna had an enforceable contract of employment by regular giving and taking of work over periods of a year or more. There was also no reason why home-workers should not thereby become employees under contracts of employment like those doing similar work at the same rate in the factory. Therefore, there was mutuality of obligation in that Nethermere had an obligation to give work to Mrs Taverna when it was there to be done and she had an obligation to do sufficient work to make it worthwhile for Nethermere to deliver the garments to her. The court implied a "global" or "umbrella" contract between Mrs Taverna and Nethermere.

Nethermere can be contrasted with *Clark v Oxfordshire Health Authority* [1998] I.R.L.R. 125 in which Clark was engaged from time to time as a "bank" nurse, namely someone who was offered work as and when an appropriate temporary vacancy occurred. The Court of Appeal agreed that Mrs Clark's relationship with the health authority as a bank nurse was not governed by a global contract of employment, in light of the lack of mutuality of obligation during the periods between engagements. According to the decision:

> "a contract of employment ... cannot exist in the absence of mutual obligations subsisting over the entire duration of the relevant period. Although the mutual obligations required to found a global contract of employment need not necessarily and in every case consist of obligations to provide and perform work, some mutuality of obligation is required. For example, an obligation by the one party to accept and do the work if offered and an obligation on the other party to pay a retainer during such periods as work was not offered, would be likely to suffice".

According to the Court of Appeal, in this case no such mutuality existed during the periods when the applicant was not occupied between assignments. The authority was under no obligation to offer the applicant work, nor was she under any obligation to accept it. She had no entitlement to any pay when she did not work and no entitlement to holiday pay or sick leave.

Accordingly, no global contract of employment between the **1–14**
authority and the applicant was in existence at any time during the three years that she was a bank nurse. Thus there was no overarching contract of employment to cover both periods when assignments were being undertaken—periods in which there was most likely to be a contract of employment—and periods between such assignments. The difference between *Nethermere* and *Clark* is that in the former there was evidence to show that throughout the period of Mrs Taverna's relationship with Nethermere there was mutuality of obligation. Nethermere had to provide work when it was available and Mrs Taverna had to do enough to justify the van making the journey to deliver and uplift garments. In the latter case,

however, the evidence did not show there was any obligation on the Health Authority to provide any work to Mrs Clark between specific assignments.

In *Clark*, while the Court of Appeal emphasised that there can be no contract of employment unless there is a mutuality of obligation subsisting over the entire duration of the relevant period, it seems to have qualified this rule by saying that it did not necessarily require that in every case there be an obligation "to provide and perform" work by accepting that it would be enough, for example, if there were an obligation on one party to accept and do the work if offered and the obligation on the other party was, for example, to pay a retainer during such periods as work was not offered. In this case, however, there was no such retainer paid and on the facts there was insufficient mutuality during the period when the applicant was not occupied during a specific engagement.

However, the importance of mutuality of obligation and personal performance has been emphasised by the House of Lords in the following decision.

Carmichael v National Power plc

[2000] I.R.L.R. 43

Mrs Carmichael and Mrs Leese were employed as station guides at the Blyth Power Stations. Their jobs involved conducting visitors on tours of the Power Stations and the advertisement to which they responded prior to appointment explained that visits were normally two hours long and could be at any time during the day. Employment was to be on a "casual as required basis" at a certain hourly rate. Mrs Carmichael and Mrs Leese were appointed after interview and were told that National Power had noted that they were "agreeable to be employed" on a "casual as required" basis. They signed a pre-typed letter that stated "confirming acceptance of this offer" and after training they were paid for the hours they worked. When they did work they had to follow instructions of National Power in relation to First Aid Responses, Uniform and the Quality of the Tours. Mrs Carmichael and Mrs Leese complained that National Power had failed to give them a written statement of particulars of employment terms as required by the Employment Rights Act 1996—an obligation required only in respect of people who had contracts of employment—but National Power claimed that they did not have contracts of employment.

The House of Lords held first that whether there is a contract of employment is a question of law to be determined by reference solely to documents only where the parties intended that *all* the terms of the contract were to be contained in those documents. Secondly, in this case there was no evidence to support the inference that there was an intention to create an employment contract which subsisted when Mrs Carmichael and Mrs Leese were not actually working.

The Lord Chancellor (Lord Irving of Lairg) stated:

> "[There were] no provisions governing when, how or with what frequency guide work would be offered; there were no provisions for notice of termination on either side; the sickness, holiday and pension arrangements for regular staff did not apply; nor did the grievance and disciplinary procedures. Significantly ... in 1994 ... Mrs Carmichael was not available for work on seventeen occasions and Mrs Leese on eight. No suggestion of disciplining them arose. The objective inference is that when work was available they were free to undertake it or not as they chose. This flexibility of approach was well suited to their family needs. Just as the need for tours was unpredictable so also were their domestic commitments. Flexibility suited both sides ... The arrangement turned on mutual convenience and goodwill ... Mrs Carmichael and Mrs Leese had a sense of moral responsibility to [National Power] but ... no legal obligation."

Personal Service

One of the distinctive features of the contract of employment is that **1–15**
neither the employer nor the employee is free to delegate performance to another. It is regarded as a contract based on personal selection. It was this factor which caused the Court of Appeal to decide that there was no contract of employment in *Express and Echo Publications Ltd v Tanton* [1999] I.R.L.R. 367. This was because there was a clause in the contract that if Mr Tanton, a driver, was "unable or unwilling" to perform the work personally "he shall arrange at his own expense entirely for another suitable person (provided he was trained and suitable) to perform the services". More recently the EAT has held that an opportunity to delegate performance to another is not fatal to the existence of a contract of employment. In *MacFarlane v Glasgow City Council* [2001] I.R.L.R. 7 it was accepted that a peripatetic gym instructor who worked for the Council and who, if she was unable to take a particular class, could arrange her own replacement (who would be paid directly by the Council) from a list of instructors approved by the Council, may still have had a contract of employment with the Council. It would depend on all the other facts and circumstances but according to the EAT the case was different from *Tanton* because delegation could only occur occasionally where

MacFarlane was "unable" to take a class, the Council paid the delegate directly and the delegate had to be on the Council's approved list. The distinction between being unable and unwilling to perform the contract has been applied in *James v Redcats (Brands) Ltd* [2007] I.R.L.R. 296, EAT so that where the contract allowed a courier to ensure a suitable substitute was available "if you are unable...which might happen during holidays or when you are ill" there was an obligation to perform the work personally.

In *Staffordshire Sentinel Newspapers Ltd v Potter* [2004] I.R.L.R. 752, EAT the contract contained the following clause: "[t]he Home Delivery Agent (HDA) is not required to discharge his/her operational responsibilities personally and in the event that he/she does not want to do so for any reason (including holiday) or is unable to do so for any reason (including illness) the HDA will ensure that he/she engages suitable people to ensure that his/her obligations under this Agreement are fully complied with". The EAT held that "*Tanton* and *McFarlane* are ... entirely consistent. The critical question is what is the relevant contractual term? Where there is no clear express term in writing then it may be necessary to look at the overall factual matrix in order to discern that term ... However, where the term is clear from the contractual document that course is unnecessary", unless it can be said to be a sham. In this case, as there was no evidence the clause was a sham, the court was not permitted to look at the "overall factual matrix". In *Ministry of Defence HQ Defence Dental Service v Kettle* (EAT Case No.0308/06) the EAT observed that to determine whether there is a contract of employment the tribunal has at the outset to determine what are the terms of the agreement between the parties. To do so the all important first question for a tribunal faced with documents said to be contractual was whether it was the intention of the parties, objectively ascertained, that all the terms of the contract be contained in the documents. This is a question of fact for the tribunal and as a general rule the more detailed and customised the contractual documentation the less likely it is that the tribunal will conclude that the contract was not intended to contain all the terms of the parties' agreement. If the parties intended that the terms of their agreement be contained exclusively in a document or documents the tribunal is generally restricted to these documents. However there is no absolute rule that parties to that effect and there may be rare cases where the tribunal is able to look outside the documents. If it was not the parties' intention that the documents should be the exclusive record of their agreement the tribunal will be entitled to look at other relevant materials including oral exchanges and the parties' conduct so that in the case of *Kettle* the tribunal was correct to look at the contractual documentation, the advertisement and the parties conduct (the employer arranging for cover during Kettle's holidays) in concluding Kettle was obliged to provide the services personally.

NAME OF CONTRACT

As previously indicated, the parties to a particular contract seek to make the status of the contact beyond doubt by giving it a name or a label. However, it is clear from decided cases (*Massey v Crown Life Assurance Company* [1978] I.R.L.R. 31) that the substance, truth or reality of a relationship cannot be altered simply by putting a label or a name on it. Nevertheless, the name the parties give to a contractual relationship will be influential if the other factors do not clearly place the contract in one category or another. Further, as in *Massey*, the name given to the contract will be more influential where it is the result of the parties genuinely seeking to change or clarify the relationship. However, the substance or reality of the relationship must be consistent with the stated terms. It is not enough simply for the parties to give their relationship a name and for the court to be bound by that (*British School of Motoring v Secretary of State for Social Services* [1978] I.C.R. 894). **1–16**

THE WORKER AND THE AGENCY WORKER

As indicated earlier only relatively recently have statutory rights been conferred on those who have contracts other than contracts of employment. The most obvious examples are the rights conferred under the laws dealing with discrimination. Statutes such as the Equal Pay Act 1970, the Sex Discrimination Act 1975, the Race Relations Act 1976 and the Disability Discrimination Act 1995 and the regulations rendering unlawful discrimination by employers on the grounds of sexual orientation, religion and belief and age (Employment Equality (Sexual Orientation) Regulations 2003, Employment Equality (Religions and Belief) Regulations 2003, Employment Equality (Age) Regulations 2006) confer protection not just on employees but on the ever increasing group of economically active persons known as "workers". The definition of a "worker" includes an individual who has entered into a contract of employment and "any other contract ... whereby the individual undertakes to perform personally any work or services for another party to the contract" who is not a client or customer of any profession or business carried on by the individual (Employment Rights Act 1996 s.230). While the legal concept of "worker" is wider than the concept of "employee" questions have arisen as to what precisely are the essentials of the worker's contact beyond an obligation to perform personally for another who is not a client or customer of the individual's business. **1–17**

In *Byrne Brothers (Formwork) Ltd v Baird* [2002] I.R.L.R. 96, EAT—a case under the Working Time Regulations which adopts the same definition of worker—has given an indication of the meaning to be attached to "carrying on business" by observing that the intention behind the definition is to create an intermediate class of protected worker, who is not an employee but who cannot in some narrower sense be regarded as carrying on a business and that the policy behind the definition is to extend the benefits of protection to workers who are in the same need of that type of protection as employees *stricto sensu,* namely, workers who are viewed as liable—whatever their formal employment status—to be required to work excessive hours (in the case of the Working Time Regulations), to suffer unlawful deductions from wages (in the case of Pt II of the Employment Rights Act 1996) and to be paid too little (in the case of the National Minimum Wage Act 1998). According to the EAT "the reason why employees are thought to need such protection is that they are in a subordinate and dependent position *vis a vis* their employers: the purpose of the (definition of worker contained in) the Regulations is to extend protection to workers who are substantively and economically in the same position. Thus the essence of the distinction must be between ... workers whose degree of dependence is essentially the same as that of employees and ... contractors who have a sufficiently arms length and independent position to be able to look after themselves in the relevant respects". To draw that distinction will involve all or most of the sane considerations as arise in drawing the distinction between a contract of service and a contract for services—but with the boundaries pushed further in the putative worker's favour. It may involve the degree of control exercised by the putative employer, the exclusivity of the arrangement and the likely duration, the method of payment, the equipment the putative worker supplies and the level of risk taken. Additionally the EAT makes it clear that even for the worker's contract there has to be mutuality of obligation because according to the EAT this (the requirement of mutuality) is not peculiar to the contract of employment but arises from the general law of contract. However mutuality has not always been expressed in such terms. In other respects it has been understood to mean that there is an obligation on the putative employer to provide work to the putative employee when it is there to be done and an obligation on the putative employee to do it when it is given to him, which may be argued to be a more specific form of mutuality. The significance of the decision of the EAT in *Byrne Brothers (Formwork) Ltd v Baird* must be reconsidered following the decision of the EAT (President Elias) in *James v Redcats (Brands) Ltd* [2007] I.R.L.R. 296 in which the EAT disagreed with the decision in *Byrne Brothers (Formwork) Ltd v Baird* that economic dependency is the critical issue on the grounds that a small business may have a large degree of dependence on a single client. A better approach is to consider the dominant purpose of the contract. Was it the execution of personal work or a contract for a particular outcome or objective? If the dominant feature of the contractual arrangements is not the obligation to personally perform work but merely a particular outcome or objective and the obligation to provide personal service is an incidental or secondary consideration the relationship will be in field of business.

Agency Workers

However, many organisations rely on workers supplied to them by agencies in the hope of avoiding the responsibilities attached to contracts of employment. The advantage for the "host" organisation is that the supply of human resources can be increased or decreased without incurring any liability for unfair dismissal or redundancy payments and without the administrative costs of maintaining a large labour force with obligations relating to payments and deduction of Income Tax and National Insurance Contributions. If any liability does exist then generally it will belong to the agency as the employer and not to the host organisation. Frequently, say, a typist or IT specialist (A) will enter a contract with an employment agency or business (B), which when work becomes available will assign him to work for different businesses (C, D, or E). In such a tripartite relationship, it will be unusual for the typist or IT specialist to have a contract of employment with the agency because the contract between him and the agency is designed to ensure that it is *not* a contract of employment, thereby avoiding liabilities like redundancy payments, and he will not be a worker because he does not perform work personally for the other party to the contract (viz. the agency—B) but for a third party (C, D or E). Some legislation now expressly applies to these "agency workers". For example the Working Time Regulations 1998 (reg.36) and the National Minimum Wage Act 1998 s.34 apply not just to "employees" and "workers" but also to "any individual who is supplied by an agent to do work for another (the principal) under a contract between the principal and the agent, provided the work is not done as part of a business or profession carried on by the individual;" and to avoid a dispute as to which of the two—the agent or the principal—is the employer of the agency worker it is expressly provided that the employer of the agency worker is whichever of the agent and the principal has responsibility for paying the worker or if neither is responsible whichever of them actually pays the worker. **1–18**

Other legislation (see for example the Sex Discrimination Act 1975 s.9, the Race Relations Act 1976 s.7, the Disability Discrimination Act 1995 s.4B, the Employment Equality (Religion and Belief) Regulations 2003 reg.9, the Employment Equality (Sexual Orientation) Regulations 2003 reg.9 and the Employment Equality (Age) Regulations 2006 reg.9) extends to "contract workers" who are individuals who are supplied to a person (the principal) who makes work available for doing by individuals but who are employed by another person (the agent). While such a definition includes those who are engaged by an agency and are then supplied to a principal or end user it may be narrower than the "agency worker" as described above as to be a contract worker the individual must be "employed" by the agent (see *Harrods Ltd v Remick* [1997] I.R.L.R. 583, CA) and for the individual to be a contract worker the principal must be in a position to influence or control the conditions under which the employee worked so that a woman who was employed by her husband's firm to sell insurance products to customers of the firm was a contract worker and entitled to bring proceedings against the insurance company which trained and authorised her and had a large say in how she carried out the work (*Jones v Friends Provident Life Office* [2004] I.R.L.R. 783).

However, even if a person is not an "agency worker" or a "contract worker" it does not prevent an individual (A) engaged by agency B either being regarded as an employee (or worker) of B (the agency) or C (the host organisation). There are several possibilities—the individual can be an employee of the agency for a particular assignment or, alternatively, his general terms of employment may mean that he is to be regarded as an employee of the agency in respect of several assignments; or the individual may be regarded as also having a contract with the host organisation; or the individual may not satisfy the definition of employee or worker in respect of either the agency or the host organisation—it is possible that the individual is not the employee or worker of either (see *Astbury v Gist Ltd* (EAT 0619/06) in which HHJ Clark demonstrate that an agency worker may well not be employed by anybody!). In the case of *McMeechan v Secretary of State for Employment* [1997] I.R.L.R. 353, the Court of Appeal stated that where the agency and the individual have committed themselves to standard terms and conditions, with the intention to apply both to the general engagement and to the individual assignments worked, those conditions have to be interpreted from a different perspective depending on whether they are being considered in the context of the general engagement or in the context of a particular single assignment. In this particular case, the general impression which emerged from this engagement, despite the label put on it by the parties, was that there existed in respect of the particular assignment a contract of employment between the individual and the agency.

McMeechan v Secretary of State for Employment

[1997] I.R.L.R. 353

McMeechan entered into a contract with an employment agency on the following terms:

> "Conditions of Service (Temporary Self Employed Workers)

You will provide your services to the contractor as a self employed worker and not under a contract of service:

You will provide your services commencing on the date shown on the time sheet until the end of the same week or such earlier date as the hirer (referred to as 'the client') may determine.

The contractor agrees to offer you the opportunity to work on a self-employed basis where there is a suitable assignment with a client but the contractor reserves the right to offer each assignment to such temporary worker ('Temporary') as it may elect in cases where that stated above assignment is suitable for one of several temporarics.

The contractor shall pay your wages subject to the deduction for the purposes of National Insurance, PAYE or any other purpose required by law. An overtime premium will be paid provided this is agreed in writing by the client.

You are under no obligation to accept any offer made under para.3 but if you do so you are required to fulfil the normal common law duties which an employee would owe to an employer as far as they are applicable. In addition, you will at all times, when services are to be performed for a client, comply with the following conditions:

You will (a) not engage in any conduct detrimental to the interests of the contractor; (b) upon being supplied to the client by the contractor, not contract with any other contractor, consultant or agency for the purpose of the supply of your temporary services of whatever nature to the client unless for a period of 13 weeks has elapsed since the time that you ceased to be supplied to the client by the contractor; (c) be present during the times or for the total number of hours during each day and/or week as they are required by the contractor or the client; (d) provide to the client faithful service of a standard as would be required under a contract of employment; (e) take all reasonable steps to safeguard your own safety and the safety of any other person who may be affected by your actions; (f) comply with any disciplinary rules or obligations in force at the premises where services are performed to the extent that they are reasonably applicable; (g) comply with all reasonable instructions/requests within the scope of the agreed services made either by the client or the contractor; and (h) keep confidential all information which may come to your notice whilst working for the client and keep secret all and any of the client's affairs of which you may gain knowledge.

The contractor is not obliged to provide and you are not required to serve any particular number of hours during any day or week. In the event of your declining to accept any offer of work or failing to attend work for any reason for any period this contract shall terminate.

You are not entitled to payment from the contractor for holidays or absence due to sickness or injury. The contractor provides no pension rights.

The contractor shall be responsible for making all statutory deductions relating to insurance and income tax under Sch.E ... and transmitting these to the Inland Revenue.

You acknowledge and confirm the nature of temporary work is such that there may be periods between assignments when no work is available.

The contractor may instruct you to end an assignment with the client at any time on summary notice to that effect.

Following the decision of the contractor that your services are no longer required on a self employed basis, you shall have the right to request a review of that decision by the relevant branch manager.

If you have any grievance ... you shall have the right to present the grievance to the manager of the branch of the contractor ... you may present the grievance for ultimate decision to the area manager.

The qualifying days for statutory sick pay shall be ...

You are required to inform the contractor no later than 10 a.m. on the first qualifying day of sickness so that the contractor can make arrangements to provide other workers to the client ..."

The Court held that construing the conditions of service in the context of a specific engagement, the general impression which emerged was that the engagement in question gave rise, despite the label put on it by the parties, to a contract of employment between the worker and the agency. On the one side, in support of a contract for services, was the express statement that the worker was to be regarded as self-employed and not to be working under a contract of service. The liberty was reserved to the worker of being able to work on a self-employed basis for a particular client.

On the other side, supporting a contract of employment, were the reservation of the power of dismissal for misconduct; the power of the agency to bring any assignment to an end; the provision of a review procedure in the event of such termination; the establishment of a grievance procedure; the stipulation of an hourly rate of pay, which was subject to deductions for unsatisfactory time-keeping, work, attitude, or misconduct; and the importation of the normal common law duties of an employee.

1–19 As *McMeechan* makes clear there is invariably a contract of some type between the agency and the individual and a contract between the agency and the host organisation. What is more difficult is to decide whether there is any contract between the host organisation and the individual. In many cases the whole point of dealing through an agency is to avoid the existence of any kind of contract with the individual. In most cases there is no written contract between the host organisation and the individual and the agreements between (a) the host and the agency; and (b) the agency and the individual frequently provide that the individual is not to be regarded as an employee of the host. In *Dacas v Brook Street Bureau* [2004] I.R.L.R. 358 the Court of Appeal, noting that a contract of employment may be express or implied, was prepared to hold that in such triangular relationships the practical reality is that the individual does not have a contract of employment with the agency but an implied contract of employment with the end user or host organisation, provided there is sufficient control and mutuality of obligation. De facto day-to-day control was sufficient, and as for mutuality, Mrs Dacas (a cleaner) was under a duty to do what she was told and attend punctually and the host/end user was obliged to pay for the work even though in practice she received her wages from the agency. A similar approach is seen in *Franks v Reuters* [2003] I.R.L.R. 423 in which the length of the period of the relationship was emphasised as being important so that a relationship may evolve into an implied contract of employment. The possibility of an implied contract was again recognised in *Cable and Wireless plc v Muscat* [2006] I.R.L.R. 354. However in *James v London Borough of Greenwich* [2007] I.R.L.R. 168, the EAT reviewed the law regarding tripartite or triangular relationships and gave guidance on how tribunals should deal with them so that *Dacas* and *Franks* must now be regarded as the high water marks; the effect of adopting the guidance in *James* can clearly be seen in *Craigie v London Borough of Haringey* (EAT 0556/06) and *Heatherwood and Wexham Park Hospitals NHS Trust v Kulubowila* (EAT 0633/06) *and Wood Group Engineering (North Sea) Ltd v Robertson* (EAT No.0081/06).

James v London Borough of Greenwich

[2007] 168 EAT

Mrs James worked for Greenwich Council until 1997 and after a break she resumed working for the Council from 2001 through an agency and in 2003 she moved to another agency which offered a better rate of pay but still worked for the Council. She had no express contract with the Council but there was a written agreement between herself and the agency called "Temporary Work agreement" which provided that she would be employed as a self-employed worker in relation to each assignment and it did not give rise to a contract of employment with the agency or the client (the Council). Under the agreement the Council paid the agency a sum to cover Mrs James's wages and she was deemed to be under the direction and control of the Council which was responsible for any of her negligence. Following a period of absence Mrs James was replaced by another individual from the agency and she claimed unfair dismissal. The employment tribunal held Mrs James did not have an implied contract of employment with the Council and she appealed to the EAT which observed that from *Dacas*, while it was correct to consider the possibility of an implied contract with the end user, Mummery L.J. cautioned against tribunals finding there to be a contract of employment whenever an individual was not self-employed. What was required for an implied contract was whether it was *necessary* to do so to give business reality to what was happening between the parties. The EAT gave the following guidance when dealing with tripartite cases:

(a) the mere passage of time is not enough to require the implication of a contract of employment; (b) agency cases are not like casual worker cases where the issue is whether there is mutuality of obligation to include periods when there is no work done; (c) the issue in agency cases is whether the way the contract is performed is consistent with the agency arrangements or whether it is only consistent with an implied contract of employment between the individual and the end user or host organisation; (d) the key feature is not whether the end user is paying the wages but whether it can insist on the agency providing the particular worker at all—provided the arrangements are genuine and the actual relationship is consistent with them it is not necessary to explain the provision of the individual's services or the fact of payment to the individual by some contract between the end user and the individual even if such a contract would also not be inconsistent with the relationship as the express contracts may explain and be consistent with the nature of the relationship and no implied contract will be justified.

When agency arrangements are genuine and, when implemented, accurately represent the actual relationship between the parties—as is likely to be the case where there was no pre-existing contract between the worker and the end user—it will be rare there will be evidence entitling the tribunal to imply a contract between the end user and the worker. If any such contract is to be inferred there must, subsequent to the relationship commencing, be some words or conduct entitling the tribunal to conclude that the agency arrangements no longer adequately reflect how the work is actually being done and that the reality of the relationship is only consistent with the implication of the contract; it will be necessary to show that the individual is working pursuant to mutuality of obligations binding him or her to the end user.

On the other hand it will be more open to a tribunal to infer a contract where the agency arrangement is superimposed on an existing contractual relationship between the end user and the individual because, there, a tribunal is strictly not implying a contract as such but rather concluding that the agency arrangements did not bring the existing contractual relationship to an end.

LAW OR FACT

Finally, it has to be considered whether the classification of the contract as one of employment or some other type is a question of law or a question of fact. This is an important matter for practical reasons because once a court or tribunal of first instance has decided questions of fact, it is extremely difficult for that fact to be challenged on appeal. On the other hand, questions of law are open to appeal to a superior court or tribunal. Opinions have varied as to whether the classification of the contract, as one of employment, is a question of law or a question of fact. The correct answer is probably to say that it is a mixed question of both law and fact. Certainly where the relationship is to be determined purely by the consideration of written documents, it is fair to say it is nothing more than a question of law. This was the case in *Davies v Presbyterian Church* [1986] I.C.R. 280, HL, concerning the status of a minister of religion in the Presbyterian church. Lord Templeman observed in this case: "[t]he question to be determined is a question of law, namely, whether on the true construction of the book of rules a pastor in the church is employed and is under a contract of service". However, as has been observed in *Lee v Chung and Shun Shing Construction and Engineering Co Ltd* [1990] I.R.L.R. 236, the opinion of whether or not a person is employed under a contract of employment is often said to be a mixture of fact and law. Only exceptionally—as in *Davies*—if the relationship is dependent solely on the terms of a written contract, it is regarded as a pure question of law. But where, as is normally the case, the relationship has to be determined by an investigation and evaluation of the factual circumstances in which the work is performed the question is to be regarded by an appellate court as one of fact and to be determined by the trial court, not susceptible to challenge on appeal so that an appellate court must not interfere in what is a question of fact. This approach has recently been approved by the House of Lords in *Carmichael v National Power plc* [2000] I.R.L.R. 43 in which Lord Hoffman stated: **1–20**

> "[T]he Rule that the construction of documents is a question of law was well established when [Employment] Tribunals were created and has been carried over into Employment Law ... [the Rule] applies in cases in which the parties intend all the terms of the contract (apart from any implied by law) to be

> contained in a document ... on the other hand it does not apply when the intention of the parties, objectively ascertained, has to be gathered partly from documents but also from oral exchanges and conduct. In the latter case the terms of the contract are a question of fact and of course the question of whether the parties intended a document ... to be the exclusive record of the terms of their agreement is also a question of fact."

In *Ministry of Defence HQ Defence Dental Service v Kettle* (EAT 0308/06) the EAT applying *Carmichae*l agreed an Employment Tribunal was correct to hold that the intention of the parties was not to confine their agreement to contractual documentation so that it was then entitled to take account of events which preceded and followed the written documentation to decide that Kettle was an employee.

EMPLOYMENT *PRO HAC VICE*

1–21 A common practice in employment today is for a business to enter into a commercial contract for the use of an expensive piece of equipment which is frequently supplied with its own skilled operator. Where this occurs and the operator negligently injures a third party the question arises as to which of the two employers is liable. Such a situation arose in the following case.

Mersey Docks and Harbour Board v Coggins and Griffiths

[1947] A.C. 1

The Mersey Docks and Harbour Board, as part of their commercial activities, hired out cranes to stevedoring companies like Coggins and Griffiths who had undertaken to load or unload ships in the harbour. Clearly the use of cranes would not be required every day by Coggins and Griffiths and it made economic sense for them to rent in a crane when an unloading or loading contract had been secured. The contract Coggins and Griffiths entered into with the Harbour Board was for the hiring out of a crane with its driver or operator. While the driver was operating the crane he negligently allowed a load to drop into the hold of a ship. The question was which of the two organisations was responsible for the driver's negligence. Was it the Mersey Docks and Harbour Board, that is to say the organisation that generally employed the driver, or should he sue Coggins and Griffiths, the stevedoring company which was making use of the crane at the particular time.

The House of Lords made it clear that in such circumstances the operator or driver remains in the employment with the first or general employer. If such a general employer wishes to discharge himself of being vicariously liable for the operator's negligence, he has to prove that the authority to control was transferred to the second employer who in turn exercised detailed control over the driver or operator. In this case, having examined the contractual relationship between the Harbour Board and Coggins and Griffiths, the court came to the conclusion that the operator remained in the employment of the Harbour Board. This was because they had not delegated to Coggins and Griffiths their right to exercise detailed control over how he was to operate his crane. According to the judgment, if Coggins and Griffiths had attempted to give the driver of the crane instructions as to how he should operate his crane, they would have received from him a "sturdy answer". As a result the Harbour Board were vicariously liable for the injury to the docker.

From *King v Fife Council* 2004 S.L.T. 2000 it is clear that transfer of control may be inferred from the facts.

SPECIAL WORKING RELATIONSHIPS

Apprenticeship Contracts

The contract of apprenticeship attracts the benefits of modern employment legislation. Thus the Employment Rights Act 1996 s.230(2) states that a contract of employment also means a contract of apprenticeship, and legislation to prevent discrimination provides that "employment means ... employment under a contract of service or of apprenticeship". In short, any statute that confers rights on a person with a contract of employment also protects a person with an apprenticeship contract. Many of the terms that are implied into the contract of employment are also present in the apprenticeship contract. However there are some differences between the two contracts. **1–22**

The primary duty of the employer under an apprenticeship contract is to instruct the apprentice in the trade or profession concerned. This is endorsed in the decision of *Royce v Greig* 1902 S.L.T. 298 and a failure to instruct or educate the apprentice will be regarded as a significant breach of contract by the employer. The correlative duty of the apprentice is to learn from the experience and instruction of his master or employer. An apprentice who demonstrated a refusal to learn, for example, by failing to attend classes as part of his training, would breach the contract by the apprentice: *Butler v Dillon* (1952) 87 I.L.T.R. 95.

In *Wiltshire Police Authority v Wynn* [1980] I.C.R. 649 a police cadet was not employed under a contract of employment or apprenticeship and therefore unable to complain of unfair dismissal. In the following conclusion, Lord Denning M.R. relied on the distinction between the contract of employment and the contract of apprenticeship:

> "The courts drew a distinction according to which purpose was the primary purpose: and which was the secondary purpose. If the primary purpose was to work for the master—and teaching a trade was only a secondary purpose—it was a contract of [employment]. But if teaching a trade was the primary purpose—and work for the master was only secondary—then it was a contract of apprenticeship. The distinction between the cases where teaching and learning is the primary purpose—and the cases where the work done is the primary purpose—is helpful in the present context ... it seems to me that throughout the cadetship the primary purpose is to teach and learn—not a trade—but as part of general education. They are not being taught a trade such as would make them an apprentice. They are neither apprentices nor [employees] ... "

1–23 More recently it has been held that a pupil barrister did not enter a contract of apprenticeship with her pupil master and was therefore unable to claim the protection of the National Minimum Wage Act 1998. In *Edmonds v Lawson* [2000] I.R.L.R. 391 the Court of Appeal reviewed the law relating to apprenticeship in England which in principle reflects the Scots position. Lord Bingham of Cornhill C.J. stated:

> "A contract of apprenticeship is in law a contract with certain features peculiar to itself. It is for instance less readily terminable by the employer than the ordinary contract of employment ... [I]t is a synallagmatic contract in which the master undertakes to educate and train the apprentice in the practical and other skills needed to practise a skilled trade or profession and the apprentice binds himself to serve and work for the master and to comply with all reasonable directions. These mutual covenants are in our view cardinal features of such a relationship."

As the pupil barrister could not—unlike an apprentice—be required to carry out any reasonable instruction given by her master (she was only required to carry out instructions that were conducive to her training and development) her relationship with her master was not a contract of apprenticeship.

Part of the employer's obligation is also to set a good example to his apprentice and to make allowances for an apprentice's immaturity and lack of experience. An apprentice is to be treated more leniently than a mature qualified employee (*Stanton v Woolfendens Cranes Ltd* [1972] I.R.L.R. 82).

As the main duty of the employer is to instruct and educate the apprentice if the employer was to breach the contract by terminating the apprenticeship before its natural expiry, resulting in the apprentice not qualifying as a professional, the apprentice may be entitled to damages in respect of his losing the opportunity of becoming a qualified professional: *Dunk v George Waller* [1970] 2 W.L.R. 1241. In calculating damages for breach of the contract, the Court took into account the fact that during apprenticeship, the apprentice normally receives low wages and that a failure to implement the contract by the employer may result in the apprentice losing the opportunity of higher earnings following qualification. In *Whitely v Marton Electrical Ltd* [2003] I.R.L.R. 197, EAT the apprentice was awarded damages for dismissal prior to the completion of the training period. It is no longer necessary that the contract of apprenticeship be created in writing, although it would be wise for the parties to enter into a written contract, relevant to the appropriate period of the apprenticeship. Although the contract of apprenticeship is a limited term contract for unfair dismissal and redundancy law there is no dismissal on its completion as it is not possible for it to be renewed under the same contract.

Company Directors

Generally, executive directors of limited companies will have contracts of employment, sometimes referred to as service agreements with the company. Where a service agreement is entered into between a company and a director, a copy of such agreement or at least a written memorandum of its terms must be kept at the registered office or principal place of business of the company (Companies Act 1985 s.318). Service agreements for five years or more require to be approved not just by the Board of Directors but also the shareholders in general meeting (Companies Act 1985 ss.318, 319(1)). **1–24**

If the director is truly an employee with a contract of employment with the company, he or she will be protected against unfair dismissal and redundancy. The director will be entitled to have his or her salary and certain other debts due to him by the company protected. These would be ranked as preferred debts in the company's liquidation (Insolvency Act 1986 s.386) and, in the event of the liquidator being unable to pay even these preferred debts, an employee will be entitled to receive payments such as arrears of wages, holiday pay, notice pay and redundancy pay, direct from the National Insurance Fund by applying to the Secretary of State for Employment. If the business of the company is sold to another employer, the contracts of employment of all employees including those who may be designed as directors will be transferred to the new employer. See Transfer of Undertakings (Protection of Employment) Regulations 1981 reg.5.

It is therefore important to determine whether or not a director is also an employee of the company. In *Secretary of State for Trade and Industry v Bottrill* [1999] I.R.L.R. 326 the Court of Appeal gave general guidance as to how the question should be answered.

Secretary of State for Trade and Industry v Bottrill

[1999] I.R.L.R. 326

Mr Bottrill had become managing director of Magnatech United Kingdom Ltd in 1994. There had been one other director and two other individuals had been employees. Only one share had been issued and Mr Bottrill held that. It had, however, been intended in the future that an American group, which supplied Magnatech with all items for sale, would hold 80 per cent of the shares in the company. A draft shareholders' agreement describing the proposed relationship between the group and Magnatech had been prepared. However, before the agreement was executed, Magnatech became insolvent and a receiver was appointed. Mr Bottrill was dismissed for redundancy and wished to recover redundancy pay from the Secretary of State. The employment tribunal, in concluding that Mr Bottrill had been an employee, had relied on its findings that Mr Bottrill's status as sole shareholder had only been temporary and any control which he had had of the company was only theoretical. The actual control had been held by the American group. The tribunal had laid stress on the fact that Mr Bottrill had paid National Insurance Contributions and Income Tax as if he was an employee, had been entitled to sick pay, worked fixed hours and had a contract with Magnatech that was described as a contract of employment.

The Master of the Rolls stated:

> "[In relation to a company director] the court did not find any justification for departing from the well established position in the law of employment generally [namely] . . . whether or not an employer/employee relationship existed could be decided only by having regard to all the relevant facts. If an individual had a controlling shareholding, that was certainly a fact which was likely to be significant in all situations and in some cases it might prove to be decisive. However, it was only one of the factors which were relevant and certainly was not to be taken as determinative without considering all the relevant circumstances. The Secretary of State had . . .

> asked the court to provide what guidance it could because of the frequency with which problems of the type exemplified by the present case arose. The court was anxious not to lay down rigid guidelines for the inquiry but the [Employment] Tribunal had to take in facts of the particular circumstances of each case, and the court hoped that the following comments might be of assistance.
>
> The first ... was whether there was or had been a genuine contract between the company and the shareholder [director]. In that context how and for what reasons the contract had come into existence, for example, whether the contract was made at a time when insolvency loomed, and what each party actually did pursuant to the contract were likely to be relevant considerations.
>
> If the tribunal concluded that the contract was not a sham, it was likely to consider next whether the contract, which might well have been labelled a contract of employment, actually gave rise to an employer/employee relationship. In that context, of the various factors usually regarded as relevant, the degree of control exercised by the company over the shareholder employee was always important. That was not the same question as relating to whether there was a controlling shareholding. The tribunal might think it appropriate to consider whether there were directors other than Mr Bottrill or in addition to the shareholder employee. The question raised as to whether the constitution of the company gave that shareholder rights that he was, in reality, answerable only to himself and incapable of being dismissed. If he was a director, it might be relevant to consider whether he was able, under the articles of association, to vote on matters in which he was personally interested, such as the termination of his contract of employment. Again, the actual conduct of the parties pursuant to the terms of the contract was likely to be relevant. It was for the tribunal as an industrial jury to take all relevant factors into account in reaching its conclusion, giving such weight to them as it considered appropriate."

One of the issues that is frequently considered is the size of a director shareholding. In the case of *Buchan v Secretary of State for Employment* [1997] I.R.L.R. 80, it had been decided that a controlling shareholder could not be an employee of the company because he could in effect always prevent his own dismissal. However, that is now regarded as wrong and a controlling shareholder may now be an employee of the company. The cases of *Secretary of State for Trade & Industry v Bottrill* [1998] I.R.L.R. 326 and in Scotland *Fleming v Secretary of State for Trade & Industry* [1997] I.R.L.R. 682 have underlined the fact that whether a director is an employee of the company depends on all the circumstances and the size of the shareholding was merely one of those circumstances and this is not in any way conclusive.

Public Employment

1–25 Many people work in the public sector but that fact alone does not affect their status as employee. What it may mean, however, is that their terms of employment are not merely those set out in their contracts of employment but have to be read as being supplemented by certain principles of the general law. In some cases an employee in the public sector is no different from an employee with an ordinary contract of employment working for a private sector employer. In some special cases however, certain personnel in the public sector have their terms and conditions of employment closely regulated by statute or even the common law. Sometimes the distinction is expressed as being employment with a statutory flavour as opposed to employment governed by law.

An example of employment with a statutory flavour is seen in the following case.

Silva v The Vidyodaya University of Ceylon

[1965] 1 W.L.R. 77

The University of Ceylon sought to terminate the employment of Silva, who held a chair in economics. Silva argued that because the University was created by statute, he held a public office and that according to the common law office-holders could not have their employment terminated without being given the opportunity of rebutting any charges against him. There was little doubt that if Silva held a public office he would have been entitled to be heard before his employment was terminated. On the other hand leaving aside issues of unfair dismissal law which in 1965 had not yet been developed, an employee whose relationship with his employer was governed simply by a contract of employment, had no right to a hearing before his contract could be terminated. Having examined the relationship between the University and Professor Silva, the court came to the conclusion that it was nothing other than an ordinary contract of employment which could be terminated with or without a hearing at the instance of the University. It may be fairly described as "employment in the public sector with a statutory flavour".

On the other hand the decision in *Silva* contrasts markedly with decisions like the following.

> *Vine v National Dock Labour Board*
>
> [1957] A.C. 488
>
> At the relevant time, in order to obtain employment in the nationalised dock industry, dockers had to be on the National Dock Register. Mr Vine had his name removed from the National Dock Register with the result that he was unable to obtain employment as a docker. However, the system of Registration of Dockers introduced under legislation in the late 1940s set down the circumstances and procedure which might lead to a docker's name being removed from the Register. In particular, Vine argued that his name was removed from the Register by the decision of a local dock committee, whereas according to the statutory scheme, removal of a docker's name from the register could only be done by the National Dock Labour Committee. The Court accepted Vine's argument that his name had been removed unlawfully and without proper authority from the Register of Dockers. In law that was a nullity and resulted in his "dismissal" as a docker being invalid.

Another important aspect of employment in the public sector is that where the employment is regulated by public law, an employee may be entitled to argue that a dismissal is not merely a breach of his contract or terms of employment, but that it is illegal and therefore a legal nullity. Both in England and in Scotland employees whose employment is regulated by law are able to seek judicial review of the employer's decision to terminate their employment. If the court is satisfied that the employer has acted unlawfully, then unlike a dismissed employee in the private sector, the public employee may have his dismissal declared a nullity resulting in his reinstatement, if only until the employer has followed the required statutory procedure.

EUROPEAN DIRECTIVES AND EMPLOYEES OF THE STATE

As indicated previously (para.1–03) employees of the State, or **1–26**
organisations which are emanations of the State, are entitled to enforce against their employer the provisions of European Community directives. This is the result of an important case decided by the European Court of Justice. See Case C-152/84 *Marshall v*

Southampton & South West Hampshire Area Health Authority (No.1) [1986] I.C.R. 335.

However, a directive may only be relied on in this way if it is unconditional and sufficiently precise in its language to allow a domestic court to apply it. Thus in *Gibson v East Riding of Yorkshire Council* [2000] I.R.L.R. 598, Mrs Gibson, a local authority swimming instructor, attempted to rely on the Working Time Directive (93/104) in order to compel her employer to give her paid annual holidays. Article 7 of the Directive provides that "Member States shall take the necessary measures to ensure that every worker is entitled to paid annual leave of four weeks in accordance with the conditions for entitlement to, and granting of, such leave laid down by national legislation and/or practice".

However, even though Mrs Gibson received no paid annual leave and tried to rely on the Directive Mummery L.J. stated:

> "The realistic recognition ... that there are gaps to be filled is significant on the issue of direct effect of Article 7. The very existence of gaps in Article 7 ... is a strong indication that the terms of the Article are insufficiently precise to have direct effect in the courts and tribunals of Member States. The right which Mrs Gibson wishes to assert against the Council is quite simply not sufficiently defined in Art.7 to be directly enforceable by an individual in national courts and tribunals. Further definition is necessary in implementing measures either by the [European] Community or by the Member State. Without further definition of the conditions of entitlement ... how could a tribunal even begin to determine a claim under Art.7 by a worker who had only worked for a week ... that he was entitled to four weeks annual leave?"

In the case of *Foster v British Gas plc* [1991] I.C.R. 84, the European Court has given guidance as to what may be an emanation of the State, and although each case will depend on its own circumstances, an emanation of the State will include "a body which has been made responsible, pursuant to a measure adopted by the state, for providing a public service under the control of the state and has for that purpose special powers beyond those which result from the normal rules applicable in relationships between individuals". As a result of the application of this definition, British Gas plc itself has been regarded as an emanation of the State, as have local authorities and privatised utilities.

Civil Servants and Office Holders

1–27 Civil servants technically do not have contracts of employment but are generally brought within the framework of modern employment law by provisions which deem them to have contracts of employment (see Employment Rights Act 1996 s.191 and the Trade Union and Labour Relations (Consolidation) Act 1992 s.273(1)).

Section 191 of the Employment Rights Act 1996 provides:

> "[t]he provisions of this Act . . . have effect in relation to Crown employment and persons in Crown employment as they have effect in relation to other employment and other employees or workers . . . In this Act Crown employment means employment under or for the purposes of a government department or any officer or body exercising on behalf of the Crown functions conferred by statutory provision . . .
>
> [I]n relation to Crown employment . . . references to an employee or a worker shall be construed as references to a person in Crown employment [and] references to a contract of employment or a worker's contract shall be construed as references to terms of employment of a person in Crown employment . . ."

The correct approach today is to regard the civil servant as having a contractual relationship with the Crown but one which can be determined at pleasure by the Crown without penalty (see *Kodees Waaran v Attorney General of Ceylon* [1972] W.L.R. 456).

McClaren v Home Office

[1990] I.C.R. 824

Mr McClaren worked as a prison officer and his letter of appointment referred to the special position of Civil Servants as servants of the Crown. Following a collective agreement concerned with working hours, between the Prison Officers' Association and the Home Office, a dispute arose about the introduction of a shift system, which the Prison Officers' Association alleged was in breach of the collective agreement. When Mr McClaren refused to work the new shift system he was suspended without pay and brought an action against the Home Office claiming breach of contract. The Home Office argued that because there was no contractual relationship between Mr McClaren and the Home Office he was not entitled to sue for breach of contract, his only remedy being judicial review, a procedure whereby the court could declare the withholding of his salary to be unlawful. The first instance Court held that there was no contractual relationship between McClaren and the Home Office, and therefore his claim in contract failed.

On appeal to the Court of Appeal, however, it was held that the relationship between the Home Office and Prison Officers like Mr McClaren could be a contractual one, and that Mr McClaren's claim in contract therefore was entitled to proceed, and not be struck out on the grounds that he had no contractual relationship with the Home Office. Woolf L.J. stated "in relation to his personal claims against an employer, an employee of a public body is normally in exactly the same situation as other employees. If he has a cause of action and wishes to assert or establish his rights in relation to his employment, he can bring proceedings for damages, a declaration or an injunction (except in relation to the Crown) . . . in the ordinary way. The fact that a person is employed by the Crown may limit his rights against the Crown, but otherwise his position is very much the same as any other employee. However, he may, instead of having an ordinary master and servant relationship with the Crown, hold office under the Crown, and may have been appointed to that office as a result of the Crown exercising a prerogative power or, as in this case, a statutory power. If he holds such an appointment, then it will almost invariably be terminable at will, and may be subject to other limitations, but whatever rights the employee has will be enforceable normal by an ordinary action (in the ordinary courts). While . . . the plaintiff can be dismissed at pleasure because he holds an office or is employed by the Crown, that does not mean that he cannot have a private law (*i.e.* contractual) right in relation to matters other than his dismissal. The fact that a Prison Officer can be dismissed at pleasure does not mean that there is not other terms of his service which are contractually enforceable, and in respect of this he can have a private law (*i.e.* contractual) remedy. There is now a considerable number of dicta which indicate that it is possible for a servant of the Crown to have contractual rights . . . In the case of Prison Officers, their (private law rights) would result from the exercise by the Home Office of its statutory powers . . . to appoint prison officers, but if they were derived from the prerogative, this would not alter the nature of the right created, only the source of the authority for creating the rights."

Most modern statutes make special provision for office holders (see for example the Sex Discrimination Act 1975 ss.10A, 10B) but the holder of an office may also derive protection from the common law; otherwise such a person must bring himself within the categories of employee or worker to obtain the benefits of employment legislation. In *Perceval-Price v Department of Economic Development* [2000] I.R.L.R. 380, NICA although chairpersons of tribunals were, as holders of statutory offices, expressly excluded from the domestic discrimination legislation it was held that they were "workers" for the purposes of Art.141 of the EC Treaty in that they were in an employment relationship regardless of the nature of the relationship and its purpose but there is no universally applicable concept of "worker" for EC law (see *Christie v Department for Constitutional Affairs* (EAT No.0140/07)). Until recently ministers of religion were not regarded as being in a contractual relationship with the church but in *Percy v Church of Scotland* [2006] I.C.R. 134 the House of Lords has held that an associate minister was employed under a contract personally to execute work and that it made no difference that her status as associate minister might be described as an ecclesiastical office in that holding an office and the existence of a contract were not necessarily mutually exclusive.

FORMATION OF THE CONTRACT OF EMPLOYMENT

Generally the legal rules relating to the formation of the contract of employment are found in the general law of contract. **1–28**

Exceptions and Special Cases

The main exception concerns a term in a collective agreement which restricts an employee's right to take industrial action. This may only be incorporated into his contract of employment if the collective agreement is in writing and that it provides for the incorporation of the clause into a contract of employment. Also the collective agreement must be reasonably accessible at the employee's place of work and the clause must have been incorporated into the individual's contract of employment (Trade Union and Labour Relations (Consolidation) Act 1992 s.180). More recently still, as a result of the Working Time Regulations 1998, a term requiring the worker to work more than 48 hours per week must be in writing. There are also two special provisions which require to be noted. First, under the Merchant Shipping Act of 1995 an agreement shall be entered in writing between the crew of merchant vessels and the ship's master, before the ship leaves a British port. Secondly, a copy of a service contract entered into between a director of the company and the company itself shall be retained at the company's registered office or, failing that, a memorandum of the terms of any unwritten contract entered into between a director and the company. Where a director's contract is to be for a period of more than five years the contract has to be approved by resolution of the shareholders of the company, not merely by a meeting of the Board of Directors of the (Companies Act 1985 ss.318, 319). **1–29**

However leaving aside those special cases the general rule is that the parties may enter into a contract of employment any way they choose. It is possible to create a contract of employment in any of the following ways or by a mixture of them: entirely by a written agreement; entirely orally; by implication through the actings and conduct of the parties. However, it is clearly advisable and common practice that a contract of employment be entered into in writing.

In both Scotland and England the parties must have an intention to enter into contractual relations although, as has been seen, the main difficulty in relation to employment is not whether there is such an intention but what sort of contractual relationship is intended. Thus, many people assume social or moral obligations but do not intend their obligation to be binding contracts. In England, although not in Scotland, for there to be a valid contract there has to be consideration namely something of value that passes between the parties when the contract is being performed; strictly the benefit (or the detriment) need not have a monetary value. In employment consideration will be wages on the one hand and the value of the work done on the other hand and where a pay increase results from negotiations consideration takes the form of the employee's continuing in the same employment (*Lee v GEC Plessey Telecommunications Ltd* [1993] I.R.L.R. 383) and where voluntary workers are concerned receipt of expenses has been enough to amount to consideration (*Migrant Advisory Service v Chaudri*, July 28, 1998 unreported, EAT). In Scotland the general rule is that where a party provides services to another it is presumed they are provided in return for payment but this may be rebutted in particular circumstances (*Thomson v Thomson's Tr* 1889 16R 333).

Implied Contracts

1–30 As indicated previously, it is possible for the contract to be entered into entirely by having regard to the conduct and behaviour of the parties. These contracts are sometimes referred to as "implied contracts". An example of the entire contract being created by implication is seen in the following case.

Taylor v Furness Ltd

[1969] K.I.R. 488

After a successful interview, the employee reported for work and was given a company identity card as well as a letter of welcome. Shortly after the employee commenced employment, however, the company terminated his employment without notice. The employee argued that under his contract of employment he was entitled to a period of notice to which the company replied that the contract of employment had not yet been entered into and had not yet been issued to him. However, the Court accepted that by issuing an identity card and a letter of welcome following interview, the company and Taylor had, by implication, entered into a contract of employment. Accordingly Taylor was entitled to claim the company had broken his contract by dismissing him without notice for no good reason.

Even when there is nothing expressly agreed between an individual and an organisation after a period of time a contractual relationship may be implied: *Dacas v Brook Street Bureau (UK) Ltd* [2004] I.R.L.R. 358, CA.

Although not a legal requirement, the current practice is for employers to issue to their employees either a written contract or written terms of employment thus preventing unnecessary disputes and arguments about rates of pay, hours of work, etc.

Written Statement of Particulars

As the common law does not require anything in writing for the **1–31**
creation of a valid contract of employment the entire contract of employment may be the subject of an oral agreement, with all of its disadvantages in terms of uncertainty of meaning and difficulty of proof. In order to ensure that employees and employers are reasonably well informed about the terms of employment, statute requires that an employer give to each employee (the obligation does not extend to "workers") a written statement of the particulars of employment. The matter is dealt with by Pt I of the Employment Rights Act 1996, which is intended to give effect to Directive 91/533 (Proof of the Employment Relationship). However, this legislation does not require the contract of employment—or even particular parts of it—to be in writing but merely that certain information is given by the employer, in writing, to his employees. Therefore, a failure to issue a written statement of particulars of employment will have no effect on the validity of any contract, which might exist between the employer and the employee (see *British Steel Corporation v Dingwall,* 1976 S.L.T. 230). On the other hand, many employers and employees will accept that the written statement of particulars is at least prima facie evidence of the contract. However, since the statement is not a contract but merely a unilateral document issued by the employer to his employee, either party is free—in the context of a dispute about the contract—to argue that the written statement is not an accurate reflection of the contract.

The Terms of the Statement

Under the Employment Rights Act, as amended by the Employ- **1–32**
ment Act 2002 (ss.35–38), a written statement of particulars of employment must include the following:

(1) name of employer;
(2) name of employee;
(3) date employment with employer began and date continuous employment began, if different, taking into account employment with associated employers and previous business owners;
(4) scale, rate or method of calculating, and intervals of, remuneration and how it is paid;

(5) terms about hours of work including normal working hours;
(6) terms about holidays/pay and entitlement to accrued holiday pay on termination;
(7) terms about incapacity for work including sick pay provision;
(8) terms about pensions;
(9) notice requirements;
(10) job title or brief description;
(11) where job is not permanent, the likely period or the period of a fixed term contract;
(12) the place of work or if the employee is required to work in different places, that shall be stated as well as the address of the employer;
(13) any collective agreements which affect the terms of employment and the parties to such collective agreements; and
(14) where the employee is required to work outside the United Kingdom for more than a month, the period of time, the currency of remuneration, any additional remuneration and benefits payable, and terms about return to the United Kingdom.

A written statement must also: (1) specify any disciplinary rules applicable to the employee, and any procedure applicable to the taking of disciplinary decisions (including dismissal) relating to the employer, or refer to a document which does so and which is reasonably accessible to the employee; (2) indicate the person to whom an employee can apply if he is dissatisfied with a disciplinary decision or if he has a grievance related to his employment; and (3) indicate if there are appeals to higher levels of management.

The written statement must be given not later than two months after the employee begins employment, subject to two qualifications: (a) if within the two-month period the employee is to begin work outside the United Kingdom for more than a month, the written statement has to be given to him before he leaves the United Kingdom; and (b) if an employee's employment ends before the period of two months he is still entitled to receive a written statement, although technically he is not entitled to receive it until the period of two months has elapsed.

The written statement may be given in instalments, provided all are given within two months of the employee starting work and the particulars relating to the matters in paras (1) to (6) and (10) and (12) above, must be included in a single document given to each employee. The particulars of any other matters may be contained in a document to which the employee is referred and this can be of considerable administrative convenience to an employer. However, if the terms in paras (7), (8) or (9) above (about incapacity and pensions or notice) are not in any document given to the employee but are set out in a document referred to, for example a collective agreement, the document must be reasonably accessible to the employee.

The Employment Act 2002 (s.37) permits an employer to substitute for the written statement a written contract or letter of engagement even where such an alternative document is given before the employment begins. This is a useful modification which recognises the need for both parties to know and have agreed the terms of a contract *before* commencing work under it and removes the need for employers to issue a written statement *after* the employment has begun where before employment had begun the employer and employee had already entered into a written contract which contained everything required to be contained in the written statement.

Changes to terms of employment, whether contained in a written statement or a written contract, must be given not later than one month after the changes have occurred or before the employee is to leave the United Kingdom (if that is earlier). However, as the written statement is not the contract, informing an employee of a change to his written statement will not mean that the contract has been changed: see para.1–29, above.

The Employee's Remedy

Until the passage of the Employment Act 2002 the employee's only **1–33** remedy was to apply to an employment tribunal which could correct or complete a statement or, if no written statement has been issued, issue a statement which ought to have been issued. However, the Employment Act 2002 (s.38) has added an incentive for employers to comply with the obligation to give a written statement by providing that in a claim made to an employment tribunal about any of the matters listed in Sch.5 to that Act (this includes unfair dismissal, redundancy, discrimination, unauthorised deductions, etc. but not a claim under Pt I of the 1996 Act itself) a minimum award of compensation shall be made unless there are exceptional circumstances which would make such a minimum award unjust or inequitable. However, there is no provision for the Tribunal to enforce any of the particulars against an employer or for declaring what meaning is to be given to a written statement. It is very unusual for an employee to ask a tribunal to correct, issue or complete a written statement but when this procedure is combined with other claims, like claims for redundancy payments or for unfair dismissal, it can (particularly after the amendment introduced by the 2002 Act) be of considerable value to an employee.

Legal Status of Written Statement

The written statement is not a contract; it is a unilateral document **1–34** issued by the employer to the employee and it merely represents the terms of employment which the employer believes to be in existence at the time it is issued. Accordingly it is not possible to alter the terms of the contract merely by issuing a new written statement. This issue was examined in detail and decided authoritatively in *Robertson & Jackson v British Gas Corporation*.

Robertson & Jackson v British Gas Corporation

[1983] I.C.R. 351

Robertson and Jackson were employed as Meter Reader Collectors by the Corporation. Their letters stated that a bonus scheme would operate. They also received a written statement which stated that bonuses would be calculated in accordance with a collective agreement. The bonus scheme operated until 1981 when British Gas terminated the collective agreement which set out the rules for the calculation of bonuses. No new bonus scheme was introduced and Robertson and Jackson sued British Gas for breach of contract. The Court held that the letters of appointment contained the contract of employment and not the written statement. Under the terms of the letter of appointment, a bonus scheme was to be operated in accordance with the National Collective Agreement. This had been incorporated into Robertson and Jackson's contract, therefore entitling them to the benefits of the bonus scheme, which could not be terminated by issuing a unilateral written statement.

The following extracts from the judgment of Ackner L.J. illustrate the difference between the contract and the written statement:

> "[T]he letter of appointment ... says in terms:
>
> 'I am pleased to inform you that ... you have been appointed ... as follows ...
>
> You will be required to undertake [certain duties are then specified] ...
>
> Incentive bonus scheme will apply.'

The material words of the statement are these:

> 'The provisions of (the collective agreement) ... will apply to you. Any payment which may from time to time become due in respect of ... bonuses ... will be calculated in accordance with the rules of the scheme in force at the time.'

I read the words which I have quoted from the letter (of appointment) as clearly laying down a contractual obligation that there be an incentive bonus for the job. One then has to

> enquire where are the terms and conditions of that incentive bonus to be found. It is common ground that one goes to the collective agreement ... As at the commencement of employment ... there was a collective scheme in existence, from which one could see quite clearly what was the bonus to be paid ... and therefore, when this employment began ... there was ... imported expressly into the contract, an obligation to pay that bonus.
>
> From time to time, the collective scheme modified the bonus which was payable, and when that occurred ... that variation became a part of the employer's obligation to pay and the employee's obligation to accept ... [but] the contract did not ... contemplate the absence of any bonus at all ... [and that] could not be affected by the unilateral determination of the collective agreement."

Thus, while the written statement is strictly not a written contract it is generally accepted as an accurate reflection of the terms of the contract at least at the time the written statement was issued or amended. In *System Floors UK Ltd v Daniel* [1982] I.C.R. 54 the EAT expressed the opinion that the written statement is prima facie or persuasive evidence of the contract, but it is not conclusive evidence. However, sometimes the employee is asked to sign a statement at the end of the written statement and, depending on how such a statement is worded, his signature may show that he has accepted the terms of the statement in which case it will become a bilateral contract. The essential distinction is between signing to accept and signing to acknowledge receipt (compare *Gascol Conversions Ltd v Mercer* [1974] I.C.R. 420, CA with *System Floors UK Ltd v Daniel*, above).

Written Contracts of Employment

Where the contract of employment is entirely in writing, it may be difficult to introduce evidence that it does not accurately represent the contract or to show that the contract contains additional terms which are not set out in writing. This particularly applies where the contract has been set out in a formal document. In England the operation of the rule can be seen in *Gascol Conversions v Mercer* [1974] I.C.R. 420, CA in which Mercer, by signing a contract which provided that his working week would be 40 hours, was not permitted to introduce evidence that a local collective agreement had increased his working week to 60 hours. Some contracts include a clause that all the contractual obligations are contained in the written documents (an entire agreement clause) in which case neither party is entitled to adduce other (extrinsic) evidence of the contract's terms (*White v Bristol Rugby Club Ltd* [2002] I.R.L.R. 205) although this rule may be modified where the issue is the **1–35** nature of the contractual relationship (*Bushaway v R.N.L.I.* EAT IDS Brief 784, 2005; *Ministry of Defence HQ Defence Dental Service v Kettle* (EAT No.0308/06)). In Scotland, as a result of the provisions of the Contract (Scotland) Act 1997, where a document appears to comprise all the express terms of a contract, it shall be presumed unless the contrary is proved, that the document does comprise all the express terms stated. However, extrinsic oral or documentary evidence is admissible to prove that the contract does include additional express terms. The effect is that where a contract of employment is contained in a document which appears to be comprehensive, the rights and duties of the parties to that contract will be regulated by that document, unless one of the parties can prove that the contract includes other express terms, even though they are not written down. In effect, the onus of proof is on the party who seeks to extend contractual obligations beyond the written document. For example, if the parties had orally agreed to amend the contract it would be possible to adduce evidence of the oral agreement. However, the 1997 Act also states that where a document provides that it comprises all the express terms of the contract, then that is conclusive. The result of this latter provision therefore is that if a contract of employment is in a written form and states that it contains all the express terms of the contract, it is not possible to bring evidence to show that other terms exist.

Collective Agreements

1–36 Many employees have the terms and conditions of their employment regulated by collective agreements made between trade unions and employers and not by individual bargaining.

There are advantages in settling terms and conditions of employment collectively. From the employer's point of view it is beneficial to have either all of his workers (or all of a particular group of workers) on the same or very similar terms of employment. This avoids invidious comparisons between one worker and another by ensuring all workers involved in similar types of employment are on the same or very similar terms of employment. From the employee's point of view, agreeing matters collectively allows for the individual employee to benefit from the strength of a co-ordinated approach to bargaining, through the medium of a trade union or other collective agent. As a result of the practice of settling terms and conditions of employment through collective agreements, it is important to understand the precise legal relationship between a collective agreement and the individual employee's relationship with his employer.

Definition

1–37 A collective agreement, as stated in s.178 of the Trade Union and Labour Relations (Consolidation) Act 1992, is:

"any agreement or arrangement made by or on behalf of one or more trade unions and one or more employer or employers' associations and relating to one or more of the following matters:

(a) terms and conditions of employment or the physical conditions in which any workers are required to work;
(b) engagement or non-engagement or termination or suspension of employment or the duties of employment of one or more workers;
(c) allocation of work or the duties of employment between workers or groups of workers;
(d) matters of discipline;
(e) a worker's membership or non-membership of a trade union;
(f) facilities for officials of trade unions; and
(g) machinery for negotiation or consultation, and other procedures, relating to any of the above matters, including the recognition by employers or employers' associations of the right of a trade union to represent workers in such negotiation or consultation or in the carrying out of any such procedures."

A collective agreement does not require to be a written document (although frequently it will be), and the use of the word "arrangement" means it may encompass informal dealings between employers and trade unions.

Edinburgh City Council v Brown

[1999] I.R.L.R. 208

Mr Brown was employed in the Council's Housing Department and applied to have his post re-graded. It was the policy of the employers to make re-gradings retrospective to the date on which the application was made. That retrospective policy was established in 1987 following a recommendation by the Council's Joint Consultative Committee. Mr Brown's contract of employment provided that from time to time variations in his terms and conditions of employment would result from negotiations and agreements with unions. In 1992 the employers decided unilaterally to abandon the retrospective re-grading policy. Mr Brown argued that the retrospective policy agreed in 1987 was contained in a collective agreement which was incorporated into his contract of employment and therefore subject to change only after agreement with two unions. The Council argued that the policy was not a collective agreement and therefore was not incorporated into Mr Brown's contract under the reference to negotiations and agreements with unions and could be changed by the Council unilaterally. However, the Employment Appeal Tribunal held that the retrospective policy recommended by the Joint Consultative Committee and accepted by the Council, emanated from a collective agreement which had been incorporated into the employees' contract of employment and which could not therefore be varied unilaterally by the employers. The Employment Appeal Tribunal stressed that there is nothing in legislation which seeks to lay down any particular way in which a collective agreement should be achieved, except that it must involve negotiation between the parties. In this case there had been discussions, negotiations and agreement between the employers and the trade unions to recommend backdating of re-grading which, after acceptance by the Council, amounted to a collective agreement.

Legal Effect of Collective Agreements

1–38 When consideration is given to the making of a collective agreement and its legal quality or status, it is of vital importance to distinguish the legal quality or status of the agreement as between the trade union(s) and employer(s) who made the agreement on the one hand, and the legal quality of the collective agreement (or a part of it) that has been incorporated into the contract of employment between employers and his employees, on the other.

Between the employer and the union, the general position is that the collective agreement does not create legal rights and duties between these parties. On the other hand, once incorporated into an individual employee's contract of employment, the terms of a collective agreement take on the attributes of a binding contract, and any part of the agreement which is incorporated into the contract, will be legally binding between the employer and the individual employee. The legal status of the collective agreement between the employers and the trade unions who enter the collective agreement reflects the historical development of industrial relations in the United Kingdom, whereby neither side of industry has wanted its agreements to be subject to adjudication by the courts—the "voluntarist" approach to industrial relations—in theory there is nothing to prevent an employer and the trade union making their collective agreement a legally binding contract but this is not the approach which has been adopted in the United Kingdom.

Collective agreements are still entered into on the grounds that there is no intention to create legally enforceable contracts, an essential prerequisite of the common for a valid contract. Indeed the common law position is now endorsed by statute which provides that a collective agreement shall be not be a legally enforceable contract unless: (1) it is in writing; and (2) it contains an express provision that it is intended to be a legally enforceable contract (see the Trade Union Labour Relations (Consolidation) Act 1992 s.179).

Incorporation of Collective Agreements

1–39 One may pose the question why protracted negotiations are spent on concluding collective agreements if they do not give rise to legally binding contracts. The answer is that individual terms of the collective agreement (like those dealing with wages, hours of work and other conditions of employment) are frequently incorporated into the contract of employment between the employer and employees. This of course results, indirectly at least, in certain terms of collective agreements giving rise to legal rights and duties not between the employer and the trade union, but between the employer and those employees into whose contracts of employment the collective agreement has been introduced or incorporated. As far as collective issues are concerned, like those dealing with procedures for negotiations, or for resolving disputes between the employer and the union, and those dealing with facilities for union officials, if they are not legally binding contracts how can the parties be called to perform their obligations? The answer to this of course, is that within the United Kingdom industrial relations system the sanction for failing to observe the collective issues is in the nature of industrial action on the part of the trade union or a simple refusal to negotiate or lock-out on the part of the employers.

Mechanics of Incorporation

1–40 Incorporation usually comes about by an express statement or reference to the collective agreement in the contract of employment. Only occasionally can incorporation be implied from the actings of the parties. From an employer's point of view, an express reference in the contract of employment has the great advantage of automatically altering the contracts of employment of all employees each time a new collective agreement is arrived at. By making reference to "collective agreements made from time to time", the employer is able to ensure that successful negotiations with the trade union will automatically allow him to treat employees, whose contracts incorporate the collective agreement, as if they had all individually agreed to the new terms of employment. However where the collective term is not incorporated conclusion of a collective agreement will have no effect on the contracts of employment: *Singh v BSC* [1974] I.R.L.R. 131, ET; *Hulse v G Embrey Ltd* (EAT 400/77).

To incorporate terms of a collective agreement into the contract of employment, it is not necessary to use any particular terms or refer expressly to collective agreements. See *Edinburgh City Council v Brown* [1999] I.R.L.R. 208 (para.1.32). What the contract of employment must do is simply indicate that the employee's terms and conditions of employment are to be "as negotiated with the relevant trade union" or words to that effect. The principles about incorporation are set out in the following case.

Alexander v Standard Telephones & Cables Ltd

(No.1) [1990] I.R.L.R. 55; *(No.2)* [1991] I.R.L.R. 286

Alexander was employed by Standard Telephone and Cables at Southampton and his terms of employment stated that they were in accordance with the collective agreements reached at plant level. The collective agreement provided that "in the event of compulsory redundancy there will be selection on the basis of service within the group". When compulsory redundancies were necessary, the union argued that the collective agreement stated selection be on the basis of "Last-In-First-Out" (LIFO) within the group, but the employer argued that they had to select to retain those with skills and flexibility best suited to the circumstances. Alexander sought an interlocutory injunction restraining the employers from terminating his employment without first going through the procedure in the collective agreement.

The principles to be applied in determining whether a part of a collective agreement is incorporated into individual contracts of employment can be summarised thus:

(1) the relevant contract is the contract of employment between the individual employee and his employer;
(2) it is the contractual intention of those two parties which is important;
(3) insofar as that intention is to be found in a written document that document must be construed on ordinary principles;
(4) insofar as there is no such document or the document is incomplete or inconclusive, the contractual intention is to be found by inference from all the other available material, including collective agreements;
(5) the fact that another document is not of itself contractual does not prevent it from being incorporated into a contract of employment, if that is the intention shown between the employee and employer;
(6) where a document is expressly incorporated by general words it is still necessary to consider, in conjunction with the words of incorporation, whether any particular part of that document is apt for incorporation, if it is inapt the correct construction may be that it is not a term of the contract; and
(7) where it is not a case of express incorporation but a matter of inferring contractual intent, the character of the document and the relevant part of it and whether it is apt to form part of the individual

> contract, is central to the decision whether or not the inference should be drawn.
>
> In the present cases, the wording of the only document directly applicable to the individual plaintiffs, and the statements of particulars under the Employment Rights Act 1996, were not sufficient to effect an express incorporation of the provisions of the relevant collective agreements since the statutory statement itself did not deal with matters of redundancy. Nor was it possible to infer as a matter of contractual intent that the selection procedures and the principle of seniority were incorporated into the contracts of employment. Where none of the other clauses of the contract are apt to be incorporated into the individual contract of employment, it would require some cogent indication that a particular clause was to have a different character and to have contractual effect. In the present case, the clauses in question when considered within the context of the joint consultation scheme of the procedure agreements as a whole, were not sufficiently cogently worded to support the inference of incorporation into individual contracts of employment.

An example of express incorporation is seen in the following case.

> *National Coal Board v Galley*
>
> [1958] 1 W.L.R. 16, CA
>
> Mr Galley's contract of employment indicated that he accepted employment on "terms negotiated from time to time with the trade unions". Although his own contract of employment made no mention of overtime or weekend working, his employer, the National Coal Board, negotiated collectively with the relevant trade unions from time to time and, in one such negotiation, it was agreed that employees like Mr Galley could be required to do a reasonable amount of overtime when requested by the mine manager. When Galley was rostered for overtime he refused to do it on the grounds that it was not in his contract of employment. The Court held that his contract of employment was that he would work on such terms as were negotiated from time to time with the trade unions, and as the trade unions and the employer had negotiated a collective agreement whereby employees could be required to work overtime, his contract had incorporated these collectively agreed terms. Galley therefore was in breach of his contract by refusing to work the rostered overtime.

Galley demonstrates that where the contract of employment makes general reference to collective agreements the effect on the individual is for him to forfeit his right of individual bargaining. If an individual employee does not agree with the terms negotiated between the employer and the trade unions, his option is either to perform his contract or terminate his employment with the employer.

The contract of employment may incorporate only a particular term of a particular collective agreement (*Pearson v Jones* [1967] 1 W.L.R. 1140), but, for maximum flexibility, references should normally be to "collective agreements from time to time in force", or "as negotiated from time to time", or "as may be current". Of course if no new collective agreement can be negotiated the employer and the employee are bound by such terms as have already been incorporated. Where, as in *Glendale Managed Services Ltd v Graham* [2003] I.R.L.R. 465 the contract of employment provided that the employee's terms would "normally" be in accordance with the collective agreement, any departure from the collective agreement would require to be preceded by notice to the employees that the employers proposes to do so.

Incorporation and Union Membership

1–41 Incorporation of a collective agreement into an employee's contract of employment does not depend upon the employee being a member of the trade union that negotiated the collective agreement. Similarly, where an employer is a member of a federation of employers which negotiates a collective agreement and subsequently leaves that federation, that will in itself not mean that it is then freed from observing the terms of the collective agreement which have been incorporated into contracts of employment between itself and its employees. However, there would be nothing to prevent a contract of employment, providing that the terms of a collective agreement were to be incorporated only while the employer was in membership of a federation. This would, however, require very clear words in the contract of employment itself. Similarly, it would be unlikely that an employer joining an employers' federation or association, after the conclusion of a collective agreement, would result in a collective agreement being incorporated by implication into the contract of employment between the employer and his employee.

Hamilton v Futura Floors Ltd

[1990] I.R.L.R. 478

Hamilton's estate sought to claim a death benefit as provided for in the National Labour Agreement for the Furniture Manufacturing Trade between the trade unions and an employers' association. In order to do so it had to prove that the collective agreement had been incorporated into his contract of employment. There was no express incorporation of the collective agreement but Hamilton argued that it had been incorporated by implication. However, the Court rejected his argument and held that the provisions of the National Agreement could not be regarded as incorporated by implication, since the employers were not then members of the employers' association. Also, the fact that the employers had subsequently joined the association, did not have the effect of altering the conditions of Hamilton's employment, so that the provisions of the collective agreement could be regarded as incorporated by implication into his contract of employment.

The constitution of the association did not contain any reference to the collective agreement nor did it seek to require members to introduce any particular terms into the contracts of employment of their employees. There was no evidence that the deceased or the employer's other employees knew that they had joined the employers' association; after they (the employers) joined there was no discussion about changes in terms of employment.

However, it should be noted that the decision of the court in *Hamilton* does leave open the possibility of the constitution of an employers' association or federation requiring that members comply with collective agreements or incorporate them into contracts of employment with their own employees. Even if this is the case however, it must be doubtful whether the employee is in a position to enforce the terms of the constitution against his own employer although it may assist an employee showing the collective agreement has been incorporated by implication.

Once a collective agreement has been incorporated into the **1–42**
contract of employment it remains in force and effective between the employer and the employee until a new collective agreement is arrived at or until the individual employee and employer agree to other terms. This is made quite clear in the following case.

Gibbons v Associated British Ports

[1985] I.R.L.R. 376

Gibbons' contract of employment provided that his "wages and conditions of service shall be in accordance with national or local agreements for the time being in force". In 1970 a collective agreement regarding wages was arrived at and in 1982 a collective agreement provided that Gibbons would have a six-day guaranteed week payment but would lose his nightshift working allowance. In 1984 Gibbons' employers gave notice to the trade union that the six-day guarantee payment was to be withdrawn. The trade unions responded by saying that they would then terminate the 1970 collective agreement regarding wages and the employers argued that if they did so Gibbons' wages would then become regulated by a national agreement which made no provision for rates of pay or any six-day guarantee payment. The Court held that the six-day guarantee payment had been incorporated into Gibbons' contract and it was not affected by the trade union terminating the 1970 collective agreement itself. It could be removed or altered only by a new collective agreement or by Gibbons agreeing to its removal or alteration.

The fact the collective agreement expressly provides that it shall not create legally binding rights and duties does not prevent the collective terms becoming legally binding on incorporation into the individual's contract of employment. The fact that the collective agreement expressly provides that it shall not be legally binding between the employer and the trade union, is of no relevance to the issue of whether a term originating in a collective agreement can become legally-binding once incorporated into a contract of employment. This is made clear by the following decision.

Marley v Forward Trust Group Ltd

[1986] I.R.L.R. 369

Marley's contract of employment incorporated a collective agreement, entered into between his union and the employers, but cl.11 of the agreement stated that "this agreement is binding in honour only, and it is not intended to give rise to any legal obligation". However, emphasising the difference between the enforceability of a collective agreement, between the union and the employer, and its effect after incorporation, Dillon L.J. stated that the collective agreement "includes clause 11: 'this agreement is binding in honour only, and is not intended to give rise to any legal obligation'. That may, no doubt, have been so as between the employers and the union, but the terms of the agreement are incorporated into the personnel manual, and they must have legal effect thereby as terms of the contract between the employee and the employers".

Collective agreements may cover issues ranging from individual matters like, rates of pay, holiday entitlement and other terms and conditions of employment, to other matters which are truly collective. Such matters would include facilities for trade union officials, procedures relating to negotiations between employers and trade unions, and representation of individual workers in matters like grievance and disciplinary disputes. The courts have emphasised this distinction when considering whether part of a collective agreement has been incorporated into an individual contract of employment, and it has been said that a term in a collective agreement will only be incorporated into an individual contract of employment if it is "suitable" for or "apt" for inclusion in an individual contract. See *Alexander v Standard Telephones & Cables Ltd* [1991] I.R.L.R. 286 (see para.1–35). It may be surprising that a collective term that said "there will be no compulsory redundancy" was held by the Court of Appeal not to be apt for incorporating into the contract of employment because, looking at the content of the term in its context, the words expressed an aspiration rather than a contractual term: *Kaur v MG Rover Group Ltd* [2005] I.R.L.R. 40, CA. The same principle applies to terms which are found not in collective agreements but in some other document containing terms and conditions of employment like a staff handbook or works rules. More recently in *Keeley v Fosroc International Ltd* [2006] I.R.L.R. 961 the Court of Appeal has held that whether it is "apt" to introduce into the contract a term from a staff handbook is to be determined by having regard to the wording of the provision itself and that if it is put in clear terms of entitlement the provision may have a life of its own and may not be neutralised by the context of which its forms part so that a provision concerned with remuneration package even if couched in terms of information or explanation or in discretionary terms may still be apt for construction of a term of the contract, with the result that a term dealing with enhanced redundancy payment was incorporated into the contract of employment.

Collective Agreements and Rules

It is important to make a distinction between contractual terms **1–43** whether they originate in collective agreements or handbooks and employers' rules. The contract of employment permits an employer to specify the method by which the contract shall be performed, with the result that where an employer has drawn up rules for the proper conduct of the work, he is free to alter these rules without obtaining the employee's consent. An example is *Cadoux v Central Regional Council*, 1986 S.L.T. 117 in which the employers were able to withdraw a non-contributory life assurance scheme, by amending their own rules. This was because the reference to the employer's own rules, as amended from time to time, showed that it was in the contemplation of the contracting parties that the employers' rules might be altered and that the employers could alter them unilaterally.

AGENCY

1–44 Only in special circumstances will trade union representatives be regarded as agents acting on behalf of the members (principals). As a general rule the trade union does not act as the agent of its members, although where union negotiators have been specifically authorised to arrive at bargains or contracts on behalf of their members, agency may operate in these special and unusual circumstances. The facts of *Edwards v Skyways Ltd* [1964] 1 All E.R. 494 were unusual in that the trade union representatives had been expressly authorised by employees like Edwards to conclude bargains on behalf of the group of employees with the employer and in *Harris v Richard Lawson Autologistics Ltd* [2002] I.R.L.R. 476, CA the shop steward was held to have ostensible authority to act on behalf of the employees.

SAMPLE QUESTIONS

1. If a European Union Directive is not implemented by a Member State, can a local government employee rely on it to obtain the legal rights contained in the Directive? What protection is afforded to an employee of a private company if a European Directive is not implemented by his Member State?

2. Why is it important to be able to distinguish a contract of employment from other contracts under which people provide services? Is the contract of employment becoming less important?

3. Identify the factors that are taken into account in deciding whether a contract of employment exists, and if the employment is of a casual nature, which factor plays an important role?

4. Riccarton College writes to Mr Brown offering him the post of marketing assistant. The salary is stated to be £25,000 pa plus three per cent of the fees paid by any student introduced to the College by Mr Brown. Mr Brown writes to the College accepting employment on the terms of the letter but after about three years he receives a letter from the College enclosing a written statement of his terms of employment. Under the heading 'Salary' it states "£25,000 pa plus three per cent of fees paid by any students introduced, up to a maximum of £5,000 pa". Mr Brown does nothing on receipt of the written statement. He has earned commission of £6,000 for the year yet he receives only £5,000. When he asks the College for the difference he is informed that he is only entitled to a maximum of £5,000 "in accordance with the written statement". Is Mr Brown entitled to the difference of £1,000? Would it make any difference of he had written to the College acknowledging receipt of the written statement?

5. Mary works as an IT specialist and approaches an Employment Agency to find work. She enters into a contract with the Agency under which the Agency offers to find work for her. The contract provides that she must keep confidential any information about any business where she is sent to work and that she keeps records of her hours of work. It also provides that when assignments are offered she is not required to accept and the Agency does not guarantee to find any assignments. However in January 2006 Mary is sent to work for Routers Ltd, a haulage company, where she works alongside other IT staff employed by Routers Ltd. She, like the other IT staff, receives her instructions from Routers' Director of IT Services and is required to attend staff briefings and meetings. She is paid by the Agency net of Income Tax and National Insurance Contributions; she has no written contract with Routers Ltd but makes a monthly return of work in progress to the Agency which the invoices Routers Ltd for her services. Mary has continued under this arrangement without a any breaks apart from short absences for illness and paid holidays until

September 2007 when she is advised by the Director of IT that her services are no longer required. Does Mary have a contact of employment with either the Agency or Routers Ltd?

SUGGESTED ANSWERS FOR CHAPTER ONE

1. An employee of an emanation of a State (a concept explained in the case of Foster v British Gas*) can rely on the terms of a Directive even although it has not been introduced into his own State's legal system. Employees of the central government and of local government would be regarded as employees of an emanation of the State. This is the case even where the laws of his own State are directly contradictory of the Directive. The only requirement is that the Directive must be in sufficiently precise and have unconditional terms so that the court or tribunal which has jurisdiction to deal with the matter can apply the Directive and provide an appropriate remedy. A good example is in the case of* Marshall v Southampton etc Area Health Board *[1986] I.C.R. 335 ECJ. The law of the United Kingdom excluded her right to claim sex discrimination when she was compulsorily retired but no such exclusion was found in the Equal Treatment Directive and being an employee of an emanation of the State (viz. the Health Board) she was able to insist on the terms of the Directive, which was clearly unconditional, being applied. By taking the Directive into account, the Tribunal was able to hold that she was the victim of sexual discrimination irrespective of the exclusion at that time found in the Sex Discrimination Act.*

An employee employed by a private sector employer cannot do so. The theory is that the State (and any of its organs or emanations) is responsible for implementing the Directive and the State must not be allowed to benefit from not complying with its duty to implement the Directive. Accordingly a private sector employee is not able to rely on the Directive in an issue with his own employer. But as the State has still failed to implement the Directive which would give him protection he is able to sue his own State for its failure to confer on him the rights contained in the Directive; this is known as the Francovich *doctrine.*

2. It is important because many employment law rights like the right not to be unfairly dismissed are given only to those who have contracts of employment.

Also, the contract of employment is a special contract which by law is deemed to include certain terms, for example, the duty of the employer to provide a safe system of work for his employees and apprentices, and the duty of the employee not to do anything, like working for a competitor, which would be likely to injure his employer's business.

Additionally an employee who is negligent in the course of his employment and causes injury to a third party renders his employer vicariously liable to the third party but this is not the case where the contract is not one of employment.

The distinction is becoming less important because many employment law rights (for example the right not to have deductions from wages made without the worker's agreement and the right to have limits on the working time) are being conferred by law on those who do not have contracts of employment but work personally for a person or a company which is not their client or customer. Such people are referred to as "workers" and not "employees". Some rights not to be unfairly terminated are not being conferred on "workers", like the right not to be dismissed or terminated for making a public interest disclosure. Also, agency workers are being covered by modern legislation like the Working Time Regulations 1998. However the very important rights like unfair dismissal and redundancy are in the main still restricted to employees.

3. The factors which are taken into account are those considered in cases like Market Investigations v Minister of Social Security *(1968) 2QB1 73, for example:*

Control

The criterion of control is clearly still an important one although it is no longer the decisive criterion.

Provision of equipment

The extent to which the person doing the work has to provide equipment at his or her own expense is significant. Generally incurring a large capital outlay to acquire equipment to perform a task is more readily associated with a contract for services rather than a contract of employment.

Hire of helpers

If the task cannot be done by the individual but requires the individual worker to hire additional helpers, that would also suggest it is not a contract of employment; a contract of employment is a contract under which there is personal performance by the workman/woman.

Financial risk

If the contract involves a degree of financial risk and requires exercising responsibility for the management of the work, it suggests it is not a contract of employment but more likely to be a contract for services.

Opportunity to profit

An opportunity to profit from the sound management of the contract will be more readily associated with a contract for services.

Label or name of contract

Frequently the parties to a contract, in an attempt to remove doubt as to the type of contract, will give the contract a particular name. However, the name the contract is given will not be conclusive because the existence of a contract of employment is a matter for a court or tribunal to decide and cannot be determined by the name or "label" it is given by the parties.

Change of status

On the other hand, where the parties have genuinely intended to change the status of the contract, the courts will bear this in mind in determining the relationship between the two parties.

Income Tax and National Insurance

Seldom will the fact that the employer does or does not deduct Income Tax or pay National Insurance Contributions, as if the person was an employee, be of much significance. In many cases whether such Income Tax or National Insurance Contributions should be deducted at source is the issue which has raised the question of the individual's status. How Income Tax is paid is of little significance.

Mutuality of obligation

Is the employer required to provide work when it is available and is the individual required to do it when it is provided?
The factor which is of most importance in casual employment is mutuality of obligation and this can be seen in Carmichael v National Power *[1999] 1 WLR 2042.*

4. The contractual relationship on which rights and duties are based will be found in the letter of appointment and not in the written statement. The written statement is not a contract but a unilateral statement issued by the employer. Accordingly Mr Brown has a contractual right to receive commission for all fees and not merely up to a maximum of £5,000. The fact that Mr Brown does nothing on receipt of the statement is immaterial, as silence will not normally amount to consent to the alteration of his contract. Even acknowledging receipt of the statement will not affect Mr Brown's right to commission, as that does not show his agreement but merely that he had received the document. However, if he had signed not just an acknowledgement of receipt but also a statement claiming he accepted the terms of the statement, he would then be bound by it as he would have in effect agreed to a change in his contractual terms.

5. Whether Mary has a contract with the Agency is determined by applying the usual multiple and variable test including mutuality of obligation. Since the contract with the Agency makes it clear that there is no duty to provide work and no duty to work when it is provided, there can be no contract of employment with the Agency as there is a minimum mutuality of obligation required for any contract of employment and that is absent here (Carmichael v National Power plc).

The next issue is whether Mary might have a contract of any type with Routers Ltd. For there to be a contract there has to be an intention to create legal relations and in the circumstances such an intention will be argued by the Routers Ltd to be absent. Routers will argue that they did not want to have any contract with Mary and that is why they chose to employ her through an agency. If there is no intention to create a contract there can be no contract of any type. The absence of a written contract between Routers Ltd and Mary, however, is not conclusive. All it shows is that there is no express contract but a contract of employment may be created expressly or by implication. Also the contract of employment is a legal concept and cannot be determined simply by a party pleading that he or she did not intend to create a contract. A court or tribunal will look at all the circumstances (the factual matrix) to determine whether there is a contract of employment. While from cases like Dacas v Brook Street Motors *and* Franks v Reuters *it is now possible to show that a contract can be created by implication where a person has provided his or her personal services to another person/company over a considerable period of time and the fact that payment is made by a third party (the Agency) is of little relevance* James v London Borough of Greenwich *seems to impose a more stringent test in reminding us (1) that it is only appropriate to imply a contractual relationship where it is necessary to do so t to give business reality to what was taking place between the parties and (2) that the issue in agency cases is whether the way the contract is performed is consistent with the agency arrangements or whether it is only consistent with an implied contract of employment between the individual and the end user or host organisation. If it is consistent with an agency arrangement there is no necessity to imply a contract of employment with the end user. The fact that control over Mary is exercised by the IT Director of Routers Ltd and that she is treated like other staff who are genuinely employees and that she has to keep secret the confidential information of Routers Ltd would provide Mary with a strong argument that she has a contract of employment with Routers Ltd but essentially it depends on whether the implication of a contract of employment is necessary.*

Chapter Two

TERMS AND CONDITIONS OF EMPLOYMENT

CONTRACT OR STATUTE

2–01 Until the 1970s nearly all terms and conditions of employment were found in the contract of employment itself. Very seldom did statute intervene to prescribe terms and conditions of employment. The main exceptions related to statutes that were designed to protect employees who worked in particular types of employment, namely mines, factories and shops and offices. The physical working conditions and hours of work of employees in these industries had for many years been regulated by basic minimum statutory standards but not issues like rates of pay and other emoluments or benefits which employees might receive under their contracts of employment. The nearest that the United Kingdom legal system came to regulating pay rates was the system of Trade Boards introduced in 1919, later to become the system of Wages Councils. The Wages Council fixed a minimum wage system for employees in particular industries but not until the 1970s did statute begin to regulate other substantive terms of employment. Thus, the Employment Protection Act 1975 introduced rights to wages in the event of being laid off (guarantee payments), pay while suspended on medical grounds (medical suspension pay), pay during maternity leave (maternity pay), and to have time off work, sometimes with pay, to participate in union activities and carry out trade union duties and public duties (time off work).

That process of creating a minimum or "floor" of statutory rights has been supplemented by statutory rights relating not merely to rates of pay but to deductions from wages, working hours (including prescription of the lengths of the working day and working week), rights to parental leave, time off for emergencies and to paid holidays. As a result, the relationship between an employee and his employer today is a complex one involving a mixture of contractual and statutory obligations and rights. An example of the entitlement to wages being determined purely by the terms of the contract is seen in the following case.

Adin v Sedco Forex International Resources Ltd

[1997] I.R.L.R. 280

Mr Adin's contract of employment provided for an annuity to be paid to him while he was unable to work because of illness, and if Mr Adin was unable to work and was unable to pursue an equivalent profession, the employers would continue to pay the annuity until his death. The employers decided to terminate Mr Adin's contract of employment and argued that thereafter he was not entitled to any further benefit. However, the Court ruled that the contractual provisions had to be interpreted in the light of their stated purpose of providing income protection when an employee could not work due to illness or injury. The contractual terms about sickness benefits formed a coherent package which entitled Mr Adin to the annuity even after his contract had been ended, notwithstanding that he was still unfit to perform work.

On the other hand the circumstances in which an employer: (a) may make deductions from wages or require payments to be made to the employer by a worker; or (b) must make payments to employees who are unable to work for reasons of sickness, maternity or lack of work and during periods of notice are regulated by the Employment Rights Act 1996. The National Minimum Wage Act 1998 entitles many workers to a minimum statutory wage irrespective of the type of work performed, and the Equal Pay Act 1970 statute requires that men and women who are doing work of equal value receive equal pay. Accordingly the wages to which a worker is entitled is determined not just by the contract itself but by the contract in the context of a somewhat complex statutory framework.

EXPRESS AND IMPLIED CONTRACTUAL TERMS

In any contract of employment there will be certain terms which are **2–02**
express and others which are implied. Where the term is express, difficulties may arise in ascertaining the true contractual intention. In this respect, however, the contract of employment is no different from other contracts which have to be construed and interpreted. Particularly for the contract of employment the *contra proferentem* rule is important. This rule of interpretation means that where a contractual term is ambiguous it generally has to be interpreted against the party putting it forward in legal argument. Usually the party putting it forward in legal argument is the party who has drawn up the contract and, as most contracts of employment are drawn up by the employer, in the event of a term being ambiguous it will be construed against the interest of the employer.

Other difficulties may arise with express terms, which seek to restrict or prevent the employee working in competition with the employer after the employment ends or terminates, and give the employer an unfettered discretion with regard to where the employee works and the type of work he can be required to carry out. In recent times, courts have become used to holding that such apparently absolute terms are subject to the implied limitation of reasonableness when an employer seeks to rely on them. This is dealt with later under the heading of particular terms (see paras 2.35 and 2.41).

Wages

2–03 Whether or not wages are due for work performed is generally simply a matter of contract law. Unlike English law, Scots law permits a valid contract to exist even where there is no "consideration", therefore it is perfectly possible to have a valid contract of employment even when the services are provided free of charge. In Scotland the general but rebuttable legal presumption, however, is that when services are given, they are given in the expectation that payment will be made in return (*Thomson v Thomson's Trustee* (1889) 16 R 333). However, entitlement to wages will normally be dealt with by an express term of the contract. The written statement (see para.1–27) must give particulars of the scale or rate of remuneration or the method of calculating remuneration and today it would only be as an oversight that the contract of employment did not make clear provision as to whether or not wages are due.

The next issue concerns the amount of wages to be paid and this may require consideration, not just of contract law, but also of statute. As far as contract law is concerned there will normally be an express term in the contract of employment. If not, it may be possible to imply a term from the custom of a particular trade. In the event of there being neither an express nor an implied term in the contract, equity requires that an employee would be entitled to payment representing the market value of his or her services, a claim based on *quantum meruit*.

Generally contracts of employment make express provision for payment of wages should no work be available, and many contracts of employment guarantee a minimum amount for a particular period of work. If there is no such provision where an employee is hourly paid and the number of hours for the week or month is specified in the contract, the employee is entitled to wages for that number of hours at the agreed rate whether or not he or she actually works the specified amount or not. A failure on the part of the employer to pay the worker at the appropriate hourly rate for the specified number of hours in the week or the month, will be a material breach of the contract by the employer, allowing the employee to rescind or bring the contract to an end and claim damages. If the employee does not wish to rescind the contract he may simply claim that there has been an unlawful deduction from wages which may be recovered by a complaint to an employment tribunal (see para.2–06). Where the contract is for piecework (where wages are in accordance with output) the employer is required to provide a steady supply of work, unless there is an established custom of a particular trade that the obligation to pay wages while the worker is idle may be suspended (see Bell's *Principles* s.192 and *Devonald v Rosser & Sons* [1906] 2 K.B. 728). The payment of pieceworkers is now also regulated by the National Minimum Wage Regulations 1999 (SI 1999/584) (see para.2–09).

In the event of an employer failing to pay wages, either in part or **2–04**
in whole, what remedies are open to the employee? If the failure to pay wages is due to an event over which neither contracting party has any control, for example the destruction of the employer's premises by fire or flood, further performance of the contract of employment itself may be impossible and there would be no further obligation to pay wages to the employee under the contract. Where the failure to pay is a breach of contract by the employer, the breach will normally be a repudiation or material breach of the contract by the employer thereby allowing the employee to bring the contract to an end by rescinding it and claim damages for his loss. As we will see later, a repudiation of the contract by the employer allows an employee to leave and, for the purposes of redundancy payments and unfair dismissal law, claim he has been "constructively dismissed" (see para.4–09). Although it was at one time argued that an act of repudiation would itself bring the contract of employment to an end, the House of Lords has reaffirmed the general principle that one party of the employment contract cannot bring it to an end merely by repudiating the contract.

Rigby v Ferodo Ltd

[1987] I.R.L.R. 516

Ferodo Ltd told its employees that it was going to reduce their wages but Rigby and other employees refused to agree with their decision. The employers argued that as they were entitled to terminate Rigby's contract by giving him 12 weeks' notice, they were also entitled to change his contract by giving by giving him 12 weeks' notice prior to the change (in this case a reduction of wages). Ferodo argued that they were merely terminating one contract and offering a new contract with different wage rates; by giving 12 weeks' notice of the reduction in the wage rates they could not be seen to be in breach of the contract since they were able to terminate the contract by giving 12 weeks' notice.

However, the House of Lords rejected the employer's argument on the grounds that there is no principle of law, that any breach which the innocent party is entitled to treat as a repudiation of the contract, brings the contract to an automatic end. It was clear in this case that Rigby and his fellow employees had not accepted the employer's repudiation of the contract as bringing it to an end with the result that it had no effect on the terms of their contract with the employer. They were able to claim successfully that they were still entitled to be paid the (unreduced) wages as stated in their contracts of employment. A repudiation of the contract, if not accepted by the other party as bringing the contract to an end, is regarded as "a thing writ in water" and of no legal effect.

Late payment of wages raises two issues. The first is whether interest is due and while there is old Scots authority to that effect (Lord Fraser, *Master and Servant* (3rd edn., T&T Clark, Edinburgh, 1882 p.138)); Umpherston, *Law of Master and Servant* ((W. Green & Son, 1904), p.61) there is no recent authority. Generally, interest does not run on a debt until there has been either a judicial demand for payment or intimation by the creditor that if payment is not made by a specified date, interest will begin to run. However, this general rule may be supplemented by either an express or implied contractual provision or by a custom of the trade (Wilson, *The Scottish Law of Debt* (2nd edn., W. Green & Son/Sweet & Maxwell, 1991), p.131). Secondly, but unusually, late payment of wages may amount to a repudiation of the contract of employment.

Hanlon v Allied Breweries

[1975] I.R.L.R. 321

Mrs Hanlon worked as a barmaid and received her wages late on two consecutive occasions. Her reaction was to rescind her contract. The tribunal held that she was entitled to do so because the employers, by their conduct, had indicated that they were not seriously intending to perform their obligations to Mrs Hanlon. This case must, however, be regarded as unusual and turning on its own facts.

Wages during sickness and Statutory Sick Pay

2–05 The statutory written statement (see para.1–31) requires that the employee receive particulars of any terms and conditions relating to incapacity for work due to sickness or injury including any provision for sick pay. The result of this is that terms regarding sick pay are dealt with expressly by the written statement or contract of employment. Unless there is an express term to the effect, generally the contract of employment does not require payment of wages or salary to an employee who is unable to work through sickness or injury. Until 1982 an employee unable to work through sickness or injury was entitled to a Sickness Benefit paid to him directly by the Department of Health and Social Security. In 1982, however, Statutory Sick Pay (SSP) was introduced by the Social Security and Housing Benefits Act 1982. The provisions are now contained in the Social Security Contributions and Benefits Act 1992. The SSP system requires employers to act as a paying agent on behalf of the State and disputes about e*ntitlement* to SSP are dealt with not by employment tribunals, but ultimately by Commissioners of Revenue and Customs. However SSP is "wages" for the purpose of Pt II of the Employment Rights Act 1996 so that an employment tribunal has jurisdiction to hear a claim that there has been an unlawful deduction from SSP: *Taylor Gordon & Co Ltd v Timmons* [2004] I.R.L.R. 180, EAT. Employers pay an amount equivalent to what would have been paid by way of State Incapacity Benefit to incapacitated employees for a maximum of 28 weeks. SSP is in addition to any contractual rights and cannot be limited or excluded by any agreement. Many contracts of employment provide that the employer will make up the difference between SSP and the employee's normal earnings and usually this contractual provision will be subject to a maximum period, for example for a set number of weeks or months, after which time, the employee's only entitlement is to the basic SSP which is paid at a flat weekly rate. On the exhaustion of SSP an employee may become entitled to Incapacity Benefit but an employer has no role in the payment of such a benefit.

In the event that there is no express contractual term dealing with the right to wages or salary whilst sick or injured, it is possible to argue that such a right is to be implied into the contract of employment. In England if the contract is not clear the presumption is that wages are to be paid until the employment is ended. See *Mears v Safecar Security Ltd* [1982] I.C.R. 626. In Scotland the employee's implied right to receive wages while unable to work through sickness or injury probably operates only with respect to long fixed-term contracts.

Method of payment of wages and deductions from wages

In the 19th century many employers of manual workers in the new **2–06**
industries of the industrial revolution paid employees in credit notes instead of cash. Credit notes could be exchanged for goods only in the employer's own shops which became known as "truck shops", reflecting the Scandinavian origin of the word "truck", meaning exchange or barter. Truck shops charged inflated prices and employees were frequently tied in to an employer because they could not clear off their debts and move to another employer; debtors at this time could be imprisoned. In addition employers frequently and without any warning made deductions from wages

for poor workmanship or indiscipline. Workers therefore were in a very vulnerable position and the Truck Acts 1831–1896 were enacted to remedy their situation. These Acts required manual workers be paid in cash, any non-cash payment being regarded as void, and provided strict rules about deductions from the wages. These Acts were in force until 1986, although they were relaxed slightly in 1960 by the Payment of Wages Act which allowed a worker to agree to be paid in a form other than cash, thereby enabling the employer to make payment by cheque or other non-cash means. The Wages Act 1986 repealed the Truck Acts and the Payment of Wages Act 1960 so that the method of paying wages or salary to any worker (manual or otherwise) is now entirely a matter for the employer and the worker to agree. In practice, of course, it is determined largely by the employer in drawing up the terms on which he is prepared to offer employment.

THE WAGES ACT 1986

2–07 Until 1986, a manual worker could insist upon being paid in cash and any non-cash payment, for example by cheque or by credit transfer, was regarded as void but that created problems of security and efficiency. The practice today is to include in the contract of employment an express term dealing with how wages will be paid. It is advisable for employers to reserve to themselves some discretion in the matter in the event that the preferred method is, if only temporarily, unavailable or not practicable.

The Wages Act 1986 also revised the law regarding deductions from wages (and any payments the workers are required to make to the employer). The Wages Act has been repealed but its provisions are now contained in Pt II of the Employment Rights Act 1996. We deal here with deductions, although the rules are in all respects almost exactly the same, whether the issue concerns a deduction from wages or a payment the worker is required to make to the employer.

Section 13 of the 1996 Act provides that:

> "(1) An employer shall not make a deduction from wages of a worker unless—
>
> (a) the deduction is required or authorised to be made by virtue of a statutory provision or a relevant provision of the worker's contract, or
> (b) the worker has previously signified in writing his agreement or consent to the making of the deduction."

Thus a deduction is lawful only if it is required by statute or the worker has: (a) agreed to it in writing; or (b) has had written notice of the existence of the unwritten contractual term, giving the employer a right to make the deduction, before any deduction is made. However, where an employer has the right to transfer an employee to work which is less well paid, a fall in the wages to which the employee is entitled is not a deduction from wages.

Hussman Manufacturing Ltd v Weir

[1998] I.R.L.R. 288

Weir had been employed for 12 years by Hussman Manufacturing Ltd on night-shift duty, when his employers decided to alter their shift system and he was moved to a day-shift rota and paid at the day-shift rate. He carried on working under protest and complained to an employment tribunal that his employers had made an unlawful deduction from his wages.

The employment tribunal found that the contract of employment allowed the employers to alter the shift pattern and change Weir's shift but not to reduce his wages. The tribunal relied on the principle established in *Bruce v Wiggins Teape (Stationery) Ltd* [1994] I.R.L.R. 536, that a unilateral reduction of an employee's pay is an unlawful deduction from wages and held that the employers had made an unlawful deduction from Weir's wages contrary to s.13 of the Employment Rights Act 1996.

On appeal by the employers to the EAT it was held that an employer who moved an employee from a night-shift to a day-shift and reduced his salary to the day-shift rate had not made an unlawful deduction from the employee's wages.

Determining the amount that is properly payable will normally turn on an analysis of the employee's contract of employment. In this case the EAT had to determine what sum was properly payable to an employee who had been moved to work on a lower-paid shift as part of a management reorganisation. The EAT distinguished the decision in *Bruce* because in this case the wages properly payable to Weir were those payable for the shift to which he had been moved. The terms of the contract of employment allowed the employers to alter the shift pattern and change Weir's shift.

There are special rules for retail workers, enacted to protect them against deductions for large losses incurred by the retail outlet, even though the worker himself was not personally responsible for the loss occurring. Some employers were inserting terms into the contracts of retail workers which permitted unlimited deductions from their wages for stock or cash shortages, whether or not the retail worker was personally responsible. The following type of clause would be found in the contracts of some retail workers:

> "You shall be liable for any stock or cash shortage occurring during any week in which you were on duty and your employer shall be entitled to deduct from wages a sum equivalent to the cash or stock shortage."

The operation of such a clause could mean that at the end of a week's work, for example, a retail worker whose gross wages amounted to £150 might have £130 deducted as a result of cash or stock shortages which may have occurred during hours when the worker was not on duty. Section 18 of the Employment Rights Act provides that where an employer of a worker in retail employment makes a deduction on account of cash shortages or stock deficiencies, the deduction shall not exceed 10 per cent of the gross amount payable on that day. However, these provisions only apply to cash shortages and stock deficiencies and while they would include deductions on account of any dishonesty or other conduct which resulted in the shortage or deficiency, they would not apply to deductions in respect of misconduct in general, e.g. lateness or other disciplinary matters. Therefore for a deduction in respect of a cash shortage or stock deficiency from the wages of a retail worker to be lawful, there must have been (a) an agreement on the worker's part that the deduction may be made; and (b) the deduction must be no more than 10 per cent of the gross pay. However, even this is subject to the qualification contained in s.22(2) which removes the 10 per cent limit of the payment in the final installment of wages. An employer who fears a retail worker will leave his employment before the full amount of a shortage or deficiency has been recovered, may terminate his employment thereby being able to recover perhaps the whole amount from the final installment of wages. This may, however, lead to an employee claiming unfair dismissal.

Excluded Deductions

2–08 There are several exceptions, however, which apply to all workers and they are set out in s.14 of the 1996 Act. None of the above rules therefore apply to the following:

- (a) deductions to recover an overpayment of wages or expenses;
- (b) deductions as a result of statutory disciplinary proceedings;
- (c) a deduction the employer is required to make by law and to pay the amount over to a public authority;
- (d) deductions agreed to in writing by the worker which the employer is required to pay over to a third person, an amount notified by that person (e.g. trade union subscriptions and payments to provident and benefit funds);

(e) deductions on account of the worker having taken part in a strike or other industrial action: see *Gill v Ford Motor Co Ltd* [2004] I.R.L.R. 840, EAT;
(f) deductions agreed to in writing by the worker to satisfy a court or tribunal order requiring the payment to be made by the worker to the employer.

Definition of wages

Wages are "any sums payable to the worker in connection with his employment including fee, bonus, commission, holiday pay or other emolument referable to his employment whether payable under his contract or otherwise" (s.27). Clearly this will include payments the employer is required to make by contract and would seem to include non contractual bonuses; although non contractual bonuses are expressly declared to be wages (s.27(3)) this is to limited to situations where the employer is not "liable to pay" bonuses but has made a one-off payment to employees (*Farrell Matthews and Weir v Hansen* [2005] I.R.L.R. 160, EAT). However where the payment is not a bonus and is purely discretionary so that the worker has no legal entitlement to the payment it may not fall within the definition of "wages" (*New Century Cleaning Co v Church* [2000] I.R.L.R. 27, CA). **2–09**

The definition of wages in s.27 also includes various statutory payments like Statutory Sick Pay and Statutory Maternity Pay. It does not include entitlement to paid holidays under the Working Time Regulations 1998 which may only be recovered by a complaint under the Regulations themselves (*Commissioners of Inland Revenue v Ainsworth* [2005] EWCA Civ 441; [2005] I.R.L.R. 465). However, the following payments are excluded from the definition of wages:

(a) advances of wages or loans;
(b) expenses incurred by the worker in carrying out his employment;
(c) pensions, allowances, gratuities, in connection with retirement or as compensation for loss of office;
(d) payments referable to redundancy; and
(e) payments to the worker otherwise than in his capacity as a worker.

Pay in Lieu of Notice

This is a lump sum payment made in lieu of, or instead of, the wages an employee would earn if he or she were permitted to work his or her period of notice. In *Delaney v Staples* [1992] I.C.R. 483, the House of Lords held that pay in lieu of notice is made in respect of a period after the contract had been brought to an end and it could not be regarded as "wages". Accordingly non-payment of pay in lieu of notice is not an unlawful deduction from wages under the Employment Rights Act. An alternative to paying an employee in **2–10** lieu of notice is to place the employee on "garden leave" during the period of notice. This means that, although the contract of employment continues during the notice period, the employee is not required to work. The employee will receive his or her wages at the usual intervals during the notice period but should the employer fail to pay wages there will be an unlawful deduction from wages because the contract of employment does not come to an end until the garden leave has expired.

Delaney v Staples

[1992] I.C.R. 483, HL

Delaney was summarily dismissed and given a cheque for £82 which she was told were wages in lieu of notice but the cheque was subsequently stopped. On the date of her leaving she was also entitled to holiday pay and commission totalling £55.

The Court of Appeal held that where an employee was summarily dismissed and given a payment in lieu of notice, which was later stopped, such a sum was properly characterised as being payable by way of damages for wrongful dismissal and lay outside the definition of wages in the Employment Rights Act 1996. Accordingly an employee could not make a complaint to an employment tribunal but had to seek recovery of the wages in lieu of notice in the ordinary court. However unpaid commission and holiday pay due under the employee's contract fell within the definition of wages in the Employment Rights Act. By not paying these sums there had been an unlawful deduction from the employee's wages and these were recoverable by a complaint being presented to the employment tribunal.

Nicholls L.J. stated the issue concerned the much vexed question of whether payments in lieu of notice were within the statutory definition of wages:

> "That phrase (pay in lieu of notice) was a loose expression used indifferently to cover recognisably different situations. There was the case where the employee ... was not given the due notice of dismissal to which he was entitled under the contract. He was claiming pay for the period of notice which he said he was entitled to have been given. The proper legal analysis of his claim in such a situation was that the claim was for damages for breach of contract. It was not a claim for payment in accordance with the terms of the contract. A payment by an employer in respect of or on account of that breach was a payment in respect of that claim for damages. In such a case the claim was in respect of a post-termination period of time".

That was to be contrasted with the "garden leave" type of case where the employer gave notice of termination but dispensed with the employee's services during the period of notice. There, the contract remained in existence until the expiry of the notice given. In such a case, a claim by the employee to be paid during the period of notice was truly [a claim] to be paid wages under his contract. Such sums would come within the statutory definition of wages."

In the present case the claim was for damages of wrongful dismissal. The definition of wages in the Employment Rights Act made no express provision regarding damages payable for wrongful dismissal. In Nicholl L.J.'s view sums so payable were not within the statutory definition of wages, rather they were to be regarded as damages for wrongful dismissal, payable in connection with the termination of a worker's contract rather than in connection with his employment. They were based on the absence of employment for the period to which the damages related and they related solely to a period after the contract had been terminated and the employer/employee nexus had been severed. They did not relate to a payment for work done nor were they connected therewith.

The House of Lords dismissed the employee's claim because a payment in lieu of notice is not "wages" within the meaning of the Act where it relates to a period after the termination of the employment. Wages are paid in return for services rendered during the employment, so that all payments in respect of the termination of the employment are excluded save to the extent that they are expressly included under s.27(1). Thus payments in respect of "garden leave" are wages within the meaning of the Act since they are (advance) payments of wages falling due under a subsisting contract of employment. But all other payments in lieu, whether or not contractually payable, are not wages since they are payments relating to the termination of the employment and not to the provision of services under the employment contract.

Accordingly payments in lieu of notice are not wages, where as in the present case, without the agreement of the employee, the employer summarily dismisses the employee and tenders a payment in lieu of notice; or where the contract of employment provides expressly that the employment may be terminated either by notice or a payment in lieu of notice; or where at the end of the employment the employer and the employee agree that the employment is to terminate forthwith on the payment of a sum in lieu of notice.

Recovering Unlawful Deductions

2–11 The great advantage of being able to show there has been an unlawful deduction from wages is that it enables a worker to present a complaint in the employment tribunal relating to such a deduction from wages. Previously the only remedy for a worker was to raise a legal action in the ordinary courts claiming his employer had broken his contract of employment by not paying him the wages due—a relatively expensive procedure frequently requiring the services of a lawyer. Under the Employment Rights Act workers may complain to the employment tribunal which is a quick and inexpensive procedure and one which does not require legal representation. However a complaint of unlawful deduction may only be made where it relates to a specific sum of money or an identifiable sum so that where employees claimed that they had not been paid the correct bonuses under an implied agreement that they would receive the same bonus as had been paid by their predecessor employer which required an investigation as to the level of underpayment a claim of unlawful deduction was not available and the employee's remedy was to sue for damages for breach of contract: *Coors Brewers Ltd v S P Adcock* [2007] EWCA Civ 19. A complaint of unlawful deduction must be made before the end of the period of three months beginning with the date of the payment of wages from which a deduction has been made or, where it is one of a series of deductions, the last deduction in the series. In the event that the Tribunal upholds the worker's complaint it shall order the employer to pay to the worker the amount of any deductions made contrary to Pt II of the Act. However, as a result of the Employment Act 2002 (s.32) and the Employment Act 2002 (Dispute Resolution) Regulations 2004 (SI 2004/752), before the employment tribunal can accept a complaint the worker must first raise the grievance in writing with his employer and allow 28 days to permit resolution of the matter without having to resort to the employment tribunal.

Itemised pay statement

2–12 It is important for the worker to be able to see how his gross and net wages have been calculated and it is for this reason that the Employment Rights Act s.8 entitles employees to receive a written itemised pay statement containing particulars of:

- (a) the gross amount of wages or salary;
- (b) the amounts of any variable and fixed deductions and the purposes for which they are made;
- (c) the net amount of wages payable; and
- (d) where different parts of the net amount are paid in different ways, the amount and method of payment of each part-payment.

There are special rules in s.9 dealing with fixed deductions which may be dealt with by a standing statement. Thus if every month £5 is deducted for union subscriptions and £5 for a provident or sick fund, the itemised pay statement need not contain separate particulars of each deduction, provided the statement does show an aggregate amount of the fixed deductions and the employee has received a standing statement of fixed deductions. This will show the fixed amounts and the intervals at which the deduction is to be made as well as the purpose for which it is made. In the event that an employer fails to give an employee an itemised pay statement, the employee may refer the matter to an employment tribunal which may declare what ought to have been contained in the itemised pay statement. The employment tribunal can then order the employer to pay to the employee the aggregate of any unnotified deductions in the period of 13 weeks preceding the complaint to the Tribunal.

NATIONAL MINIMUM WAGE

Until the National Minimum Wage Act 1998 there was no general **2–13** protection against low pay. Under the Wages Councils system which had operated until 1986 the pay rates and other terms of employment in certain categories of industry were maintained by statute. However, the system of Wages Councils was abolished by the Wages Act 1986, initially for employees under 21 and then for all employees. This meant that many employees in industries, which had no collective bargaining employees, could be paid whatever wages the employer was prepared to offer. The 1998 Act with the National Minimum Wage Regulations 1999 introduces a scheme to ensure a minimum level of pay across all sectors of industry. The scheme applies to employees, workers and agency workers. Those who are under 18 are not protected and there are different rates for those between 18 and 21 and those 22 and over. (The Secretary of State may refer matters, including the level at which the Minimum Wage is set, to the Low Pay Commission: National Minimum Wage Act s.6.) The rate is expressed as an hourly rate and the rates expected to operate from October 1, 2007 are: £5.52 for those 22 and over and £4.60 for 18–21 years old. (The "development rate" which applied to a worker who is 22 or over who spent six months in employment in nationally accredited training in accordance has been abolished.) The Government accepted the Low Pay Commission's recommendation that there should be a new rate of £3.40 for 16 and 17 year olds who are above compulsory school leaving age but who are not in apprenticeships. Some groups are excluded and these include many people in work: apprentices under 26 years of age during the first year of their apprenticeship; any apprentice under 18 years of age; students on work experience which is for less than a year; those who work in sheltered work schemes for homeless people; voluntary workers; share fishermen; prisoners; and those in family work like carers or au pairs.

In order to decide whether the appropriate rate is paid it is necessary to determine the pay reference period, the total pay received and the total hours worked during that period. The pay reference period is one month or such other shorter period; accordingly the reference period for workers paid weekly is a week, for those paid daily, one day, and for those paid at longer intervals, e.g. two months, is one month (reg.10). Wages which are earned during one pay period but not received until the following period (payment in arrears) are allocated to the period in which they are earned, although this can be extended where workers have to keep records or timesheets. Thus where X works 40 hours in March, 30 hours in April and 50 hours in May and is paid (in arrears) £160 in April, £120 in May and £200 in June, it appears that for May he will receive only £2.40 per hour. Regulation 30(b), however, allocates the £120 to April and the £200 to May making the hourly rate for April and May (the months in which the money was earned) £4.00. The total pay is the gross pay which includes all commission, bonuses and gratuities paid through the payroll, but does not include benefits in kind like luncheon vouchers and use of a company car (reg.9). Accommodation provided by the employer is taken into account but only up to the maximum of £30.10 per week (reg.36). Special shift rates are excluded.

The hours to be used in arriving at the hourly rate vary depending on whether it is time work (where the worker is paid according to the hours worked), salaried work (where the worker is paid for a basic number of hours per year for which he gets an annual salary paid in 12 equal monthly installments or 52 equal weekly installments), output work (where hours vary but the worker is paid for the number of units of work completed) or unmeasured work (where there are no specified hours but the worker is required to work when needed or work is available) (regs 3–6). The hours to be taken into account situation may be summarised as follows:

Time work: hours done in reference period.

Salaried work: basic hours plus any hours for which the worker received extra payments.

Output work: the actual hours in the reference period; instead of paying an output worker the NMW (National Minimum Wage) for the actual hours worked in the reference period an employer may pay in accordance with a fair piece rate system whereby the worker (who must be given written notice of the system) is paid at a rate which reflects the number of units which the average worker can produce.

Unmeasured work: the actual hours in the pay reference period or hours in a "daily average" agreement.

Enforcement

Employers are required to keep records to show that the worker is paid the NMW and a worker has the right to see such records (reg.3). This is a right enforced by complaint to an employment tribunal which awards a sum equal to 80 times the NMW rate (National Minimum Wage Act ss.10, 11). **2–14**

Enforcement of payment of the NMW is by the Inland Revenue issuing of an Enforcement Notice on an employer and by a worker making a complaint to an employment tribunal that there has been an unlawful deduction from wages under Pt II of the Employment Rights Act 1996 (National Minimum Wage Act ss.17–24). Where such a complaint is made, it is presumed the worker qualified for the NMW and that she was paid less than that wage (National Minimum Wage Act ss.28).

If a worker is dismissed or subjected to a detriment for seeking to enforce his right to the NMW, a complaint will also lie to the Employment Tribunal (National Minimum Wage Act s.24; Employment Rights Act 1996 s.104A) and an employer who wilfully refuses to pay the NMW, fails to keep adequate records, keeps false records, or obstructs an Enforcement Officer, commits a criminal offence (National Minimum Wage Act s.31).

HOURS OF WORK AND TIME OFF

Until the Working Time Regulations 1998 (SI 1998/1833), which give effect to the Working Time Directive (93/104) and the Young Workers Directive (94/33) (subject to the employer's duty to take reasonable care for the employee's health and safety), generally employers and employees were free to make such contractual arrangements as they wished regarding hours of work. **2–15**

The Regulations, which are accompanied by guidance issued by the Department of Trade and Industry, apply to employees, workers and agency workers but initially certain sectors of activity were excluded, namely air, road, rail and sea transport, activities of doctors in training, activities of the armed forces and the civil protection services which inevitably conflict with the regulations. The significance of these exclusions was seen in the decision of the ECJ in *Bowden v Tuffnells Parcels Express Ltd* [2001] I.R.L.R. 838 to the effect that office-based clerical workers employed by a road transport business were excluded from Directive 93/104. However, Directive 2000/34, which supersedes Directive 93/104 became effective in 2003 and removed or modified many of the exclusions and the provisions of Directive 2000/34 are now reflected in the Working Time (Amendment) Regulations 2003 (SI 2003/1684) and the Working Time (Amendment) (No. 2) Regulations 2006 which together make substantial changes to the 1998 Regulations.

The position under the amended Regulations may be summarised as follows.

The Regulations are entirely excluded from:

(a) workers covered by the European Agreement on the working time of seafarers;
(b) workers on board sea going fishing vessels; and
(c) workers on ships on inland waterways or lakes (reg.18).

Certain regulations dealing with the length of the working week, night work and rest periods do not apply to workers in services like:

(a) the armed services and police;
(b) mobile staff (air crew) in civil aviation covered by Directive 2000/790; and
(c) workers covered by Directive 2002/15 on working time of persons performing mobile road transport activities (reg.18).

Special provision is now also made for mobile workers in these industries who are not covered by their respective Directives (reg.24A).

The working time of doctors in training and workers employed in offshore oil work (work on offshore installations in connection with exploration and extraction of mineral resources)—including such work performed in the territorial waters of the UK adjacent to Great Britain or any area designated under s.1(7)of the Continental Shelf Act 1964—is now regulated (regs 2, 25A, 25B).

Protection to other workers may be reduced if certain conditions are met. Regulation 21 contains many special circumstances in which the regulations do not apply for example (a) where place of work and residence or places of work are distant from each other including offshore work; (b) where the work involves security and surveillance which requires permanent presence; (c) where there is a need for continuity of service and production; (d) where there is foreseeable surge of activity; and (e) where there are exceptional events and accidents. However, even in such special circumstances it is a requirement to give compensatory time off or other "appropriate protection". Also in several other respects the scope of the Regulations may be extended or modified by collective or workforce agreements (reg.23).

Working Time

2–16 "Working time" means any period during which the worker is working, at the employer's disposal and carrying out his activity or duty, any period during which the worker is receiving relevant training and "any additional period which is to be treated as working time . . . under a relevant agreement" so that if an employer and employee are in doubt about whether an additional period is to be treated as working time they are able to enter an agreement by which that uncertainty is removed. Such an agreement might provide that all contractual working hours or all times during which the worker is on the premises of the employer are to be regarded as working time. However, in *Sindicato de Medicos de Assistencia Publica (SIMAP)* [2000] I.R.L.R. 845, the European Court of Justice in a case dealing with primary care health workers held that time spent on call by doctors in primary health care teams must be regarded as working time where their presence at the health centre is required.

Sindicato de Medicos de Asistencia Publica v Conselleria de Sanidad y Consumo de la Generalidad Valenciana

[2000] I.R.L.R. 845, ECJ

The Spanish Court had referred to the European Court of Justice certain questions regarding the meaning of the Working Time Directive (93/104) in a case dealing with primary care health workers and particularly whether their time "on call" was working time for the purpose of the Directive.

The European Court of Justice stated that time spent on call by doctors in primary health care teams must be regarded as working time where their presence at the health centre is required. In the scheme of the Directive, working time is placed in opposition to rest periods, the two being mutually exclusive. Accordingly in the present case the fact that doctors are obliged to be present and available at the workplace with a view to providing their professional services means they are carrying out their duties. However, where doctors are on call by being contactable without having to be at the health centre, only time linked to the actual provision of primary care services must be regarded as working time within the Directive. In that situation even if they are at the disposal of their employer, in that it must be possible to contact them, they may manage their time with fewer constraints and pursue their own interests.

The Directive provides that a worker may not be required to work more than 48 hours per week on average, unless the worker has consented to work more than this. The European Court held that where trade union representatives gave consent to workers exceeding 48 hours in a collective or other agreement, that was not equivalent to consent given by a worker individually, which is what is required by the Directive (Art.18).

In *Landeshauptstadt Kiel v Jaeger* [2003] I.R.L.R. 804 the ECJ confirmed that working time included all the time a doctor was required to be present at a hospital even though he was permitted to rest or sleep when his services were not required. Particularly because the amended Directive applies to doctors in training who perform most of the on call duties the Commission launched a consultative document and has now produced a proposal for an amending Directive which seeks to distinguish between active and inactive on call time with only the former always counting as working time. The strictness of the approach of the ECJ is seen in *Dellas v Premier Ministre* [2006] I.R.L.R. 225 in which the ECJ also emphasises that in the Directive the concept of working time is placed in opposition to rest periods, the two being mutually exclusive.

Dellas v Premier Ministre

[2006] I.R.L.R. 225

Mr Dellas was employed as teacher in a residential school and his job required him to spend nights on call at the school. His working time was calculated in accordance with French law which provided that where a person worked at an establishment run by a charity the first nine hours of on call time were weighted as three hours and each following hour treated as one half hour.

The ECJ held that the Working Time Directive prevents Member States from operating such a weighting system where the hours were spent at the employer's premises. The Directive does not allow for any intermediate category and the intensity of the work done by an employee and his output are not among the characteristic elements of the concept of working time. On call duty performed by the employee where he is required to be physically present on the employer's premises must be regarded in its entirety as working time regardless of the work actually done and the fact that on call duty includes some periods of inactivity is completely irrelevant and that this was so even where the national legislation applied a limit of 44 hours to the working week in place of the Directive's 48 hours.

MacCartney v Oversley House Management

[2006] I.R.L.R. 514, EAT.

Ms MacCartney was employed as a care manager and was provided with a flat at the top of one of the estate's main buildings. She worked for four days per week providing 24 hour cover. She could carry out the bulk of her duties including visiting residents between 8am and 6.30pm but she also had to respond to emergencies and to do so was required to be available by mobile phone and remain within three minutes radius of the estate on the days she worked so that in effect she was on call from 6.30pm to 8am.

The EAT held that the whole of the time she was on call constituted working time as she was required to remain at or within a very short distance of her home which was located within her place of work and contained her office. She had to be available at a place determined by her employer with a view to performing her services if need be. Unless the likelihood of being called out is so insignificant to be trifling the extent to which the worker is likely to be called out is not decisive of whether or not she is working. Nor was it important to ascertain whether the accommodation provided by the employer might constitute the worker's home as the ECJ in Jaeger made it clear that periods of rest are characterised by the fact that the worker is not subject to any obligation to the employer which may prevent her from pursuing freely and without interruption her own interests in order to neutralise the effects of her work on her health and safety. Those conditions are not met where the worker is required to be on call in tied accommodation which is part of the workplace.

Thus MacCartney was not being allowed her entitlements of: (a) 11 hours consecutive rest in each 24 hour period; or (b) an uninterrupted rest break in a working day which exceeded six hours. While her employer could have relied on reg.21which allows these entitlements to be exchanged for compensatory rest at a later time it does not apply where the issue is the length of the working week.

Maximum working week

A worker's average working time—including overtime—shall not exceed 48 hours for each seven day period (reg.4). The normal reference period for calculating the average is 17 weeks but this may extended to 52 weeks by collective or workforce agreement but an employer and a worker are free to agree in writing that (for a particular period or indefinitely) the 48 hour limit shall not apply to that worker. The only exceptions permitted from the 48 hour limit are in respect of (1) domestic servants and (2) workers whose working time "is not measured or predetermined or can be determined by the worker himself" on account of the specific characteristics of the activity in which the worker is engaged (for example, executives and workers with autonomous decision-making powers, family workers and religious celebrants) (regs 19, 20). Although in Directive 93/104 the opportunity for Member States to derogate from the 48 hour week was envisaged as being temporary the Commission has proposed that it be continued subject to the **2–17** following modifications: (a) an employer and an individual worker will be able to opt out of the 48 hour week only where there is no collective bargaining arrangements in force; (b) an agreement to work in excess of 48 hours per week shall be valid only for a renewable period not exceeding one year; (c) agreement given at the time the contract of employment is entered into or during a probationary period shall be null and void; (d) no worker may work more than 65 hours in any week unless permitted by collective agreement; (e) employers keep up-to-date records of all workers who work more than 48 hours per week and the number of hours they actually work (Art.22). However to date the proposal has not yet been adopted.

Night work

2–18 Except where the work involves special hazards or heavy strain (in which case the night worker must not work for more than eight hours in any 24 hour period) a night worker's normal hours shall not exceed an average (measured over 17 weeks or longer by collective or workforce agreement) of eight hours in a 24 hour period (reg.6). A worker may not be assigned to night work before the opportunity of a free health assessment and where a night worker suffers from health problems related to night work (confirmed by medical practitioner) he is to be transferred to other suitable (non-night) work whenever possible (reg.7). Records of night work for two years must be kept (reg.9). The limits on night work are excluded in many cases when certain conditions apply and may be excluded or modified by collective or workforce agreement (regs 21, 23).

Rest periods

2–19 There are exceptions for shift workers (reg.22) but generally a worker is entitled to a daily rest break of 11 consecutive hours and a weekly rest period of not less than 24 hours. However, an employer is entitled to substitute two uninterrupted period of 24 hours each in a 14-day period or one uninterrupted period of 48 hours in a 14-day period (regs 9, 11, 12). The weekly rest period is in addition to the daily rest period unless objective technical or work organisation conditions justify it. Where a worker's working day is more than six hours he is entitled to a rest break (away from his work station) of not less than 20 minutes, uninterrupted unless a collective or workforce agreement provides otherwise (reg.12).

Annual leave

2–20 A worker is entitled to four weeks' paid annual leave (reg.13). Currently this is inclusive of public holidays but with effect from April 2009 the entitlement is to be increased to 28 days. Entitlement to paid annual leave cannot be modified or excluded by collective or workforce agreement and except where the employment is terminated, there can be no payments in lieu and the ECJ in *Federatie Nederlandse Vakbeging v Staat der Nederlanden* [2006] I.R.L.R. 561 has held that it is not consistent with the Directive to allow a worker to carry unused leave over to the next year and receive a payment in lieu although it does allow unused leave can be carried over to next year, although this is not allowed by the Working Time Regulations. However where termination occurs during the leave year, special provision is made to ensure that the worker receives a payment in respect of leave not yet taken (reg.14). Where the worker has at the point of termination taken more leave than that to which he is *pro rata* entitled, the employer may recover such excess if there is a binding agreement to that effect between the employer and the worker, or a workforce agreement or a collective agreement. Although there are provisions regarding when leave may be taken they may be varied by agreement between the worker and the employer or by collective or workforce agreement (reg.15). Many employers attempted to avoid the administrative work associated with paying for holidays at the time the fell due particularly to workers who were temporary or short term by augmenting the worker's basic hourly or weekly rate to be inclusive of holiday pay. This was known as "rolling up" entitlement to holiday pay and while it was convenient for the employer it could also mean that a worker who had been in effect paid his holiday pay in advance had no funds to support him during the holiday period and would be tempted to

continue working thereby defeating the objective of the Directive which was to ensure the worker enjoyed a period of annual rest. There were conflicting domestic decisions and the matter was referred to the ECJ which declared such rolled-up schemes to be unlawful although where payments under pre-existing and transparent rolled-up schemes had already been made they could be offset against entitlement under the Directive but any such schemes may not be continued.

Robinson-Steele v RD Retail Services Ltd

[2006] I.R.L.R. 386.

There was a term in the worker's contract that "the worker agrees that payment in respect of entitlement to paid annual leave shall be made together with and in addition to the worker's hourly rate at 8.3% of his hourly rate". Robinson-Steele had worked for almost two years in which time he had had only one week's leave at Christmas and for which he had not received separate payment. Similar issues had arisen in other cases and the courts in England and Scotland had reached different conclusions on whether rolling up holiday pay was consistent with the Directive. The Court of Appeal referred the matter to the ECJ where the workers argued that payment for annual leave must take place at the time the holiday is actually taken and any arrangement to the contrary would be a payment in lieu which was contrary to Art.7(2) of the Directive or acted as an obstruction to taking leave and discouraged in particular low paid workers from taking leave at all.

The ECJ held (1) remuneration must be maintained for the duration of annual leave and Art.7(1) precludes part of the remuneration payable to the worker for work done from being attributed to payment for annual leave without the worker receiving a payment additional to that for work done; (2) while the Directive does not expressly lay down the point at which the payment for annual leave must be made, it treats entitlement to annual leave and to a payment on that account as being aspects of a single right and the purpose of the requirement of payment for leave is to put the worker during such leave in a position which is, as regards remuneration, comparable to periods of work so that the point at which the payment for annual leave is made must be fixed so that the worker is put in a position comparable to periods of work; (3) Art.7 does not preclude setting off money paid under a rolled up holiday pay arrangement against entitlement for a specific period of leave provided the arrangements are transparent and comprehensible.

Enforcement and remedies

2–21 There are three ways in which the Regulations can be enforced:

(1) Criminal offences under Health and Safety at Work Act 1974:

- 48 hour working week;
- length of night work and entitlement to health assessment and transfer to non-night work;
- provision of rest breaks for monotonous or fixed-rate work;
- keeping records in respect of the working week, night work and health assessments.

(2) Breach of statutory duty by action for damages in ordinary court:

- a worker suffers injury by employer's failure to comply with these Regulations by action in ordinary courts. However in *Sayers v Cambridgeshire County Council* [2006] EWCA Civ 2029 the High Court has held that reg.4(1) (which restricts the working week to 48 hours) does not confer such a right of action because Parliament had not intended to create such a right of action when it provided in reg.29 for enforcement of reg.4(1) by criminal proceedings. Where an employee sues an employer at common law for breach of the employer's duty to take reasonable care for the employee's safety there is no reason why breach of reg.4(1) cannot be relied on to prove that the injury caused by long hours was foreseeable: *Hone v Six Continents Retail Ltd* [2006] I.R.L.R. 49, CA.

(3) Complaint by workers to the employment tribunal:

- daily rest;
- weekly rest;
- rest breaks during working day;
- annual leave (including failure to pay wages during);
- compensatory rest.

Where a complaint is well founded the tribunal shall make a declaration to that effect and may award compensation that is just and equitable (reg.30). However a complaint for failure to pay holiday pay may be made only under the Working Time Regulations and not as an unlawful deduction from wages (*Commissioners of Inland Revenue v Ainsworth* [2005] EWCA Civ 441). Complaint may also be made to the employment tribunal that a worker was dismissed or subjected to a detriment for:

- not complying with a requirement imposed in contravention of the employer's duties under the Regulations;
- refusing to forego a right under the Regulations;
- failing or refusing to sign a workforce agreement;
- being a representative of the workforce or a candidate in an election for representatives;
- bringing proceedings against the employer or alleging that an employer infringed a right conferred on the worker (regs 31, 32).

Time Off Rights

Statute now provides that employees are entitled to time off for **2–22** certain purposes. On some occasions time off is with pay, while on other occasions it is unpaid time off. This section deals only with time off rights and the circumstances in which maternity, paternity and adoption leave are required are dealt with in Ch.7, below.

Trade union duties and activities

An official of an independent trade union recognised by an **2–23** employer is entitled to paid time off to carry out his duties connected with negotiations with his employer and concerned with the receipt of information and consultation (and for training associated therewith), relating to redundancies and required by the Transfer of Undertaking Regulations 1981 and the Trade Union and Labour Relations (Consolidation) Act 1992. An employee is also entitled to unpaid time off to take part in the activities of a recognised trade union. In each case, the amount of time off to which an employee is entitled is such time off as is reasonable (in respect of which see the guidance given by the Code of Practice issued by ACAS) and complaints that an employer has not permitted time off, lie to an Employment Tribunal (Trade Union and Labour Relations (Consolidation) Act 1992 ss.168, 170). The Court of Appeal has held that it was not reasonable for all the shop stewards to be given time off to attend a union meeting on the busiest day of the week (*Allen v Thomas Scott & Sons Bakers Ltd* [1983] I.R.L.R. 329).

Public duties

2–24 Employees who hold certain public offices, e.g. Justice of the Peace, or are members of certain public bodies, e.g. local authorities, statutory tribunals, national health service trusts, school boards, etc. are also entitled to reasonable time off without pay to perform their public duties (Employment Rights Act 1996 s.50; see for example *Borders Regional Council v Maule* [1993] I.R.L.R. 199, EAT). Jury service is treated by the ordinary law which provides that it is an offence to fail to attend for jury service (Criminal Procedure (Scotland) Act 1995 s.85 and jurors are entitled to expenses for loss of wages and benefits (Juries Act 1949 s.24 (as amended)). Jurors are now protected against dismissal and detrimental treatment but it is not detrimental treatment for an employer not to pay an employee during a period of jury service (Employment Rights Act 1996 s.43M).

Finding work

2–25 An employee who is under notice of redundancy is entitled to reasonable time off with pay (a maximum of half a week's pay) to look for other work or to arrange training for new employment; he must have two years' continuous employment but need not be entitled to a redundancy payment (Employment Rights Act 1996 s.52).

Ante natal leave

2–26 A woman who is pregnant is entitled to paid time off for ante natal care where the appointment has been made on the advice of a registered medical practitioner, midwife or health visitor and an employee who is dismissed for asserting her right to time off is treated as unfairly dismissed (Employment Rights Act 1996 ss.56, 104).

Domestic incidents

In part implement of the Parental Leave Directive the Employment Rights Act 1996 s.57A entitles employees to a reasonable amount of time off during working hours to deal with a domestic incident, for example: **2–27**

- when a dependant falls ill, is injured or dies or to arrange care for such a dependant;
- where the care arrangement for such dependant unexpectedly end; for example where arrangement for baby-sitting fell through at the last minute (*Truelove v Safeway Stores plc* EAT 0295/04; *Qua v John Ford Morrison* [2003] I.C.R. 482, EAT);
- where the employee's child is involved in an unexpected incident at school.

Employee representatives

An employee who is a representative for purposes of redundancy or business transfer consultation is entitled to reasonable paid time off to perform his duties or to act as a candidate in election of representatives (Employment Rights Act s.61). **2–28**

Safety representatives

Safety representatives appointed by a recognised trade union and elected representatives of employee health and safety are entitled to such time off with pay as is reasonable in accordance with the HSC Code of Practice to perform their functions and to receive training (Safety Representatives and Safety Committee Regulations 1977 (SI 1977/500); Health and Safety (Consultation with Employees) Regulations 1996 (SI 1996/1513)). **2–29**

Study and training

Employees who are between 16 and 18 years of age and not in full time education are entitled to reasonable time off with pay to undertake study or training which leads to a relevant qualification (Employment Rights Act 1996 s.63A(1)). **2–30**

OTHER CONTRACTUAL TERMS AND DUTIES

As indicated earlier the contract of employment contains many implied terms. This is largely due to the fact that formerly the contract would be created orally with few of the terms being agreed expressly between the employer and the employee or in the older law, the master and the servant. The contract of employment may be regarded as a nominate contract, that is to say a contract which conforms with certain basic fundamental legal principles. The result **2–31** of this is that where A agrees to enter a contract of employment with B, provided the contract is clear regarding the nature of the work or the position to be held, the remainder of the contract is in-filled by the law implying or introducing certain terms into the contract. By way of example, let us assume that Mr Smith writes to Mrs Jones in the following terms:

> *"Dear Mrs Jones*
>
> *DRIVER*
>
> *I hereby offer to employ you as the driver of my limousine on the following terms and conditions:*
>
> *(a) You will work 40 hours per week between the hours of 8a.m. and midnight, Monday to Friday.*
> *(b) You may be required to work overtime in excess of 40 hours up to a maximum of eight-hours per week.*
> *(c) You will be paid at the rate of £7.50 per hour for your basic hours and £12.00 per hour for any overtime worked.*
>
> *Please let me know if you accept this offer of employment.*
>
> *Yours faithfully*
>
> *Mr Smith"*

Mrs Jones replied in the following terms:

> *"Dear Mr Smith*
>
> *DRIVER*
>
> *I hereby accept your offer of employment on the terms stated in your letter of yesterday's date.*
>
> *Yours faithfully*
>
> *Mrs Jones"*

The exchange of the above letters results in Mr Smith employing Mrs Jones under a contract of employment. In addition to the terms of contract expressed in the letters there will be, implied by law, a series of obligations which when considered as a whole, result in there being a comprehensive contract.

2–32 It is tempting to think of the implied duties of the contract of employment as specific duties relating, for example, to the obedience of the employee and his obligations to carry out his employer's instructions, and likewise the employer's duty to take reasonable care for the health and safety of the employee. Undoubtedly there are categories into which the employee's and employer's duties may conveniently be located. However, the underlying obligation in the relationship today may be stated simply as an obligation on both parties not without proper and reasonable cause to act in such a way that is likely to, or calculated to, destroy or seriously damage the trust and confidence on which the employment relationship is ultimately based. The generality of the duty of trust and confidence is illustrated by the following two cases.

Malik v Bank of Credit and Commerce International SA

[1997] I.R.L.R. 462, HL

The House of Lords held that an employer could be in breach of the implied duty of trust and confidence by operating his business in a dishonest and corrupt way and an employee who was unable to secure employment in the future as a result of having worked for such an employer is entitled to damages for that loss.

Lord Nicholls of Birkenhead stated:

> "Employers may be under no ... implied contractual term of general application, to take steps to improve their employees' future job prospects. But failure to improve is one thing, positively to damage is another. Employment and job prospects, are matters of vital concern to most people. Jobs of all descriptions are less secure than formerly, people change jobs more frequently, and the job market is not always buoyant. Everyone knows this. An employment contract creates a close personal relationship, where there is often a disparity of power between the parties. Frequently the employee is vulnerable. Although the underlying purpose of the trust and confidence term is to protect the employment relationship, there can be nothing unfairly onerous or unreasonable in requiring an employer who breaches the trust and confidence term to be liable if he thereby causes continuing financial loss of a nature that was reasonably foreseeable."

Employers must take care not to damage their employees' future employment prospects, by harsh and oppressive behaviour or by any other form of conduct which is unacceptable today as falling below the standards set by the implied trust and confidence term.

TSB Bank plc v Harris

[2000] I.R.L.R. 157

Harris was unaware that customer complaints about her conduct were not passed to her for comment and in many cases was unaware that customer complaints had been made against her. When Miss Harris sought another employment, TSB were approached for a reference. The reference stated that 17 complaints had been made against her, of which four were upheld and eight were outstanding, and as a result of that reference the new employers refused to engage Miss Harris. When Miss Harris discovered that there had been so many complaints against her, in respect of which she was given no opportunity to comment or explain she resigned and claimed a constructive dismissal. The employment tribunal held that the employers were in breach of the implied term of trust and confidence in providing a reference which made mention of previously unregistered complaints and was misleading and potentially destructive of the employee's career in financial services. That decision was upheld by the Employment Appeal Tribunal on the grounds that where an employer undertakes to give a reference in respect of an employee, there is an implied contractual obligation to ensure that it is a fair and reasonable reference, and a failure to do so may be a breach of the implied term of trust and confidence. While referring to previously lodged complaints was nothing more than true and accurate, that was not necessarily a reasonable and fair reference. As a result of the employers were in breach of contract.

It is important to note that there is breach of the duty of trust and confidence only where there is no proper or reasonable cause for the employer's or employee's conduct and in the context of unfair dismissal claims the EAT has held that whether the employer had reasonable or proper cause for his conduct is to be measured by considering whether the employer's conduct was within the range of reasonable responses. Thus in *Abbey National plc v Fairbrother* (EAT No.0084/06) where Fairbrother complained that Abbey National plc had breached the duty of trust and confidence in its handling of a grievance he had raised, as the employer's handling of the grievance was within the range of reasonable responses there was no breach by the employer and the employee's claim of constructive dismissal failed. Similarly in *Barratt v Accrington and Rossendale College* (EAT No.0099/06) there was no breach of the duty of trust and confidence by the employer when it refused to dismiss Barratt's fellow employee after he had assaulted Barratt because having regard to the fellow employee's record it was not possible to say that it had acted outwith the range of reasonable responses. In *Fairbrother* the EAT indicated that deciding whether there has been a breach of the duty of trust and confidence should be done by asking the following questions: (1) What was the conduct complained of? (2) Did the employer have proper and reasonable cause for the conduct? (3) If Yes, the employee cannot complain of constructive dismissal. (4) If No, the employment tribunal should ask whether the conduct was likely to, or calculated to, destroy the trust and confidence between the employer and the employee. On the other hand in *Hilton v Shiner Ltd* [2001] I. R. L. R. 727 another EAT suggests that the first question to ask is whether, ignoring any cause, one party has committed acts which *prima facie* are likely to damage the trust and confidence of the relationship and only then to consider whether there is reasonable cause for the acts.

Having underlined the generality of the obligations on both the employer and employee and the flexibility of the duty of trust and confidence it is convenient to categorise the implied duties of the employee under the following headings:

Obedience

An employee must carry out the instructions given to him by his employers for the purpose of performing his contract so that in the example given earlier, if Mr Smith was to instruct Mrs Jones to drive himself and friends to the grouse moor, Mrs Jones would not be entitled to refuse on the grounds that she was against field sports. On the other hand, if Mrs Jones was instructed to drive the car back to Edinburgh with game that had been taken illegally, she may well be able to refuse to carry out that instruction because it may mean her performing an illegal act and no employee in a contract of employment is required to perform an act that is illegal or immoral. Examples can be seen in the case of *Morrish v Henlys (Folkestone)* [1973] 2 All E.R. 137, in which Mr Morrish who was employed as a petrol pump attendant refused to falsify the sales records at a time when the business was to be put up for sale. He was entitled to refuse to carry out the instruction because it would have resulted in him performing an illegal (fraud) and immoral act. A similar example is seen in the case of *Pagano v H G S Ltd* [1976] I.R.L.R. 9 in which Mr Pagano was held entitled to refuse to carry out an instruction to drive a vehicle which was unsafe and sufficiently unroadworthy that had he driven the vehicle on the roads he would have been guilty of an offence under the Road Traffic Acts. **2–33**

An employee is not required to perform an act which is outside the scope of his contract. This situation frequently occurs where the duties of the employee are not expressed in any detail. Generally, an employee is entitled to resist instructions which will require him to perform work not intended by the contract. A simple example is seen in the case of *Moffat v Boothby* (1884) 11 R 501 in which the court held that a shepherd was entitled to refuse to obey instructions to tend cows. However, this rule is subject to qualification. First of all an employee is expected to be flexible in emergency situations. This is particularly the case where preservation of life or the avoidance of serious injury is concerned. Thus in the case of *Smith v St Andrew Ambulance* (July 12, 1973, unreported NIRC) in which an ambulance driver, who was due to finish his spell of duty, was instructed to pick up a child who was seriously ill. The driver refused on the grounds that the return journey would take him beyond his contractual finishing time, but the tribunal held that because of the emergency the employee ought to have shown flexibility by extending his working time.

Another situation in which the employee is required to be flexible is seen in the case of *Sim v Rotherham Borough Council* [1986] I.C.R. 897. This case involved school teachers taking industrial action which resulted in them refusing to teach classes of colleagues who were absent on the grounds of illness. Undoubtedly the contract of employment of *Sim* did not expressly require him to cover for absent colleagues but the Court came to the conclusion that Sim, as a professional school teacher, owed an obligation of flexibility and co-operation in circumstances where fellow teachers were absent through illness.

2–34 The scope of the contract may also be limited by terms of place and time. An employee is generally entitled to adhere to the contractual hours. Thus in *Kennell v Sanders & Sanders Ltd* [1972] I.T.R. 399, Kendal was entitled to refuse to type a letter which would have meant her staying on beyond her normal finishing time. Even if the employee's contract of employment may require him or her to attend and perform work at certain times, that is subject to the employer's implied obligation to take reasonable care for the health and safety of the employee. This issue arose in *Johnstone v Bloomsbury Health Authority* [1991] I.R.L.R. 118 in which Dr Johnstone, employed as a junior doctor by the health authority, was required by his contract to work a standard working week of 40 hours and additional availability on call up to an average of 48 hours a week. The result was that in some weeks Dr Johnstone worked in excess of 88 hours which he contended affected his health. Although the judges in the Court of Appeal disagreed, the following statement of Sir Nicolas Browne-Wilkinson is probably an accurate reflection of law:

> "There was in the contract of employment no incompatibility between Dr Johnstone's duty on the one hand and the authority's right, subject to the implied duty as to health on the other hand. The implied duty did not contradict the express term of the contract. There must be some restriction on the authority's rights. In any sphere of employment other than that of a junior hospital doctor an obligation to work up to 88

> hours per week would be rightly regarded as oppressive and intolerable. The authority's right to call for overtime under (the contract) was not an absolute right but must be limited in some way. Therefore not withstanding (the express term in the contract) the authority could not lawfully require the plaintiff to work so much overtime in any week as it was reasonably foreseeable it would damage his health."

The place an employee is required to work must be stated in the written statement of particulars and where the contract is clear an employer will have no right to insist on the employee working in another place. In some cases, however, the contract does not say expressly where the place of employment is and this has to be determined by looking at all the facts and circumstances from which it may be possible to imply a term regarding the place of work. Adopting such an approach in the case of *O'Brien v Associated Fire Alarms Ltd* [1968] 1 W.L.R. 1916 the Court of Appeal came to the conclusion that O'Brien's place of work was "the Liverpool area" and he could not therefore be required to work in Barrow-in-Furness. In some cases the contract will include an express term allowing the employer to move the employee from one place of work to another. Also, it may be the case that such a term can be implied into a particular contract by considering all the facts and circumstances. An example can be seen in the case of *Prestwick Circuits v McAndrew* [1990] I.R.L.R. 191. However, an implied right to transfer an employee from one place of work to another is itself subject to the implied qualification that the employee be given reasonable notice of any proposed transfer. In *McAndrew* the Court of Session stated that the implied right of an employer to transfer an employee is itself subject to giving reasonable notice and reasonable distance.

Where there is an express term in the contract allowing the **2–35**
employee to be transferred from one place to another, this too has to be applied in such a way as not to make it impossible for the employee to perform his contract. An example of this is seen in the following case.

United Bank Ltd v Akhtar

[1989] I.R.L.R. 507

There was a term in Mr Akhtar's contract of employment which allowed the bank to transfer him to any place of business which the bank had in the United Kingdom, either permanently or temporarily; the contract also provided that the bank may make a contribution to the employee's removal costs. The bank, in reliance on this term, required Mr Akhtar to move from one town in the Midlands to another, without indicating whether the move would be temporary or permanent and without indicating whether they would make a contribution to Mr Akhtar's removal costs. Initially Mr Akhtar was given only a weekend's notice, which the bank later extended to almost a week. The court came to the conclusion that although the employer appeared to have an unfettered discretion to transfer Mr Akhtar from one place to another it could not use that contractual term in such a way as to make it virtually impossible for Mr Akhtar to perform his contract. It is clear therefore that even an express mobility clause in a contract of employment has to be operated in such a way that it is not virtually impossible for the employee to comply with it.

The scope of the contract is also limited by the implied understanding that employees will not be required to undertake unforeseen and unreasonable risks in carrying out the contract. An early example of this is seen in the case of *Burton v Pinkerton* (1867) L.R. 2 Ex. 340 in which the captain of a sailing vessel, who had taken charge of the ship carrying normal peace-time cargo from Spain to the South Americas, was entitled to refuse to carry on with the voyage when war broke out between the two countries and the cargo became guns and ammunition. Similarly, in the case of *Ottoman Bank v Chakarian* [1930] A.C. 277, the Privy Council held that Mr Chakarian, who was an employee of the Ottoman Bank and worked in Greece, could not be required to take up a position with the bank in Turkey where, as a result of discrimination against Armenians, Mr Chakarian had been sentenced to death. More modern cases demonstrate that less substantial risks may justify an employee refusing to carry out the contract because of the risk that is involved. For example in the case of *Ferrie v Western District Council* [1973] I.R.L.R. 162 an employee was entitled to refuse to clean ponds in remote locations where the ponds were deep and steep-sided and presented a serious risk to non-swimmers, like Mr Ferrie, who might drown in the event of him slipping or falling into the pond while carrying out the cleaning operation. Similarly, in *Wasilewski v Associated Tunnels* [1973] I.R.L.R. 346, Mr Wasilewski, who suffered from a heart condition, refused to cross a picket line of fellow employees on his way to work; and in the case of *Knight v Barra Shipping* (Case No. 187/92, unreported) it was accepted that requiring an employee to work on the stern deck of a trawler with insufficient grab and safety rails might be subjecting an employee to "intolerable conditions" which he would not be required to put up with.

Although the issue may now have been subsumed within the more all-embracing implied obligation of trust and confidence, it is important to learn in the meantime that any instructions or orders given to an employee must be given in a way which demonstrates there is a degree of mutual respect between an employer and employee. Modern law requires that instructions be given in a way that does not undermine trust and confidence. An example of this is seen in the case of *Wilson v Racher* [1974] I.R.L.R. 114, in which undoubtedly the employee had demonstrated a degree of disobedience to his employer but the court came to the conclusion that this was provoked by the employer's lack of respect for the employee, by humiliating him in front of others.

Employer's Duty of Safety

As indicated previously in addition to the many statutory duties in relation to health and safety there is in the contract of employment an implied duty on the employer to take reasonable care for the employee's safety. While the duty is general it is often considered in terms of a duty to provide a safe system of work, competent staff, safe plant and materials and a safe place of work and while an employer may often entrust the safety of his employees to others who occupy premises or are subcontractors the duty to provide a safe system of work is non delegable. Thus in *McDermid v Nash Dredging and Reclamation Co Ltd* [1987] I.C.R. 917, HL, McDermid was injured while working under the instruction of a tugboat captain who was employed by a subsidiary of McDermid's employer when the tugboat captain failed to operate the system he had devised for McDermid's safety. In holding McDermid's employer liable for his injuries Lord Brandon stated that "an employer owed his employee a duty to exercise reasonable care to ensure that the system of work provided for him was a safe one; the duty has been described as personal or non-delegable which meant that if it was not performed it was no defence for the employer to show that he had delegated its performance to a person – whether his employee or not – whom he had reasonably believed to be competent to perform it". The duty has been developed so that it includes not just physical injuries but also mental illnesses or psychiatric conditions which result from stressful working conditions. The most extensive examination of the law in the area of stress related injuries is *Sutherland v Hatton* [2002] I.R.L.R. 263, CA in which guidance was given as to when an employee's psychiatric illness or condition was reasonably foreseeable. Amongst the factors or guidance the Court of Appeal stated that an employer is usually entitled to assume that an employee can withstand the normal pressures of a job unless he knows of some vulnerability the employee has and that for the employer's duty to be triggered the indications of harm to the employee's health must be plain enough for any reasonable employer to recognise that he should do something about it; and an employer who offered a confidential counselling service was unlikely to be found in breach of his duty. However in *Barber v Somerset County Council* [2004] I.R.L.R. 475, **2–36**

HL, the House of Lords emphasised that while the factors identified in *Hatton* were helpful the overall test is the conduct of the reasonable and prudent employer taking positive thought for the safety of his workers in the light of what he knows or ought to know. Psychiatric illnesses may result from the employer's management style, bullying or harassment by fellow employees or work overload.

Hone v Six Continents Retail Ltd

[2002] EWCA Civ 922, CA

Hone was employed by Six Continents Retail Ltd as a Licensed House manager. He complained to management about his long hours of work and kept records which he claimed showed that he had worked between 89 and 90 per week. He suffered headaches and insomnia and was referred by his GP to a consultant. However within a couple of weeks he collapsed at work and sued his employers for failing to take reasonable care for his safety. It was found that shortly before Hone visited his GP two key employees had left which resulted in significant extra burdens being placed on him; about the same time his manager expressed concern that Hone had not opted out of the 48 hour working week and Hone had told his manager there was lack of support and complained about feeling tired. His manager recognised he needed help and seemed to accept that an assistant manager should be appointed. The Court held that after that time the employer ought to have reasonably foreseen an injury to Hone's health attributable to stress at work. The Court of Appeal dismissed the employer's appeal against the High Court's finding that injury was reasonably foreseeable because Hone had suffered no prior history of mental illness before his collapse, had had no absences from work before then and had not told anyone his health was being affected by his workload. The Court of Appeal observed that prior to collapsing Hone had complained about excessive workload and feeling tired and had asked for an assistant. That Hone was recording working hours of about 90 per week showed either that he was worker far more than that which could be expected of him or that he was making irrational entries as a cry for help. Although breach of the Working Time Regulations did not itself give rise to liability it did go towards the issue of foreseeablity in an action for breach of the employer's duty of care.

Employee's Duty of Careful Performance

An employee must perform his contract with reasonable care. **2–37**
Failure to do so is a breach of contract and will allow the employer to rescind the contract and claim damages. This may mean that the employee will be dismissed and that the employer will seek to recover damages for loss which flows from the employee's breach of contract. The principle is exemplified in the cases of *Clydesdale Bank v Beatson* (1882) 10 R 88; and *Janata Bank v Ahmed* [1981] I.R.L.R. 57. Beatson was employed as a teller by the Clydesdale Bank and through negligence on his part gave out ten £100 notes instead of ten £10 notes; the Court held that the bank was entitled to recover from Beatson the difference. Mr Ahmed who was employed by the Janata Bank granted a loan to a client without making even the most rudimentary enquiry into the client's creditworthiness. When the client failed to pay back the money the court held that Mr Ahmed had been in breach of his contractual obligations to perform his duties with reasonable care.

Lister v Romford Ice and Cold Storage Ltd

[1957] A.C. 555

Romford Ice Cold Storage Ltd employed Mr Lister senior and Mr Lister junior (father and son). The son drove a lorry and the father acted as the driver's assistant or mate. When Lister senior was giving manoeuvering instructions to his son, he was injured as a result of his son's careless driving. In accordance with the normal rules of vicarious liability Lister junior's employers, Romford Ice and Cold Storage Company Ltd, were liable to Mr Lister senior for his injuries. Romford Ice and Cold Storage Ltd called upon their insurance policy and their insurers duly made payment to Lister senior. However, relying on their subrogation clause in the contract of insurance, the insurers then insisted that Romford Ice and Cold Storage Company Ltd used their right to require Lister junior to perform his contract with reasonable care to recover from Lister junior the payments the insurance company had to make to Lister senior. Although it was argued that this seemed to turn the economics of the employment relationship upside down, the House of Lords reaffirmed the principle that an employee who breaches his contract by performing his obligations without reasonable care is required to indemnify the employer for any loss which follows.

The trade unions suggested that the legislation should be passed to prevent an employee being required to indemnify an employer, where the employer was already covered by adequate insurance.

However, legislation was never passed and the matter was resolved (and remains so today) by an undertaking being given on behalf of the members of the British Insurance Association that no insurance company will require an employer to exercise his right of indemnity against an employee in circumstances similar to those which arose in *Lister*. However, this undertaking does not in anyway affect the underlying legal principle.

Even where no insurance is involved but there is another means by which the employer can recover his losses, the courts are reluctant to require employees to indemnify employers who themselves can have a claim against others (employers).

Morris v Ford Motor Company

[1973] 2 Q.B. 792

Morris was employed by a contractor who had a contract to clean a factory belonging to Ford Motor Company. He was injured as a result of negligence of a Ford Motor Company employee and, on the principles of vicarious liability, Morris sued the Ford Motor Company and was awarded damages. However, as part of the cleaning contract entered into between Ford and the contractor (Morris' employer) the contractor had to indemnify the Ford Motor Company for any liability Ford might incur to the employees of the contractor even if this was caused by one of Fords own employees. Relying upon this right of indemnity the Ford Motor Company recovered the damages it had to pay to Morris from Morris' own employer. The contractors, using the same kind of arguments that were used successfully in *Lister*, attempted to rely upon Ford's own right of indemnity against the negligent employee but were denied the right to do so because it would not be "just and equitable".

It is important to remember, however, that where there are no complications relating to indemnity clauses or insurance, the underlying legal principle illustrated by *Beatson* and *Ahmed* continues to operate.

Employee's Duty of Fidelity

2–38 This implied duty binds an employee to protect his employer's business in the form of commercial assets and trade secrets and other confidential information and is relevant to the freedom of an employee to take on secondary or part-time employment. The general rules are stated simply and are found in cases like *Graham v Paton,* 1917 S.C. 203; and *Faccenda Chicken v Fowler* [1986] I.C.R. 297. At its simplest, it requires the employee to use all reasonable means to advance his employer's business and, secondly, to refrain from doing anything which would injure his employer's business. The first limb has to be seen in the context of the scope of the contractual duties so that a gardener who develops an expertise in the stock market is not required to advise his employer against risky investment.

In *Sanders v Parry* [1967] 1 W.L.R. 753 Parry worked for a firm of solicitors doing the work of a major client who expressed his dissatisfaction with the firm's charging rates and approached Parry with a view to him taking up employment with the client; it was held that Parry's first obligation was to have alerted his employer to the client's dissatisfaction instead of exploiting that dissatisfaction to his own benefit.

Competition

There is no general rule that an employee may not deal in commodities in which his employer deals or is prohibited from working for a competitor of his employer in his own time (*Graham v Paton*, above). It depends on the work the employee does, there being important distinctions between employees doing mundane and relatively unskilled work and those whose work gives access to strategic and confidential information. Only with regard to the latter would the court be inclined to prevent an employee working for a competitor: *Hivac v Park Royal Scientific Instruments Ltd* [1946] Ch.169. On the other hand, an employer is entitled to the exclusive performance of the contract at the times stated in the contract (*Cameron v Gibb* 1967 3 S.L.R. 282). **2–39**

However employees, who, even outside their contracted working hours, take on other work which affects the efficient performance of their duties under their main contract of employment, may be in breach of the main contract of employment (*Currie v Glasgow Central Stores* 1905 12 S.L.T. 651). Under the Working Time Regulations 1998 it is unlawful to employ a person for more than 48 hours, on average, per week unless the employee has agreed in writing to do so and as the weekly limit takes into account work for all employers, some employers now require an employee to inform them if they have secondary work so that the necessary written agreement is obtained.

Trade secrets and confidential information

The employee's implied duty of fidelity and loyal service requires protection of trade secrets or confidential information, and breach would permit the employer to terminate the contract of employment summarily and take other action to prevent further disclosures or misuse of confidential information. Even after the contract of employment has come to an end a diluted form of this duty continues. **2–40**

Faccenda Chicken v Fowler

[1986] I.C.R. 297

Fowler left his employment with Faccenda Chicken to set up in competition. There was no restrictive covenant in Fowler's contract of employment and Faccenda Chicken therefore could only rely on Fowler's implied duty not to disclose or use confidential information after the contract came to an end. The information which the employer claimed to be confidential in this case included the names and addresses of customers and their requirements, the most convenient routes for delivery vehicles and customers' preferences for delivery days and times and the pricing structure used for particular customers. The Court of Appeal held that while an ex-employee must not disclose secret processes of manufacture or other truly confidential information, the obligation of the ex-employee did not extend to information which was confidential only in that, had it been disclosed during the contract, it would have breached the implied duty of fidelity.

The factors which are relevant to determining whether or not information is truly confidential include:

- the nature of the job;
- the nature of the information;
- can it be equated with a trade secret;
- has the employer stressed the confidentiality of the information during the period of employment; and
- can the confidential information be isolated from other general information to which an employee is exposed in the course of employment?

Having regard to these matters in this case, the Court of Appeal came to the conclusion there had been no breach of Fowler's implied duty because he necessarily acquired the information in performing his job, it was widely known throughout the company even at the most junior levels, and the employer had never stressed the confidentiality of that information to Fowler, or any other employee.

However in *Helmet Integrated Systems Ltd v Tunnard* [2007] I.R.L.R. 126, CA the Court of Appeal has emphasised that while an employee must not compete with his employer during the employment the duty of fidelity does not prevent him from competing with his former employer once the contract has been terminated. This freedom carries with it a freedom to prepare for future activities that the employee intends to undertake following termination of his employment with the result that Tunnard was not in breach of his duty of fidelity in designing a safety helmet that would be marketed in competition with his employer's own product, because while employed Tunnard had undertaken no competitive activity nor made any offer to sell his design. However just because activities are described as "preparatory" does not mean that they are permitted; thus in *Shepherds Investments Ltd v Walters* [2007] I.R.L.R. 110 the preparatory activity included diverting business opportunities and disclosing confidential information and was in breach of the duty of fidelity. Of course an employee will develop his own skills and knowledge while in employment and they become part of the employee's own "stock in trade" which he is allowed to use in developing his career and earning potential *United Sterling v Mannion* [1974] I.R.L.R. 314; but see the interesting case of *PennWell Publishing (UK) Ltd v Ornstein* [2007] EWHC 1570, QB that data of a journalist held on employer's computer was the property of the employer.

Until recently while company directors had been held to owe fiduciary duties—which are additional to and potentially more restrictive than the employee's duty of fidelity–to the company such duties had never been applied to ordinary employees who were not also directors. The cases of *Tunnard* and *Walters* however show that similar duties may be owed by senior- and middle-ranking employees who are not directors although the extent of the duties is likely to vary depending on whether the director was a director in name only (*Foster Bryant Surveying Ltd v Bryant* [2007] I.R.L.R. 425, CA).

RESTRICTIVE COVENANTS

Because it is sometimes difficult to differentiate between an employee's own personal knowledge and experience and information which is regarded as confidential by the employer, most employers will seek to protect their legitimate interests like business connections, knowledge of customers and confidential information by inserting into contracts of employment clauses by which employees may be prevented from working for competitors both during and after their employment comes to an end; such clauses are referred to as restrictive covenants. The advantage over merely having to rely on the implied duty is seen when the case of *Fowler* above in which there was no covenant and the outcome in case of *Thomas v Farr plc* (below) in which there was a covenant. Covenants may be designed to prevent a current or an ex-employee from simply competing with a current or previous employer (non-competition) or more specifically to prevent ex-employees from approaching clients of the former employee (non solicitation), to prevent ex-employees from doing business with clients of the former employer (non-dealing) or to prevent ex-employees from inducing former colleagues to leave and work for the ex-employee or his new employer (non-solicitation of staff). In all cases the covenant must **2–41** be reasonable but particularly in cases of non-solicitation and non-dealing covenants a covenant designed to prevent an ex-employee from having dealings with an ex-employer's clients may be unreasonable because it also prevents the ex-employee from simply making use of the services of such clients. Accordingly in *Dunedin Independent plc v Welsh* [2006] CSOH 174a covenant which prohibited Welsh from having "business dealings" was unenforceable because it would have prevented Welsh making use of the services provided by any of the clients of his former employer even if that ultimately led to him being employed by them.

A covenant which prevents an employee from competing with his employer after leaving employment is regarded as a *pactum illicitum* and will be unenforceable unless it is necessary to protect a legitimate interest of the employer. The mere exclusion of competition by an ex-employee is not itself a legitimate interest and in order to be enforceable a restrictive covenant must protect confidential information or trade connections (*A & D Bedrooms v Michael*, 1984 S.L.T. 297). However, even then for the covenant to be enforceable it must be reasonable and in the public interest.

Reasonableness can be determined by having regard to the time of the restriction, the area to which it applies and the job function to which it relates. Thus in *Hinton & Higgs Ltd v Murphy* [1989] I.R.L.R. 519 a covenant, by which Murphy, an ex-employee of Hinton & Higgs, undertook not to work for any previous or present client for 18 months after his employment, was void as being unreasonably wide as there was no area limit and the ex-employee had worked only in Scotland so that he had no knowledge of clients outside that area. However, each case depends on its own circumstances and a worldwide restriction for two years which prevented the ex-employee providing any services for any competitors has been upheld.

Bluebell Apparel v Dickinson

1980 S.L.T. 157

The case appeared to be a dispute between Mr Dickinson, a trainee manager, and Bluebell Apparel, a company for which he had previously worked but it was in reality a dispute between the major businesses in the denim jeans industry, namely Levi Strauss and Wrangler. Dickinson's contract of employment provided that he would not, for two years after the termination of his employment, perform any services for any competitors anywhere in the world. Having regard to the nature of the jeans industry and the confidential information which Mr Dickinson had access to the Court upheld the validity of the covenant. The Court noted the covenant was necessary to protect trade secrets in a worldwide industry. It remarked that "prohibition against disclosing trade secrets is worthless unless accompanied by a restriction upon the employee possessed of secrets against entering the employment of rivals".

Spencer v Marchington

[1988] I.R.L.R. 393

The covenant in the employee's contract of employment prohibited him from working for any employment agency within a 25 mile radius of Banbury where the employer's business was located. However, the existing customers of the employers were all within a 20 mile radius of Banbury, most were within a 15 mile radius and there were no customers at all in certain large towns within the 25 mile radius, namely Rugby and Oxford. The restriction would have prevented the ex-employee offering his services to people who lived outside the radius, but who would look to towns inside the radius for the services of an employment agency. As a result, the restriction was held to be invalid as being unreasonably wide.

Thomas v Farr PLC

[2007 I.R.L.R. 419, CA

Thomas was employed as Managing Director of Farr plc-an insurance broker specialising in social housing insurance which was a small and specialist market. When he terminated his contract he accepted an offer of work from a company in competition with Farr plc. There was a term in Thomas' contract that for 12 months after termination of his employment he would not be engaged or concerned or interested in any business which is the same as or is in competition with Farr plc. The Court of Appeal upheld the High Court's decision that the covenant was enforceable. The High Court found that as a result of his position Thomas was familiar with and had access to the strategic plans and information relating to its exploitation of new markets and pricing and financial information relating to clients and insurers but held that the non solicitation and confidentiality clauses were not themselves sufficient because there were problems of practical application and enforcement. The Appeal Court held that in order to establish that the inclusion of a non-competition clause was reasonably necessary for protecting an employer's interest in confidential information the first matter the employer needs to establish is that at the time of the contract the nature of the proposed employment was such as would expose the employee to information of the kind capable of protection beyond the term of the contract. Provided the employer overcame that hurdle it was no argument against a restrictive covenant that it might be very difficult for either the employer or the employee to know where exactly the line might lie between information which remained confidential after the employment ended and information which did not. The fact that that distinction could be very hard to draw might support the reasonableness of a non-competition clause. The fact that there might be serious difficulties in identifying precisely what was or what was not confidential information mean that a non-competition clause could be the most satisfactory form of restraint provided it was reasonable in time and in space. In this case there was clear evidence that Thomas' appointment as managing director exposed him to information which Farr plc was entitled to require to be kept confidential after termination of his employment; the clearest example was financial and pricing information. That information was not in the public domain and was important in determining the price which Farr could afford to quote to its clients within its financial strategy. Knowledge of such information would be valuable to a competitor in how to undercut Farr in its dealings with clients and insurers. There would be difficulty in policing the non-solicitation clause and confidentiality clauses; it would not be easy to detect a breach of the covenant in that respect and the solicitation of clients would not be done by Thomas but by staff below him.

The covenant must not be against the public interest which generally requires access to services in a free market.

Bull v Pitney Bowes

[1967] 1 W.L.R. 273

It was a term of Bull's contract of employment that on retirement he would receive a company pension. However, this was conditional on him not entering the employment of any competitor after retirement. Bull took up employment with a company that was in competition with his previous employers, who then withheld his company pension because he was in breach of contract.

The covenant was unenforceable as being contrary to the public interest because in the knowledge that he would lose his company pension from Pitney Bowes, Mr Bull would then demand a higher than normal salary from his new employers and this would be contrary to the public interest in that the new employer's price of goods to the public would be inflated by paying Bull a higher than normal salary.

An obligation of confidence to an employer may also be overridden by public interest so that where an employee, who believed his employers were practising illegal price syndication, proposed to reveal this, the court held that the employers could not rely on the contract of employment to prevent this disclosure by their ex-employee on the grounds that there can be no duty of confidence in an iniquity (*Initial Services Ltd v Putterill* [1958] 1 Q.B. 396). Today such an employee would be protected by the Employment Rights Act 1996 (s.43J(2), as inserted by the Public Interest Disclosure Act 1998) which provides that any agreement which purports to preclude a worker from making a protected disclosure is void.

If a covenant consists of several discrete obligations or clauses **2–42** and one obligation is unenforceable that part may be severed or deleted leaving the remainder to stand. This severance or deletion of part of a covenant is referred to as "blue-pencilling" but it can only be done if it does not change the character of the obligation. However, while a court is free to sever or delete an offending part of a covenant, it will not re-word a covenant to make it enforceable. Similarly, an invalid covenant cannot be cured by asking the court to enforce it only to the extent that it is reasonable because if a covenant is invalid it cannot serve as the basis for a court order (*Agma Chemicals Co Ltd v Hart,* 1984 S.L.T. 246).

A covenant may attempt to avoid the possibility of a court declaring it unreasonable by inserting a declaration within (or "*in gremio*") the covenant itself that it is reasonable between the parties. However, such a declaration of reasonableness is of no effect because in practice, it seeks to oust the jurisdiction of the court. Further, since a covenant must also be in the public interest allowing the parties to decide what is reasonable it would deprive the court of its jurisdiction of protecting the public interest.

Some covenants provide that the covenant, if otherwise reasonable, will be enforceable whether or not the termination of the contract has been lawful so that the covenant may be relied on even where the employer breaks the contract by wrongfully dismissing the employee. Such phraseology does not necessarily render the covenant unlawful but it will not permit the employer to enforce the covenant where his breach of contract results in the contract being terminated (*Aramark plc v Sommerville*, 1995 G.W.D. 8-407).

SAMPLE QUESTIONS

1. Bill works as a night shift worker at a 24-hour petrol station. In January 2007 his employers decide to discontinue the night shift and transfer Bill to day-shift working with the result that Bill loses his shift allowance of £50.00 per week. Bill is informed at the end of January 2007 that he will be transferred to day shift working from March 1, 2007. Bill is reluctant to do day-shift but agrees to do so after his employer points out that in his contact of employment there is a clause that Bill will "work such shifts as management may determine provided at least four weeks' notice of any change of shift is given". Bill works on the day shift from March 1, 2007 until August 1, 2007 when he tells management that he cannot accept the wage cut any more because of a change in his personal circumstances. Management refuses to reinstate the night-shift allowance and Bill wonders if he has any redress against his employers for reducing his wages. How would you advise Bill?

2. By her contract, Mary is entitled to four-weeks' notice of termination of her employment. Her employer is dissatisfied with her work and gives her four-weeks' notice but tells her that she need not attend work during that period. He also gives her a cheque for four-weeks' wages but when Mary takes it to the bank she is told that the employer has instructed that the cheque not be paid. You meet Mary at a party about three months after she was given notice and she asks you if she can require the employer to pay her wages by presenting a complaint to the employment tribunal.

3.(a) John works as the Marketing Manager for a large international company. His working week often exceeds 48 hours and he has not agreed to work in excess of 48 hours a week. When he raises the issue of working hours with his boss he is told that the company's success depends on "managers putting in the number of hours the job requires".
(b) Barbara works as a typist in a transport company and is permitted to take only two-weeks paid holiday a year. Her boss says that she can take another two weeks if she wants more holidays but she will not be paid for them.
(c) Christine is a nurse at the local hospital who is required to be on-call for six hours after her normal duties have ended. This requires that she carries a "pager" with her and if called must return to the hospital within 15 minutes. When her on call hours are added to her normal hours the total hours are about 50 hours each week. Michael is an X-ray technician who is sometimes required to remain at the hospital during critical operations in case X-ray equipment needs to be repaired urgently. In fact he is seldom required to do any work and spends most of his on call hours playing snooker in the hospital staff room or asleep. He has not signed any agreement by which he agrees to work more than 48 hours per week but his trade union has agreed

on behalf of all technicians that if required they will work more than 48 hours a week.

SUGGESTED ANSWERS FOR CHAPTER TWO

1. The first possibility is to consider whether by reducing Bill's wages his employer has broken his contract. If there has been a breach, Bill will be entitled to sue for damages in the ordinary court as in Rigby v Ferodo Ltd *[1987] I.R.L.R. 516. Also, if Bill wishes, he will be able to terminate his contract and claim that he has been constructively dismissed. This would allow claims for a redundancy payment and unfair dismissal to be lodged (see Chs 4 and 5, below). However it is unlikely that Bill's contract has been broken as it clearly gives the employer the right to change the shift patterns on four-weeks' notice and Bill has received such notice in this case.*

The second issue is whether by reducing Bill's wages as a result of transferring him to day shift the employer has made an illegal deduction from wages. However, in Hussman Manufacturing Ltd v Weir *1998 I.R.L.R. 288 it was made clear that where an employer has a contractual right to transfer an employee to other work the fact that the other work is less well paid does not mean that there has been an unlawful deduction from wages. In Bill's case the employer has a contractual right to move Bill to day-shift and if that means he is no longer contractually entitled to the night-shift allowance there will be no unlawful deduction from wages. He is receiving the wages that are properly payable.*

If Bill had agreed in writing to the reduction in wages he would not be able to claim his employer had acted unlawfully as s.13 permits deductions where the employee has agreed in writing to the deduction being made.

Finally one has to consider whether a claim under s.13 of the Employment Rights Act would be in time. According to the Act a claim has to be made in three months from the date the wages (from which the deductions was made) were due or where the deduction was one of a series, the last date on which one of a series of payments were due. In this case, on the assumption that wages were still being paid at the day-shift rate on the date on which the claim was presented to the employment tribunal, Bill's claim would still be in time. However if Bill were to leave his employment, his claim to the employment tribunal would have to be presented within three months of the date on which his last payment of wages occurred.

2. Mary's case has to be distinguished from one in which the employer terminates a contract of employment without notice but gives wages in lieu of notice. Mary has been placed on what is termed "garden leave"; namely that she has been given notice that her employment will end on the expiry of the notice given by her employer but that she not required to perform any work during that period, i.e. she can spend the time tending her garden. In such a situation the payment she is to receive from her employers is in effect an advance payment of the wages that she would earn during the period of notice, if she had worked during that period. It therefore relates to a period during the time the contract exists and is regarded as falling within the statutory definition of wages in s.27 of the Employment Rights Act. Mary can therefore present a complaint to the employment tribunal to require the employer to make the payment due. The payment in Mary's case is different from the payment in lieu of notice that occurred in Delaney v Staples [1992] I.C.R. 483. *Where the employer terminates the contract without giving notice but gives the employee a payment in lieu of (or instead of) notice the contract comes to an end immediately and the payment made by the employer is not given in return for work done but as a payment of damages or compensation for the contract being broken by the employer not giving adequate notice. It therefore relates to a period after the contract has come to an end and is not within the statutory definition of wages in the Employment Rights Act.*

Where the employer does not give pay in lieu of notice an employee is not able to claim that there has been an unlawful deduction from wages under the Employment Rights Act. The employee would have to sue the employer for damages for breach of contract in the ordinary courts because for a time the employment tribunal did not have the jurisdiction to hear claims for breach of contract. That position was changed in 1994 when employment tribunals were given the jurisdiction to hear certain claims for breach of the contract of employment including cases in which the employer being due to pay wages in lieu of notice had failed to do so.

However, Mary's claim falls into the category of unlawful deductions from wages and she can present a claim to the employment tribunal but such a claim has to be presented within three months of the date of the payment. In this case the date of the payment was the date the employer gave Mary the cheque so provided that the complaint is presented to the employment tribunal within three months of that date it will be in time. Even if it is not however an employment tribunal has a discretion to admit a later claim if it is satisfied that a claim in three months was not reasonably practicable, for example if the employee had been ill or in hospital and unable to make the compliant in the time limit.

3.(a) Regulation 4 of the Working Time Regulations provides that unless the employee has agreed in writing his working time shall not exceed 48 hours per week on average, the average being calculated over 17 weeks. As John has not agreed to this however he cannot be required to work more that 48 hours unless some other regulation applies to him. Regulation 20(1) provides that reg.4 does not apply to a worker whose working time is not measured or is set by the worker himself on account of the work he does. Managing executives or others who have "autonomous decision making powers" are given as examples of such types of worker. It is arguable that in his position of

Marketing Manager for a large company with international business he would be expected to set his own working hours. Accordingly it is unlikely that his employer will have failed to comply with the Working Time Regulations.

(b) Regulation 13 entitles Barbara to four weeks paid holiday per year. Although some of the entitlements given by the Regulations may be excluded because of the type of work done by the worker (for example because the worker, like John, is a worker who sets his own working hours (reg.20), or because the work requires continuous service or production (reg.21)) entitlement to paid holidays cannot be excluded in this way. Although previously it was (reg.18) provided that the regulations did not apply at all to certain sectors of activity including air, road rail, sea and inland waterway transport and it would have necessary to decide whether Barbara worked in such an excluded secto butr the Working Time Regulations 1998 were amended with effect from August 1, 2003 by the substitution of a new reg.18. This removed the previous exclusion of entire sectors of industry whose effect was vividly illustrated by Bowden v Tuffnell's Parcels Express Ltd *[2001] I.R.L.R. 838, which confirmed that the entire industrial sector of road transport was excluded. The result of the amendment to reg.18 is that she is now entitled to be paid for the additional two weeks holiday her employer allows her to take.*

(c) For Christine and Michael the critical distinction is between working time and other time. Working time and rest time are mutually exclusive.

The definition of working time is found in reg.2 and is any time the worker is working, at his employer's disposal and carrying out his activities, time when the worker is receiving training and any additional time agreed to be working time by the employer and worker. Neither Christine nor Michael are being trained during their on call hours and there is no agreement regarding their on call hours. The question is whether their on call hours are periods when they are working, at the employer's disposal and carrying out their duties.

The decision of the ECJ in Sindicato de Medicos de Assistencia Publica (SIMAP) [2000] I.R.L.R. 845 is that time when the worker has to be present at his place of employment, even if only on call, must be regarded as working time. Therefore Michael's on call hours would be treated as working time and would be added to his normal hours to ascertain his average weekly working hours. In Christine's case however she is able to spend her on call hours as she likes even although she has to be able to report within to 15 minutes to the hospital. Accordingly her on call hours would not be taken into account in calculating her working hours. If Christine was required to occupy a separate flat provided by her employer at or near her place of work her situation would be analogous to that in MacCartney v Oversley House Management [2006] I.C.R. 510.

CHAPTER THREE

TERMINATION OF THE CONTRACT AND WRONGFUL DISMISSAL

TERMINATION BY NOTICE

3–1 Unless the contract is for a fixed period the contract of employment can be ended by either party giving notice of termination. Such notice need not be given in writing although the contract itself may require this in order to avoid disputes, not just about whether it has been given but the date it was given and the date it expired. Where verbal notice is given it does not start to run until the day following the day on which it is given (*West v Kneels Ltd* [1986] I.R.L.R. 430) and the giving of notice involves no particular words to be used; it is very much a matter for the court to consider the meaning attached to the words used. Thus where the employee stated "I am left with no option but to resign ... I look forward to hearing from you within seven days", it was legitimate to read the letter as meaning resignation would take effect if there was no reply within seven days (*Walmsley v C & R Ferguson Ltd,* 1989 S.L.T. 258). Notice, once given, cannot unilaterally be withdrawn before it expires (*Riordan v The War Office* [1960] 3 All E.R. 774; *Norwest Holst Administration v Harrison* [1985] I.C.R. 668).

Usually the contract will provide for the length of notice required to terminate the contract, and provided this does not permit notice shorter than that required by the Employment Rights Act 1996, the parties may agree whatever notice term they wish. However, if the contract makes no provision (express or implied) for termination by notice the common law provides that either party may terminate the contract by giving reasonable notice of termination (*Forsyth v Heathery Knowe Coal Company* (1880) 7 R 887). What is reasonable depends on the circumstances of the case including the seniority of the employee and how long it is likely to take him to find other work or the employer to find a replacement. In *Hill v C A Parsons Ltd* [1972] Ch. 305 a senior engineer was entitled to six months notice of termination.

THE EMPLOYMENT RIGHTS ACT 1996

Since 1963, statute has provided for minimum periods of notice. **3–2**
Provided an employee has been continuously employed for a month or more he is entitled to the period of notice specified in the Employment Rights Act and any contractual term which deprives the employee of that right is void (Employment Rights Act s.86(3)). The length of minimum notice to which an employee is entitled depends on the length of his continuous employment and for every year of continuous employment an employee is entitled to one week's notice. Thus an employee who has been continuously employed between one month and two years is entitled to one week's notice, with a week being added for each year of continuous employment, until the maximum of 12 weeks is reached. Accordingly, under the Act an employee who has been continuously employed for two years is entitled to two weeks' notice; an employee who has been employed for 10 years is entitled to 10 weeks' notice and so on up to the maximum of 12 weeks after 12 (or more) years' continuous employment. Such a sliding scale does not apply to the notice the employee is required to give; under the Act an employee is not required to give more than one weeks' notice but his contract of employment will often require that he gives more.

This does not mean that employment cannot be ended before the expiry of the relevant notice period, as either party is free to waive his rights either to the notice or accepting pay in lieu of notice (Employment Rights Act s.86(3); *Trotter v Forth Ports Authority* [1991] I.R.L.R. 419) and either party is free to terminate the contract summarily where that is justified by the other's conduct (Employment Rights Act s.86(6)). However, there must be evidence to justify dismissal or resignation without giving notice, as it is not enough for the employer merely to describe the employee's conduct as "gross misconduct" and thereby claim release from his statutory obligation to give notice or money in lieu thereof (*Lanton Leisure Ltd v White & Gibson* [1987] I.R.L.R. 119). The rights to minimum periods of notice are contractual and are not to be regarded as independent statutory rights (*Westwood v Secretary of State for Employment* [1985] I.C.R. 209); the rights are enforced through the law of contract with there being no independent statutory remedy for either the employer or the employee failing to give statutory notice. While it is not competent to claim that a failure to pay wages in lieu of notice by an employer who does not allow the employee to work out his notice is an unlawful deduction from wages (*Delaney v Staples* [1992] I.R.L.R. 191), a claim for breach of contract may be made to the employment tribunal in the event of an employer dismissing without notice or pay in lieu thereof when summary dismissal is not justified (Employment Tribunals Extension of Jurisdiction (Scotland) Order 1994).

The provisions in the Employment Rights Act 1996 regarding minimum periods of notice do not apply when a contract is terminated by operation of law under the doctrine of frustration; they are concerned with situations where a contract is terminated by one of the parties, whereas by definition, frustration of a contract occurs through no fault or act on the part of the party designed to achieve that result (*G.F. Sharp & Company Ltd v McMillan* [1998] I.R.L.R. 632).

PARTNERSHIP DISSOLUTION

3–3 Many employees are employed by partnerships. In Scots law there are two kinds of partnerships. The first and most common type is that regulated by the Partnership Act 1890 which recognises that a partnership possesses a quasi legal personality distinct from the personalities of the partners themselves but lacks the distinct legal personality of a limited company (Partnership Act 1890 s.4(2)). The result is that a change in the composition of the partnership technically results in a change in the personality of the employer. Strictly every time a partner resigns or a new one is assumed the legal personality of the employer changes. In practice, employees agree to continue to work under the new partnership. However, the dissolution of such a partnership will operate to terminate contracts of employment between the firm and employee. Where the dissolution is the result of the death or incapacity of one of the partners, the contract of employment will be regarded as frustrated because the legal personality of the employer has been brought to an end by extraneous circumstances (*Hoey v McEwan & Auld* (1867) 5 M 814). However, where the partnership continues, contracts of employment with the firm are deemed to include an implied term that the death, resignation or assumption of a partner or partners will be accepted by the firm's employees (*Berlitz School of Languages v Duchene* (1903) 6 F. 181). Indeed the Employment Rights Act 1996 s.218(5) provides that continuity of employment is preserved where there is an alteration in the composition of a partnership. One of the great disadvantages (from the point of view of the partners) of a partnership is that the partners are not able to limit their liability, each partner being jointly and severally liable for the debts of the firm. However, since 2001 it has been possible to form a limited liability partnership (Limited Liability Partnership Act 2000). In addition to being able to limit the liability of the partners such a partnership is regarded as a body corporate with a legal personality separate from the legal personalities of its individual members. Accordingly the ordinary law of partnership does not apply to a limited liability partnership which has unlimited capacity to enter into contracts of employment. Where such a partnership is the employer the contract of employment is with the body corporate whose legal personality is not affected by any change in the partners who make it up. From the employee's point of view it is like being employed by a limited company rather than a partnership. The Limited Liability Partnership Act is likely to be of more effect in England where a partnership has no legal personality distinct from its members. The effect of the dissolution of a limited liability partnership on contracts of employment is analogous to the effect of a company being wound up.

WINDING UP, RECEIVERSHIPS AND ADMINISTRATION ORDERS

Many people are employed by limited companies. Such business **3–4**
organisations have a separate legal personality and have perpetual succession so that contracts of employment with such companies are not affected by the change in the shareholders or the directors, although in very special circumstances a change in the shareholders may also amount to a change in the ownership of the business or undertaking of the company where, for example, the businesses of a subsidiary and parent company following a share transfer become closely integrated (*The Print Factory (London) 1991 Ltd v Millam*, CA, IDS Brief 829—discussed in Ch.5, below). However, where companies are wound up the effect on the contracts of employment depends on the nature of the winding up and the circumstances surrounding it but generally a court order which winds up a company (a compulsory winding up order) operates as notice of termination of the contracts of employment between the company and its staff (*Day v Tait*, 1900 8 S.L.T. 40). On the other hand a resolution to voluntarily wind up a company may operate to terminate contracts of employment depending upon the facts and circumstances of each case (*Ferguson v Telford, Grier & McKay & Co* [1967] I.T.R. 387). It may be necessary therefore to distinguish a voluntary winding up to cease business on insolvency (*Reigate v Union Manufacturing Company (Ramsbottom) Ltd* [1918] 1 K.B. 592) from a voluntary winding up, merely to facilitate a takeover or business reconstruction (*Midland Counties Bank Ltd v Attwood* [1905] 1 Ch. 355).

Often where a company is in financial difficulty the creditors or the court may appoint a receiver or administrator who will try to keep the business (or a part of it) going in the hope that it might be sold, thereby increasing assets for distribution to the creditors. Where a receiver is appointed, existing contracts of employment are not terminated by virtue of his appointment (Insolvency Act 1986 s.57(4)). However, the appointment of a receiver may be inconsistent with continued employment of one or more employees; in this case the appointment of the receiver will terminate these contracts of employment (*Griffiths v Secretary of State for Social Services* [1974] Q.B. 468). Of course the receiver himself may expressly dismiss employees by his conduct, for example by selling the business, or repudiate existing contracts of employment and it is provided that where existing contracts of employment are continued or adopted by a receiver, he is personally liable on such contracts (Insolvency Act 1986 s.57(3)). A similar situation appears to operate with regard to administrators. Nothing the receiver does within the first 14 days of appointment is to be taken as evidence of his adoption of contracts (Insolvency Act 1986 s.57(5)) but an administrator, liquidator or receiver who continues the contracts of employees beyond the 14-day period will be held to have adopted the contracts even though he has stated expressly that he is not doing so (*Powdrill v Watson* [1995] I.R.L.R. 268). He cannot have his cake and eat it too! Following that decision, Parliament enacted the Insolvency Act 1994 under which the liability of administrators (s.19) and administrative receivers (s.44) on contracts of employment adopted by them was restricted to qualifying liabilities, namely payment of wages, salaries and contributions to a pension scheme in respect of services rendered after the adoption of the contract. Significantly qualifying liabilities do not include wages in lieu of notice, liability for the remainder of a fixed term contract or contributions to a pension scheme in respect of the period prior to adoption of the contract.

Frustration

3–5 Like any other contract the contract of employment may, by operation of extraneous circumstances and events, become impossible to perform or "frustrated". The death of either party frustrates the contract of employment (*Hoey v McEwan and Auld* (1867) 5 M 814) as does the serious or protracted illness of either party. In *Condor v Barron Knights* [1966] 1 W.L.R. 87 the contract of the drummer in a pop group was frustrated when he developed an illness which prevented him from working the schedule the pop group required. Where the illness of the employees is concerned a great deal depends on the circumstances of the employment and the nature of the illness as well as the prospect of recovery. In *Marshall v Harland & Wolf Ltd* [1972] 2 All E.R. 715 the following were stated to be relevant:

- terms of the contract;
- the nature of the employment and its expected duration if no illness;
- the nature of illness and prospects of recovery;
- period of past employment;
- possibility of acquisition of statutory rights by the replacement employee; and
- continued payment of wages during absence.

Sharp & Company Ltd v Mcmillan

[1998] I.R.L.R. 632

McMillan was employed by Sharp & Co Ltd as a joiner. In October 1994 he injured his left hand and never worked for the employers again. On December 4, 1995 he told the managing director he was permanently unfit for work as a joiner but they agreed to keep him on their books so that he could get a more generous pension once he reached 60 years old in March 1996. However, Sharp & Co Ltd considered his contract of employment frustrated as a consequence of his ill health and that his employment with the company would terminate on November 22, 1996.

It was held that a contract of employment which has come to an end by reason of frustration cannot be treated by the parties as subsisting. If a contract is frustrated by operation of law there is nothing to revive and a nullity has to be declared. There is nothing to prevent parties entering into a new contract but they must do so with the clear intention to achieve that result otherwise there is no *consensus ad idem* because if the parties both think that the previous contract is still subsisting there is no intention to create a new contract.

The contract of employment came to an end by reason of frustration, at least by the date the applicant told his employers he would remain permanently unfit to work as a joiner. Thereafter the relationship between the parties was not regulated by a contract of employment properly understood. The arrangement whereby the employers agreed to continue to treat the applicant as an employee for pension purposes was not the same as a contract of employment.

Also the statutory provisions regarding minimum periods of notice do not apply when a contract is terminated by operation of law under the doctrine of frustration. They are concerned with situations where a contract is terminated by one of the parties, whereas by definition, frustration of a contract occurs through no fault or act on the part of the party designed to achieve that result. Therefore McMillan was not entitled to a period of notice.

Being sent to prison or interned (or being on bail with a condition that the employee did not attend work) does not necessarily frustrate the contract although again it will depend on the length of the sentence and the nature of the employment. It is not the conduct of the employee that is regarded as preventing him from performing the contract but the act of the court in sending him to prison.

F.C. Shepherd & Co Ltd v Jerrom

[1986] I.R.L.R. 358

The contract of an apprentice who, during his apprenticeship, had been convicted of conspiracy to assault and affray which resulted in him being given a borstal sentence, was frustrated after he had served 39 weeks in borstal.

Lawton L.J. stated:

> "The apprentice's criminal conduct was deliberate but it did not have by itself any consequences on the performance of the contract. What affected the contract was the sentence of borstal training which was the act of the judge and which he (the apprentice) would have avoided if he could have done . . . In this case the facts did frustrate the contract."

3–6 It is competent for the contracting parties to provide that an event which may ordinarily frustrate the contract will not do so, so that contractual provisions which provide for long periods of sick leave would suggest that the parties had anticipated such an eventuality and had provided that lengthy sickness absence would not frustrate the contract. In *Four Seasons Healthcare Ltd v Maughan* [2005] I.R.L.R. 324, EAT the provision of a detailed contractual disciplinary procedure which provided for summary dismissal in the event of physical abuse of residents inhibited a finding of frustration in respect of an employee whose bail condition prevented him attending work because although there was information on which the employer could have dismissed the employee it chose to suspend without pay pending the outcome of the trial.

A contract can also be frustrated by becoming illegal and this has meant that where an employee becomes legally disqualified from performing certain work, his contract may be brought to an end by frustration. Therefore where a contract of employment requires the employee to hold a valid qualification, a relatively short period of legal disqualification can result in the contract being frustrated (*Tarnesby v Kensington & Chelsea & Westminster Area Health Authority* [1981] I.R.L.R. 369—doctor's registration being temporarily suspended; *Dunbar v Baillie Brothers* 1990 G.W.D. 26-1487—HGV driver, losing licence following a heart attack).

The doctrine of frustration will apply more readily to fixed term contracts of employment which cannot be determined by giving proper notice (*Notcutt v Universal Equipment Co Ltd* [1986] I.C.R. 414). Particularly in relation to contracts which may be ended by giving notice, employment tribunals have been urged not to readily find the contract of employment frustrated as this could deprive employees of valuable statutory rights. This is so because where the contract is brought to an end by frustration there is no dismissal for the purpose of unfair dismissal or redundancy law (*Williams v Watson Luxury Coaches Ltd* [1990] I.R.L.R. 164).

Rescission

The general rule is that one party cannot bring to an end his contractual obligations merely by repudiating the contract or breaking it in a material or fundamental way; repudiation merely allows the innocent party to rescind the contract so that a repudiation of the contract by a unilateral wage reduction did not itself terminate the contract. Therefore where the employee continued to work, his contract of employment did not come to an end and he was therefore entitled to the wages stated in his contract. **3–7**

Rigby v Ferodo Ltd

[1988] I.C.R. 29

Ferodo Ltd gave its employees notice that it was going to reduce wage rates but Rigby and other employees refused to agree. When his wage was reduced Rigby sued for the difference but Ferodo argued that the notice to reduce the wages should be construed as a 12–week notice to terminate the contract of employment with the offer of a new contract containing the reduced wage rate.

Lord Oliver stated:

> "There was no reason in law or in logic why, leaving aside the extreme cases of outright dismissal or walk out, a contract of employment should be on any different footing from any other contract, regarding the principle that an unaccepted repudiation was a thing writ in water and of no value to anybody.

... [T]he employers had no intention of terminating the contracts of their workforce except by compelling the acceptance of the new contractual terms which the employees were not willing to accept. Faced with that the employers could have terminated the contracts on proper notice. They chose not to do so. They could have dismissed them out of hand and faced the consequences. They chose not to do so. They continued to employ them week by week under contracts which entitled them to certain levels of wages but withheld from them part of that entitlement. In those circumstances there could be no answer to the employee's claim.

It had been argued that since the employers could have terminated the employee's contract by 12–weeks' notice they must be treated as if they had done so, so that the claim for

> damages was limited to the shortfall in wages during that period. [But] that argument rested on a fallacy. It assumed the very proposition already rejected namely that the employment under the contract had come to an end. But here there were claims for sums due under a continuing contract which had never terminated and there was no room for the application of the principle referred to."

However, where a party rescinds the contract, he has to communicate that one way or another to the party alleged to be in breach (*Edwards v Surrey Police* [1999] I.R.L.R. 456) and the conduct of either party may be regarded as inconsistent with rescission and may indicate an affirmation of the new contract (*Bashir v Brillo Manufacturing Company* [1979] I.R.L.R. 295).

TERMINATION BY PERFORMANCE AND PASSAGE OF TIME

3–8 Where the contract is to perform a particular and finite piece of work, it is brought to an end or discharged when the work is completed (*Brown v Knowsley Burgh Council* [1986] I.R.L.R. 102; *Ironmonger v Movefield* [1988] I.R.L.R. 461). Where the contract is for a fixed period, it comes to an end when the term expires and neither party is required to give notice of impending expiry (*Lennox v Allan & Sons* (1880) 3 R 38).

Agreement

3–9 Since contracts are based on consent, it follows that, in spite of any express or implied contractual terms to the contrary, parties to the contract of employment can at any time agree that it be terminated. From the point of view of contract law, such a procedure is unremarkable. However, the termination of a contract by agreement will in most cases deprive the employee of any statutory rights. For example, as will be seen when redundancy and unfair dismissal are examined in Chs 4 and 5, below, termination by agreement does not amount to a dismissal which is a pre-requisite for claiming a redundancy payment or unfair dismissal. An agreement to terminate a contract with a view to pre-empting any unfair dismissal or redundancy application is void. The Employment Rights Act 1996 s.203 provides that any agreement is void insofar as it purports (a) to exclude or limit the operation of any provision of the 1996 Act; or (b) to preclude a person from bringing any proceedings under the 1996 Act before an employment tribunal. However, s.203(2) provides that certain types of agreement which purport to do these things may be valid. These include (a) compromise agreements (following independent advice) including those by which unfair dismissal cases are referred to ACAS; and (b) agreements following action by an ACAS Conciliation Officer.

Whether a contract has been ended by the employee being dismissed or by agreement it requires consideration of the question—Who actually terminated the contract?—which is an issue of fact. Where an employer argues that there has been no dismissal because the contract has been ended by agreement, an employment tribunal will wish to be satisfied that the agreement has been freely arrived at.

Hellyer Bros v Atkinson

[1992] I.R.L.R. 540

The employer requested Mr Atkinson sign a termination agreement but the employment tribunal held that the employee was in fact dismissed. The finding was upheld by the Employment Appeal Tribunal which stated that where an employee's voluntary act in compliance with the employer's request is the physical event which marks the termination of the contract of employment, there is no rule of law that that amounts to an agreement to terminate the contract unless there is duress or pressurisation. The employment tribunal was therefore entitled to find that in signing off when requested to do so an employee was agreeing to fill in the appropriate form and not to termination of his contract of employment.

Wrongful Dismissal

Wrongful dismissal is the term which denotes dismissal in breach of **3–10**
contract and is to be contrasted with unfair dismissal which is primarily concerned with the reasonableness of the employer's actions. Although in unfair dismissal the question as to whether an employer has broken the contract in dismissing the employee will be relevant, it is only one of all the circumstances the employment tribunal is required to take into account. Dismissal by a public body can sometimes be challenged by judicial review—a procedure in the Court of Session or High Court by which the legality of an employer's action in dismissing an employee may be declared unlawful, for example, because the public body has acted outwith its statutory powers and such a dismissal may also be described as wrongful. Leaving aside the issue of judicial review the remedies for wrongful dismissal are the remedies afforded by the law of contract.

Remedies

3–11 The law regards the contract of employment as a contract involving the provision of personal services—a personal relationship based on mutual trust and confidence. One result of this is that the common law provides that the remedy of specific implement is not available (*Murray v Dumbarton County Council*, 1935 S.L.T. 239) and this rule is now enshrined in s.236 of the Trade Union and Labour Relations (Consolidation) Act 1992 which provides the following:

> "No court shall be way of—
>
> (a) an order for specific performance or specific implement of a contract of employment, or
> (b) an injunction or interdict restraining breach of threatened breach of such a contract,
>
> compel an employee to do any work or attend at any place for the doing of any work."

The result is that where a breach involves, on the employee's part a wrongful resignation like leaving without giving the notice required by the contract or, on the employer's part a wrongful dismissal like dismissing without notice where the conduct of the employee does not merit it, the courts will generally not grant any order whose effect would be to compel the continuation of the employment relationship. Thus a court order preventing an employer from appointing a replacement will generally not be granted (*Page One Records Ltd v Britton* [1968] 1 W.L.R. 157; *Skerret v Oliver* (1893) 23 R 468). However in England the Courts have restrained a wrongful dismissal by the granting of an injunction and the Scottish Courts have followed this trend. The English courts have been willing to grant injunctions restraining dismissal where there is clear evidence that there is no breakdown of the trust and confidence on which the employment relationship is based.

Ali v Southwark London Borough Council

[1988] I.C.R. 567

Mrs Ali was employed as a care assistant by the Borough Council in an old people's home, in respect of which concern had been expressed as to the standard of care the residents received, but witnesses were unwilling to give evidence freely, and as a result the Council set up an independent panel of inquiry. In the panel's report Mrs Ali and others were named as being to blame and it was recommended that they be dismissed immediately. Detailed allegations were set out against each of the employees named but the source of the information on which the allegations were based was not given.

Disciplinary charges were laid against Mrs Ali but no details of the evidence on which the charges were based were given and she sought an injunction to restrain the employers from proceeding with the disciplinary hearing without disclosing the evidence on which the charges were based.

Held, that even if the court had been satisfied that the disciplinary procedure was in breach of the employee's contract of employment, injunction would not be granted as the employers had no confidence and trust in Ali as an employee.

Millett J stated:

> "I would decline to grant injunctive relief. Even if I had come to the conclusion that what was proposed would be a breach of contract. I would have concluded that the appropriate remedy for the plaintiff (Ali) sounded in damages. The court will intervene by way of injunction in an employment case to restrain dismissal only where it is satisfied that the employer still retains the trust and confidence in the employee or if he claims to have lost such trust and confidence on some irrational basis.

In the present case it is quite plain that the defendants (the Borough Council) have lost all confidence in the ability of the employee to carry out the work of caring for others. They have not lost that confidence irrevocably but they have certainly lost it for the moment on reasonable grounds because of the advice they have been given by the independent panel."

Similarly where the contract provides for a specific procedure prior to dismissal, the English courts have been prepared at least to postpone the otherwise wrongful dismissal until proper procedures have been carried out.

Irani v Southampton and South West Hampshire Health Authority

[1985] I.C.R. 590

Irani held a permanent post with the Health Authority and a dispute arose between him and one of his senior colleagues. After an inquiry the Authority concluded that the differences were irreconcilable and the Health Authority wrote to Irani giving him proper contractual notice of termination, although the letter also offered to allow him to resign on terms to be negotiated. There was no complaint as to the conduct or competence of Irani, while the letter of termination offered the right of appeal. Irani did not exercise that right of appeal but sought an injunction restraining his employers from implementing their letter of notice because they had failed to observe the procedures for resolving dispute between employers and employees which were incorporated into Irani's contract from the Whitley Council "blue book"—the collective agreement for Health Authority employees.

The Court held Irani was entitled to an injunction to ensure he had the protection of the contractual "blue book" in circumstances in which there was no criticism of his conduct or professional competence and damages would not be an adequate remedy. If an injunction were not granted Irani would not be allowed to rely on the "blue book" procedures because by the time his case came to court for a full hearing he would no longer be an employee of the defendants.

3–12 A similar approach is seen in *Gryf-Lowczowski v Hitching Brooke Healthcare NHS Trust* (2005 EWHC 2407) where the court had to decide whether a consultant surgeon's contract with an NHS Trust was frustrated where owing to an external assessment of his abilities, he was required to undertake a re-skilling programme with another Trust before continuing with his contractual duties. Although the re-skilling training was proving difficult to arrange it was held that as long as it remained a realistic possibility, the contract was still capable of performance and was not therefore frustrated and in the circumstances, it granted an injunction to restrain the dismissal without first-of-all complying with its own contractual disciplinary procedures.

Examples of the Scottish courts being prepared to grant interdicts to restrain a dismissal are laid out in the following cases.

Anderson v Pringle of Scotland

[1998] I.R.L.R. 64

Pringle employed Anderson as a textile worker from 1959. The statement of terms and conditions of employment issued by Pringle referred to a collective agreement between Pringle and the trade union entered into in 1986 and set out the precise steps to be followed in the event of redundancies being necessary. These procedures required selection to be on the basis of Last-In-First-Out.

Pringle intimated its intention to alter the basis of selection to a matrix based on other selection criteria but the union would not agree to such an alteration. Nevertheless Pringle informed each employee individually that the new procedure would be used.

Anderson petitioned the court for interdict. The interim

orders were granted as the court accepted that as the redundancy procedures contained in the collective agreement were capable of being incorporated into an individual's contract the court was merely being asked to enforce the *mechanisms* of dismissal rather than preventing dismissal completely.

Lord Prosser stated:

> "Whatever may be the outcome . . . after [a full hearing of the case] I am prepared at this stage to see the case as one where (as in *Irani*) the mechanisms of dismissal rather than the principle of dismissal is at the heart of the matter. In the contemporary world where even reinstatement is a less inconceivable remedy, intervention before dismissal must . . . be seen as a matter of discretion rather than impossibility. If there were any question of mistrust the position would no doubt be very different; but at least on the material before me . . . there is [no] true analogy between the [employer's] preference for other employees and the need for confidence which is inherent in the employer/employee relationship. It may be very difficult or inconvenient for the employer to abide by the priorities they have agreed to; but they can hardly call it unfair to be held to their own bargain . . . such exceptional cases as there have been give no very clear picture of the criteria for intervention. . . . [T]here remains the question of the balance of convenience. If interdict was not pronounced the petitioner would lose his job whereas the employers were not at any immediate risk of disaster . . . the balance of convenience favours maintaining the status quo."

Peace v The City of Edinburgh Council

[1999] I.R.L.R. 417

Peace was employed as a teacher by the City of Edinburgh Council and was suspended pending an investigation of allegations of professional misconduct. In 1997 the Council published new disciplinary procedures but Peace contended that according to the terms of his contract of employment, which incorporated agreements made between the Scottish Joint Negotiation Committee for Teaching Staff as supplemented by local agreements, any disciplinary proceedings should take place under terms agreed by that Committee in 1975. This stated all material stages of a disciplinary procedure should take place before elected members of the authority. Peace petitioned the court for an interdict to restrain the Council from breaching his contract of employment by adopting the new disciplinary procedures. The Council argued that the petition was incompetent and that the employee's only remedy was damages.

It was held that the petition was competent. Where the parties agreed that a contract of employment should subsist, albeit in a qualified form, there was no reason in principle for not enforcing provisions which do not require any greater degree of co-operation than the parties are prepared to accept.

Accordingly, because the Council was not refusing to employ Peace but merely insisting on dealing with him in accordance with the new procedures to which Peace had not agreed and was therefore in breach of his contract of employment it was possible to grant an interdict; however, if the effect of the petition had been to prevent dismissal at all it would have been regarded as incompetent and interdict would not have been granted. The trend of granting interdict in such special circumstances is also seen in *Harper v Tayside University Hospitals NHS Trust* 2001 G.W.D 1-50, in which the court emphasised that interdict would be granted as the contract had not been terminated; the circumstances were exceptional and the employee was entitled to the protection contained in the contractual mechanisms before dismissal could be lawfully carried out.

Damages

3–13 As these cases make clear, the remedy of interdict or injunction for a wrongful dismissal is exceptional and the most common remedy for wrongful dismissal is an action of damages at the instance of the employee. Damages are designed to compensate the employee for the loss he has sustained as a result of the contract being broken. If the contract is for a fixed term, damages will include the salary and other benefits which the employee would have received if the contract had run its full course subject to the employee's duty to mitigate his loss. If the contract could have been lawfully ended by the employer giving notice, the damages will compensate the employee for what he would have received in salary and other benefits during the period of notice. In each case damages will include compensation for loss of all of the parts of the remuneration package to which the employee was contractually entitled. This would include subscription to a private health insurance scheme, the free use of a car, pension and insurance benefits, rent free accommodation, share option schemes and an entitlement to a share in the profits (*Shove v Downs Surgical plc* [1984] I.C.R. 532). By restricting the loss to the period of the contract or the notice it required, the court is giving effect to the right of the party in breach to perform the contract in the least burdensome way. Thus the party in breach cannot be required to compensate the innocent party for any losses not resulting from the failure to perform obligations under the contract.

Morran v Glasgow Council of Tenants

[1998] I.R.L.R. 67

Morran was dismissed in breach of his contract. If his contract had been performed by the employers he would have received either four weeks' notice of termination or pay in lieu of notice. In fact he received neither and argued that if he had been given four weeks' notice he would have had enough continuous employment to claim unfair dismissal. He therefore claimed damages for loss of the right to claim unfair dismissals.

Held that in an action for damages for breach of the contract an employee is entitled to recover damages which will put him in a position he would have been in had the employers fulfilled their contractual obligation. Where as here the contract gives the employer the option of terminating by giving due notice or making a payment in lieu thereof, the less burdensome way for them is to dismiss the employee and make a payment in lieu of notice. If the employers had dismissed the employee with pay in lieu of notice, his employment would still have terminated before he had the necessary service to claim unfair dismissal.

In *Morran* the employer had an express right to terminate the contract by giving pay in lieu of notice and the Court declined to say what would be the position where the right to terminate by giving pay in lieu of notice was not express. However, in England it has been held in a case in which there was no express right to terminate by giving pay in lieu of notice (*Virgin Net Ltd v Harper* [2004] I.R.L.R. 831) that even where an employer terminated the contract by giving pay in lieu of notice so that by the date of termination the employee did not have the one year's employment necessary to claim unfair dismissal (see Ch.5, below) the damages should not include a sum in respect of the loss of the right to claim unfair dismissal because Parliament had deliberately restricted the right to claim unfair dismissal to those with one year's employment and Harper had not suffered any loss by being dismissed before she had one year's employment because at that time she had not acquired the right not to be unfairly dismissed.

For some time the decision of the House of Lords in *Addis v Gramophone Company Ltd* [1909] A.C. 488 has been regarded as **3–14**
precluding an award of damages in respect of injury to the

employee's feelings. However, in *Malik v BCCI S.A.* [1997] I.R.L.R. 462 the House of Lords has distinguished *Addis* and has held that an employee is entitled to damages for the financial loss he suffered (through, for example, not being able to find other employment) as a result of the employer being in breach of the implied duty of trust and confidence by, for example, running his business in a dishonest and corrupt way. Thus "stigma" damages may now be awarded for loss of reputation caused by the breach of contract.

Malik v Bank of Credit and Commerce International S.A. (in compulsory liquidation)

[1997] I.R.L.R. 462, HL

Two employees, Mr Malik and Mr Mahmud, were employed by the Bank (BCCI) in London. They claim that their association with BCCI placed them at a serious disadvantage in finding new jobs. They had both worked for the bank for many years.

For the purpose of this case it was assumed that BCCI operated in a corrupt and dishonest manner, but that Mr Mahmud and Mr Malik were innocent of any involvement. Following the collapse of BCCI its corruption and dishonesty became widely known, and in consequence Mr Mahmud and Mr Malik were at a handicap on the labour market because they were stigmatised by reason of their previous employment by BCCI consequently suffering loss.

It was agreed that the contracts of employment of these two former employees each contained an implied term to the effect that the bank would not, without reasonable and proper cause, conduct itself in a manner likely to destroy or seriously damage the relationship of confidence and trust between employer and employee.

Lord Nicholls of Birkenhead stated:

> "Exceptionally ... the losses suffered by an employee as a result of a breach of the trust and confidence term may not consist of, or be confined to, loss of pay and other premature termination losses. Leaving aside injured feelings and anxiety, which are not the basis of the claim in the present case, an employee may find himself worse off financially than when he entered into the contract. The most obvious example is conduct, in breach of the trust and confidence term, which prejudicially affects an employee's future employment prospects. The conduct may diminish the employee's attractiveness to future employers.

The loss in the present case is of this character. BCCI promised, in an implied term, not to conduct a dishonest or corrupt business. The promised benefit was employment by an honest employer. This benefit did not materialise ... Are financial losses of this character, which I shall call 'continuing financial losses', recoverable for breach of the trust and confidence term? This is the crucial point in the present appeals. In my view, if it was reasonably foreseeable that a particular type of loss of this character was a serious possibility, and loss of this type is sustained in consequence of a breach, then in respect of the loss principle damages should be recoverable.

This approach brings one face to face with the decision in the wrongful dismissal case of *Addis v Gramophone Co. Ltd* [1909] A.C. 488. It does so, because the measure of damages recoverable for breach of the trust and confidence term cannot be decided without having some regard to a comparable question which arises regarding the measure of damages recoverable for wrongful dismissal. An employee may elect to treat a sufficiently serious breach of the trust and confidence term as discharging him from the contract and, hence, as a constructive dismissal. The damages in such a case ought, in principle, to be the same as they would be if the employer had expressly dismissed the employee. The employee should be no better off, or worse off, in the two situations.

In my opinion these observations cannot preclude the recovery of damages where the manner of dismissal involved a breach of the implied duty of trust and confidence and this caused financial loss. *Addis* was decided before the implied term of trust and confidence was adumbrated. Now that this term exists and is normally implied into every contract of employment, damages for its breach should be assessed in accordance with then ordinary contract law principles."

Johnson v Unisys Ltd

[1999] I.R.L.R. 90, CA

Johnson was employed as a manager by Unisys Ltd until he was summarily dismissed for misconduct and claimed damages for breach of contract for wrongful dismissal, alleging that because of the manner of his dismissal, he suffered a mental breakdown.

The Court of Appeal held that he was not entitled to damages for losses, arising from his inability to obtain employment after suffering a mental breakdown, as a result of the manner of his dismissal. Where there is an express dismissal *Addis v The Gramophone Company* remains authority that damages cannot include compensation for the manner of dismissal, for the employee's injured feelings or for the fact that he may find it more difficult to obtain employment from the dismissal itself.

The breach of contract in *Addis* was confined to the manner of dismissal, whereas *Malik* was not a wrongful dismissal case but a complaint relating to the breach of trust and confidence on behalf of the employer, owed to the employees during the period of their employment. In the present case since the complaint was only about the manner of his dismissal, *Addis* was fatal to his claim.

[2001] I.R.L.R. 279, HL

On appeal to the House of Lords it was held that in light of the development of the remedy of unfair dismissal, it would be improper for the courts (as opposed to Parliament) to develop a common law remedy for the manner in which an employee is dismissed. As a result, it would not be wise for the courts to develop a separate implied term in the contract of employment that the power of dismissal would be exercised fairly and in good faith, even though *Addis v The Gramophone Company* which prevents an employee recovering damages for injury to his feelings, distress and damage to his reputation as a result of the manner in which he was dismissed, would not stand in the way of recovering damages for breach of another term of the contract, as in *Malik*.

However, where the breach does not take the form of wrongful dismissal, damages may be awarded for psychiatric illness (to be distinguished from mere injury to feelings and upset) caused by the breach of contract:

Gogay v Hertfordshire County Council

[2000] I.R.L.R. 703

Gogay was employed by the Council as a care worker and received a letter suspending her, saying that an alleged issue of sexual abuse had to be investigated. Gogay was upset, although following investigation no allegation of sexual abuse had been made. Gogay suffered from depression brought about by the suspension and sued for damages for personal injury brought about by the employer's breach of contract.

The Court of Appeal held the actions of the Council amounted to breach of the duty of trust and confidence. To say that here had been an allegation of sexual abuse was putting it far too high. Regarding damages the High Court had not erred in awarding damages for the psychiatric illness which had been caused by the suspension in breach of contract. There is a clear distinction between a psychiatric illness and hurt, upset and injury to feelings. The present case was therefore distinguishable from *Addis* in that the employee in this case suffered psychiatric illness rather than hurt feelings. This case is also distinguishable from *Addis* and *Johnson v Unisys* in that this was a suspension of employment rather than dismissal.

Mitigation and taxation

The award of damages of course is subject to the rules of mitigation. This means that an employee who is wrongfully dismissed must make reasonable efforts to mitigate his loss by attempting to find other work; a failure to do so will result in a reduction of any damages that might be awarded. Although initially he can reject employment on less favourable terms than those he enjoyed under his previous employment contract, he will eventually be required to lower his sights (*Yetton v Eastwoods Froy* [1967] 1 W.L.R. 104). Also taxation has to be taken into account so that where an award of damages for loss of earnings is made, the Income Tax the employee would have paid if he had actually earned the salary is deducted and compensation for loss of employment in excess of £30,000 is itself subject to tax under s.148 of the Income and Corporation Taxes Act 1988. **3–15**

Pay in lieu of notice

In Scots law, the employer has an implied right to terminate the contract by paying wages and giving other contractual benefits due to the employee in lieu of notice. It follows that where an employer does this in the ordinary case, no action for damages will lie because no breach of contract will have occurred. In England the position is not as straightforward in that there is no implied or automatic right to end the contract by paying wages and other benefits in lieu of notice. However, many contracts of employment, both in England and in Scotland, expressly provide that the employer may end the contract by giving pay in lieu of notice in order to put it beyond doubt that there will be no breach by the employer making a payment in lieu of notice instead of allowing the employee to work out notice. Unless the conduct of the employee justifies summary **3–16** dismissal, an employer who dismisses without notice or without paying in lieu of notice will be liable in damages to the employee for a sum equivalent to wages in lieu of notice and the employee may sue for such in either the ordinary courts or an employment tribunal, but the amount of damages that may be awarded by an employment tribunal is limited by statute to £25,000 (Employment Tribunals Extension of Jurisdiction Orders 1994 (SI 1994/1623 and SI 1994/1624)). However, in a claim for damages for wrongful dismissal in breach of a contract of employment, which provided that the employers might make a payment in lieu of the stipulated notice of six months, the correct measure of damages was the amount the employee would have earned had the employment continued but the employee had to give credit for any earnings received in new employment obtained within the period of notice (*Cerberus Software Ltd v Rowley* [2001] I.R.L.R. 160, CA).

Cerberus Software Ltd v Rowley

[2001] I.R.L.R. 160, CA

The employee, a sales and marketing director with the employers from 1994, was summarily dismissed on June 26, 1996 and found alternative employment weeks later on August 1, 1996.

Ward L.J. stated that the contract of employment was in very different terms to that in *Abrahams v Performing Right Society Ltd* [1995] I.C.R. 1028. This case was relied on by the Industrial Tribunal. It gave either party the right to terminate the contract on not less than six months notice, but the all-important words were: "It is agreed that the employer may make a payment in lieu of notice to the employee".

That meant that the employer was given the right to elect whether or not to make a payment in lieu of notice.

Where the company was given the choice whether to pay or not to pay, the language was totally inconsistent with a contractual right given to the employee to insist that he should be paid six months salary in lieu of notice.

The claim was for damages for breach of contract, that is, damages for wrongful dismissal. The measure of damages was the amount that the employee would have earned had the employment continued according to contract, but then the ordinary rule applied that the employee had to minimise his loss by using due diligence to find other employment.

His Lordship readily understood the employee's incredulity that the employers might be permitted to behave with bad faith yet not pay for it. In other circumstances the employer might have to pay dearly for such conduct.

Such an employer was not only in breach of contract giving

rise to a claim for damages for breach of contract at common law. In addition the employee had the statutory remedy for unfair dismissal.

If the present employee had not been successful in finding alternative employment the employers would have been liable to compensate him for the time he was out of work beyond the six-month period of notice, that is, he would recover more than would be awarded under his common law claim.

The fact remained, however, that he did find better paid employment shortly after his unhappy experiences with the employers and the damages awarded to him had to be mitigated accordingly. He was badly treated but the appeal had to be allowed.

The sum awarded by the industrial tribunal would be set aside and there should be substituted for it the appropriate amount of damages for the period from the date of dismissal to the commencement of the new employment.

Sedley L.J. dissented.

However, the precise wording of the contract is important. In *Abrahams v Performing Right Society Ltd* [1995] I.C.R. 1028, CA, the contract provided that in the event of the termination of the contract the employee would be "entitled to a period of two years' notice or an equivalent period in lieu". When the employment was terminated without notice the employee claimed pay in lieu for the notice period. The employers argued that the employee's claim was for damages and accordingly he could only sue for what he had lost and that he (the employee) had to give credit for any earnings from employment during the two-year period. The Court of Appeal held that he was entitled to the full salary during the period because his was not a claim in damages but a claim for a debt due under the contract. In Scotland even where there is no express term in the contract it is arguable that a claim against an employer who summarily dismisses without cause and without pay in lieu notice is properly an action of debt and not damages so that there is no duty on the employee to account for any earnings he might receive from employment during the notice period.

SAMPLE QUESTIONS

1. Pat is an accountant who has been employed by Riccarton University since 1992. His contract of employment provides "Termination of employment:
This contract may be terminated at any time by either party giving the other one month's notice in writing".
In 2007 the University decided to terminate Pat's contract and after consulting the terms of his contract, the Secretary writes to Pat giving him one month's notice. Pat brings his contract to you and asks if the University has acted lawfully. What advice would you give to Pat? Would your advice differ if Pat told you that just before he was given notice he had admitted that while attending a meeting about University business in the centre of Edinburgh he had left a portable computer belonging to the University in his car, unlocked, in a public car park and as a result of which the computer was stolen?

2. James was employed as one of 10 salesmen by Biotech Ltd. He had been employed for 12 years by Biotech and in that time had been off for three months in 2000 following a nervous breakdown. Towards the end of 2006 James began to suffer heart problems and his doctor advised him to take three months off work, which he did. On his return he became tired easily and after about a month back at work he was admitted to hospital for heart surgery. The operation was successful and his doctors expected that he would be able to resume normal work within two months. Just before he was due to return to work he received a letter from Biotech that the company regarded his contract as having been brought to an end by his illness. James has heard that Biotech is having financial difficulties and were to make some employees redundant and he wonders whether he will be able to claim a redundancy payment. When he asks Biotech about this he is told that as his illness frustrated his contract he is not entitled to a redundancy payment. What advice would you give James and would it be any different if his contract provided that "you are entitled to sick pay for any period of six months in any calendar year"?

3. Jack is employed as a nurse at Riccarton Nursing Home. He has frequently found that there are inadequate supplies of linen and dressings so much so that some patients' relatives have complained to Jack about the standard of care the patients are receiving. Jack has read in the local newspaper that patients and relatives have written to the manager of the home alleging poor nursing care and unacceptable standards of hygiene. The Nursing Home is closed within a few days of the newspaper article being published and Jack receives a letter giving him notice of termination of his employment. According to Jack's contract he was entitled to three months' notice but the Nursing Home has given only one month's notice. You meet Jack in a rather depressed mood as he has had his feelings hurt by the way he has been dismissed; he has been trying to find a new job but at various interviews after he said he had previously worked at the Riccarton Nursing Home he was told his applications were unsuccessful. He wonders if he might be entitled to compensation for having his contract terminated?

SUGGESTED ANSWERS FOR CHAPTER THREE

1. According to the Employment Rights Act, Pat is entitled to a minimum period of notice related to his length of continuous employment. In Pat's case the minimum period of notice is eight weeks. The Act also provides that any contractual term which is less than the minimum period is void and of no effect. Thus the term in Pat's contract of employment that he is entitled to one month's notice is of no effect and he is entitled to eight weeks notice of termination. As his employer has failed to give Pat the required notice he is in breach of his contract of employment and must pay damages to Pat equalling the money Pat would have earned if the employer had given him the correct notice, i.e. another four weeks' pay. Pat would be able to sue for the damages either in the employment tribunal—the cheaper and quicker procedure—or the ordinary court.

Your advice would differ if Pat had accepted that he left the University's computer in his unlocked car thus by doing so he would be in breach of his contract, an implied term of which is that he will perform his duties with reasonable care. If Pat was in breach of his contract the University would not be bound to give any notice at all as the Employment Rights Act (s.86(6)) provides that it does not affect the right of either party to terminate the contract without notice by reason of the conduct of the other party. It could be strongly argued that Pat was in breach of his contract by leaving the computer in his unlocked car and depending on the circumstances, including the value of the computer and what information it contained, his conduct entitled the University to terminate his contract without notice.

2. It is true that a contract which is brought to an end by frustration will mean the employee has not been dismissed and therefore not entitled to a redundancy payment (see Chapter 5 below). A contract which is frustrated by illness or other cause over which the parties have no control (i.e. death or imprisonment) is brought to an end by operation of law and not by the act of either of the contracting parties. However, while the illness of an employee may result in the law regarding the contract as frustrated and not capable of further performance, everything depends on the circumstances of the employment, the nature of the illness and the prospects of recovery and the other factors set out in Marshall v Harland and Wolff Ltd *[1972] I.R.L.R. 90. In light of the doctors' expectation that James would be fully fit to resume normal working, the fact that he was not a unique employee but one of a sales team of 10 and that he had had a similar length of absence before for health reasons, it is likely that his contract would not be regarded as frustrated. If James had been*

employed in heavy physical work which his heart condition required him to avoid the, decision might have been different.
The fact that his contract provided that he would be entitled to six-months sick pay in any year suggests that the parties accepted that long periods of illness, if they occurred, would not frustrate the contract as the parties had made special provision to take account of such an eventuality.

3. Until the decision of the House of Lords in Malik v Bank of Credit and Commerce International SA *[1997] I.R.L.R. 462, Jack would not have been able to recover any more than the wages he would have earned during the period of notice that the employers required to give him under his contract of employment. As Jack has received only one month's notice, when by his contract, he was entitled to three months' notice, he will be entitled to damages amounting to what he would have earned during the two months notice he did not work. After the decision in* Malik *where an employer has broken the term of trust and confidence which is found in every contract, an employee who suffers a loss as a result of that breach will be entitled to damages calculated according to the ordinary rules of contract law. They therefore may include a sum representing the employee's disadvantage in the labour market by being unable to find new employment. These damages are referred to as "stigma" damages. The issue for Jack is whether the Nursing Home, by not providing adequate supplies of linen, would be seen to be in breach of their implied duty not to act in a way that was likely to damage the trust and confidence between them and Jack. In* Malik *it was accepted for the purpose of the case that the Bank had operated in a dishonest and corrupt manner. Whether the Nursing Home had breached the contract by failing to provide adequate supplies for the patients would depend on the circumstances but even then the decision in* Metiard v St Edmunds College *(IDS Brief 624, 1998) shows that a distinction may be made between running the business in a dishonest and corrupt way* (Malik) *and running it in a way which falls below acceptable standards of patient care. If the Nursing Home has not breached the implied term of trust and confidence, Jack will not be able to claim stigma damages for not being able to find new employment. If Jack can show that the Nursing Home's conduct did amount to a breach of the implied duty of trust and confidence, he will be entitled to damages representing his financial losses by being out of work as a nurse for longer than he otherwise would have been.*

However he will not be entitled to damages for the way in which he was dismissed. In Johnson v Unisys Ltd *[2001] I.R.L.R. 279 the House of Lords has held that the decision in* Addis v Gramophone Co Ltd *[1909] A.C. 488 still prevents an employee recovering damages for injured feelings, distress or damage to his reputation as a result of the manner of dismissal. Accordingly Jack would not be able to claim damages for the distress caused to him by the manner of dismissal.*

CHAPTER FOUR

UNFAIR DISMISSAL

INTRODUCTION

Dismissal is the ultimate sanction the employer can impose in the event of the employee breaching the contract of employment or acting in some other way which renders continued employment unacceptable to the employer. Less serious disciplinary measures would include warnings, suspensions, demotion and withholding of wages. Where an employer dismisses an employee without good reason the dismissal may be characterised as wrongful or unfair. 4–1

WRONGFUL DISMISSAL AND UNFAIR DISMISSAL

Occasionally the term "wrongful dismissal" describes a dismissal of a public office holder. This is where the dismissal is illegal in that it does not conform with certain procedures prescribed by common law or statute. However, it is more likely it indicates a dismissal that is in breach of contract for which the remedy, until 1995, lay in the ordinary courts in the form of an action for breach of contract leading to an award of damages. Since 1995, by virtue of the Employment Tribunals Extension of Jurisdiction Order 1994 (SI 1994/1624), it has been competent to complain of wrongful dismissal in the employment tribunals as well as in the ordinary courts. This can have the advantage of being an informal legal procedure that can be conducted without the aid of professional lawyers. However, an employment tribunal may not award more than £25,000 in damages and may only hear complaints which are lodged within three months of the employment being terminated. 4–2

Whether a dismissal is wrongful depends entirely on whether the contract has been broken; courts and tribunals do not consider the employer's motive for terminating the contract. Thus a wrongful dismissal occurs when an employee is dismissed without notice (summary dismissal) in circumstances which do not justify summary dismissal. Conversely there is no wrongful dismissal where an employer dismisses an employee with proper notice (or with no notice but paying wages in lieu thereof) even though the employer's motive was questionable.

Unfair dismissal describes a dismissal which is contrary to certain standards of reasonableness or other rules of law. These are currently contained in the Employment Rights Act 1996, the Transfer of Undertakings (Protection of Employment) Regulations 2006 and the Trade Union and Labour Relations (Consolidation) Act 1992 (TULR(C)A). In determining whether a dismissal was unfair, the employment tribunal is permitted to take into account the provisions of the ACAS Code of Practice on Disciplinary and Grievance Procedures. Although of considerable value and guidance, the ACAS advisory handbook on Discipline and Grievances at Work is not required to be taken into account by tribunals. Unlike wrongful dismissal, unfair dismissal is concerned with the employer's reason and motives for dismissal and how it is carried out; it is dealt with exclusively by employment tribunals and may lead to orders of re-instatement, re-engagement or compensation.

WHO IS PROTECTED AGAINST UNFAIR DISMISSAL?

4–3 Like most statutory rights, unfair dismissal protection is currently conferred only on employees who meet prescribed statutory conditions, although s.23 of the Employment Rights Act 1996 permits the Secretary of State to extend the protection to other groups. The most significant qualifying condition is the requirement to have been continuously employed for a period of one year at the effective date of termination (Employment Rights Act s.108). However, there are various exceptions (see paras 4–18 to 4–27, below), such as where the dismissal is for union membership/non-membership (TULR(C)A s.152), for pregnancy (Employment Rights Act s.99) or for certain health and safety reasons (s.100). In such special cases no continuous employment is required before a complaint may be lodged.

Until June 1999 it was necessary (as a result of the Unfair Dismissal (Variation of Qualifying Period) Order 1985 (SI 1985/000)) in the ordinary case for an employee to have had two years' continuous employment before he or she was entitled to complain of unfair dismissal. This was challenged—ultimately unsuccessfully—in *R v Secretary of State for Employment Ex p. Seymour-Smith and Perez* [1999] I.R.L.R. 253, ECJ; [2000] I.R.L.R. 263, HL, where the applicants sought judicial review of the 1985 Order. They claimed that the proportion of women who could comply with the two-year qualifying period was considerably smaller than the proportion of men, so as to amount to evidence of prima facie indirect discrimination against women. Therefore, they argued that the two-year qualifying period, unless justified, was contrary to the EC Equal Treatment Directive (76/207). The House of Lords eventually held that whilst the two-year qualifying condition was a condition with which a considerably smaller proportion of women could comply, the Secretary of State had been able to show that the condition was still objectively justified at the date of the applicants' dismissals and so the applications failed. Nevertheless, since June 1,

1999, to claim unfair dismissal in the ordinary case, an employee only requires to have one year's continuous employment with his or her employer (or any associated employer).

The Employment Equality (Age) Regulations 2006 (SI 2006/1031) removed the upper age limit for claiming unfair dismissal for dismissals taking effect on or after October 1, 2006. Prior to these Regulations, in most cases, employees lost the right to complain of unfair dismissal when they reached the non-discriminatory normal retiring age for the position they held or, in any other case, the age of 65.

Generally an employee cannot contract out of his or her statutory right not to be unfairly dismissed or to complain to an Employment Tribunal (Employment Rights Act s.203). However, there are two important exceptions to this: **4–4**

(1) where there has been agreement following action by an ACAS conciliation officer; and
(2) where the employee has entered into a settlement or compromise agreement having received independent advice from a lawyer or other authorised advisor.

Formerly, where the employee was employed under a fixed term contract for one year or more it was lawful for him or her to agree that the right to claim unfair dismissal was excluded so that where the fixed term contract expired without being renewed there was no right to claim unfair dismissal. The opportunity to exclude unfair dismissal rights in fixed term contracts was removed by the Employment Relations Act 1999 s.18(1) in relation to contracts entered into after October 25, 1999.

Those employed in the police service are excluded from protection against unfair dismissal unless the dismissal is for health and safety reasons under s.100 or for making a protected disclosure under s.103A (s.200). Those employed by the Crown are protected against unfair dismissal except for the special protection in relation to Sunday working (s.191). Civil servants who are members of the Security Service, the Secret Intelligence Service or the Government Communications Headquarters, in addition, may not claim the special protection of the protected disclosure provisions (s.193). Members of the armed forces are now entitled to claim unfair dismissal with certain exceptions including health and safety dismissals, trade union membership dismissals, working time dismissals and flexible working dismissals. Service personnel may be required to use the "service re-dress procedures" before complaining to an employment tribunal (ss.191, 192).

Until October 25, 1999 those employees who ordinarily worked outside Great Britain (s.196) were excluded from complaining of unfair dismissal. The Employment Relations Act 1999 s.32(3) repealed s.196 of the Employment Rights Act but it was unclear when employees based outside Great Britain would be protected by the unfair dismissal provisions.

Serco Limited v Lawson

[2006] I.R.L.R. 289, HL

L was a British national employed by Serco Limited who were registered in the UK and based in England. His job was as a security supervisor based in the Ascension Islands where Serco provided security to the RAF. His salary was paid into a UK bank account but he paid no tax in the UK as he was based abroad. He resigned and claimed constructive dismissal. The Court of Appeal held that the tribunal had jurisdiction where there was "employment in Great Britain". In this case although there were strong connections to Britain, the Court of Appeal decided that L was employed on Ascension Island and not in Great Britain. The case was appealed to the House of Lords who allowed the appeal. Lord Hoffman gave the following guidance on the correct approach to determining jurisdiction in such cases.

What should be considered was where in reality the employee was working at the time of his dismissal, regardless of any contractual provision. However, in relation to peripatetic workers such as airline pilots and salesman, the question should be where the employee is based and this will involve consideration of the terms of the contract of employment. Lord Hoffman stated that it would not normally be sufficient merely that someone is employed by a British company even if the employee is himself British:

> "Something more may be provided by the fact that the employee is posted abroad by a British employer for the purposes of a business carried on in Great Britain. He is not working for a business conducted in a foreign country which belongs to British owners or is a branch of a British business, but as representative of a business conducted at home. I have in mind, for example, a foreign correspondent on the staff of a British newspaper, who is posted to Rome or Peking and may remain for years living in Italy or China but remains nevertheless a permanent employee of the newspaper who could be posted to some other country. He would in my opinion fall within the scope of section 94(1).
>
> Another example is an expatriate employee of a British employer who is operating within what amounts for practical purposes to an extra-territorial British enclave in a foreign country. This was the position of Mr Botham working in a military base in Germany. And I think, although the case is not quite so strong, that the same is true of Mr Lawson at the RAF base on Ascension

> Island. While it is true that Mr Lawson was there in a support role, employed by a private firm to provide security on the base, I think it would be unrealistic to regard him as having taken up employment in a foreign community in the same way as if Serco Ltd were providing security services for a hospital in Berlin."

CONTINUOUS EMPLOYMENT

Continuous employment is a statutory concept whose existence depends on the provisions contained in the Employment Rights Act ss.210–219. Until February 6, 1995, broadly speaking, weeks of employment were not to be taken into account in calculating a period of continuous employment unless the week was one in which the employee worked or would, in accordance with his contract of employment, normally have worked 16 hours. However, as a result of the decision of the House of Lords in *R v Secretary of State for Employment* [1994] I.R.L.R. 176 in which it was held that the discounting of weeks in which fewer than 16 hours were worked indirectly discriminated against women, the law was changed by the Employment Protection (Part-time Employees) Regulations 1995 (SI 1995/31). Now, subject to what follows, any week counts towards continuous employment provided that during that week the relationship is governed by a contract of employment. Thus a week in which an employee is by contract required to work—no matter for how long—will count towards his continuous employment. **4–5**

The rules relating to continuous employment may be summarised as follows:

(1) periods of continuous employment are made up of weeks that "count";
(2) except where there is a strike or lock out, a week which does not count breaks continuity and the employee has to start accumulating continuity all over again;
(3) once employment with an employer has begun it is presumed to be continuous unless the employer proves otherwise;
(4) the following weeks count as continuous employment:

- a week during the whole or part of which the employee's relations are governed by a contract of employment;
- a week in which the employee is incapable because of illness, pregnancy or childbirth;
- a week during which the employee is absent on account of a temporary cessation of work (for example a break

between two fixed term contracts) or an arrangement whereby continuity is maintained;
- a week of absence because of pregnancy where a woman has exercised her statutory right to return to work;
- a week which occurs between dismissal and re-engagement or which occurs in the period of statutory notice the employee should have received.

Normally the rules of continuous employment permit consideration of employment only with one (the dismissing) employer; however where certain changes of employer occur, the law permits continuity to be maintained.

Where a business or undertaking has been transferred, employment with the transferor counts along with employment with the transferee. Also where one body corporate is substituted by another Act of Parliament, employment with both counts towards continuous employment. Similarly where an employee transfers to an employer who is an associated employer of the other employer, this means the employment with both employers counts towards continuous employment. Employers are associated where one is a company that the other controls or where two or more are companies controlled by a third person (*Merton London Borough Council v Gardiner* [1980] I.R.L.R. 472).

WHAT IS A DISMISSAL?

4–6 For unfair dismissal the meaning to be attached to "dismissal" is defined by the Employment Rights Act s.95. This is important because the definition is exhaustive; if an employee cannot prove that he or she has been "dismissed" in accordance with the definition, the case is bound to fail.

Termination of Contract by Employer with or without Notice

4–7 Where the employer with or without notice terminates the contract of employment, the employee is dismissed. Where the employer behaves in such a way that it is clear it intends the contract to end, then such a termination will be effective and the contract will end when the wish is communicated to the employee (*Brown v Southall and Knight* [1980] I.C.R. 617). Where a letter communicates dismissal, the dismissal does not take effect until the employee has read the letter or has had a reasonable opportunity of doing so, although an employee cannot avoid being dismissed by deliberately not reading the letter.

The main difficulty is where the words of the employer or a member of management are liable to be misunderstood or are in some way ambiguous. However, even unambiguous words of dismissal can be withdrawn if uttered in the heat of the moment; but the withdrawal must be almost immediate (*Martin v Yeoman Aggregates Ltd* [1983] I.C.R. 314). In the case where the language is ambiguous it is for the tribunal to consider the context in which they were made and how the employee might reasonably interpret them. It is also dismissal for an employer to impose unilaterally radically different terms and conditions if these can be construed as a withdrawal of the old contract (*Alcan Extrusions v Yates* [1996] I.R.L.R. 327, EAT).

In the case where the employee uses unambiguous language consistent with dismissal, there is no obligation on the employer to investigate if the employee really means what has been said or done (*Kwik-Fit (GB) Ltd v Lineham* [1992] I.R.L.R. 156). The employer is entitled to treat unambiguous words of resignation as such unless there are special circumstances due to personality conflicts or individual characteristics or circumstances. Thus a refusal to allow an immature or disabled employee to withdraw a clearly stated resignation may be regarded as a dismissal due to the existence of special circumstances (*Barclay v City of Glasgow District Council* [1983] I.R.L.R. 313).

Being told by an employer to "resign or be dismissed" is a dismissal even where the employee resigns (*Sheffield v Oxford Controls Ltd* [1979] I.R.L.R. 133). This is also the case where the employee is pressurised into resigning because of employer fraud (*Caledonian Mining Co Ltd v Bassett* [1987] I.C.R. 425, EAT). The critical issue is to establish a causal link between the employer threat and the employee's termination (*Haseltine, Lake & Co v Dowler* [1981] I.C.R. 222, EAT). The critical question in each is case is who caused the employment to be terminated.

Caledonian Mining Co Ltd v Bassett and Steel

[1987] I.R.L.R. 165, EAT

The employers, Caledonian Mining Co Ltd, had proposed to make Bassett and Steel redundant and had offered to find them alternative employment within the group of companies. In fact the employers entered an agreement with the National Coal Board who offered Bassett and Steel employment and on receipt of that offer they resigned from Caledonian Mining Co Ltd. However that company refused to pay a redundancy payment saying that there was no dismissal.

The EAT held that it must be resolved whether there is a dismissal or a constructive dismissal and not merely by looking at the label put on the termination. The fact that there has been a resignation is not enough to say that the employer could not have terminated the contract.

> "Whatever the respective actions of the employer and employee at the time the contract was terminated, the relevant question is; Who really terminated the contract of employment? In the present case it was clearly the employers who caused the employee to resign. The reality of the matter was that it was the employers who terminated the contract. Therefore the employees were dismissed in law ...
>
> The employment tribunal had said that if the applicants were inveigled into leaving the respondent's employment that was a dismissal ... it was clearly the employers who caused the applicants to resign. The fact the applicants gave notice when they resigned is an irrelevant factor. The reality of the matter is that it was the employers who terminated the contract by inveigling the applicants to resign in circumstances to which we have already referred."

Expiry of Limited Term Contract without Renewal

4–8 Where an employee is employed on a contract for a limited term the expiry of that contract without its renewal is a dismissal of the employee. Thus if an employee is employed on a contract which is from January 1, 2005 until December 31, 2005 (what may be described as a "real" fixed term contract) he is dismissed if the contract is not renewed on its expiry. Of course the dismissal may be fair but it is nevertheless a dismissal. The original provisions of the ERA referred to the non-renewal of a "fixed-term contract". In *Dixon v BBC* [1979] I.C.R. 281 the Court of Appeal held that a contract for a fixed term also included a contract for an apparent fixed term, namely a contract which is stated to be for a fixed term as above (from January 1, 2005 to December 31, 2005) but which either party could end before the expiry date merely by giving the other party notice. Accordingly when a real fixed term contract or an apparent fixed term contract comes to an end there is a dismissal if it is not renewed and if, in the case of an apparent fixed term contract, the employer gives notice to terminate the contract before its expiry date there will also be dismissal.

The 2002 Employment Act amended the definition of dismissal to include the non-renewal of a "limited term contract" instead of a "fixed-term contract". This encompasses "real" and "apparent" fixed term contracts as above, but also includes contracts which come to an end on the occurrence or non-occurrence of a specific event or on the completion of a specific task.

Constructive Dismissal

This occurs where a contract is terminated by the employee, with or without notice, but in circumstances such that he or she is entitled to terminate without notice by reason of the employer's conduct. **4–9**

The test for whether an employee is entitled to terminate the contract without notice is contractual and it is not enough for the employee merely to show that the employer's conduct had been unreasonable in some way (*Western Excavating ECC Ltd v Sharp* [1979] I.C.R. 221; *GGHB v Pate,* 1983 S.L.T. 90). In effect, the employer's actions must show that it repudiated the contract by committing a significant breach of it, which goes to the root of the agreement or shows that the employer no longer wishes to be bound by one or more of its essential terms. In such circumstances, the employee is entitled to rescind. Obvious circumstances where an employee would be justified in rescinding the contract would be where the employer unilaterally reduces pay, demotes or removes important parts of the employee's duties without authority or changes the employee's place of work without contractual approval.

Whilst there has to be a material breach of contract, this can take the form of breach of an implied term; i.e. the implied term that the employer will not act in a manner that is calculated or likely to damage or seriously destroy the trust and confidence on which the employment contract rests (*Woods v W M Car Services (Peterborough) Ltd* [1981] I.R.L.R. 347). This particular implied term may also limit the exercise of any contractual discretion granted to the employer (*McLory v Post Office* [1993] I.R.L.R. 159, EAT). Equally, a constructive dismissal could arise where the employer breaches the implied term not to apply a contractual disciplinary power harshly or oppressively (*Beckett v BBC* [1983] I.R.L.R. 43), refuses to deal promptly with an employee's grievance (*W A Goold (Pearmark) Ltd v McConnell* [1995] I.R.L.R. 516), fails to treat a complaint of sexual harassment seriously (*Bracebridge Engineering Ltd v Darby* [1990] I.R.L.R. 3) or does not take reasonable care for an employee's health and safety (*Waltons & Morse v Dorrington* [1997] I.R.L.R. 488, EAT). However, it is not a material breach to merely perform the contract where there is dispute about its terms (*Financial Techniques v Hughes* [1981] I.R.L.R. 32).

Whitbread plc (t/a thresher) v Gullyes

(EAT Case No. 478/92, unreported)

Ms Gullyes was employed as a branch manager of an off-licence by Whitbread plc. She held this position for almost four years until she accepted a post at a larger branch which had suffered from staff and operational problems. She accepted the offer on the basis that she would be transferred to another branch if she so requested. Her contract required her to work 39 hours per week but in the new job she in fact worked an average of 76 hours per week and she was provided with only 152 staff hours per week by way of assistance. While she was on holiday and without consulting her, the area manager transferred two experienced staff to other branches. On her return Gullyes found that she could not cope and when her request for a transfer to another branch was refused, she resigned and complained that she had been constructively dismissed and that this dismissal was unfair.

The tribunal held that Gullyes had been constructively dismissed. The area manager had offered Gullyes the job knowing that she did not have sufficient experience to take the post unless she received considerable support. The employers failed to provide this support. The number of staff hours allocated to Gullyes was insufficient to enable her to carry out her contractual duties, which included the opening of the shop at set hours, hiring and supervising staff, preparing staff rotas and stocktaking. The removal of the two experienced staff member's made Gullyes' position "untenable".

There was a repudiatory breach by the employers of an implied term in Gullyes's contract of employment, namely, that the employers should not behave in such a way as to prevent Gullyes from being able to carry out her part of the contract. The employers had by their conduct made it "difficult or impossible" for Gullyes to carry out her contractual duties. By resigning, Gullyes accepted the breach and was entitled to treat the contract as at an end.

The EAT dismissed the employer's appeal.

The employers had argued that the implied term, relied upon by the tribunal, only applied where the employers had made it impossible for the employee to perform the contract, rather than just very difficult. However, the EAT, rejected this argument although it agreed that performance of the contract by Gullyes had to be rendered more than just difficult by the employer's actions but held that the facts found by the tribunal satisfied this stricter test. The employers knew that Gullyes had insufficient experience and their failure to provide the necessary back-up prevented her from performing her contract to any acceptable extent.

If the EAT was wrong in this, the employers had breached the implied term of trust and confidence also contained in the contract. The employers' response to this was to argue that they had complete trust and confidence in Gullyes but that was approaching the matter from the wrong perspective as it was Gullyes who had lost confidence in her employers. Without the support that Gullyes was entitled to expect from her employers, her position became impossible and she

> resigned. On the findings of fact made by the tribunal, the EAT found that she resigned as a direct result of the breach by the employers of the implied term of trust and confidence.

In order to establish that he or she has been constructively dismissed it is not enough for the employee to show that the employer broke the contract or indicated that he or she would do so; he or she must also show that the breach was what caused him or her to leave. While a long delay before acting on the breach will make it difficult for an employee to show a constructive dismissal he or she is not required to leave without notice and giving notice may allow the employer to recognise that a breach has occurred and seek to rectify it.

There are two other situations that are worthy of note:

(1) In a case where the employer has given notice but the employee wishes to leave before the employer's notice has expired, although the employee's act is the act which brings the contract to an end he or she is still regarded as dismissed for the original reason (Employment Rights Act s.95(2)).

(2) Where there has been a transfer of an undertaking (see Ch.5, below) and the transfer would involve a substantial change in an employee's working conditions to his detriment, the employee may treat the contract as having been terminated by the employer with notice. This gives protection to an employee if the change is not of a nature that would allow the employee to claim constructive dismissal (TUPE 2006 reg.4(9)).

Therefore unless the employment relationship is ended in a way which is regarded as a dismissal, there can be no claim for unfair dismissal. Consequently where the employment contract is ended by one of the following methods the employee has no complaint.

Resignation which is Genuine and Intended

Where the contract is ended by the genuine, mutual agreement of the parties there is no dismissal even though the last act leading to termination may be that of the employer (*Birch v Liverpool University* [1985] I.C.R. 470). **4–10**

Operation of Law (Frustration)

This occurs, for example, where the employee becomes so incapacitated that he or she cannot perform the contract. If the contract is found to be frustrated then it comes to an end by operation of law. Crucially this means that it is not terminated by the employer and there is no "dismissal". **4–11**

In *Marshall v Harland and Wolff Ltd* [1972] I.C.R. 101 the following factors were suggested that a tribunal should take into account when considering whether the illness of the employee has frustrated the contract. These are:

- the terms of the contract, including provisions regarding sick pay;
- how long was employment to last;
- is the employee in a key post;
- nature of illness and prospects for recovery;
- period of past employment;
- need for replacement to be appointed;
- risk of acquiring statutory duties regarding replacement employee;
- have wages continued to be paid; and
- acts of employer, including failure to dismiss.

However employment tribunals will require clear evidence to demonstrate frustration of the contract. Where the employer feels the employee's illness is so severe as to render him or her incapable of performing the contract it has the power of dismissal on these grounds. In such a case, of course, the employee would be entitled to claim unfair dismissal since the employer has dismissed and that would then require the employer to show the reason for the dismissal.

Other instances of frustration would include imprisonment of the employee (*FC Shepherd and Co Ltd v Jerrom* [1986] I.C.R. 802) and legal disqualification from continuing to hold a particular post (*Tarnesby v Kensington Area Health Authority* [1981] I.R.L.R. 369).

STATUTORY PROCEDURES

4–12 The Employment Act 2002 introduced standard minimum dismissal and disciplinary procedures (DDPs) and grievance procedures (GPs) which require to be followed by all employers and employees regardless of size from October 1, 2004. Details of the procedures are contained in the Employment Act 2002 Sch.2 Pt 2 and in the Employment Act 2002 (Dispute Resolution) Regulations 2004 (SI 2004/752). The procedures are very simple but are intended to encourage employers and employees to attempt to resolve disputes without recourse to tribunals. Employees who have not initiated the appropriate GP will be prevented from bringing a complaint to the tribunal and in the case of dismissal, where an employer fails to use the correct DDP, the dismissal will be automatically unfair under s.98A of the Employment Rights Act and it will not be possible for the employer to justify the dismissal by arguing that the dismissal was reasonable. The employee will be entitled to compensation of at least four week's pay apart from exceptional cases where this would result in injustice to the employer. There are also financial penalties, in most cases, for failing to complete the relevant statutory minimum procedure—a reduction or increase in compensation of between 10 and 50 per cent depending on whether the fault is that of the employee or the employer.

The standard DDP applies in most cases where an employer wishes to dismiss an employee (including the non-renewal of a fixed term contract but not constructive dismissal) or to take disciplinary action (apart from warnings or paid suspension) that is alleged to be on grounds of conduct or capability. The procedure involves three steps:

(1) Notice in writing to the employee setting out the circumstances which have led the employer to consider dismissal or disciplinary action and inviting the employee to attend a meeting.
(2) The meeting should take place before any action (apart from suspension) is taken and should not take place until the employee has been informed of the basis for the information in the Step 1 notice and had an opportunity to consider his response. After the meeting the employer informs the employee of the decision and advises him or her of their right to appeal.
(3) If the employee wishes to appeal the employer must hold another meeting but this need not take place before the dismissal or other disciplinary action takes place. The employer must notify the employee of his final decision.

In very exceptional circumstances, where the employee has been guilty of gross misconduct, the employer has dismissed the employee immediately he became aware of the conduct and it was reasonable for the employer to dismiss without any investigation, a modified two step procedure applies as follows:

(1) Notice in writing to the employee of the reasons for the dismissal and advising him or her of their right to appeal.
(2) If the employee wishes to appeal the employer must invite him or her to a meeting. After the meeting the employer must advise the employee of the final decision.

In relation to grievances there is a similar three step standard procedure, except that it is instigated by written notification sent by the employee to the employer setting out the grievance. The two step modified GP consists of the employee giving written notice to the employer of the grievance and the basis for it and the employer sending a written response. This should only be used where the employment has ended and where both parties agree to use the modified procedure. Neither GP applies where employment has ceased, neither procedure has been started and it has ceased to be reasonably practicable for the employee to commence either procedure. Neither GP applies where the grievance relates to dismissal by the employer (apart from constructive dismissal) or to other disciplinary action unless that action constitutes unlawful discrimination in which case special provisions apply (reg.7).

4–13 There are further exceptions when the procedures do not apply or may be treated as having been completed: where the dismissal is one of a number of collective dismissals; where employees are dismissed for taking industrial action; where it is not possible for employment to continue (for example where the factory has been destroyed or continued employment would be illegal); where one party has reasonable grounds to believe that complying with the procedure would result in a significant threat to himself, his property or others; or where one party has been subjected to harassment and has reasonable grounds that following the procedure would result in continued harassment.

Timing and location of meetings should be reasonable, they should be conducted in a way that allows both parties to explain their cases and, in the case of an appeal meeting, the employer should, if possible, be represented by a more senior manager than at the initial meeting. The ACAS Code of Practice on Discipline and Grievance at Work (2004) gives further guidance on how the procedures should be followed.

THE REASON FOR DISMISSAL

4–14 Assuming the statutory dismissal procedures have been complied with, once the employee has satisfied the tribunal that he or she has been "dismissed" the onus transfers to the employer to show that the dismissal was for a potentially fair reason. These are set out in Employment Rights Act s.98(2). If the employer can do this the tribunal then considers whether the employer has acted reasonably. Where the employee has less than one year's employment (the qualifying period for ordinary unfair dismissal claims) and is claiming that he or she has been unfairly dismissed for one of the special reasons mentioned later, the onus is on the employee to prove that he or she was dismissed for that specific reason. The one exception to this is if the employee alleges that he has been dismissed for trade union reasons (see below), the onus of proof is on the employer to show that this was not the reason for the dismissal.

The Fair Reasons

4–15 (1) *Related to the capability or qualifications of the employee for the work he or she is employed to do.* Capability and qualifications are widely defined; the former includes skill, aptitude, health and mental capacity while the latter includes technical, academic and professional qualifications. The phrase "work employed to do" indicates an examination of contractual job descriptions or job duties will be necessary. Thus in *Tayside Regional Council v McIntosh* [1982] I.R.L.R. 272 the dismissal of an HGV driver who by his contract of employment was required to hold the appropriate driving licence was for a reason that related to his capability or qualifications. Ultimately, however, the issue of capability must be resolved by reference to the work the employee was doing at the time of dismissal (*Shook v Ealing London Borough Council* [1986] I.R.L.R. 46).

Shook v London Borough of Ealing

[1986] I.R.L.R. 46, EAT

Shook had a contractual term which allowed her employer to transfer her to any work for which her qualifications were appropriate. On her dismissal she argued that she was not incapable of doing all the kinds of work that her contract required. Her employers had therefore shown their reason for her dismissal was not related to her capability for the work she was employed to do.

The EAT held it was not necessary for the employer to show Shook was incapable of doing all the tasks which the employer was entitled by law to call upon her to discharge. In this case, however widely her contract was construed, her incapability related to her performance of her duties under her contract, even though her performance of all of them may not have been affected. There is a distinction between the reasons set out in Employment Rights Act s.98(2)(a) (capability); and (2)(b) (conduct); and the reasons in (2)(c) (redundancy); and (2)(d) (breach of statute).

According to the EAT the former two are couched in terms of "relation" whereas the latter two are couched in terms of actuality.

Dismissal for incapability is most appropriate where the employee's failure arises from a basic incapacity to perform the work. Where the employee's incapability can be attributed to carelessness or idleness it would be more appropriate to regard the reason for dismissal as one relating to conduct (*Sutton & Gates (Luton) Ltd v Boxall* [1978] I.R.L.R. 486). Incapability cases can also arise through the employee's ill health and an employer considering dismissal should take account of the following factors:

- warnings are not inappropriate where the circumstances leading to the incapacity are within the employee's own control (*A Links & Co Ltd v Rose* [1991] I.R.L.R. 353):
- prior consultation with the employee would normally be required in such circumstances (*Taylorplan Catering Scotland Ltd v McInally* [1980] I.R.L.R. 53);

- employers should avoid rigid rules such as dismissal on expiry of sick leave entitlement;
- employers must consider proper medical (specialist) advice;
- employers should ensure that in dismissing for incapacity they are not contravening the Disability Discrimination Act 1995 (see Ch.6, below).

4–16 (2) *Related to the conduct of the employee*. Although statute does not state this expressly, it is implied that there must be a connection between the conduct and the employee's responsibilities to his or her employers. This is sometimes referred to as the "conduct in context test". The case, *Thomson v Alloa Motor Co Ltd* [1983] I.R.L.R. 403, indicates that the conduct must in some way reflect on the employer/employee relationship. Thus damage caused to employer's property when a learner driver was leaving the garage forecourt after her duties had ended (which did not involve driving), was not a reason related to her conduct. It follows therefore that acts of misconduct, including criminal activities away from work, can have a sufficient connection with the employment relationship to relate to the conduct of the employee; this would be the case particularly where dishonesty was involved and the employee had responsibility for money or property or where the employee held a senior (management) position (*Norfolk County Council v Bernard* [1979] I.R.L.R. 222). In essence the employer must be able to show that there is some connection between the criminal conduct and the continued employment of the employee, though this may come about through the impact of the offence upon trust and confidence (*Moore v C & A Modes* [1981] I.R.L.R. 71). Certainly, an employer would be expected to consider the impact of the misconduct on trust and confidence if contemplating the summary dismissal of the employee (*Neary v Dean of Westminster* [1999] I.R.L.R. 288).

4–17 (3) *Retirement*. Retirement at 65 or over or at an objectively justified normal lower retiring age has become a "potentially fair reason" for dismissal within the meaning of s.98 of the Employment Rights Act 1996 by virtue of the Employment Equality (Age) Regulations 2006. Whether the dismissal is for retirement is to be determined in accordance with ss.98ZA to 98ZF of the Employment Rights Act 1996. Briefly , this means that the reason will be taken to be "retirement" where the dismissal takes place on a planned retirement date and the employee has been given between 6 and 12 months notice of the retirement date and of the reason for dismissal. If the dismissal takes place before the planned date it will NOT be retirement. Otherwise it will be for the tribunal to decide what the reason is, taking into account issues such as how much notice has been given and whether the employer complied with the rest of the procedure in Schedule 6.

4–18 (4) *The redundancy of the employee*. Redundancy is legally defined in the Employment Rights Act s.139(1) to mean a reduction in the needs of the business for employees to do work of a particular kind or a cessation (temporary or permanent, actual or expected) of the business, completely or in the place where the employee is employed. This is dealt with in more detail in Ch.5, below. However even where the employer can show that the reason for dismissal is redundancy, the dismissal may nevertheless become unfair by virtue of how the redundancy has been handled and this is examined later in the context of the reasonableness of the employer's actions. A redundancy may also be unfair by virtue of the special provisions in Employment Rights Act s.105 which deals with unfair selection for redundancy for certain reasons including health and safety; trade union reasons; assertion of statutory rights; making a protected disclosure; enforcing the national minimum wage or the Working Time Regulations, for being a part-time worker, for making a request for flexible working, being absent on jury duty, being an employee on a fixed term contract, an employee representative or trustee of an occupational pension scheme.

(5) *Contravention of a statutory enactment, either by the employer or employee, if the employee's employment were to be continued.* This would apply to the continued employment of a doctor whose registration had been terminated or an employee who is required to have a work permit but whose permit had expired. It is important to note, however, that it is not sufficient for the employer to believe that an enactment would be broken; there must be an actual breach of a statutory provision by continued employment. However, where an employer relies on reputable advice as to the continuing need for a permit it may be able to show that, although there was no actual breach of the law by its continuing to employ the employee, there was some other substantial reason for the dismissal, namely reliance on reputable advice. Thus in *Bouchaala v Trust House Forte* [1980] I.R.L.R. 382 the employer had relied on the advice of the Home Office regarding the need for Bouchala to hold a valid work permit. **4–19**

(6) *Some other substantial reason (SOSR) justifying the dismissal of the employee from the position he or she held.* This reason is frequently pleaded as an alternative to conduct particularly where the employer is unsure of overcoming the "conduct in context test". It usually involves establishing that the particular ground will have a negative impact upon the employer's business. It has been successfully pleaded in the following situations: **4–20**

- *Singh v London Country Bus Services Ltd* [1976] I.R.L.R. 176: criminal conviction unconnected with work.
- *Treganowan v Robert Knee & Co Ltd* [1975] I.C.R. 405: personality clashes resulting from disclosures of private life.
- *Scott Packing & Warehousing Ltd v Paterson* [1978] I.R.L.R. 166: reaction of best customer against conduct of employee.

- *Saunders v Scottish National Camps Association* [1981] I.R.L.R. 277: sexual proclivities of employee which made parents less likely to send their children to the camps.

There will be SOSR for a dismissal where business conditions require the employer to introduce changes in conditions or terms of employment which employees refuse to accept, so long as it can be shown that there are pressing business needs constituting the reason for the introduction of the changes. In such circumstances an employer would be justified in dismissing those employees who refused to accede to the new conditions (*Hollister v National Farmers' Union* [1979] I.R.L.R. 238).

Hollister v National Farmers' Union

[1979] I.R.L.R. 238, CA

Mr Hollister was employed by the NFU as a group secretary in Cornwall but after a reorganisation of its operations in Cornwall he was asked to accept different terms of employment and working conditions. Mr Hollister protested but he was given an ultimatum to accept the new contract or be dismissed. He refused and was dismissed.

The Court of Appeal held that where, as in the present case, it is essential as a result of a reorganisation that new contracts of employment be made and the only sensible way to deal with it is to terminate the existing contracts, offering the employees reasonable new ones, and an employee refuses to accept the new agreement, that is a substantial reason of a kind such as to justify dismissal within the meaning of s.98(1)(b).

Selfridges Ltd v Malik

[1998] I.C.R. 268, EAT

In February 1992 Selfridges Ltd, who paid employees a Christmas bonus, started negotiations with trade unions and employees with a view to discontinuing the bonus, to which the employees were contractually entitled. Because of poor trading conditions, savings had to be made. To compensate employees for the loss of the bonus, Selfridges offered a 3 per cent increase in wages for that year. After some months of meetings and discussions, all but 50 of the company's 1,500 employees accepted the proposed variation of their contracts of employment. Selfridges then wrote to the 50 employees who would not agree to the loss of their annual bonus stating that their contracts would be terminated with three months'

> notice, after expiry of which new contracts under which no Christmas bonus would be paid would immediately come into effect. Following the termination of their contract employees submitted complaints of unfair dismissal.
>
> The EAT had been entitled to find that the alleged "other substantial reasons" which Selfridges put forward did not really exist, as there was no economic reason for the termination of the contracts of the 50 employees who had not agreed to the loss of their Christmas bonus at a time when the other 1,450 had accepted the change. It did not make economic sense to say that poor trading conditions did not allow the continuation of the bonus while offering staff the 3 per cent increase by way of compensation. Accordingly the EAT rejected the employer's contention that the reason was SOSR.

Statute also provides:

(1) that the dismissal of an employee to accommodate the return of an employee from maternity leave or adoption leave or from medical suspension is for SOSR provided the dismissed employee has been informed in writing when engaged that this will be the position (Employment Rights Act s.106); and

(2) where there has occurred a transfer of a business and there is an economic, organisational or technical reason entailing changes in the workforce of the transferee or transferor either before of after transfer, the dismissal of an employee shall be for redundancy or for SOSR (Transfer of Undertakings (Protection of Employment) Regulations 2006 reg.7).

These provisions only go to help the employer establish a potentially fair reason. The employer will still require to show that the dismissal is reasonable in all the circumstances.

It follows that if the employer is not able to show that one of the above reasons was the principal reason for the dismissal, the employee's complaint must succeed.

Retirement Dismissals

Where the reason for dismissal is retirement then the fairness of the **4–21** dismissal is assessed quite differently from any other reason. There is no consideration of the reasonableness of the employer's actions as there would be if the dismissal was for misconduct for example. Instead, the dismissal will be deemed to be fair provided that the employer has complied with the procedure for allowing employees to make a request to stay on past retirement under Sch.6 (see para.4–22 below). Conversely, a dismissal for retirement will be automatically unfair if the employer has not told the employee of the intended retirement date and of his right to make a request under Sch.6 at least 14 days before the date of dismissal. The statutory dismissal procedures do not apply.

Right to request to continue working beyond the retirement date

4–22 Schedule 6 to the Employment Equality (Age) Regulations 2006 introduces a right for an employee to request to work on beyond the proposed retirement date. If an employer intends to dismiss an employee by reason of retirement then that employer has a duty to notify the employee:

a. of the employee's right to make a request to continue working beyond retirement; and
b. of the date on which he intends the employee to retire.

The notification of the above information must be given in writing not less than six months and not more than one year prior to the dismissal. If an employer has failed to notify the employee of the foregoing s/he has a continuing duty to do so until the 14th day before dismissal.

An employee has the right to make a request in writing to the employer not to retire on the intended date between three and six months before the intended retirement date. If the employer has failed to give the information noted above then a valid request can be made right up to the intended date of retirement.

If a request is made by the employee then the employer has a duty to follow the requirements set out in Sch.6. This obliges the employer to hold a meeting, which both parties must take all reasonable steps to attend, to discuss the request and to give a decision in writing as soon as reasonably practicable. If the employer agrees to the request without a meeting then that is acceptable. If it is not reasonably practicable to hold the meeting then the request can be considered without a meeting although the employer is obliged to consider any representations made by the employee and to notify the decision in writing to the employee as soon as reasonably practicable. If the employer confirms the decision to retire then s/he must state the date of dismissal, at the same time advising the employee of a right of appeal.

If an employer fails to notify the employee of the right to request to continue working between 6 and 12 months before the intended retirement date, then a tribunal shall make such award as it considers just and equitable of up to eight weeks pay (limited by the statutory cap on a week's pay).This is in addition to any other rights the employee may have.

The issue of reasonableness—substantive matters

4–23 For all reasons other than retirement, once the employee has been able to prove that he or she has been dismissed, and the employer has shown that he has complied with any relevant statutory procedure, the next question is whether the employer has acted reasonably and shown a sufficient reason for dismissing the employee (Employment Rights Act s.98(4)). Strictly the onus of proving that the employer acted reasonably and that the reason justified dismissal is neutral but in practice employers approach it as a stage at which the onus is on them. In considering the issue of reasonableness, it is recognised that there is a band of reasonable responses to the employee's conduct, of which an employer might reasonably take one view and another quite reasonably take another. Ultimately, it is for the tribunal as an industrial jury to decide whether the employer's decision fell within this band. It is not for the tribunal to substitute their views for those of the employer (*Iceland Frozen Foods Ltd v Jones* [1983] I.C.R. 17). A tribunal which seeks to avoid the band of reasonable response approach and substitute their views for those of the employer commits an error of law (*Post Office v Foley* [2000] I.R.L.R. 827). The present approach is exemplified in the following case.

Beedell v West Ferry Printers Ltd

[2000] I.R.L.R. 650

Mr Beedell was dismissed for fighting after almost 30 years exemplary service with the company. He complained of unfair dismissal and argued that no proper assessment of his part in the incident had been made, that dismissal was too severe in the circumstances given his length of service and work record and that when a similar incident had occurred previously the non-aggressor had received a written warning only. Applying the band of reasonable responses test the EAT concluded that although dismissal might have been harsh it was a reasonable response which a reasonable employer might take. In addition, the EAT reiterated that it is not for the employment tribunal to put themselves in the place of management to decide whether they, the tribunal members, would have dismissed in the circumstances.

The band of reasonable responses approach may, however, be criticised in that it does not set any objective standard. This is illustrated in the following case.

Scottish Midland Cooperative Society v Cullion

[1991] I.R.L.R. 261, SC

This case seems to suggest that provided the employer has conducted a proper investigation and had grounds for believing the employee had been guilty of misconduct or breach of rules, the dismissal will be fair whether or not the tribunal itself was satisfied the employee had committed the act in question. The fact that there was no allegation of dishonesty but merely a breach of till procedure was to be seen in perspective, namely that the employers attached great importance to till procedures; nor did the fact that the employee had an unblemished record of 14 years and that the amount involved was small (£1.43) mean that the employers had acted outwith the band of reasonable responses.

Admissible Evidence

4–24 Contrary to the position in cases involving alleged wrongful dismissal, in unfair dismissal employers are restricted to producing evidence of which they were aware at the time they took the decision to dismiss. Thus information or evidence of misconduct which comes to light after the decision to dismiss has been taken cannot be relied on by the employer to show the reason for the dismissal or that its conduct in dismissing the employee was reasonable (*W Devis & Sons Ltd v Atkins* [1977] I.C.R. 662). It can, however, be taken into account when the tribunal is considering the remedy to afford the employee and evidence which is discovered after the decision to dismiss is taken, may result in compensation being reduced to nil.

Frequently the decision to dismiss will be subject to an internal appeal by the employee; where this occurs the employer is required to reappraise the decision to dismiss in the light of all the evidence which emerges during the process of termination (*Tipton v West Midlands Cooperative Society* [1986] I.C.R. 192). However, where the appeal process upholds the appeal but discloses evidence which will support dismissal for another reason the dismissal process will require to be commenced afresh (*National Heart and Chest Hospital v Nambiar* [1981] I.C.R. 441).

The issue of reasonableness—procedural matters

4–25 To determine whether an employer acts reasonably it is necessary to have regard to the guidance given by the House of Lords in *Polkey v A E Dayton Services Ltd* [1987] I.R.L.R. 503.

Polkey v A E Dayton Services Ltd

[1987] I.R.L.R. 503, HL

Mr Polkey had been dismissed by his employers as redundant without any warning or prior consultation and he argued that his dismissal was unfair because of that failure in pre-dismissal procedure. The employers claimed that they had behaved reasonably in the circumstances because had they complied with the procedure it would have made no difference to their decision to dismiss. The House of Lords declared that the correct approach to the issue of procedure was to ask whether the employer had been reasonable or unreasonable in deciding that the reason for dismissing the employee was a sufficient reason, not that the employee would have been dismissed in any event even if there had been prior consultation and warning. Whether the employers could reasonably have concluded that the failure to consult or warn would be useless, so that the failure would not necessarily render the dismissal unfair, was a matter for the tribunal to consider in the light of the circumstances known to the employer at the time of the decision to dismiss.

Lord Mackay of Clashfern LC declared that:

> "if the employer could reasonably have concluded in the light of the circumstances known to him at the time of the dismissal that consultation or warning would be utterly useless he might well act reasonably even if he did not observe the provisions of the [procedure]. Failure to observe the requirements of the [procedure] relating to consultation or warning will not necessarily render a dismissal unfair. Whether in any particular case it did so is a matter for the employment tribunal to consider in the light of the circumstances known to the employer at the time he dismissed the employee."

Lord Bridge of Harwich indicated that in the "great majority of cases" an employer will not be acting reasonably, unless in incapability cases the employee is given fair warning and an opportunity to mend his or her ways and show that he or she can do the job; in misconduct cases the employer must investigate the complaint fully and fairly and hear the employee's defence in mitigation or explanation and in redundancy cases the employer warns and consults the affected employees or their representative, adopts a fair basis for selection and takes reasonable steps to avoid or minimise the redundancies through redeployment within the organisation. He concluded by stating that "it is quite a different

> matter if the tribunal is able to conclude that the employer, himself, at the time of dismissal, acted reasonably in taking the view that, in the exceptional circumstances of the particular case, the procedural steps normally appropriate would have been futile, could not have altered the decision to dismiss and therefore could be dispensed with".

The rule in *Polkey* may be summarised that where there is a serious flaw in the employer's pre-dismissal procedure, the dismissal would be unfair unless the employer, on the information available to it, would be acting reasonably by adopting no (or no further) procedure because such a (further) procedure would be "utterly futile" on the basis of information known to the employer at the time of dismissal. The Employment Act 2002 restricts the impact of this rule as follows:

> "As we have seen, where the basic statutory procedures have not been complied with the dismissal will be automatically unfair and it will not be possible for an employer to argue that his actions were 'reasonable'".

However, where there have been procedural shortcomings relating to matters beyond the statutory minimum requirements, whether these are contractual or otherwise, these failures will no longer necessarily lead to a conclusion that the dismissal was unfair if the employer can show that on the balance of probabilities (more than a 50 per cent chance) the dismissal would still have resulted even if a proper procedure had been followed (Employment Rights Act s.98A(2)).

If the tribunal comes to the conclusion that a proper procedure would have made a difference to the outcome it will find the dismissal to be unfair but is required to consider the percentage chance of the outcome being different and the employee not being dismissed. Thus if the tribunal concludes that after a proper procedure there was 30 per cent chance that the employee would still have been dismissed it will reduce any compensation it awards by that percentage. This percentage should never exceed 50 per cent as in that case the tribunal should have found that on the balance of probabilities the dismissal would still have taken place and was therefore either fair or if it is found to be unfair, this was on substantive rather than procedural grounds.

What is the Effect of *Polkey* Now?

4–26 While the Employment Act has restricted the effect of the *Polkey* rule, it is still an important decision for those cases where, although the relevant statutory procedures have been followed (or did not apply in the particular case), there have been procedural failures and the tribunal is not satisfied that the dismissal would still have resulted even if the procedures had been followed. It sets out guidelines for procedures that should normally be followed prior to dismissal.

Where the reason for dismissal is incapability

Although in *Polkey* Lord Bridge seemed to indicate that an ill **4–27** health dismissal which had not been preceded by a warning would be unfair, in *A Links & Co Ltd v Rose* [1991] I.R.L.R. 353, the Court of Session explained that Lord Bridge was talking of incapacity in the very general sense and that the correct approach is to consult with the employee. Essentially, what the tribunal must do in these cases is to assess what consultation was necessary in the circumstances of the case, what consultation, if any in fact took place, and whether or not the consultation process was adequate in all the circumstances. Thus consultation is usually required although there will be exceptional circumstances in which any consultation might be avoided as in *Eclipse Blinds Ltd v Wright* [1992] I.R.L.R. 133 where to have consulted with the employee would have meant revealing how serious her illness was. However, there might still be scope for warnings where the illness flowed from circumstances within the employee's own control, for example where an employee had refused to comply with medical advice to cope with obesity which had led to absences.

The tribunal will balance the needs of the employer to have the employee back at work against the employee's need to have time to recover but in all cases it is important for the employer to discover the true medical position (*East Lindsey District Council v Daubney* [1977] I.R.L.R. 181). Ultimately, although the employer must consult and seek medical advice, the final decision lies with the employer in the light of all the relevant facts. However, especially in large enterprises, employers will not act reasonably if they do not consider the possibility of transfer to different work.

Where the reason for dismissal is conduct

Undoubtedly *Polkey* raised the significance of pre-dismissal pro- **4–28** cedures. As the case makes clear, at the very least, a reasonable employer would be expected to conduct an investigation, to hold a hearing and usually to give the employee an opportunity to appeal the decision to dismiss. (Some form of meeting and a right of appeal, of course, now form part of the minimum statutory procedures but in many cases, a reasonable employer would carry out a more thorough investigation than the statutory procedures require.) The purpose of the hearing is to enable the employer to form a judgment as to the employee's guilt. It is not necessary for the employer to prove the employee's guilt, it is enough if it has a genuine belief in that guilt. This proposition stems from the following case.

British Home Stores Ltd v Burchell

[1978] I.R.L.R. 379, EAT

Burchell was dismissed for suspected dishonesty. The EAT indicated that the following issues should be addressed in cases of misconduct. First, there must be established by the employer the fact of a belief in the employee's guilt. Secondly, that the employer had in his mind reasonable grounds upon which to sustain that belief. And thirdly that the employer at the stage at which he formed that belief on those grounds, has carried out as much investigation into the matter as was reasonable in all the circumstances of the case.

It is now clear that the first element of the *Burchell* test relates to the reason for the dismissal and the last two elements concern the issue of reasonableness (*Post Office v Foley* [2000] I.R.L.R. 827). *Burchell* is important not only in dishonesty cases but also to other cases of breach of discipline, *Distillers Co (Bottling Services) Ltd v Gardner* [1982] I.R.L.R. 42. It is also important to appreciate that the level of investigation will vary with the circumstances of the case so that the investigation may be relatively superficial where the employee is caught red-handed and relatively extensive where the case is based on inference (*Inner London Education Authority v Gravett* [1988] I.R.L.R. 497). Although an employer would be expected to provide some evidence as to its grounds for a belief in the employee's guilt, tribunals must avoid placing the onus of proof on the employer and deciding that once the employer has failed one or more of the three elements there has been an unfair dismissal (*Scottish Daily Record and Sunday Mail (1986) Ltd v Laird* [1996] I.R.L.R. 665).

4–29 As *Polkey* makes clear, the right to be heard in defence or mitigation is a critical step in any misconduct dismissal.

Spink v Express Foods Group Ltd

[1990] I.R.L.R. 320, EAT

Spink was alleged to have falsified weekly returns and failed to visit customers. He was called to an interview but was given no advance indication of the purpose of his interview nor details of the complaints against him. The EAT concluded that at the very least an employee should know the case against him or her, hear or be told the important parts of the evidence, have the opportunity to criticise or dispute that evidence and be permitted to adduce his or her own evidence and argue the case.

Where informants are concerned a reasonable procedure should ensure that the employee sees the witness statements (*Louies v Coventry Hood & Seating Co Ltd* [1990] I.R.L.R. 324) although there may be exceptional circumstances where it would be useless or futile to disclose the witness statements, for example in the following case.

Fuller v Lloyds Bank plc

[1991] I.R.L.R. 336, EAT

Witness statements over an alleged assault in a pub were not disclosed to the employee but he knew the case against him and the identity of witnesses from police witness statements. The EAT held that Fuller's dismissal was not unfair because the non-disclosure did not make the procedure intrinsically unfair and overall the employer had applied a fair procedure.

It is impossible to prescribe rules to apply in every case but generally a fair pre-dismissal procedure will include the following:

- to require a proper investigation is conducted;
- to ensure the employee is heard;
- to ensure he or she knows the complaints against him or her;
- to ensure he or she can examine the evidence on which the case is based;
- to permit him or her to introduce his or her own evidence;
- to ensure that internal disciplinary procedures are followed;
- to avoid informal discussions of cases by those who will eventually decide;
- to ensure the employee is informed of any appeal rights; and
- to ensure that at the end of the process the employer had a reasonable belief in the employee's guilt.

Appeals

The importance of granting an employee a right of appeal in misconduct cases was stressed by the House of Lords in *West Midland Cooperative Society Ltd v Tipton* [1986] A.C. 536. Here the employee was still challenging the decision to dismiss but was denied a right of appeal even though this was specified in the disciplinary procedure. The House of Lords held that where an employee is still resisting the decision to dismiss and is denied a right of appeal which is provided by the contract, this factor alone may constitute a sufficient procedural defect to make the employer's decision to dismiss unreasonable. The right of appeal is now a key element of the statutory procedure but it may be that the contract sets out a particular appeal procedure or the appeal hearing itself may be found to be unfair. In *Westminster City Council v Cabaj* **4–30**

[1996] I.R.L.R. 399 where the membership of the appeals' panel was different from that specified in the disciplinary code, the Court of Appeal accepted that this defect alone could have made the decision to dismiss Cabaj unreasonable. Adherence to appeal rights may also cure earlier procedural defects.

> *Whitbread & Co plc v Mills*
>
> [1988] I.R.L.R. 501
>
> Mrs Mills was called to an interview which she thought was about her allegations towards the company doctor and his improper behaviour during an examination. Instead, it was a disciplinary interview to consider her dismissal. She subsequently exercised her right to appeal against the decision to dismiss. An important issue for the EAT was whether the appeal process could cure the obvious earlier procedural mistake. It was held that this was possible. The EAT held that this depended upon the degree of unfairness at the original hearing and the nature of the appeal, particularly whether it involves an opportunity for an earlier procedural defect to be cured by a rehearsal or re-hearing of the case. Although a defective procedure will be enough to make a dismissal unfair, defects at the initial stage can be cured by an internal appeal so long as the appeal is in effect a re-hearing.

Ultimately employers must consider each case on its merits including:

- the previous service of the employee;
- consistency of penalty but a tariff approach is inappropriate;
- mitigating circumstances should also be considered; and
- taking account of the provisions of the employers own disciplinary rules (if they exist) and the ACAS Code of Practice on Disciplinary and Grievance Procedures, even if not expressly referred to by the parties.

Redundancy

4–31 In *Polkey* Lord Bridge observed that a redundancy will be unfair unless the employer warns, consults, adopts a fair procedure and, where possible, avoids the redundancy by redeployment. Thus where employees complain that they have been unfairly selected for redundancy, tribunals are expected to consider three issues—that the unfairness incorporates unfair selection, lack of consultation and a failure to consider alternative employment (*Langston v Cranfield University* [1998] I.R.L.R. 172). The Inner House in *King v Eaton Ltd* [1996] I.R.L.R. 199 has taken a relaxed view of what information about selection is to be disclosed to employees and the extent to which the employer can justify his selection in the employment tribunal, holding that where an employer had chosen a method of selection and applied it, a tribunal to whom an appeal has been taken must be satisfied that redundancy selection has been achieved by adopting a fair and reasonable system and applying it fairly and reasonably as between one employee and another. In general, the employer who sets up a system of selection which can be reasonably described as fair and applies it without any overt sign of conduct which mars its fairness, will have done all that the law requires of it provided the employee receives sufficient information about the selection process to establish that the exercise has not been a sham (*King v Eaton Ltd (No. 2)* [1998] I.R.L.R. 686).

A key aspect of the *King* case was the Inner House's explanation that fair consultation involves consultation when the redundancy proposals are still at an early stage, the provision of adequate information to enable a response, adequate time in which to respond and a conscientious consideration by the employer of responses. As a result great emphasis has been placed on the need for effective consultation and this can be seen in *Ferguson v Prestwick Circuits Ltd* [1992] I.R.L.R. 266 where it was held that an employer had not consulted properly even where the employer argued that the reason (for not consulting) was because some of the employees whose jobs were under threat and who had been threatened with redundancy on a previous occasion had indicated that they did not want to go through the process again and preferred just to be told on the day. Neither the size of the employer's business, nor the urgency of the need to make redundancies, can in themselves excuse a failure to consult (*De Grasse v Stockwell Tools Ltd* [1992] I.R.L.R. 269). Even where there is a recognised trade union, it may be necessary to consult with the individual employees—particularly where consultation with the union has broken down (*John Brown Engineering Ltd v Brown* [1997] I.R.L.R. 90).

Mugford v Midland Bank plc

[1997] I.R.L.R. 208

Mr Mugford was a branch manager of the bank who lost his job when the bank went through a major restructuring. Around 3,000 employees were made redundant (including 858 managers). He argued that the bank's failure to consult with him made his dismissal unfair. However, the EAT held his dismissal was fair because even though there had been no consultation with him individually there had been consultation with the union. A key factor was that consultation was available to him if had chosen to take advantage of it.

The EAT sought to summarise the law as follows: (1) where

> there has been no consultation on redundancy the dismissal will be unfair unless the tribunal finds that a reasonable employer would have concluded that consultation would have been an utterly futile exercise in the circumstances of the case; (2) consultation with the trade union over selection criteria does not of itself release the employer from considering with the employee individually whether he or she is being selected for redundancy; (3) it will be a question of fact and degree to decide whether consultation with the individual and/or the union was so inadequate as to make the dismissal unfair.

As discussed above, where an employer has failed to reach the procedural standards set by *Polkey*, for example by not consulting with the employee, provided the statutory minimum procedure has been followed, it is now possible under s.98A(2) of the Employment Rights Act to argue that, on the balance of probabilities, the dismissal would have resulted even if the desired procedure had been followed and that the dismissal was otherwise fair on procedural grounds.

SPECIAL SITUATIONS

4–32 What has been stated above applies to dismissal for the ordinary reasons viz., conduct, capability, redundancy, breach of statute and some other substantial reason. However special rules exist for some special categories of dismissal and these are discussed now.

Industrial Action and Lock-Outs

4–33 Formerly, the law recognised two forms of industrial action for the purpose of unfair dismissal law, i.e. official and unofficial industrial action with different legal consequences relating to any dismissal. Where the action is official (broadly this means that the action has been authorised by the employee's trade union) or where the dismissal is during a lock-out, the position is regulated by TULR(C)A s.238 and an employment tribunal may only entertain an application if one or more relevant employees has not been dismissed. Where the action is unofficial employees who are dismissed while taking part have no right to claim unfair dismissal even if other employees who also took part were not dismissed.

Protected industrial action

4–34 However, since the Employment Relations Act 1999 introduced s.238A into TULR(C)A a third category of industrial action has been added, i.e. protected industrial action. This is essentially industrial action authorised by the union which attracts immunity for the trade union which calls the action. Where an employee takes part in protected industrial action his or her dismissal will be unfair if one of three conditions is satisfied:

— where the dismissal took place within twelve weeks of the start of the action (Any days in which the employees were locked out extend the period of protection);
— where the dismissal took place outwith the protected period but the employee had stopped taking part in the action before the eight week period ended; or
— where the dismissal is outwith the protected period and the employee is still taking part in it but the employer has failed to take reasonable procedural steps to resolve the dispute.

The above right is to be construed as one with unfair dismissal rights. There is, however, no qualifying period.

Official industrial action

The rules in s.238 of TULR(C)A about official industrial action which denied an employment tribunal jurisdiction, where there was no evidence of selectivity in dismissal or re-engagement, are now only relevant for dismissals beyond the 12-week period and for dismissals in connection with a lock-out. The critical question in this situation is to consider the position of one or more relevant employees who have not been dismissed, or one or more relevant employees who have been offered re-engagement within three months of being dismissed, while the applicant has not. A relevant employee is: (a) where the dismissal occurs during a lock-out, any employee directly interested in the dispute; and (b) where the dismissal occurs during industrial action, any employee taking part at the date of the claimant's dismissal. **4–35**

The effect of s.238 is to prevent any employee dismissed from having a claim of unfair dismissal provided all relevant employees are dismissed and none is offered re-engagement within three months. However, it has to be emphasised that a failure to dismiss just one relevant employee will permit all other employees who are dismissed to make claims; whether the dismissals are unfair will depend on the tribunal applying the usual rules and in particular determining whether any employees have been treated unfairly. Because of its exceptional nature tribunals will scrutinise an employer's reliance on s.238 very carefully. Whether there is industrial action or a lock-out does not require either the employee or the employer to be acting in breach of contract; what is important is the purpose and effect of the action or lock out (*Power Packing Casemakers v Faust* [1983] I.C.R. 292).

Unofficial action

4–36 As already noted, the third category of rule arises where the action is unofficial. This category is regulated by TULR(C)A s.237. In such a case, employees who are dismissed while taking part have no right to claim unfair dismissal even if other employees who also took part were not dismissed; selective dismissals can therefore occur with impunity. Ironically action is not unofficial where no employee who takes part is a member of a trade union and to avoid the classification of action as unofficial by the mass resignations of members from their trade unions, it is provided that if an employee is a member of a trade union when the action commences he or she is treated as a member throughout the action.

UNION MEMBERSHIP AND ACTIVITIES

4–37 Individual employees receive certain rights to allow them to join and to participate in the activities of an Independent Trade Union (ITU). Thus TULR(C)A (ss.152, 153) provides it is unfair to dismiss (or select for redundancy) an employee who:

(a) is or proposes to become a member of an ITU;
(b) has taken part or proposes to take part in the activities of an ITU or made use of trade union services at an appropriate time;
(c) is not a member of any trade union or of a particular trade union;
(d) has refused to become or remain a union member; or
(e) failed to accept an inducement not to do any of the above.

It is also unfair to dismiss an employee who refuses to pay a sum or suffer deduction from wages in lieu of membership. In the case of the dismissal of a non-union member, a third party (for example, the trade union itself) may be joined as a respondent in the proceedings as well as the employer.

"Appropriate time" means times which are outside the employee's working hours or within his or her working hours with the employer's consent. Consent can be given by implication as well as expressly. It is for the employment tribunal to find as a fact whether or not the reason or principal reason for dismissal related to the applicant's trade union membership. This should be decided not only by reference to whether the employee had simply joined a union but also by reference to whether the introduction of union representation into the employment relationship had led the employer to dismiss the employee.

Speciality Care plc v Pachela

[1996] I.R.L.R. 248, EAT

The applicants who were employed as carers in a nursing home complained that they were dismissed for a reason related to trade union membership or activities. The applicants joined an Independent Trade Union after the employers decided to alter their shift patterns. However, the applicants refused to work the new shifts and were subsequently dismissed.

The employment tribunal found that, although their refusal to work their reassigned duties might have been one factor behind the decision to dismiss the applicants, the principal reason was that they had joined the union and had sought to use the union as the means of making their protest. The tribunal held that the principal reason for their dismissal was joining the union and the dismissals were automatically unfair by reason of s.152 of TULR(C)A.

The employers appealed to the EAT which allowed the appeal on the ground that the Tribunal had failed to set out its reasoning sufficiently. The case was remitted to another Tribunal and it was necessary for the EAT to give guidance to the new Tribunal on s.152.

The EAT noted that the employment tribunal had decided the case after the Court of Appeal's decision in *Associated Newspapers Ltd v Wilson* [1994] I.C.R. 97 but before that of the House of Lords ([1995] 2 A.C. 454). In the Court of Appeal, Dillon L.J. had stated that the decision in *Discount Tobacco and Confectionery Ltd v Armitage* [1995] I.C.R. 431 meant that it was open to an employment tribunal to hold that an employee had been dismissed for being a member of a union, if he had been dismissed for invoking the assistance of the union in relation to his employment.

Accordingly, it would be for an employment tribunal to find as a fact whether or not the reason or principal reason for dismissal related to the applicant's trade union membership, not only by reference to whether he had simply joined a union, but also by reference to whether the introduction of union representation into the employment relationship had led the employer to dismiss the employee. Tribunals should answer that question robustly, based on their findings as to what had really caused the dismissal.

The word "activities" is not defined but this is deliberate since the word covers a wide variety of possibilities dependent upon the circumstances of the case. It certainly includes forming a union branch or complaining about safety representation. However, not every act of a union member involves the activities of a trade union, so that if the employee is pursuing a personal matter or acts in a malicious or unwarranted way, or it is the employer's reaction to trade union activity in general as opposed to the individual's union activities, these are not the activities of the union (*Lyon v St James Press Ltd* [1976] I.R.L.R. 413). In *Therm-a-stor Ltd v Atkins* [1983] I.R.L.R. 78 employees were dismissed because of the employer's reaction to a union request for recognition, not their taking part in the activities of the union, but special provision is now made by the Employment Relations Act 1999 for dismissals in connection with union recognition and these are dealt with at para.4–39 below.

4–38 Where a dismissal is unfair by virtue of ss.152 or 153 the tribunal is not concerned with the reasonableness of the employer's action; the dismissal is declared to be automatically unfair. Where an employee alleges that the reason for the dismissal falls within ss.152 or 153, the onus of proof is on the employer to show that the reason was not a prohibited one. Further, the employee is not required to satisfy the qualifying rules (one year's continuous employment).

Where the dismissal takes the form of selection for redundancy, it is necessary that the circumstances constituting redundancy applied to one or more other employees who held similar positions and who were not dismissed and that the reason was union membership, taking part in union activities or using union services or failing to accept inducements not to do any of these or non-union membership. In such a case it is not necessary that the employer has acted deliberately or intentionally to discriminate against union members in the selection (*Dundon v GPT Ltd* [1995] I.R.L.R. 403). However, there must be evidence of disparity of treatment between employees who hold similar positions on union membership grounds.

Dundon v GPT Ltd

[1995] I.R.L.R. 403, EAT

Mr Dundon had been employed by GPT Ltd for 20 years when he was dismissed on grounds of redundancy. He was an active trade unionist and for many years had been a union representative. When he became a senior representative the employers recognised that he would need to spend more time on his union duties and he was given a less demanding job.

However, the employers considered that Mr Dundon was spending too much time on his union duties and not enough time on his work. Eventually, a "half-and-half" arrangement was agreed and set out in a letter dated January 30, 1990 but Mr Dundon still spent less than 20 per cent of his time on company work. This was made worse by the fact that when he did work, his time-keeping was poor.

The method of selection for redundancies was based on six

criteria—quality of work, quantity of work, co-operation, attendance/time-keeping, special knowledge and experience, and length of service. Those carrying out the selection were told that employees should not be penalised because of their union duties.

Mr Dundon was assessed as "very poor" under the heading "quantity of work". The manager hearing his appeal against the assessment was concerned that it might have been distorted as a result of his union activities and the assessors were instructed to be guided by the "half-and-half" arrangement but the selection of Mr Dundon for redundancy was confirmed.

When Mr Dundon complained that his selection was unfair under ss.152 and 153 of TULR(C)A, the employment tribunal rejected his claim because although "his union activities were relevant to his selection", the employers had not deliberately selected him because he was a union activist.

Mr Dundon appealed to the EAT against the finding that he had not been selected for redundancy because of his union activities, and against the level of contribution.

The EAT held the employment tribunal had erred in holding that the appellant had not been unfairly selected for redundancy by reason of his trade union activities. Although his union activities were relevant to his selection, the employers had not deliberately or maliciously selected him based on those activities.

According to the EAT "an employer does not have to be motivated by malice or a deliberate desire to be rid of a trade union activist in order to fall within the provisions now set out in ss.152(1)(b) and 153 of TULR(C)A. These sections make it automatically unfair to select an employee for redundancy by reason of his participation in union activities at an appropriate time".

> "... the tribunal's finding that the feature of the employee's working life which made the employers select him, was that he was spending far too much time on trade union duties, was the same as saying that "the reason" they selected him was because he was spending too much time on trade union duties. Had the tribunal approached the matter correctly and gone on to consider whether those activities had been carried out at an appropriate time, it would inevitably have concluded that the reason why the employee was selected for redundancy was because he had taken part in trade union activities at times at which, in accordance with consent given by the employers (albeit tacitly and reluctantly), it was permissible for him to do so."

O'dea v ISC Chemicals Ltd

[1995] I.R.L.R. 799, CA

The Court of Appeal rejected the claim by a senior trade union shop steward—employed and paid as a technical services operator, but who spent half his working time as an Isceon packaging operator and the other half on trade union activities—that he was unfairly selected for redundancy despite the fact that the other two technical services operators kept their jobs. They were not comparators because they did that job all the time and the appellant did not. Equally, he could not compare himself with the other Isceon packers since his status and conditions of work were different and it was important that the tribunal have regard to the status, nature of work and terms and conditions of employment, taken as a whole, and not only rely on the nature of the work performed.

Union Recognition Dismissals

4–39 Until the Employment Relations Act 1999 an employer could not be compelled to recognise a trade union for collective bargaining purposes. The 1999 Act has introduced such a right (see TULR(C)A Sch.A1 as amended by the Employment Relations Act 2004) by which the Central Arbitration Committee is authorised to consider applications by independent trade unions for recognition by employers for the purposes of collective bargaining and special rules, now make it unfair to dismiss employees in connection with union recognition. It is unfair to dismiss employees who seek to obtain, support or prevent union recognition or the ending of bargaining arrangements or who vote or seek to influence the way others vote in a ballot about union recognition (TULR(C)A Sch.1A para.161). It is also unfair to select employees for redundancy in a discriminatory way if the reason for their selection was one concerned with union recognition (TULR(C)A Sch.1A para.162). There is no qualifying period for such dismissals.

HEALTH AND SAFETY DISMISSALS

4–40 Although special protection was accorded to employees engaged in the offshore industries who were seen as especially vulnerable to dismissal should they complain about safety standards, employees on the mainland continued to depend on the ordinary rules of unfair dismissal law. In particular they required to have sufficient qualifying service. To remedy the situation the Trade Union Reform and Employment Rights Act 1993 introduced special protection for all workers, irrespective of their length of service, who take measures to protect their own health or safety or that of others. The present provisions are to be found in Employment Rights Act s.100 where it is declared that dismissal of an employee for any of the following reasons will be unfair:

(a) carrying out health and safety duties by an employee designated by the employer to carry out such duties (for example a safety officer);
(b) carrying out functions as health and safety representative or safety committee member;
(c) taking part in consultations with the employer as a representative of employee safety or seeking election to such a post;
(d) bringing circumstances to his employer's attention by reasonable means where there are no safety representatives or safety committee or it is not reasonably practicable to use them and the employee reasonably believes these circumstances were harmful to health or safety;
(e) leaving the place of work in circumstances of danger which the employee reasonably believed to be serious and imminent and which he or she could not reasonably be expected to avert;
(f) taking appropriate steps to protect him or herself, or others (including members of the public) from danger which he or she reasonably believed to be serious and imminent.

As regards this final protection, the appropriateness of the steps is to be judged by reference to all the circumstances including the employee's knowledge and the facilities and advice which were available and it is a defence if the employer can show that it would have been negligent for the employee to take those steps (Employment Rights Act s.100(2) and (3)). There is no qualifying period for the above protections.

Harvest Press Ltd v McCaffrey

[1999] I.R.L.R. 778

Mr McCaffrey worked with one other employee on the night shift. He made a complaint to management about this other employee, who consequently found out that it was Mr McCaffrey who had complained and became extremely abusive towards him. Following on from this, one night Mr McCaffrey walked off the job. He indicated that he would only return to work if his fellow worker were removed from the night shift. The company refused this request and argued that Mr McCaffrey had resigned when he left work in the middle of his shift. The issue for the EAT was whether the circumstances of Mr McCaffrey's case were caught by Employment Rights Act s.100(1)(d) so as to enable him to leave his place of work because of serious and imminent danger. His employers had argued that "danger" should be limited to dangers associated with the workplace itself. Mr McCaffrey's position, however, was that it covered dangers caused by the behaviour of fellow employees. The EAT held that "danger" did encompass dangers caused by co-workers and concluded that the word should be construed broadly so as to cover any danger, however originating.

ASSERTING A STATUTORY RIGHT

4–41 It is unfair to dismiss an employee if the reason was one of the following:

(1) he or she brought proceedings against the employer to enforce a statutory employment right;
(2) he or she alleged that the employer had infringed a statutory employment right (Employment Rights Act s.104).

It is not necessary to show that the employee actually had the right in question so long as the claim to the right is made in good faith and the qualifying period does not apply. This provision only applies to certain statutory rights, namely those described in Employment Rights Act s.104(4). They include:

- rights conferred by the Employment Rights Act which can be enforced by employment tribunals;
- the right conferred by Employment Rights Act s.86 (to minimum notice of termination);
- rights conferred by TULR(C)A ss.68, 86, 146, 168, 168A, 169 and 170 (i.e. deductions from pay, union activities and time off);
- rights conferred by the Working Time Regulations 1998; and
- rights conferred by the Transfer of Undertakings (Protection of Employment) Regulations 2006.

Mennell v Newell & Wright (Transport Contractors) Ltd

[1997] I.R.L.R. 519, CA

From March 1993 until November 1994 the employee was employed as a driver. In September 1994 the employer wished all drivers to sign a new contract which allowed the employer to deduct from the employee's final pay the cost of certain training they had provided.

Mr Mennell had refused to sign, although all his colleagues

had done so. He was dismissed and complained of unfair dismissal. He claimed his dismissal was for asserting a statutory right, namely protection against unlawful deductions from pay contrary to the Employment Rights Act.

The employment tribunal decided that it had no jurisdiction to hear the complaint because on the alleged facts no statutory right could come into effect until the deduction or failure to pay money had actually taken place.

The EAT had held that s.104 applied where an employee alleged in good faith that his employer had infringed a relevant right and there was no requirement that the right be actually infringed. Thus if the employer sought by threat of dismissal to impose a variation of the contract of employment to incorporate a term which negated the employee's statutory right not to suffer a reduction of wages without his consent, that was or might be an infringement of his statutory right at the time the threat was made. A worker might present a complaint that the employer had made an illegal deduction from his wages but that right only arose where the employer "has made a deduction form his wages". There was no jurisdiction to complain about a threatened deduction from wages, there had to be an actual deduction.

The Court of Appeal stated that the critical question raised by the employee's reliance on s.104 was "what was the reason for his dismissal by the employer?" The Court of Appeal held that it was sufficient if the employee had alleged that his employer had infringed his statutory right and that the making of that allegation was the reason for his dismissal. However, the employee could not succeed in establishing that such an allegation was the reason for his dismissal, because he was unable to identify when, where, to whom or in what terms he had alleged that the employer had infringed his relevant statutory rights. Section 104 is not confined to cases where the relevant statutory right had been infringed, but included cases where the employee alleged that the reason for dismissal was that he had alleged that his employer had infringed his statutory right. Provided it was made in good faith such an allegation need not be correct either as to the entitlement to the right or to its infringement. However, on the facts in the instant case the employee had been unable to establish that he had made any such allegation.

PREGNANCY AND FAMILY LEAVE

By the Employment Rights Act s.99 (which is not dependent on a **4–42**
period of continuous employment) a dismissal is unfair if the reason or the principal reason for it is prescribed by relevant regulations

(see below) and relates to pregnancy, childbirth or maternity or taking any of the family leave entitlements.

Regulation 20 of the Maternity and Parental Leave etc. Regulations 1999 (SI 1999/3312) provides that an employee who is dismissed (or selected for redundancy) is unfairly dismissed if: (a) the principal reason for the dismissal (or selection for redundancy) is one of those specified in reg.20(3); or (b) the principal reason for the dismissal is that the employee is redundant and alternative employment has not been offered in accordance with reg.10 of the 1999 Regulations.

Regulation 20(3) specifies the following as reasons which make the dismissal (or selection for redundancy) automatically unfair:

(a) the pregnancy of the employee;
(b) the employee has given birth to a child and dismissal ends her maternity leave;
(c) because of a legal requirement or a recommendation under a Health and Safety Code of Practice, the employee was suspended from work on the ground that she was pregnant, had recently given birth or was breast-feeding;
(d) she took, sought to take or availed herself of the benefits of, ordinary maternity leave;
(e) she took or sought to take—
    (i) additional maternity leave;
    (ii) parental leave;
    (iii) time off under s.57A of the Employment Rights Act 1996 (family emergencies);
    (iv) paternity leave;
    (v) adoption leave;
(f) she declined to sign a workforce agreement relating to maternity, parental or family emergencies;
(g) performed (or proposed to perform) any functions or activities as a representative or candidate in relation to a workforce agreement;
(h) she failed to return after maternity leave or additional adoption leave when proper notice had not been given.

WHISTLE-BLOWING

4–43 The Public Interest Disclosure Act 1998 conferred protection against dismissal on all employees irrespective of length of employment or age by inserting a new Pt IVA and s.103A into the Employment Rights Act 1996. The effect of these new provisions is to make it unfair to dismiss an employee who makes a protected or qualifying disclosure which means:

"any disclosure of information which in the reasonable belief of the person making the disclosure, tends to show one or more of the following:

- a criminal offence has been committed;
- someone is failing to comply with a legal obligation;
- a miscarriage of justice has occurred or may occur;
- the health and safety of any individual is likely to be endangered;
- the environment is likely to be damaged; or
- information regarding any of the above is likely to be deliberately concealed."

However, this is not a "whistle-blowers' charter" in that dismissal is unfair only where the disclosure is made to certain people, i.e. an employer, a legal adviser, a Minister of the Crown who has appointed an employer, or a person designated by the Secretary of State (see the Public Interest (Prescribed Persons) Order 1999 (SI 1999/1549) to whom the disclosure may be made (Employment Rights Act ss.43C–43F).

There will, however, be circumstances in which disclosure to the employer cannot be expected, for example where a worker may fear that he or she will be subjected to a detriment by the employer or where the disclosure has already been made to the employer; also where the conduct or failure which is to be disclosed is of an exceptionally serious nature it may be a qualifying disclosure depending on the person to whom it was made, Employment Rights Act ss.43G, 43H. In all cases, however, the disclosure must be made in good faith. Where the main reason for the disclosure was personal antagonism, the Court of Appeal has held that there was no qualifying disclosure (*Street v Derbyshire Unemployed Workers Centre* [2004] I.R.L.R. 687). No continuous employment is required and the normal limit for unfair dismissal compensation does not apply.

In *Stephens v Hall* (unreported) the Tribunal held that although there was a qualifying disclosure, the employee's constructive dismissal was not for making the disclosure but because the other employees refused to work with her because she took frequent cigarette breaks leaving others to do her work. *Bladon v ALM Medical Services Ltd* [2002] I.C.R. 1444, CA, deals with an employee who does not make the protected disclosure to his employer but to a body, in this case the Social Services Inspectorate, which was not a prescribed body under the Regulations. The Court held that it was reasonable to disclose to the Social Services Inspectorate as it was an appropriate investigatory body, the information (standard of patient care) was serious and the employers did not have a disclosure policy. In *Fernandes v Netcom Consultants (U.K.) Ltd* (Case No.648, unreported) an accountant (Fernandes) employed by Netcom faxed a report (to an accountant in the parent company) that he (Fernandes) believed a Director of the company was failing to provide receipts for personal expenditure. Fernandes was advised that no action would be taken and to destroy the fax. Fernandes persisted in drawing the matter to the attention of senior employees including the company chairman who told him he was a bad accountant and had lost the respect of everyone. The Tribunal held that Fernandes was dismissed for making a qualifying disclosure and was awarded £293,441 in compensation. In a narrow interpretation of the provision, in *Kraus v Penna Plc* [2004] I.R.L.R. 260, the EAT upheld the tribunal's decision that informing a client that their actions could be in breach of employment legislation was not a qualifying disclosure as it had not been established that the employer was under any legal obligation and it was not sufficient that the claimant reasonably believed that it was.

JURY SERVICE

4–44 It will be automatically unfair to dismiss someone for being called for jury service or for being absent for work as a result. However, there is an exception where the employee's absence will cause substantial injury to the employer, this has been brought to the attention of the employee and the employee has not applied to be excused from service or to have the service deferred (Employment Rights Act s.98B).

OTHER SPECIAL CASES

4–45 It will also be automatically unfair to dismiss for any of the following reasons:

- in connection with an employees rights under the Working Time Regulations, the National Minimum Wage Act or in relation to tax credits;
- for being an employee representative, a trustee of an occupational pension scheme or for accompanying a fellow worker to a disciplinary or grievance hearing;
- for exercising rights to request flexible working or to be accompanied to disciplinary or grievance hearings;
- for refusing to work on a Sunday when entitled to do so (this applies to most workers in shops and betting shops);
- for exercising rights as a part-time or fixed term worker;
- because of a spent conviction.

There is no qualifying period in any of these cases.

Remedies for Unfair Dismissal

The remedies for unfair dismissals are themselves a complicated area and in this guide it is appropriate to set out only the essential principles. The Employment Rights Act (ss.111–132) creates a framework of remedies for unfair dismissal. The primary remedy is supposed to be re-employment (either reinstatement or re-engagement) but this has not been the case in practice. There is also a right to compensation where either the Tribunal refuses to order re-employment or the employee does not seek this remedy. Compensation is made up of two elements—the basic award and the compensatory award. There is also a right to an additional award where the tribunal has ordered re-employment and this has not been complied with by the employer. **4–46**

Reinstatement and re-engagement

An order of reinstatement is an order from the tribunal requiring the employer to treat the complainant in all respects as if he or she had not been dismissed (Employment Rights Act s.114(1)). To take the employee back on less favourable terms does not constitute reinstatement. The order must specify the following: **4–47**

(a) the amount payable by the employer for benefits not received by the claimant, including arrears of pay;
(b) any rights and privileges, including seniority and pension rights which must be restored; and
(c) the date for compliance with the order.

A tribunal can make an order of re-engagement on such terms as it may decide that the complainant be engaged by the employer, or by a successor employer, or by an associated employer, in employment comparable to that from which he or she was dismissed or other suitable employment (see Employment Rights Act s.115(1)). The order must specify the terms on which re-engagement is to take place, including the following:

(a) the identity of the employer;
(b) the nature of the employment;
(c) remuneration;
(d) amount payable by the employer for benefits which the employee might reasonably have been expected to receive, including arrears of pay;
(e) rights and privileges, including seniority and pension rights, which must be restored; and
(f) date for compliance with the order.

There is a clear order of priorities as regards re-employment. First, the tribunal must consider reinstatement, and only if this is not ordered should it consider re-engagement and on what terms. In conducting this exercise the tribunal must consider the following:

(a) the wishes of the claimant;
(b) whether it is practicable for the employer to comply; and
(c) where the claimant caused or contributed to the dismissal, whether it would be just to make the order (see Employment Rights Act s.116(1)).

It is for the employer to show that re-employment is not practicable. The employer has two opportunities to show this. First, when the tribunal is contemplating making the order; and secondly, when the order has been made and not complied with and additional compensation becomes payable. At this latter stage the additional award can be avoided if the employer can satisfy the tribunal that it was not practicable to comply with the order (Employment Rights Act s.117(4)(a)). There may be circumstances where personal relationships can be an issue as far as practicability is concerned (*Enessy Co SA v Minoprio* [1978] I.R.L.R. 489) and there are special rules which apply where the employer has hired a permanent replacement.

Where the employer fails to comply with the order, the tribunal can make an additional award (subject to the practicability issue again). The additional award will be between 26 and 52 weeks' pay (currently £310). Tribunals can exceed the statutory maximum of the compensatory and additional awards, to ensure that the aggregate of the compensation awarded reflects fully the amount specified in the re-engagement order. This is so that a complainant is compensated fully where an order for re-employment has been made but not complied with (Employment Rights Act s.117(2)).

Compensation

4–48 A complainant's compensation is made up of two elements—a basic award and a compensatory award.

The basic award

4–49 The basic award is calculated by reference to the period, ending with the effective date of termination (EDT) during which the employee has been continuously employed, by starting at the end of that period and reckoning backwards the number of years of employment and allowing:

(a) one and a half weeks' pay for each year in which the employee is over 41;
(b) one week's pay for each year in which the employee was between 22 and 41; and
(c) half a week's pay for each year of employment under 22 (Employment Rights Act s.119(2)).

The maximum number of years that can be taken into account is 20 and the maximum amount of a week's pay is currently £310.The amount of the award can be reduced for the following reasons:

(a) where the employee has received a redundancy payment, or an ex-gratia payment which is intended to satisfy his or her legal rights (Employment Rights Act s.122(4));
(b) on grounds of justice and equity where claimant has unreasonably refused an offer of re-instatement (Employment Rights Act s.122(1)); or
(c) where it would be just and equitable because of the claimant's conduct prior to dismissal where (Employment Rights Act s.122 (2)).

In cases of dismissal for union membership or activities, or for carrying out duties of: (1) a health and safety representative; (2) a representative in connection with the Working Time Regulations collective; (3) an employee representative in connection with consultation on collective redundancies or TUPE; or (4) a trustee of an occupational pension scheme, there is a minimum basic award of £4,000 (Employment Rights Act s.120(1)). Where an employee is dismissed and the statutory dismissal procedures are not followed, there is a minimum basic award of four week's pay unless this would cause injustice to the employer.

Compensatory award

Section 123(1) of the Employment Rights Act declares that the **4–50**
amount of the compensatory award will be such amount as the tribunal considers just and equitable in all the circumstances having regard to the loss sustained by the complainant in consequence of the dismissal, insofar as that action is attributable to action taken by the employer. The award is subject to a statutory maximum that is currently £60,600, although the maximum does not apply to health and safety dismissals or for dismissals associated with a protected disclosure. The purpose of this part of the award is to compensate for loss. In particular, it can compensate:

(a) any expenses reasonably incurred by the complainant in consequence of the dismissal; and
(b) loss of any benefit which the complainant might reasonably have been expected to have had but for the dismissal (Employment Rights Act s.123(2)).

Complainants have a duty to mitigate their losses and an award will be reduced if they have failed to do so (Employment Rights Act s.123(4)). The compensatory award can also be reduced on a just and equitable basis where the tribunal finds that the dismissal was to any extent caused or contributed to by the action of the complainant (Employment Rights Act s.123(6)). Once again the award could be reduced substantially in procedural unfairness cases so long as the flaws are genuinely procedural and not substantive (*King v Eaton Ltd (No.2)* [1998] I.R.L.R. 686). However, as tribunals are no longer required to find a dismissal unfair on procedural grounds, where they find that the dismissal would have occurred even if proper procedure had occurred, this deduction should not exceed 50 per cent. If the chance of the dismissal occurring anyway exceeds 50 per cent then the tribunal should find that the dismissal was fair (or unfair on substantive rather than procedural grounds). A tribunal is directed to ignore any pressure exercised on the employer through a real or threatened strike or other industrial action when calculating the award (Employment Rights Act s.123(5)). If a relevant statutory procedure was not followed and the non-completion was wholly or mainly attributable to the failure by the employer to comply with the requirements of the procedures, the tribunal must increase the compensatory award by at least 10 per cent and up to 50 per cent. If the failure to complete the relevant statutory procedure was wholly or mainly due to the failure by the claimant to comply with its requirements, or to exercise a right of appeal under the procedure, the award must be reduced by between 10 per cent and 50 per cent. In either case, the adjustment need not be made if it would not be just and equitable. These adjustments should be made before any reductions for contributory conduct by the employee.

The principles for calculation of the compensatory award were first discussed in *Norton Tool Co Ltd v Tewson* [1972] I.C.R. 501 where the most important heads of loss were stated to be as follows:

(a) *Immediate Loss of Wages*: This is compensation for actual loss of wages from the date of dismissal to the date of the hearing. It can include the loss of other benefits such as the loss of a company car or cheap loan facilities.
(b) *Future Loss*: Where the complainant is still out of work at the date of the hearing the tribunal can make an award to cover future loss of wages. The tribunal may be required to speculate on such factors as the likely period of continued unemployment and the rate of pay when employment is obtained. In considering these questions the tribunal should rely on its collective knowledge of industrial relations in the area (*Bateman v British Leyland (UK) Ltd* [1974] I.R.L.R. 104).
(c) *Loss of Pension Rights*: The sum here might be substantial, particularly where the complainant contributed to an occupational pension scheme and remains unemployed.
(d) *Loss Arising from the Manner of the Dismissal*: An employee has no right to compensation for the distress caused by dismissal or for injury to feelings. However, occasionally, employees may be entitled to compensation where there is cogent evidence that the manner of dismissal may have caused financial loss (does it become more difficult to find other work?).
(e) *Loss of Statutory Protection*: There may be occasions where the loss of service-related rights, such as the right to

long notice, can be compensated under this head. It is normally a nominal sum of around £250.

INTERIM RELIEF

In certain cases (trade union-related dismissals for making a protected disclosure dismissals, health and safety and working time cases, dismissals for making a protected disclosure and dismissals of employee representatives and trustees of occupational pension schemes) employees can apply to an employment tribunal for interim relief. This is an order that the employee's contract, if terminated, will continue in force as if it had not been terminated and, if not terminated, that it will continue in force, in either case until the complaint is settled or determined by the tribunal. The continuation covers pay and other benefits such as pensions and seniority rights and for determining the period of continuous employment. **4–51**

SAMPLE QUESTIONS

1. Jim is an accountant employed by Lothian Magnates Ltd. He has been employed in that capacity for several years but recently his appraisals have not been good. After the accounts of the company were audited Jim was asked to meet his boss to "discuss his performance". Jim went along to the meeting with his boss to be told that "after examining your performance over the last year, I have come to the conclusion that you are incapable of carrying out your responsibilities". Jim is taken aback and tries to offer as an explanation the fact that his health has been poor and that his workload has been increasing. However, his boss is not interested and merely recites to Jim a catalogue of accounting errors which he says are Jim's responsibility. Without even being given a chance of looking at the report, to which Jim's boss is referring, Jim is told that he is dismissed and that he should leave the company's premises immediately. Jim asks if he can appeal against the dismissal but his boss tells him "the case against you is so cleat there is no point in you appealing".

You bump into Jim in the pub later the same day when he is drowning his sorrows. He asks you if he might have any claim for unfair dismissal and he also tells you that he thinks the reason he has been dismissed is because he had complained that his employer was not observing health and safety laws.

On your advice Jim presents a complaint of unfair dismissal and shortly thereafter he receives a letter from Lothian Magnates saying that since his employment came to an end they have discovered that he appears to have been involved in embezzling several thousand pounds of their money.

In the context of the law of unfair dismissal what issues foes the above raise?

2. To be successful in a complaint of unfair dismissal an employee must prove he or she has been dismissed and the employer must show that the reason for the dismissal was one recognised by law. In what circumstances is an employee deemed to be dismissed and what reasons are recognised by law as the basis of a fair dismissal?

3. In what circumstances is an employee protected against unfair dismissal where he or she has not been employed for a year?

4. On January 5, 2007, Mary enters into a contract to work on a research project for Riccarton University. The contract is to last for the duration of the project. It contains the following clause: "I agree that on the expiry of this contract in the event of it not being renewed I will not be entitled to complain of unfair dismissal".

The research project is completed in January 2008 and Mary is not offered another contract and asks you if she can claim unfair dismissal.

How would you advise Mary?

5. What remedies are available to an employee who has been found to be unfairly dismissed?

6. Bob works for a company which makes sportswear and employs its own drivers to deliver it goods to shops. In order to make savings it decides to sell its sportswear by mail order only and it disposes of its fleet of vehicles and dismisses the drivers. Although Bob and the other drivers have heard rumours for some time, that are surprised to be called in to the manager's office on Friday morning to be told that their employment is to be terminated at the end of the working day. All the drivers are dismissed at the same time. None of them is given any opportunity of suggesting ways of avoiding their dismissal and although the company Procedural Rules provide that any employee dismissed is entitled to appeal to the company board of Directors, Bob who used to work in the despatch section of the company where some new employees have been recruited to deal with the increase in the mail order business, is advised that any appeal will be pointless.
Assuming Bob was unfairly dismissed, that he had 10 years' continuous employment and earned £320.00 gross per week with a take home pay of £280.00 per week, how might a tribunal calculate his compensation?

SUGGESTED ANSWERS FOR CHAPTER FOUR

1. The first issue to be addressed in this scenario is whether the employers have complied with the statutory pre-dismissal procedures set out in the Employment Act 2002 (Dispute Resolution) Regulations 2004 which came into force on October 1, 2004. With a few exceptions, these procedures must be followed whenever an employer wishes to dismiss an employee (for any reason (with the exception of constructive dismissal) or take other disciplinary conduct on grounds of capability or conduct). There is a standard three step procedure which applies unless the employee is being dismissed for gross misconduct and in all the circumstances it would be reasonable for the employer to use a modified two step procedure. In Jim's case, the standard procedure would be the appropriate one. The employer should have set out in writing the circumstances that have led him to consider dismissal, which would be the alleged accounting errors. Jim should have been invited to a meeting to discuss the matter. This meeting should not take place until the employee has been informed of the basis of the employer's allegations and been given reasonable time to consider his response. After the meeting, the employer should notify Jim of his decisions and Jim should be given an opportunity to appeal. As the employer has not complied with this procedure, the dismissal is automatically unfair, regardless of the employer's grounds for dismissal, and further, any compensatory award will be increased by between 10 and 50 per cent as a result.

Even if the employer had complied with these minimum provisions, there might still be issues of procedural unfairness. For example the *employee might feel that the person who held the appeal was already biased against him for personal reasons or witnesses might be asked to attend a disciplinary hearing without the employee having a chance to cross-examine them. In these circumstances the dismissal might be unfair in terms of s.98(4) of the Employment Rights Act which requires that the fairness of the dismissal is to be judged having regard to whether, in the circumstances, the employer acted reasonably or unreasonably in treating the reason as a sufficient reason for dismissing the employee and that question shall be determined in accordance with equity and the substantial merits of the case. Also, in line with the decisions in* Iceland Frozen Foods Ltd v Jones *[1982] I.R.L.R. 439 and* British Home Stores v Burchell *[1980] I.C.R. 303, EAT, before dismissing an employee, an employer is expected to carry out such an investigation as is reasonable.*

However, an important amendment in s.98A(2) provides that, where the minimum procedures have been complied with, other procedural unfairness may be disregarded if the employer can show that a dismissal would have resulted even if a fair procedure had been followed.

2. To be successful in a complaint of unfair dismissal, an employee must prove that he has been dismissed, however, he or she is assisted by the provisions of the Employment Rights Act s.95 which provides that in certain circumstances an employee is deemed to be dismissed. These are where the employer terminates the contract under which he or she is employed either with, or without, notice. However, an employer who utters words of dismissal on termination in the heat of the moment (e.g. in the course of a work place argument) is able to withdraw such words soon after uttering them and if he or she does so, and the employee persists in leaving his or her employment, a Tribunal may find that the employee has terminated the employment, not the employer. The second circumstance is where the employee is employed under a contract for a limited term which expires and is not renewed. This is also deemed to be a dismissal. The final form of dismissal is where the employee terminates the contract with or without notice in circumstances in which he or she is entitled to terminate it without notice by reason of the employer's conduct. This is referred to as a constructive dismissal. However, before an employee can claim to have been constructively dismissed, two things must occur. First of all, the employer must be in material breach of the contract and the second is that the employee leaves as a result of that breach. The failure to permit an employee to return to work after maternity leave is also regarded as a dismissal and where the employer has given notice of termination, and the employee leaves before the expiry of that notice, the employee is still deemed to be dismissed. This last rule permits employees who are under notice of dismissal to leave before the notice expires where, for example, they have found other employment which is available only immediately.

It follows, therefore, that genuine consensual termination of the contract is not a dismissal, nor is a resignation by an employee a dismissal. However, where an employee resigns, if he or she has resigned in the heat of the moment or if there are circumstances which suggest to the employer that his or her intention to resign is not genuine, an employer may require to permit an employee to withdraw a resignation and a failure to do so by an employer can result in the Tribunal concluding that it was the employer who terminated the employment.

Similarly, where a contract is brought to an end by operation of law, for example by the contract becoming illegal of performance or impossible of further performance, there is no dismissal. Examples include where an employee who is required to have a particular qualification loses that qualification and it is illegal to continue his or her employment, or where an employee becomes so seriously ill or incapacitated, that further performance of his or her contract becomes impossible. An example might be where a machine operator loses the power of a hand and is therefore unable to continue to perform his or her contract. Where an employee is sent to prison for a considerable period of time, that may also frustrate his contract but he or she will not be regarded as dismissed, even though his or her own misconduct led to the period of imprisonment. The law regards the decision of the Judge as the cause of the employee being unable to perform his or her contract and as such, the contract is regarded as being frustrated.

The Employment Rights Act recognises certain reasons as to why a dismissal may have been fair. They are set out in s.98 of the Employment Rights Act and include reasons which relate to the capability or qualifications of the employee and to the conduct of the employee. Other reasons are that the employee was redundant or that it would be contrary to the law to continue to employ him or her. Finally, if the reason is not any of these specific reasons, but is of such a kind as to justify the dismissal of the employee holding the position he or she held, the reason is a reason for which the dismissal may be fair.

It is important to note that where the reason relates to capability or qualifications of the employee, they have to be regarded in the context of the kind of work the employee was employed to do. This frequently requires an examination of the contract of employment to find out precisely what duties the employee was employed to do. If an employee who was not employed to do driving work was dismissed because he no longer held a driving licence, the reason for the dismissal would not relate to his capability or qualifications. Where the reason relates to the conduct of the employee, it will only satisfy the legal test if the conduct of the employee is judged in the context of his or her employment but this may mean that the conduct of an employee committed away from work is still relevant. For example, an employee who was engaged in a position requiring integrity and honesty and who, away from work, committed a crime of dishonesty could be dismissed for a reason related to his or her conduct.

3. The general rule is, in order to be able to complain of unfair dismissal, employees must have one year's continuity of employment by the date of the termination of their employment, known as "the effective date of termination". Thus, if an employee is dismissed for misconduct, incapability, redundancy, breach of statute, or for some other substantial reason, he or she cannot complain of unfair dismissal if he or she has less than one year's employment by the effective date of termination.

However, certain dismissal rights are regarded as being so important that they are not dependent upon any period of continuous employment. If an employee is dismissed for taking part in the activities of an independent trade union at an appropriate time, namely outside his or her working hours or inside working hours but with his or her employer's consent, or if he or she is dismissed for being a member of an independent trade union, or if is dismissed for not being a member of any trade union, his or her dismissal is automatically unfair irrespective of the continuity of employment (Trade Union and Labour Relations (Consolidation) Act 1992 s.152). Similarly, an employee who is dismissed for a reason set out in s.100 of the Employment Rights Act (health and safety cases) does not require any continuity of employment before being able to complain of unfair dismissal.

No continuity of employment is required before an employee can complain of unfair dismissal for having made a qualifying disclosure under s.103A of the Employment Rights Act, or where an employee has asserted a statutory right and the reason for the dismissal is covered by s.104 of the Employment Rights Act. A full list of the reasons where continuity of employment is not required is set out in this chapter. In cases where the employee does not require to have any continuity of employment prior to claiming unfair dismissal, the usual rule is that dismissal is automatically unfair and does not depend upon whether the employer acted reasonably or not.

4. Prior to the changes made by the Employment Act 2002, the definition of "dismissal" for the purposes of unfair dismissal included the non-renewal of a "fixed-term contract". This included any contract with a fixed end-date (whether or not it could be terminated earlier by notice) but did not include a contact like Mary's which has no specific end-date but came to an end on the completion of a task or the occurrence or non-occurrence of an event (such as renewal of funding). Therefore, Mary will be unable to claim unfair dismissal as, under the provisions operating at the time, she had not been "dismissed". However the Employment Act amended s.95 of the Employment Rights Act which now provides that dismissal includes the non-renewal of a "limited-term" contract and a "limited-term contract" includes contracts which come to an end on the completion of a task or the occurrence or non-occurrence of a specific event. So if Mary's contract had come to an end on the later date, she would have been "dismissed" and able to claim unfair dismissal. Note that the statutory dismissal procedures apply to the non-renewal of limited term contracts and failure to follow the applicable procedure will mean that the dismissal will be automatically unfair.

5. The normal remedies for unfair dismissal are reinstatement, re-engagement, and compensation. Only where the dismissal is alleged to have been for certain reasons (e.g. trade union membership to activities or for having made a qualifying disclosure) is it possible to have the remedy of Interim Relief which requires that the employment contract is continued until the complaint is heard by the employment tribunal. The principal effect of this is that the employee is entitled to be paid between the date of dismissal and the time the case is heard by the Tribunal.

While an employee is asked to express his/her preference regarding which remedy he or she wishes, the employment tribunal will only grant the remedies of re-instatement and re-engagement where it is practicable for the employee to be re-instated or re-engaged. In many cases, because of the breakdown in the relationship caused by the dismissal, a successful employee will not wish to be re-instated or re-engaged. Ultimately however, it is a matter for the Tribunal to exercise its discretion in determining whether or not it would be reasonably practical to re-instate or re-engage the employee.

Where an employee has indicated in his/her application to the Tribunal that he/she wishes to be re-instated or re-engaged, the employer who seeks to challenge the practicability of such an order may be required to produce evidence to the Tribunal and in the event the employer requires an adjournment, the Tribunal may award expenses against the employer.

In the event that a Tribunal orders re-instatement or re-engagement, an employer is free to ignore the order, but must however accept that the Tribunal may increase the compensation which it then awards to take into account the fact that the employer has either not complied entirely or at all with its order for re-instatement or re-engagement. Re-instatement means that the employee is put back into the position he/she had lost as if he/she had not been dismissed; re-engagement means that the employee is taken back on not less favourable terms than those that operated before his/her dismissal but perhaps in a different department or place of employment. Where there has a been a breakdown in the relationship between the dismissed employee and other staff it may not be practicable to re-instate him/her but it may be practicable for him/her to be re-engaged.

The most common remedy for an employee who has been unfairly dismissed is to receive an award of compensation. The award of compensation is made up of two parts. The basic award which is calculated having regard to the employee's earnings subject to a weekly limit, his/her age and the length of his continuity of employment, subject to a maximum number of years (20). The basic award is calculated in almost exactly the same way as a redundancy payment is calculated. The basic award may be reduced for several reasons, such as where the employee has received a redundancy payment or refused and offer of reinstatement and, importantly, because of the conduct of he employee. It cannot be reduced however because of a failure to mitigate loss. In some circumstances a minimum basic award is specified by statutory provision. For example where there has been a failure to comply with a statutory dismissal procedure there is a minimum basic payable of four week's pay.

The other part of the compensation award is the compensatory award and this seeks to compensate the employee for the losses he/she has sustained as a result of being dismissed. It would include awarding him/her earnings that he/she has lost between the dismissal and the date of finding new employment and the loss of any other benefits he/she enjoyed under his/her contract from which he/she has been dismissed. A Tribunal is entitled to reduce the amount of the compensatory award as a result of (1) any contributory fault on the part of an employee; (2) failure by the employee to mitigate his loss; or (3) where the tribunal otherwise considers it to be just and equitable to reduce the award. This latter might include a situation where conduct later comes to light which would have justified the dismissal had the employer known about it at the time or where these was procedural unfairness but the tribunal considers that the dismissal would have happened even if a fair procedure had been followed. Any redundancy or other payments which have not already been deducted from the basic award are deducted from the compensatory award. Where either party is to blame for the non-completion of the statutory minimum procedures, the compensatory award must be reduced or increased as appropriate by between 10 and 50 per cent unless this would be unjust to the affected party. Finally, the compensatory award is subject to a statutory maximum, except where the dismissal is for certain health and safety reasons or for making a protected disclosure.

6. The Tribunal would make an award of compensation to Bob taking into account his age, length of service, and his weekly wage. In order to calculate the basic award, however, only £310.00 of gross weekly wage can be taken into account. This is as a result of a statutory limitation.

Accordingly, although Bob actually earns £320.00 per week, the law only permits £310.00 to be taken into account in calculating his basic award. Bearing in mind Bob's age and length of employment, his basic award would be 10 x £310.00 x 1.5. The multiplier in Bob's case is 1.5, as all of his years of employment occur after he has reached the age of 41. In accordance with s.119(2)(a), he is entitled to one and a half week's pay for each year of employment. The amount of Bob's basic award therefore would be £4,650.

When calculating Bob's compensatory award, the Tribunal will take into account his actual loss which will be based on his take-home pay. Clearly an employee who would normally pay income tax and national insurance will lose only the net or take-home pay. Accordingly, the Tribunal will take £280.00 per week as the basic figure. It will then consider how long Bob has been out of work (past losses) and it will seek to estimate how long he will remain out of work after the date of the employment tribunal hearing (future losses). It will take into account any evidence placed before it with regard to the nature of the work and the state of the economy in the locality where Bob lives; the employment tribunal is able to rely upon its own knowledge as well as considering evidence placed before it. If we assume that ten weeks had elapsed since Bob's dismissal and the date of the employment tribunal hearing, the Tribunal will award £2,800 in respect of those weeks and if it estimates taking into account any evidence placed before it, that Bob is likely to remain out of work for a further ten weeks and the efforts he has made to find new work, it will award £2,800 for those ten weeks making a total compensatory award of £5,600. An employee who is dismissed is require to take all reasonable steps to minimise the loss by, for example, attempting to find new work and an employee who does not make such reasonable efforts will have the compensatory award reduced by such percentage as the tribunal deems fair and appropriate. At the tribunal hearing an employee would be expected to show how he/she had attempted to reduce his losses by producing letters of application for new work or other evidence of his/her attempts to find new work.

Clearly the employer has not complied with the statutory DDP and therefore we can assume that the dismissal was automatically unfair. However, prior to making the required adjustment to reflect this failure, the Tribunal is also required to take into account, under the law as declared in Polkey v A E Dayton Services Ltd *[1987] I.R.L.R. 503, the effect of adopting a fair procedure. In this case, we know that Bob was not given any opportunity of suggesting ways of avoiding his dismissal and that he was advised that any appeal to the Board of Directors would be pointless. In view of the employer's decision to dispense with all of its vehicles and its drivers, the employer might be able to argue that even if it had adopted a wholly fair procedure by inviting Bob and his fellow employees to make suggestions as to how their redundancy might be avoided, it would have been of no effect because their dismissal was inevitable. A Tribunal could conclude that if a dismissal was inevitable, even after a wholly fair procedure that no compensation should be awarded. It is possible for an employment tribunal to make a 100 per cent reduction in the compensatory award if it concludes that even in the event of a wholly fair procedure being adopted, the outcome would have been no different. In this case, however, had Bob been invited to express his views about avoiding dismissal and they had been fairly considered by his employers in light of the fact that he had previously worked in the dispatch section which has just recruited employees to deal with a mail order business, it is arguable that a Tribunal could have been persuaded that a fair procedure would have resulted in a different outcome, namely that Bob would have been given employment in the dispatch section, thereby avoiding his redundancy completely. It would be for Bob to argue therefore that if a fair procedure had been adopted, including but not limited to the statutory DDP, there was a considerable chance that he would not have been dismissed. The employment tribunal is required to weigh up such a chance or probability and express it in percentage terms. In this case, in view of the fact that Bob had previously worked in the dispatch section, a Tribunal could well take the view that there was a very high chance that his redundancy would be avoided, had a fair procedure been adopted, and to reduce his compensation by only a small percentage, say 10 per cent or 20 per cent, or not at all. There is nothing in the facts to suggest that Bob might have contributed to his own dismissal so there would be no reduction in compensation for that reason. Had the amounts been larger the amount would then be subject to the statutory maximum. Finally, because the employer had not complied with the statutory procedure there will require to be an adjustment upwards of between 10 and 50 per cent unless there are "exceptional" circumstances which do not appear to exist here.*

CHAPTER FIVE

REDUNDANCY PAYMENTS AND TRANSFERS OF UNDERTAKINGS

INTRODUCTION

The roots of the legal provisions which require that employees who are dismissed on the grounds of redundancy are found in the economic circumstances that prevailed in the 1950s when British industry was required to modernise. The legislation was part of the government's overall manpower planning policy aimed at inducing employees to accept the results of economic and technological change. 5–1

> "By the early sixties there was growing awareness that the modernisation of manpower constitute a major barrier to substantial long term economic expansion. [The Redundancy Payments] Act was one of several measures intended to facilitate modernisation and change in industry. It was part of an overall manpower policy aimed at securing a greater acceptance by workers of the need for economic and technological change and at mitigating the social and economic consequences of such changes for those workers involved. Thus although certain features of the policy were designed to effect greater change in the distribution and utilisation of manpower at the same time it was intended that future changes in this sphere would not bring serious economic and social hardship to those individuals affected." *The Effects of the Redundancy Payments Act*, Parker *et al* (1971)

The system for compensating employees for loss of employment when dismissed on account of redundancy was first introduced by the Redundancy Payments Act 1965 which used the concept of continuous employment established by the Contracts of Employment Act 1963. Although both Acts are now repealed, the equivalent provisions are contained in the Employment Rights Act 1996 with very little change to the original legislation. Compensation for redundancy is calculated having regard to the employee's length of continuous employment, age and weekly pay. The maximum length of employment that may be considered is 20 years and the week's pay is "capped" by statute (currently at £310.00 per week but subject to annual up-rating). While the Employment Equality (Age) Regulations 2006 (SI 2006/1031) repealed ss.156 and 162(4), (5) and (8) of the Employment Rights Act 1996 which (1) excluded entitlement where the employee at the date of dismissal had reached 65 (or an earlier normal retirement age); and (2) reduced the amount of a redundancy payment by one twelfth for every month worked after the employee had reached his/her 64th birthday, it left untouched the other provisions which take account of the employee's age so that the maximum payment is £9,300 (20 years multiplied by 1.5 multiplied by £310), hardly a princely sum for loss of employment held for 20 years. Nevertheless the theory is that such a sum, which is not liable to Income Tax, will render employees more malleable when industrial or business restructuring is required.

Various legislative provisions touch on redundancy. For example the Trade Union and Labour Relations (Consolidation) Act 1992 ss.188 et seq, requires that an employer who is proposing to dismiss employees on the grounds of redundancy must provide information and consult with their representatives. The Employment Rights Act 1996 s.98(2)(c) recognises that in the law of unfair dismissal "redundancy" is a fair reason for the dismissal of an employee while under the discrimination statutes, particularly the Sex Discrimination Act 1975 and the Disability Discrimination Act 1995, the criteria an employer uses to select employees for redundancy may be indirect sexual or marital status discrimination; similarly, taking into account periods of absence resulting from an employee's disability for purposes of selection for redundancy might breach the Disability Discrimination Act 1995. However, this chapter is concerned only with the legislative provisions dealing with redundancy payments.

GENERAL PRINCIPLES

5–2 The provisions relating to redundancy payments are now contained in the Employment Rights Act 1996 Pt XI. Provided an employee has two years' continuous employment he becomes entitled to a redundancy payment on being dismissed for redundancy or after a spell of lay-off or short time (Employment Rights Act ss.135, 155). In *Barber v Guardian Royal Exchange Assurance Group* [1990] I.C.R. 616, the European Court of Justice made it clear that a redundancy payment is to be treated as "pay" for the purposes of Art.141 and this has required that the conditions which require to be satisfied for entitlement are neither direct not indirect sex discrimination. Thus in *Rankin v British Coal* [1993] I.R.L.R. 69 when Mrs Rankin, who was over 60, was dismissed on the grounds of redundancy in March 31, 1987 she was able to argue that the relevant domestic legislation which at that time excluded women over 60 and men over 65 from entitlement to payment was directly discriminatory and contrary to Art.141. Eventually the offending legislation was repealed in January 16, 1990.

In *Lloyd-Briden v Worthing College* (EAT 0065/07), the EAT has held that the Employment Rights Act 1996 s.109 (which until the coming into force of the Employment Equality (Age) Regulations 2006 excluded unfair dismissal claims from employees over 65) was not contrary to the EC Equal Treatment Framework Directive as explained in *Mangold v Helm* (IDS Brief 803) which applied only to cases in which the Member State had introduced discriminatory laws after the date the Directive was adopted, namely November 2000. Like s.109, s.156 of the Employment Rights Act was introduced before November 2000 so that it is not possible to argue that the exclusion contained in s.156 should be set aside as being contrary to the fundamental principle of non-discrimination on the grounds of age in respect of dismissals before the repeal of s.156.

Although the repeal of s.156 of the Employment Rights Act by the Employment Equality (Age) Regulations has—thankfully—rendered the matter academic, in *Rutherford v Secretary of State for Trade and Industry (No. 2)* [2006] I.R.L.R. 551 the House of Lords has held that s.156 did not indirectly discriminate against men on the grounds that the statistical evidence that more women than men retire before 65 did not show that the statutory bar discriminated against men. The correct comparison was between men and women who wanted to work on after 65 and be protected against redundancy and as there was no disproportionate effect on the people in that group (i.e. those who want that protection and are still in the workforce at 65) s.156 did not indirectly discriminate against men.

In *R v Secretary of State for Employment Ex p. Seymour-Smith (No.1)* [1997] I.R.L.R. 315, HL; [1999] I.R.L.R. 253, ECJ; *(No.2)* [2000] I.R.L.R. 263, HL, the period of qualification for unfair dismissal (in 1985 two years) was challenged on the ground that it excluded a greater proportion of woman than men as being contrary to Art.141, but was held to be justified by factors unrelated to sex, like the legitimate social and employment policy of the State. On that basis it is unlikely on current figures that the two-year qualifying period for entitlement to a redundancy payment would be contrary to Art.141.

DISMISSAL

Dismissal is defined variously by the Employment Rights Act ss.136 **5–3** and 137 and includes the failure to permit the return of pregnant employees and implied termination. Section 136 is equivalent to the definition of dismissal for unfair dismissal in the Employment Rights Act s.95(1) which has been explained in Ch.4, above. For redundancy payments law, it is specially provided, however, that a lock-out will not support a constructive dismissal (Employment Rights Act s.136(2)) and where an employee is under notice of redundancy and wishes to leave before the expiry of the employer's notice, his notice must be in writing and given during the "obligatory period" (Employment Rights Act s.136(3)). Section 136(5) provides that where in accordance with an enactment or rule of law (a) an act on the part of an employer; or (b) an event affecting an employer (including an individual employer's death) operates to terminate the contract of employment, that act or event shall be taken to be a termination of the contract by the employer. There is no equivalent provision in unfair dismissal law but for redundancy payments law, the death of an individual employer or the dissolution of partnership or the winding-up of a company is a dismissal. Also, an event affecting an employer is wide enough to include the destruction of work premises. The result is that certain circumstances, which would otherwise be regarded as a frustration of the employment contract, are deemed to be dismissals, thereby preserving the employee's right to claim a redundancy payment if otherwise qualified.

VOLUNTEERS FOR REDUNDANCY

5–4 The critical distinction is between an agreed termination, referred to sometimes as termination by mutual consent, and a dismissal. Where an employee volunteers for redundancy there are two possible analyses: (1) he agrees to be dismissed in which case he is entitled to a redundancy payment; and (2) the contract is ended by mutual consent in which case there is no dismissal and he is not entitled to a payment. Thus where an employee "volunteers" for redundancy, there is a dismissal provided the causative act (to bring the employment to an end) is that of the employer alone, so that where employees applied for early retirement and the employer accepted their applications there was no dismissal but rather termination by mutual consent (*Birch & Humber v Liverpool University* [1989] I.R.L.R. 165). However, in *Caledonian Mining Ltd v Bassett and Steel* [1987] I.R.L.R. 165 (see para.4–7) the EAT has emphasised that the real question is: "who really terminated the employment?" The EAT held in that case that whether there is a dismissal or constructive dismissal it must be resolved not merely by looking at the label put on the termination and, in accordance with the views expressed by Sir John Donaldson in *Martin v Glynwood Distribution (t/a MBS Fastenings)* [1983] I.R.L.R. 198, whatever the respective actions of the employer and employee at the time the contract was terminated, the relevant question is, who really terminated the contract of employment? In the present case it was clearly the employers who caused the employee to resign. The reality of the matter was that it was the employers who terminated the contract. Therefore the employees were dismissed in law and were entitled to redundancy payments. A similarly sympathetic approach to "volunteers" is seen in *Scotch Premier Meat Co Ltd v Burns* [2000] I.R.L.R. 639, EAT in which the employment tribunal—upheld by the EAT—held that as the employees who had volunteered for redundancy had not made an informed choice because the employers had not indicated to them that instead of redundancy there was a possibility the business could be sold—an event which in fact did not take place—the employees were dismissed. Lord Johnston in the EAT makes no bones about the approach to be adopted: "We consider that it is the proper approach of this Tribunal and the employment tribunal to assess the matter in the way most favorable to the retention of rights that the employees have and there can be no greater right than the right to claim unfair dismissal if the redundancy procedure is inadequately handled by the employer", although that may confuse the question of has there been a dismissal with whether proper procedures have been followed. There is no right to claim either a redundancy payment or unfair dismissal unless there has been a dismissal and it is doubtful whether such a relaxed approach to dismissal would be followed in unfair dismissal law.

Even if not dismissed an employee may become entitled to a redundancy payment by being placed on short-time or laid off for the specified number of weeks (Employment Rights Act ss.135(1)(b), 147). The purpose of these provisions is to prevent an employer merely placing an employee on short-time or laying him off for a long period. By not being dismissed the employee would not be able to claim a redundancy payment. The effect of the provisions in ss.135 and 147 is to allow an employee laid off or on short-time to serve notice on his employer that he intends to terminate the employment and claim a redundancy payment. Unless the employer can show that full time employment is to be resumed, the employee will become entitled to a redundancy payment. However, the procedure is strictly applied and failure to comply results in loss of entitlement (*Allinson v Drew Simmons Engineering* [1985] I.C.R. 488).

REDUNDANCY

For purposes of redundancy payments the definition of redundancy is set out in the Employment Rights Act 1996 s.139. This is different from the definition of redundancy in TULR(C)A s.188, which requires an employer to consult a trade union, where dismissal as redundant means "a dismissal not related to the individual concerned". **5–5**

Section 139 provides an employee is dismissed by reason of redundancy if the dismissal is attributable wholly or mainly attributable to the following:

(a) the fact that his employer has ceased or intends to cease, (i) to carry on the business for the purposes of which the employee was employed by him, or (ii) to carry on that business in the place the employee was employed; or

(b) the fact that the requirements of that business, (i) for employees to carry out work of a particular kind, or (ii) for employees to carry out work of a particular kind in the place the employee was employed have ceased or diminished either permanently or temporarily.

There are thus two "limbs" to the definition of redundancy. The first and easier to apply is where the employer ceases the business for the purpose of which the employee was employed either completely or at the place the employee has been employed. The second deals with the more complex issue of whether the requirements of the business for employees to do "work of a particular kind" have ceased or diminished. Whether a "business" ceases is a question of fact and the judicial approach is illustrated by *Melon v Hector Powe Ltd,* 1981 S.L.T. 74, HL.

Melon v Hector Powe Ltd

1981 S.L.T. 74, HL

A company (Hector Powe Ltd) owned a factory at which men's suits were made for sale in the company's retail outlets. They sold the factory and its equipment to another company (Executex Ltd) which made suits for sale in the retail market generally but not for dedicated retail outlets. The employees remained and did the same kind of work (making suits) working for Executex but the House of Lords held that there was a transfer of the assets of the business but not the transfer of the business. Making suits for dedicated retail outlets, also owned by the factory, was a different business from making suits for sale to any wholesaler for onward retail sales. Hector Powe Ltd had ceased to carry on the business of making suits for its own retail outlets when it sold the factory and its equipment to Executex Ltd.

An example of redundancy by the cessation of a business is in *Glenboig Union Fireclay Co Ltd v Stewart* [1971] I.T.R. 14 in which the brickworks at which Stewart worked was closed down.

In the definition of redundancy, the place the employee is employed is important. The fact that an employer no longer needs employees to work in a particular place (for example a factory or a branch or any other place of employment) will satisfy the definition of redundancy even though the need for employees to do the same work remains or is increasing at another place. To establish the place of employment and the kind of work for which there is a reduced requirement, the contract test was at one time applied (*Haden Ltd v Cowen* [1982] I.R.L.R. 314). This involved an examination of the employee's contract to see if the employer had the right to transfer the employee to another place; if the employer had that right, even if there was a reduction in the requirements of the business for a particular kind of work in the place the employee actually worked, redundancy would not be the reason for dismissal. Thus an employee would not be redundant if work was available for him at a place at which he could be required by his contract to work. The result was that where an employee's contract allowed his employer to require him to work at a different place, the fact that the employer no longer needed his services at his current place of work would mean that he was not dismissed for redundancy and therefore not entitled to a payment.

The "contractual" approach to determining what is the **5–6**
employee's place of employment has now been expressly rejected by the EAT in the following case.

Bass Leisure Ltd v Thomas

[1994] I.R.L.R. 104

Mrs Thomas was employed by Bass Leisure Ltd as a collector for more than 10 years working from their Coventry depot, which was about 10 minutes drive from her home. The job involved driving around a number of public houses to collect the takings from fruit machines. She returned to the depot at the end of each day to report back to her manager and collect her schedule of visits for the next day. She normally stated out at about 7.30am and was home shortly after 2pm. The job therefore fitted in with her role as a housewife.

In 1991, the company decided to close the Coventry depot and Mrs Thomas was offered relocation in Erdington, some 20 miles west of Coventry. She reluctantly agreed to give the move a try. It soon became apparent to her, however, that it meant her having to spend much more time at work. First because of the longer drive between her home and the depot and, secondly, because certain organisational changes meant that she was unable to leave the depot until much later in the afternoon. She consequently terminated her employment and sought a redundancy payment.

The employers relied upon para.3.2 of her contract of employment which provided that:

> "The company reserves the right to transfer any employee either temporarily or permanently to a suitable alternative place of work and to change the terms and conditions of employment in order to meet the needs of the business. Domestic circumstances will be taken into account in reaching a decision if relocation is involved."

and para.8.3 that "your geographic area may be altered, provided that it remains realistically accessible from your normal residence".

The EAT held that the employee was entitled to terminate her contract by reason of the employers' conduct in requiring her to move from the Coventry depot to one some 20 miles away, notwithstanding a clause in her contract under which the employers reserved the right to transfer her because "the place" where an employee was employed for the purposes of s.139(1) does not extend to any place where he or she could contractually be required to work. The question of what is the place of employment concerns the extent or area of a single place, not the transfer from one place to another. The location and extent of that "place" must be ascertainable whether or not the employee is in fact to be required to move and therefore before any such requirement is made (if it is), and without knowledge of the terms of any such requirement, or of the employee's response, or of whether any conditions upon the making of it have been complied with. Accordingly, the question is primarily a factual one and the only relevant contractual terms are those which define the place of employment and its extent, rather than to make provision for the employee to be transferred from one "place" to another. Applying the correct criteria in the present case, the respondent's "place of employment" was the Coventry depot.

In *High Table Ltd v Horst* [1997] I.R.L.R. 513 the Court of Appeal has endorsed that view by stating the question of where the employee was employed was to be answered primarily by consideration of the factual circumstances pertaining prior to his dismissal. If an employee only worked in one location, according to the Court of Appeal, it defies commonsense to widen the extent of the place of employment by referring to mobility clauses in the contract and "it would be unfortunate if the law were to encourage the inclusion of mobility clauses only to exclude the entitlement to a redundancy payment".

Hours of Work

5–7 While the place the employee is employed is important to the definition of redundancy, the time at which the work is done is not expressly mentioned. Accordingly, requiring employees to work different hours will generally not mean that an employee who is dismissed because he is unwilling or unable to work the new hours will be dismissed for redundancy. The critical question is whether the change in working hours is such that it can be said that the requirements of the business to do work of a particular kind have ceased or diminished.

Johnson v Nottinghamshire Combined Police Authority

[1974] I.C.R. 170, CA

Johnson worked for the Police Authority as a clerk working a standard five-day week over 38 hours. In an effort to release police officers from clerical work, the Authority requested Johnson to do the same kind of work for the same number of hours but at different times of the day and on Saturdays. When Johnson refused, he was dismissed and the question was whether the reason for his dismissal was redundancy. The Court of Appeal, noting that the definition of redundancy made special mention of the place of work, held that the change in time did not alter the essential nature of the work or, in terms of the statute, work of a particular kind, namely, clerical work.

This can be contrasted with the following case:

Archibald v Rossleigh Commercials Ltd

[1975] I.R.L.R. 231

Archibald had been employed as a night shift mechanic whose hours of work were from 10pm to 8am six nights a week. When the employer decided that it would no longer keep the premises open 24 hours a day Archibald was offered work as a day mechanic but refused and claimed a redundancy payment. The employment tribunal upheld his claim because the employers' requirement for employees to do work of a particular kind which the applicant was employed to do—work of a night mechanic—had ceased. The Tribunal pointed out that his duties were different from those of the day shift, in that Archibald was required to attend to emergencies which arose during the night; it was not merely a change of the time at which the work was done.

To determine the requirements of the business for employees to do work of a particular kind, it may be necessary to distinguish an employee's skills or abilities from other attributes. Thus in *Vaux Breweries v Ward* (1969) 7 K.I.R. 309 Mrs Ward was not redundant because the employer still required waitresses although the ambience of the pub had been changed, so that the employers now preferred to employ younger female staff who might have a better rapport with the new type of customer the pub was trying to attract. There was no reduction in the requirements of the business for waitresses and the fact that Mrs Ward did not possess the qualities of younger female staff was irrelevant. However, in *BBC v*

Farnworth, The Times, October 7, 1998 it has been held that an employee with a narrow range of experience and ability, who was replaced by a producer with a broader range of experience, was dismissed on grounds of redundancy but the critical issue in each case is: "Have the requirements for work of a particular kind ceased or diminished?" and that requires a careful examination of the work the employer requires to be performed. The statutory language focuses on "particular kind" and may be contrasted with the terminology of the Equal Pay Act which refers to "work of the same or similar nature". Accordingly it would be correct to hold that a manager of a conventional grocery shop replaced by someone capable of managing a supermarket would be dismissed for redundancy; while they are both involved in retail management, the particular kind of work could be very different: *Sartin v Co-operative Retail Services Ltd* (1969) 7 K.I.R. 382.

Bumping

5–8 Until recently it has generally been accepted that the dismissal of one employee to accommodate, and prevent, the dismissal of another redundant employee is also to be regarded as a dismissal on the grounds of redundancy. The concept, known as "bumping", means that an employee whose job continues may nevertheless be seen to have been dismissed by reason of redundancy. The reason for this is because the definition of redundancy in s.131(1)(b) of the Employment Rights Act does not expressly require that the redundant employee be an employee who is employed on the particular kind of work the requirements of which have ceased or diminished. The consequence of permitting an employer to argue that a "bumped" or displaced employee is dismissed by reason of redundancy is that while the "bumped" employee will receive a redundancy payment (if otherwise qualified) the employer will also be able to overcome the first obstacle in defending an unfair dismissal complaint by proving the reason for dismissal was redundancy. Thus, an employer who gives up its fleet of delivery vehicles with the resultant redundancy of the five drivers, some of whom had long service, might decide to retain one of the drivers (A) who is also able to work in, say, the despatch section. To do so the employer may have to dismiss a newly recruited employee (B) in despatch. The result will be that instead of having to pay a redundancy payment of several thousand pounds to A the employer may be able to reward A for his long service by transferring him to despatch and, if B has less than two years' employment, dismiss him without having to make him a payment at all.

This approach to a "bumped" redundancy was endorsed by the EAT in *Safeway Stores Ltd v Burrell* [1997] I.R.L.R. 200. In *Murray v Foyle Meats Ltd* [1999] I.R.L.R. 563 the House of Lords finally dispatches the contract test and endorses the approach in *Safeway Stores Ltd v Burrell.*

Murray v Foyle Meats Ltd

[1999] I.R.L.R. 562, HL

The employers operated a slaughterhouse where the applicant was employed as a meat plant operative. He normally worked in the slaughter hall but under his contract could be required to work elsewhere and had occasionally done so. Importantly other employees who did not work on the slaughter hall line had similar terms of employment.

Following a decline in business fewer employees were needed in the slaughter hall and the employers had proposed to make about 35 employees, including Murray, redundant. Murray was dismissed and claimed unfair dismissal arguing that the employers had not shown that the reason for his dismissal was redundancy.

The employers argued that the dismissals were by reason of redundancy in that the dismissals had been wholly attributable to the fact that the requirements of the business for employees to carry out work of a particular kind, namely on the slaughtering line, had diminished.

Murray argued that requirements for employees to carry out work of a particular kind meant "requirements for employees contractually engaged to carry out work of a particular kind". Therefore, there should be no distinction between those who worked in the slaughter hall and those who worked elsewhere but could be required to work there and it had been wrong for the employers to select for redundancy only those who normally worked in the slaughter hall. They should have selected from everyone working under the same contract of employment.

According to the House of Lords the language of the Act was simplicity itself. It asked two questions of fact. The first was whether one or other of the various types of economic affairs existed. In this case the relevant one was whether the requirements of the business for employees to carry out work of a particular kind had diminished. The second was whether the dismissal was attributable wholly or mainly to that state of affairs. That was a question of causation.

> "The tribunal had found as a fact that the requirements of the business for employees to work in the slaughter hall had diminished and that state of affairs had led to the applicants being dismissed. That was the end of the matter."

The House of Lords agreed with the decision in *Safeway Stores Plc v Burrell*. Cases like *Nelson v BBC* [1977] I.C.R. 649

had been treated as authority for what has been called "the contract test" which required one to consider whether there was a diminution in the kind of work for which according to the terms of the contract the employee had been engaged. According to the House of Lords the contract test and the function test missed the point. The key word in the act was "attributable" and there was no reason in law the dismissal of an employee should not be attributable to a diminution in the employers need for employees irrespective of the terms of his contract or the function he performed. In some circumstances the dismissal of an employee who could perfectly well have been re-deployed (under his contract) or who had been doing work unaffected by the fall in demand might require some explanation to establish the necessary cause or connection. However that was a question of fact and not one of law.

The result was that the employers had shown that the reason for Murray's dismissal was redundancy because it was attributable to a diminution in the requirements of the business for employees to carry out work of a particular kind, namely, the work of meat plant operative.

Renewal and Re-engagement

5–9 Where an employee is dismissed by reason of redundancy his entitlement to a redundancy payment may be lost if he refuses an offer of suitable alternative employment made by his employer or an associated employer. Provided certain formalities are observed in the making of the offer the employee's unreasonable refusal excludes receipt of a payment (Employment Rights Act s.141). The offer need not be in writing; it may be a collective one (or advertised on a notice board) but it must be made before the end of the prior contract and must begin within four weeks of the end of a prior contract. If the offer is on the same terms as the employment which has ended it is deemed to be of suitable employment. Where the offer is of different terms the position varies, depending on whether the employee rejects it outright or accepts it. If the latter, a statutory—without prejudice—trial period of four weeks is brought into play (Employment Rights Act, s.138(2)). If termination by either party occurs during a trial period the original dismissal is reinstated, but if termination is by the employee his right to a payment is dependent on his refusal being reasonable or the job being unsuitable (s.141(4)(d)). If the employee rejects it outright, whether he is entitled to a payment depends on whether an employment tribunal finds the offer one of suitable employment. If it is, the employee may still lose his entitlement by unreasonably refusing the offer. If the employment offered is not suitable the employee is entitled to receive a redundancy payment. Where an employee accepts alternative employment that does not prevent him from claiming unfair dismissal in respect of the original employment (*Jones v Governing Body of Burdett Coutts School* [1998] I.R.L.R. 521, CA).

Whether alternative employment offered is suitable and whether the employee's refusal is reasonable requires a consideration of all facts and circumstances but in *Standard Telephone Cables Ltd v Yates* [1981] I.R.L.R. 21 it was held that work which required less skill and was regarded as a step backwards could properly be regarded as unsuitable while the fact that the employee believes that the alternative job might last only 12 to 15 months did not mean it was unsuitable although the temporary nature of alternative employment was a relevant consideration: *Morganite Crucible v Street* [1972] I.C.R. 110.

Cahuc, Johnson & Crouch v Allen Amery Ltd

[1966] I.T.R. 313

The three employees were previously employed in Hackney, London E2 and were offered, but refused, alternative employment in EC1. The employment tribunal held that the offer was unsuitable because each employee lived very close to the old premises but the new premises involved a bus journey of at least 40 minutes. One employee had a widowed mother whom she had been able to look after while she worked at the old premises but would not be able to do so at the new ones. The tribunal observed "The third factor ... was the inconvenience and the time in travelling. It is manifest that it is a great advantage to have a job which does not involve travel in London. If she accepted the offer it would take about 40 minutes in each direction. There is no need to underline the inconveniences of waiting for and the difficulty of catching buses in rush hours, bad weather etc. ... We find ... the offer was not of suitable employment in relation to the employees."

Bruce v National Coal Board

[1967] I.T.R. 159

As the alternative employment offered to Bruce, who was a diabetic, would have involved him working three shifts instead of two, his routine would be sufficiently disturbed to allow him to reasonably reject the offer.

Misconduct and Strikes

5–10 Where there is a redundancy situation and the employer has given notice of termination or the employee has given notice of intention to claim a payment but the employer justifiably terminates for misconduct of the employee, the special provisions in ss.140 and 143 of the Employment Rights Act operate. Entitlement to a redundancy payment depends on whether an employment tribunal thinks it is just and equitable to make a payment (*Lignacite Products Ltd v Krollman* [1979] I.R.L.R. 22). Where the misconduct takes the form of an employee going on strike, the employee does not lose his right to a payment (Employment Rights Act s.141(2)). See *Simmons v Hoover* [1977] I.C.R. 61. However, participation in a strike after notice of termination for redundancy permits the employer to delay, by service of a "notice of extension", the date of termination by the days lost through the strike. Failure to comply with such a notice may result in the employee losing his right to a payment (Employment Rights Act s.143(3), (4) and (5)).

THE ONUS OF PROOF

5–11 Location of the onus of proof varies according to the issue being contested. Where the issue is dismissal the onus is on the employee to bring his case within the exhaustive definitions in s.136 of the Employment Rights Act (*Dixon v BBC* [1978] I.C.R. 357). On the other hand an employer is required to prove compliance with formalities relating to an offer of alternative employment (*Cartin v Botley Garages Ltd* [1973] I.T.R. 150). Once the employee has proved he has been dismissed and that he is not excluded from entitlement, an employee can rely on the presumption that the reason for dismissal is redundancy (Employment Rights Act s.163(1)) and that employment is continuous with the dismissing employer (Employment Rights Act s.210(5)).

MAKING THE CLAIM

5–12 The need to make the claim in time is not merely procedural (*Secretary of State for Employment v Atkins Auto Laundries* [1972] I.C.R. 76) but affects the substantive entitlement. To preserve his entitlement the claimant must, within six months of the relevant date (which is usually the date when notice of termination expires), (1) agree and receive a payment, (2) serve written notice of claim on ex-employer, (3) refer entitlement to an employment tribunal under the Employment Rights Act 1996 s.163, or (4) present an unfair dismissal claim (Employment Rights Act s.164(1)). Provided it is made within six months of the expiry of the initial six-month period, an employment tribunal may admit a late claim (Employment

Rights Act s.164(2)). As a result of the Employment Rights (Dispute Resolution) Act 1998 s.11, a claim for a redundancy payment may be settled via ACAS.

However as a result of the Employment Act 2002 and the Employment Act 2002 (Dispute Resolution) Regulations 2004 (SI 2004/752) before an employment tribunal can accept a claim for a redundancy payment the employee must first—and no later than one month after the expiry of the normal time limit—lodge a written grievance with his employer and wait 28 days for a reply. A failure to comply with this rule has the harsh effect of excluding the employee's right to complain the employment tribunal completely and to mollify it this rule it is provided (Employment Act 2002 (Dispute Resolution) Regulations 2004 (SI 2004/752) reg.15) that where a claim for, inter alia, a redundancy payment is (a) presented to an employment tribunal within the time limit set out in the Employment Rights Act 1996 s.163 but the employee has not lodged his written grievance or waited 28 days for a reply; or (b) presented to an employment tribunal after the expiry of the normal time limit but the employee has lodged his written grievance within that time limit, the normal time limit is extended by three months.

Where an employer makes a redundancy payment otherwise than as a result of a decision of an employment tribunal, the employer shall give the employee a written statement showing how the payment has been calculated and a failure to do without reasonable excuse is a criminal offence (Employment Rights Act s.165).

Exclusions

The main exclusion operates in relation to domestic servants related **5–13** to the employer and employed in a private household (Employment Rights Act s.161(1)). Formerly employees on fixed term contract for more than two years were able to exclude their right to a redundancy payment on the expiry of the term without it being renewed but that applies only to contracts entered into before October 1, 2002 (Fixed-term Employees (Prevention of Less Favourable Treatment) Regulations 2002 (SI 2002/2034)).

Payments

Payments are calculated in accordance with statutory rules which **5–14** apply a formula consisting of (i) the length of the employee's continuous employment prior to the relevant date (which is usually the date the notice of termination expires); (ii) the employee's week's pay; and (iii) the age of the employee (Employment Rights Act s.162(1), (2)); depending on the employee's age a different multiplier is applied: for years below 22 a multiplier of 0.5, for years between 22 and 41 a multiplier of 1.0 and for years over 41 a multiplier of 1.5 (Employment Rights Act 1996 s.162(2)). Previously service below 18 years did not count (Employment Rights Act s.211(2)) and employees over 65 (Employment Rights Act 1996 s.156) were excluded but as a result of the Employment Equality (Age) Regulations 2006 (SI No 2006/1031) employment before 18 and after 64 years is taken into account. However the provision whereby different multipliers are applied to calculate the payment has been retained on the Government's view that they can be justified: see also Ch.6, para.6.37, below. The week's pay is subject to variable statutory limit, currently £310. A statement showing how the payment is calculated must be given (Employment Rights Act s.165(1)).

Payments on insolvency

5–15 Frequently dismissal by reason of redundancy occurs when a business becomes insolvent and in order to prevent employees' claims for redundancy payments being defeated by such circumstances, s.166 of the Employment Rights Act 1996 provides that an employee whose claim for a redundancy payment is defeated by the insolvency of his employer may apply to the Secretary of State who may make the payment from the National Insurance Fund. Other payments may also be made by the Secretary of State from the Fund in the event of the employer's insolvency. In implementation of Council Directive 80/987 Pt XII of the Employment Rights Act 1996 requires the Secretary of State to pay from the Fund specified debts due to the employee after the termination of his employment in the event of the employer's insolvency.

The payments are:

- up to eight weeks' arrears of pay;
- minimum notice pay;
- up to six weeks' holiday pay;
- a basic award of compensation for unfair dismissal; and
- an apprenticeship fee.

In the event of the Secretary of State refusing to make a payment, an employee may apply to an employment tribunal which may declare the amount of any payment which it finds the Secretary of State ought to make (Employment Rights Act s.188).

TRANSFER OF AN UNDERTAKING

Introduction

5–16 Until 1981 employees who worked in businesses that were sold to or acquired by another employer could find that the person who acquired the business did not wish to employ the existing workforce at all, or was only prepared to offer them employment on less favourable terms than those that they had enjoyed with the previous employer. Whether the existing workforce was offered work with the new owner of the business depended almost entirely on whether the new owner wished to employ them. Thus employees who had served an employer's business faithfully for many years could find that the work they had done in that business was to be done by newly recruited employees or employees who were already employed by the new owner. In effect they had no right to work with the new employer/owner of the business. To remedy this situation the EC Acquired Rights Directive was adopted. The Directive was implemented in the United Kingdom by the Transfer of Undertakings (Protection of Employment) Regulations 1981 (TUPE) (SI 1981/1794). The Directive was amended in some minor respects in 1998 but, in order to reflect decisions of the ECJ, it was revoked and replaced by a new Directive (2001/23) which is implemented in the United Kingdom by the Transfer of Undertakings (Protection of Employment) Regulations 2006 (SI 2006/246) which replace the 1981 Regulations. In one very important change the new Regulations make express provision for when there occurs not strictly the transfer of a business but the replacement of one employer/contractor by another; until the new Regulations such a change of contractor could be regarded as a transfer of part of a business but in order to clarify some of the decisions of the ECJ the Directive 2001/23 and the new Regulations now expressly deal with changes of contractors as a "service provision change."

Relevant Transfer

The Regulations apply only to a relevant transfer which is defined **5–17** to mean a transfer of an undertaking to another person or a service provision change which is defined to mean that activities previously carried out by one person are thereafter carried out by another person. There has to be a transfer of a business or undertaking (or a service provision change) from one legal persona to another legal persona so that the acquisition of shares in a limited company—even to such an extent that there is a change in the control of the company—is not a transfer for the purpose of the Regulations. The ownership of the shares will have changed but the business remains in the ownership of the company. In *Brookes v Borough Care Services* [1998] I.C.R. 1198 the EAT held that a change in the ownership of shares does not amount to a transfer even where this is done to avoid the application of the Regulations. However the acquisition of shares does not prevent there being a relevant transfer. In *Millam v The Print Factory (London) 1991 Ltd* [2007] EWCA Civ 322, where the shares in one company (F) were sold to another company (M) which then incorporated F's business into its own and took over the payment of F's employees' wages, managed its occupational pension scheme, took over F's sales functions and gradually took over 50 per cent of F's work even though the two companies remained separately registered, the facts were consistent with a transfer of an undertaking from F to M because M had the power which it exercised to change contracts of employment of F's employees, took all the important decisions relating to F's business strategy, and channelled work to and from F.

Although the 1981 Regulations made no reference transfers of contracts it had become clear from decisions of the ECJ (see for example *Rask v ISS Kantineservice A/S* [1993] I.R.L.R. 133, ECJ; *Schmidt v Spar und Leihkasse der fruheren Ampter Bordesholm Kiel und Cronshagen* [1994] I.R.L.R. 302, ECJ; *Suzen v Zehnacker Gebaudereinigung* [1997] I.R.L.R. 258, ECJ) that the Directive applied not merely to the transfer of businesses and undertakings in the traditional sense but also to any organisation that was an "economic entity" and the result of this interpretation meant that the Directive and therefore the implementing Regulations applied to the many circumstances in which one employer/contactor was replaced by another. Particularly in the 1990s many organisations chose to "contract out" certain functions from cleaning and maintenance to IT support (and even legal advice, training and representation) and a question arose as to whether when such contracts were let, re-let or even taken back in-house there was a transfer of an economic entity. In order to assist in resolving this question the 2006 Regulations in reg.3 now expressly provide they apply not merely to a sale of a business or parts of one which is described as:

> "a transfer to another person of an undertaking (or part of one) where there is a transfer of an economic entity which retains its identity which means an organized grouping of resources which has the objective of pursuing an economic activity whether that activity is central or ancillary,"

but also to a situation where there is a change of contractor which is described—rather prosaically—as a service provision change in which (i) activities cease to be carried out by a person (client) on his own behalf and are carried out instead by another person on the client's behalf (contractor); (ii) activities cease to be carried out by a contactor on a client's behalf and are carried out instead by another person (subsequent contractor) on the client's behalf; or (iii) activities cease to be carried out by a contractor or subsequent contractor on a client's behalf and are carried out instead by the client on his own behalf. These three circumstances in practice describe (a) contracting out, (b) change of contractor and (c) contracting in. However there is no service provision change unless immediately before the change there is an organised grouping of employees which has the principal purpose of carrying out the activities concerned on behalf of the client, the client intends the activities will after the service provision change be carried out by the transferee other than in connection with a single specific event or task of short term duration and that the activities do not consist wholly or mainly of the supply of goods (but not services) for the client's use. In *Hunt v Storm Communications Ltd* (ET No.2702546/06) an employment tribunal has held that there was a service provision change where Hunt spent 70% of her time servicing the public relations needs of one particular client when that client transferred its contract to another public relations business.

While the new Regulations seek to give legislative effect to the principles and examples enunciated by the ECJ and domestic courts nevertheless difficult issues still arise in dealing with dismissals in connection with a transfer of an undertaking namely (a) is there a business or undertaking (or part of one) and (b) has that been transferred. It is easy to conflate these two issues but it is important to keep them apart, as it is possible to find that while there was an undertaking or business, which the old owner has ceased, strictly it has not been transferred. To an extent this has been in part due to the need to interpret and apply the Regulations in a way that gives effect to the Directive which it is intended to implement. The Directive and Regulations are concerned with whether an "economic entity" existed, whether it has retained its identity and whether it has been transferred to a new owner/employer. In *Cheesman v R Brewer Contracts Ltd* [2001] I.R.L.R. 144 the EAT has attempted to give guidance on how these two questions should be approached.

Is There an Undertaking?

- There needs to be a stable economic entity, whose activity is not limited to the performance of a single works contract, an organised grouping of persons and assets enabling the exercise of an economic activity which pursues a specific objective. **5–18**
- The undertaking must be sufficiently structured and autonomous but will not necessarily have significant tangible or intangible assets.
- In certain sectors of industry, such as cleaning or surveillance, the assets are often reduced to the most basic and the activity is only manpower.
- An organised grouping of wage earners permanently assigned to a common task may, even in the absence of other factors of production, be an economic entity.
- Economic activity itself is not an entity and the identity of an entity emerges from other factors like the workforce, management staff, its operating methods and resources available to the entity.

Is There a Transfer?

- The decisive criterion is whether the entity has retained its identity as indicated by the fact that its operation is continued or resumed (by the new owner). **5–19**
- In a labour intensive sector an entity can retain its identity where the new owner not merely pursues the activity but also takes over a major part of the employees assigned by the old owner to the specific activity.

- Consideration should be given to all the factors characterising the transaction (between the old owner and the new owner); these factors include the type of undertaking, whether tangible assets are transferred and the value of intangible assets, whether the majority of employees and customers are taken over and the degree of similarity of activities carried on before and after the transfer.
- The fact that assets are not transferred does not mean there cannot have been a transfer.
- Where no employees are taken over, the reason for not taking them over (e.g. attempting to avoid the conclusion there has been a transfer of an undertaking) is relevant.

Thus, in *Cheesman v R Brewer Contracts Ltd* [2001] I.R.L.R. 144, EAT, when Brewer Ltd won a local authority maintenance contract previously awarded to Onyx (UK) Ltd, the EAT held that the employment tribunal had erred in holding that there was no transfer of an undertaking because the existing workforce of Onyx (UK) Ltd was not taken over by Brewer Ltd. Of course the guidance set out in Cheesman was pronounced before the new Regulations and some of these difficulties will be resolved by the 2006 Regulations expressly providing that a relevant transfer includes a service provision change.

The Regulations apply to public and private undertakings engaged in economic activities whether or not they are operating for gain but are expressly excluded from applying to an administrative reorganisation of public administrative authorities or the transfer of administrative functions between such authorities (reg.3(4), (5)).

The Effect of the Regulations

5–20 The Regulations essentially do two things for employees who work in businesses which are sold or transferred by their existing employer (transferor) to a new owner (transferee) or who work for an employer/contractor (transferor) on a particular contract which is lost or given to another contractor (the transferee) in the new Regulations described as a "service provision change". First, by reg.4 the contractual rights and duties that the employees enjoyed with the transferor are automatically transferred and become binding on the transferee (the new owner or contractor); in effect the transferee steps into the contractual shoes of the transferor and becomes the employees' new employer. However this is subject to the following two important qualifications: the employees must have been employed by the transferor and assigned to the organised grouping of resources or employees that is the subject of the transfer; and any employee is free to object to his contract being transferred and if he does so his contract is deemed to be terminated but the employee is not to be regarded as having been dismissed by the transferor so that such an employee has no claim for a redundancy payment or unfair dismissal (reg.4).

Secondly, by reg.7(1), in order to complement the transfer of contracts, the dismissal of an employee because of the transfer, or a reason connected with it, is declared to be unfair. An employee who is dismissed for a reason connected with the transfer of an undertaking or service provision change has the right to complain that he or she was unfairly dismissed so long as the normal qualifying period for unfair dismissal is satisfied.

Economic, Technical or Organisational Reasons

By reg.7(2) it is a defence for the employer to show that the dismissal was for an "economic, technical or organizational" (ETO) reason entailing "changes in the workforce". According to the Court of Appeal in *Berriman v Delabole Slate Ltd* [1985] I.C.R. 546 the latter phrase requires there is a change in the number of employees or their functions. It is not enough for one employee to be replaced by another because changes in the identity of the individuals who make up the workforce do not constitute changes in the workforce if the overall numbers and functions of the employees remain unchanged. On the other hand there can be a change in the workforce where the same people are kept on but are given entirely different jobs provided the workforce is engaged in a different occupation (*Crawford v Swinton Insurance Brokers Ltd* [1990] I.R.L.R. 42, EAT). Regulations 7(1) and 7(2) are mutually exclusive so that if the reason for dismissal is the transfer or a reason connected therewith which is not an ETO reason the dismissal is automatically unfair. Where the dismissal is for such an ETO reason by reg.7(3) it is deemed to have been for redundancy or for a substantial reason of a kind such as to justify the dismissal of the employee and whether it is fair or unfair will depend upon the general issue of reasonableness determined in accordance with the provisions of unfair dismissal law (see Ch.4 para.4.23). **5–21**

Who are Protected against Unfair Dismissal?

The unfair dismissal protections granted by the Regulations apply to employees who are dismissed either before or after there has been a transfer of an undertaking or a service provision change if the transfer (or change) or a reason connected with them is the reason for their dismissals. Even under the 1981 Regulations it was clear from the decision of the House of Lords in *Litster v Forth Dry Dock & Engineering Co Ltd*, 1989 S.C. 96, HL that even when the employees are dismissed before the transfer their claims for unfair dismissal will be against the transferee (i.e. the person who has acquired the undertaking or the contract) so long as their dismissals were for the transfer or a reason connected with the transfer. This decision prevented the transferee from instructing the transferor (the seller of the undertaking or holder of the contract) to dismiss staff prior to the transfer so as to acquire the business or contract without having to honour the continuing contracts of employment **5–22** of the employees in the undertaking or the contract. If the transferee sought to do this then the employees would have an unfair dismissal claim against the transferee even though they were never employed by the transferee and were actually dismissed by the transferor. This principle is now enshrined in the Regulations themselves (see reg.4 (3)) and in *Kerry Foods Ltd v Creber* [2000] I.C.R. 556, the EAT has formulated the following principles for dealing with reg.7: (a) every dismissal is effective to terminate the employment relationship; (b) a dismissal by the transferor by reason of the impending transfer will be automatically unfair; (c) the employees concerned will enforce their remedies in relation to that dismissal against the transferee in accordance with the *Litster* principle; (d) if the main reason for the dismissal by the transferor is an ETO reason neither reg.7(1) nor the *Litster* principle will apply; (e) if the reason for the dismissal is an ETO but the dismissal is nonetheless unfair the principle in point (d) remains true and the employee may recover only from the transferor as it is only where reg.7(1) applies that the *Litster* principle operates.

What is the Reason for the Dismissal?

5–23 It can be difficult sometimes to determine whether the sole or principal reason for a dismissal is either the transfer (or the service provision change) or a reason connected with the transfer (or a service provision change). In *Harrison Bowden Ltd v Harrison* [1994] I.C.R. 186 the ultimate purchaser of a business (transferee) was held liable for the pre-transfer dismissal of the employee by the receiver even though at the time of dismissal no specific purchaser had come forward. On the other hand, in *Ibex Trading Co Ltd v Walton* [1994] I.R.L.R. 564 the EAT concluded that there was no dismissal for a reason connected with the transfer when in similar circumstances an administrator dismissed staff before any particular purchaser had been identified and in *Morris v John Grose Group Ltd* [1998] I.R.L.R. 499 the EAT, disagreeing with *Walton*, has held that the words "the transfer" do not have to refer to the relevant particular transfer which has actually taken place provided the identity of the transferee, the date of the transfer and the terms of the transfer have all been decided by the time the matter comes before the employment Tribunal.

Changing the Terms of Employees

5–24 The effect of the Regulations is that a transferee also acquires the employees who were employed there on the same terms and conditions as they had with the transferor. Regulation 4(4) now provides that except where the transferor is subject to insolvency proceedings any change to these terms (and this is so even if the employee agrees) is void if the reason for the change is the transfer or a reason connected with the transfer unless it is an ETO reason "entailing changes in the workforce". This latter phrase presumably has the same meaning as it does in relation to dismissal (discussed above) so that a change that does not affect the number or functions of the employees will not be within the scope of the exemption. If the reason for the change in the terms is because the transferee wishes to harmonise the terms and conditions of the transferred employees with those of existing staff, any change be void even if agreed to by the relevant employees and even if the new terms are overall more favourable than the existing ones; in order to be effective the transferee must show that the real reason for the change was an economic, organisational or economic reason entailing changes in the workforce and an exercise in harmonisation is unlikely merely to meet the conditions required by the Court of Appeal in *Delabole Slate*.

Dismissal and Re-engagement by the Transferee

Equally, there may well be successful unfair dismissal claims if the **5–25** transferee chooses to dismiss the staff previously employed by the transferor and then seeks to re-hire them on new and different contracts. This is because the dismissal of an employee on the transfer of an undertaking is effective and operative creating enforceable statutory unfair dismissal rights so long as the dismissal is connected with the transfer. These points were made by the House of Lords in *British Fuels Ltd v Baxendale* [1998] I.R.L.R. 706 where Lord Slynn of Hadley, having considered the terms of the Regulations, stated:

> "[The Regulations] ... seem to me to point to the dismissal being effective and not a nullity. If there is no dismissal there cannot be compensation for unfair dismissal. It is because the dismissal is effective that provision is made for it to be treated as unfair for the purposes of awarding compensation under employment legislation.
>
> British Fuels Ltd were right to point out ... that the Regulation affects many transfers which occur as an everyday matter—not just on the merger of giants but in the sale of a business or part of a business, or in the re-distribution of a business or part of a business or in the re-distribution of a business between subsidiary companies. Changes may be needed in order to harmonise terms and conditions of the combined workforces—either by agreement or by dismissal (which, if it is unreasonable, will attract compensation) followed by an offer of re-engagement. It does not follow, British Fuels Ltd submit, that an obligation to take on the entire workforce on the existing terms is necessarily in the best interests of employees. It could deter transfers which overall would be in the interest of the employees. Moreover where adjustments have to be made to working conditions, detailed questions may fall to be litigated as to whether the various adjustments do

mean that the employee's terms overall are less favourable. This also applies to whether the employer has discharged the onus of showing that the 'economic technical or organisation' reason relied on was one 'entailing changes in the workforce' and whether it was the reason or a principal reason for dismissing the employee.

It follows in my opinion that under the regulation the dismissals are not rendered nullities; nor is there an automatic obligation on the part of the transferee to continue to employ or find work for the employees who have been dismissed."

Pension Rights

5–26 Although the 2006 Regulations themselves make no provision for the transference of pension rights protection of participation in pension schemes is now dealt with by the Pensions Act 2004 and the Transfer of Employment (Pension Protection) Regulations 2005 (SI 2005/649) which apply where the Transfer of Undertakings (Protection of Employment) Regulations apply. Briefly, where an employee of a transferor is a member of an occupational pensions scheme the transferee must ensure that the employee is eligible to become an active member of a pension scheme in relation to which the transferee is the employer and, if it is a money purchase scheme, the transferee must make contributions equal to the employee's contributions (subject to an upper limit of 6 per cent of basic pay) or make equivalent contributions to a stakeholder pension scheme of which the employee is member. If the transferee's scheme is not a money purchase scheme the Transfer of Employment (Pension Protection) Regulations 2005 provide that either the value of the benefits provided for by the transferee's scheme must be at least 6 per cent of pensionable pay for each year of employment or that the scheme must provide for the employer to make relevant contributions on behalf of the employees for each period for which the employee contributes to the scheme and that the transferee's contribution must equal the employee's contributions subject to an upper limit of 6 per cent of his basic salary. These provisions make a great change to the position which prevailed under the Transfer of Undertakings (Protection of Employment) Regulations 1981 which conferred only a modest entitlement to pension protection.

SAMPLE QUESTIONS

1. Mr Smith is a teller employed by the United Kingdom Bank and by a term in his contract of employment he is required to "work at any branch office of the United Kingdom Bank situated in the United Kingdom". For several years Mr Smith has worked at the Edinburgh branch but that is to be closed down as a result of efficiency savings introduced by the new managing director. Mr Smith is advised that on the closure of the Edinburgh branch he will be dismissed but he not receive a redundancy payment because his place of employment is the United Kingdom and not the Edinburgh branch. Is Mr Smith's employer correct?

2. Mrs Jones is employed by Hermiston Electronics Ltd (HEL) as its catering manageress with responsibility for the staff restaurant. In order to concentrate on its core business HEL contracts out the provision of staff meals to Gourmet Meals Ltd (GML). GML takes on all the catering staff including Mrs Jones and receives a fee based on the average number of staff meals provided less the cost of services provided by HEL (gas, electricity and water). After she receives her first pay from GML Mrs Jones notices that it no longer includes £50 per month in respect of management responsibility allowances. When she raises the issue with GML she is told that GML "does not pay responsibility allowances to any employees". Mr McDonald was employed by HEL as kitchen porter and restaurant cleaner but is dismissed by HEL just before GML take over the contract because he will be "surplus to requirements". What claims might Mrs Jones and Mr McDonald have and against which company would they be brought?

SUGGESTED ANSWERS FOR CHAPTER FIVE

1. The first question to be addressed is whether the reason for Mr Smith's dismissal is that he is redundant. According to the Employment Rights Act s.139, a dismissal is for redundancy where it is attributable to either the fact that the employer has ceased or intends to cease to carry on business in the place where the employee was employed, or that the requirements of the business for employees to carry out work of a particular kind have ceased or diminished. The circumstances in Mr Smith's case would seem to refer to the first situation, namely, that the employer intends to cease to carry on business at the Edinburgh branch—that branch is to be closed down. Accordingly the next issue is to consider whether that was the place Mr Smith was employed. At one time according to the decisions in cases like Haden Carrier Ltd v Cowen *[1982] I.R.L.R. 314, CA and* Nelson v BBC *[1977] I.C.R. 649 the place an employee was employed was to be decided by having regard to the terms of the contract. This is so if an employee could be transferred to another place, his place of employment would be anywhere to which he could be transferred and provided there was work available at any such place it would not be correct to say that the closure of the branch at which the employee generally worked would mean that he was redundant. The result was that the very existence of such contractual provisions meant that an employee whose employer closed down the branch where the employee worked would not be entitled to a redundancy payment provided work was available for him at a place to which he could be transferred. That approach—the contract test—has now been overruled in cases like* High Table Ltd v Horst *[1997] I.R.L.R. 513 because it permitted employers to include contractual mobility clauses principally to avoid paying redundancy payments. The current approach is shown in* Curling v Securicor Ltd *[1992] I.R.L.R. 549. Applying that approach the place where Mr Smith was employed would be the Edinburgh branch and as that branch was to be closed he would be dismissed on the grounds of redundancy and entitled to a redundancy payment. According to the EAT in* Curling *"an employer who does not invoke a mobility clause cannot be heard to say that its mere existence entitles him to claim, after he has closed down the workplace where the employees were employed, that he might have required them to work elsewhere, although he did not effectively do so, and therefore they were not redundant".*

Would the position of Mr Smith have been different if the United Kingdom Bank had required him to move to the Glasgow branch but Mr Smith had refused? The answer is ***no*** *because the reason for his dismissal would still be attributable to redundancy in that the place an employee is employed—which is the critical issue for the definition of redundancy—is to be distinguished from other places to which the employee may be transferred. This is the effect of the decision in* Bass Leisure Ltd v Thomas *[1994] I.R.L.R. 104 where the EAT held that the employee was entitled to terminate her contract by reason of the employers' conduct in requiring her to move from the Coventry depot to one some 20 miles away. Notwithstanding a clause in her contract under which the employers reserved the right to transfer her because "the place" where an employee was employed for the purposes of s.139(1) does not extend to any place where he or she could contractually be required to work. The question of what is the place of employment, concerns the extent or area of a single place, not the transfer from one place to another.*

2. The legal position of Mrs Jones and Mr McDonald depends on whether HEL has transferred an undertaking (or part of one) to GML. If it has, the employment rights of the employees employed in the part transferred will be transferred to GML. Whether there has been a transfer of an undertaking (or part of one) is a question of fact. Until the Transfer of Undertaking (Protection of Employment) Regulations 2006 were adopted whether contracting out of an in-house facility was decided by considering whether the activity contracted out was to regarded as the transfer of an economic entity which retained its identity (see for example, Rask v ISS Kantine-service A/S *[1993] I.R.L.R. 133). The 2006 Regulations now make express provision for the contracting out of activities. Regulation 3 provides that the new Regulations apply not just to a transfer of an undertaking or part of one but also where there is a "service provision change". Looking at the facts here there appears to have been such a change on the assumption that there was an organised grouping of employees whose principal purpose was the provision of staff meals. According to reg.4 the contractual rights of Mrs Jones will be enforceable against GML after the service provision change and she will be able to claim breach of contract against GML. If GML continue to refuse to pay the management allowance Mrs Jones will also be entitled to leave and claim constructive dismissal against GML (see Ch.4, above).*

Mr McDonald will also be able to claim unfair dismissal. Regulation 7 applies to employees employed at the time of the transfer or the sevice provision change and, as a result of the decision in Litster *[1989] I.R.L.R. 161, (HL) (and now enshrined in the 2006 Regulations (reg.4(3)) to employees dismissed by the transferor (HEL) before, but because of the transfer or service provision change. If his dismissal was because of the (imminent) service provision change in the form of the transfer of the in-house facility he will be able to claim unfair dismissal against GML. His dismissal would be automatically unfair. If it could be shown that the reason for Mr McDonald's dismissal was an economic, technical or organisational reason entailing changes in the workforce the reason for McDonald's dismissal will be redundancy or some other reason and whether his dismissal is unfair depends on s.98(4) of the Employment Rights Act.*

CHAPTER SIX

DISCRIMINATION

6–1 Until legislation was enacted in the 1970s the law of the United Kingdom did little to prevent employers treating job applicants and employees less favourably on account of their sex, sexual orientation, race, colour, nationality, religion, political opinions, age or disability. Since that time however, legislation, often rooted in European Union directives, has made it unlawful to treat applicants and employees less favourably on various grounds. Domestic law must be interpreted in light of, and to give effect to, any relevant European directive. Further, the European Convention on Human Rights, introduced into UK law by the Human Rights Act 1998, guarantees certain rights such as the freedom of religious belief and the freedom of expression. The 1998 Act requires that domestic legislation be interpreted wherever possible in ways that are consistent with these guarantees and in that respect may extend the scope of existing domestic legislation. In most of the situations where the law provides that dismissal will be automatically unfair for a particular reason (see Ch.4, above) for example being a trade union member, making a protected disclosure, refusing to work on Sundays, etc.—the employee is also protected against detrimental treatment short of dismissal for that reason.

This chapter deals with discrimination on grounds of: (1) sex, pregnancy and marital status; (2) gender re-assignment; (3) race, colour, ethnic and national origins and nationality; (4) sexual orientation; (5) religion or belief; (6) age; (7) disability; (8) being part-time workers; and (9) being fixed term contract employees. It also covers the various family-related leave rights.

SEX, PREGNANCY AND MARITAL STATUS

6–2 The Sex Discrimination Act 1975 (SDA) and the Equal Pay Act 1970 (EPA) are the central UK legislative provisions in this field, the former dealing with non-contractual issues like selection for employment, subjecting employees to a detriment by, for example, not promoting them and the latter dealing with contractual issues mainly relating to the payment of wages or other contractual benefits. UK law in this area, however, is subject to Art.141 of the EC Treaty (equal pay for work of equal value) as amplified by the Equal Pay Directive (75/117) and the Equal Treatment Directive

(76/207) (as amended by Directive 02/73) which eliminate less favourable treatment on grounds of sex and marital or family status.

Although the UK courts were initially unsure of whether discrimination on the grounds of pregnancy fell within the ambit of sex discrimination that matter was resolved by the European Court of Justice.

Dekker v VJV Centrum

[1991] I.R.L.R. 27, ECJ

Mrs Dekker applied for a post with VJV Centrum but was refused employment because the employer would have suffered financially during a period of maternity leave to which Mrs Dekker would have been entitled.

The ECJ held that whether a refusal to employ results in direct sex discrimination on grounds of sex depends on whether the most important reason is one which applies without distinction to employees of both sexes or whether it exclusively applies to one sex. As only women can be refused employment because of pregnancy, such a refusal is direct discrimination on grounds of sex and an employer acts contrary to the principle of equal treatment contained in the Equal Treatment Directive if he refuses to enter a contract with a female applicant who is suitable for the post in question because of the possible adverse financial consequences of employing a pregnant woman; it is not important that there are no male applicants.

Webb v EMO Air Cargo (U.K.) Ltd

[1994] I.R.L.R. 482, ECJ

Mrs Webb had been engaged by EMO with a view to replacing a pregnant employee, Mrs Stewart, during the latter's maternity leave. Shortly afterwards, she had discovered that she herself was pregnant, her baby being expected at roughly the same time as Mrs Stewart's, and EMO had then dismissed her. The House of Lords was unsure of whether her dismissal constituted sex discrimination and referred the matter to the European Court of Justice.

The European Court held (1) that the Equal Treatment Directive (Art.2(1) read with Art.5(1)) precludes dismissal of an employee who is recruited for an unlimited term with a view, initially, to replacing another employee during the latter's maternity leave and who cannot do so because, shortly after recruitment, she is herself found to be pregnant; and (2) the situation of a woman who is incapable by reason of pregnancy of performing the task for which she was recruited cannot be compared with that of a man similarly incapable for medical or other reasons.

When the case returned to the House of Lords it was noted that it was apparent from the ECJ's ruling that it had been considered to be a relevant circumstance that Mrs Webb had been engaged for an indefinite or unlimited period. According to Lord Keith of Kinkel that suggested the possibility of a distinction between such a case and the case where a woman's absence due to pregnancy would have the consequence of her being unavailable for the whole of the work for which she had been engaged, for example, where the work was of purely seasonal duration or where staff were required for some specific event such as the Wimbledon fortnight or the Olympic Games. If such a situation did not fall to be distinguished, the result would be likely to be seen as unfair to employers and as tending to bring the sex discrimination law into disrepute.

The possibility of such an exception has since been rejected by the ECJ.

Tele Danmark A/S v Handles-og Kontorfunktionaerernes Forbund I Danmark

[2001] I.R.L.R. 853, ECJ

B was to work for six months in the company's customer service department, starting July 1, 1995, and the first two months were set aside for training. In August 1995 she told her employers that she was pregnant and the baby was due in early November. The employers dismissed her with effect from September 30.

The employers argued that the reason they had dismissed B was not the pregnancy itself but the fact that she was unable to perform a substantial part of the contract. Further, the employers considered that by not informing them that she was pregnant at the recruitment stage, B had breached the duty of good faith required in employment relations, and that that, in itself, justified dismissal. They also argued that EC law would only be contravened by an employer refusing to employ a pregnant woman or dismissing her where the contract was for an indefinite period and the employee's obligations would continue beyond her maternity leave (the "*Webb* exception").

The ECJ held:

> "The Equal Treatment Directive and the Pregnant Workers Directive prohibit dismissal of a worker on the ground of pregnancy even where she was recruited for a fixed period and where because of her pregnancy she was unable to work during a substantial part of the term of that contract."

The ECJ pointed out that while this might seem unfair to employers, were they to allow an exception in these circumstances, there would be nothing to prevent unscrupulous employers putting all workers on short fixed term contracts and then, should an employee fall pregnant, not renewing it at the appropriate time.

They held that there was no breach of good faith by failing to disclose the pregnancy as the employer would not be permitted to take this information into account in deciding whether or not to appoint the woman.

The SDA now specifically provides that less favourable treatment on grounds of pregnancy or in relation to maternity leave will be sex discrimination. (ss.3A and 3B)

Direct sex discrimination occurs where an employer treats (or **6–3** would treat) a person less favourably than a person of the opposite sex on the grounds of his or her sex (SDA s.1). Direct marital status discrimination occurs where an employer treats (or would treat) a married person less favourably than an unmarried person of the same sex (SDA s.3). In each case the relevant circumstances must not be materially different (SDA s.5(3)) but the subjective motive of an employer is not relevant. An example of direct sex discrimination in employment is seen in *Dunlop v RSA* (IT Case No. S/3696/76, unreported) in which a female was not allowed to do night shift or weekend working thereby losing the value of unsociable hour rates. The RSA's motive, not to place Miss Dunlop in a vulnerable position, although laudable, was not relevant and did not excuse the act of direct discrimination. In *Moyhin v Barts and London NHS Trust* [2006] I.R.L.R. 860, a male trainee nurse succeeded in a claim of direct sex discrimination. Male trainee nurses were required to be chaperoned when carrying out intimate procedures on female patients but female trainees did not require to be chaperoned when carrying out similar procedures on male patients. The fact that the reason was the Trust's concern to safeguard female patients could not justify the discriminatory treatment.

In *James v Eastleigh Borough Council* [1990] I.C.R. 554, in which female pensioners were not required to pay for entry into a local authority pool while male pensioners, like Mr James, were the House of Lords held that the test which should be applied in assessing whether there was direct discrimination was the "but for" test, namely, would the applicant have received different treatment from the respondent but for his or her sex? But for Mr James' sex he would have been entitled to free entry to the swimming pool. *James* focused on the idea of the application of gender-based criteria as a basis for a decision—if you base your decision on such it will amount to direct discrimination.

The "but for" test has since been criticised as overly simplistic (see *Chief Constable of West Police v Khan* [2001] I.R.L.R. 830 H.L.). Further guidance is given in the following case:

Shamoon v Chief Constable of Royal Ulster Constabulary

[2003] I.R.L.R. 285

S was a Chief Inspector in the RUC. Complaints had been made about the way S had carried out appraisals of junior officers. As a result she was no longer asked to carry out appraisals. S claimed that she was directly discriminated against, citing the examples of two male chief inspectors who were still carrying out appraisals. The House of Lords held that the two male Chief Inspectors were not appropriate comparators. This was not a like-for-like comparison as similar complaints had not been made against the male officers. In such circumstances, the tribunal should construct a hypothetical comparator, being a male chief inspector against whom similar complaints had been made. The tribunal should then ask whether she had been treated less favourably than such a male officer would have been treated and, if so, was it on grounds of her sex? Although the question breaks naturally into two parts, there was no need for the issue to be addressed in this way and in some cases it might be appropriate to ask first what the reason for the treatment was or alternatively to combine the two questions.

Lord Nicholls said:

> "Chief Inspector Shamoon claimed she was treated less favourably than two male chief inspectors. Unlike her, they retained their counselling responsibilities. Is this comparing like with like? Prima facie it is not. She had been the subject of complaints and of representations by Police Federation representatives, the male chief inspectors had not. This might be the reason why she was treated as she was. This might explain why she was relieved of her responsibilities and they were not. But whether this factual difference between their positions was in truth a material difference is an issue which cannot be resolved without determining why she was treated as she was. It might be that the reason why she was relieved

of her counselling responsibilities had nothing to do with the complaints and representations. If that were so, then a comparison between her and the two male chief inspectors may well be comparing like with like, because in that event the difference between her and her two male colleagues would be an immaterial difference.

I must take this a step further. As I have said, prima facie the comparison with the two male chief inspectors is not apt. So be it. Let it be assumed that, this being so, the most sensible course in practice is to proceed on the footing that the appropriate comparator is a hypothetical comparator: a male chief inspector regarding whose conduct similar complaints and representations had been made. On this footing the less favourable treatment issue is this: was Chief Inspector Shamoon treated less favourably than such a male chief inspector would have been treated? But, here also, the question is incapable of being answered without deciding why Chief Inspector Shamoon was treated as she was. It is impossible to decide whether Chief Inspector Shamoon was treated less favourably than a hypothetical male chief inspector without identifying the ground on which she was treated as she was. Was it grounds of sex? If yes, then she was treated less favourably than a male chief inspector in her position would have been treated. If not, not. Thus, on this footing also, the less favourable treatment issue is incapable of being decided without deciding the reason why issue. And the decision on the reason why issue will also provide the answer to the less favourable treatment issue."

GENUINE OCCUPATIONAL QUALIFICATIONS AND POSITIVE DISCRIMINATION

Positive discrimination (sometimes referred to as affirmative action) **6–4** means the more favourable treatment of a person on grounds of sex in order to overcome the fact that his or her sex is under-represented in a work group. Generally this is not permitted. The only exceptions to this in employment, permit an employer to encourage one sex to apply for jobs in such work groups or to discriminate in favour of the under-represented sex in offering training opportunities to existing employees (SDA ss.47, 48). Even where there is such an under-representation in a work group an employer is not permitted to recruit an applicant of one sex in preference to a better qualified applicant of the other sex. This issue has also been considered in light of the European Equal Treatment Directive. In *Kalanke v Freie Hansestadt Bremen* [1995] I.R.L.R. 660 the ECJ held that an unconditional priority over equally qualified men accorded to women in competition for certain public sector jobs (in order to ensure better representation of women in such jobs) was contrary to the Equal Treatment Directive. However, the Directive is not breached where special reasons specific to an individual male candidate permit the priority for female candidates to be overridden (*Marschall v Land Nordrhein-Westphalen* [1998] I.R.L.R. 39). Article 141 now gives Member States greater freedom to allow positive discrimination. However, the United Kingdom has not taken this opportunity to date.

In certain carefully circumscribed circumstances an employer is entitled to defend discrimination in the form of not selecting a person for employment by bringing the case within situations in which the law recognises there is a good reason for selecting a member of one sex. These are set out in SDA s.7 and are known as Genuine Occupational Qualifications (GOQs) and apply in the following circumstances:

(1) Where the essential nature of the job calls for a man (or woman) for reasons of physiology (but not strength or stamina) or, in dramatic performances, authenticity.
(2) Where the job needs to be held by a man (or woman) in order to preserve decency or privacy because it is likely to involve physical contact with women in circumstances in which they may reasonably object, or women might object to the job being done by a man because they are in a state of undress or using sanitary facilities or the job involves working in a private home and objection may be taken to a woman having social contact or knowledge of intimate details of life of person living there, as seen in the following cases.

Snell v Exclusive Cleaning And Maintenance (Northern) Ltd

(ET Case No. 1298/123, unreported)

Held that being a man was a GOQ for job of men's toilet cleaner as the employer operated a 24 hour shift system and toilets could not be closed to allow cleaning.

Banks v Viroy Cleaning Services Ltd

(ET Case No. 17934/84, unreported)

Held being a woman was not a GOQ for job of women's toilet cleaner as the office closed at 5pm by which time most staff had gone home.

Main v Ministry of Defence

(ET Case No. 3101031/97, unreported)

A male nurse was rejected in preference for a female nurse who was less experienced and with poorer qualification. It was held that a distinction had to be drawn between professional people and, for example, those supervising changing facilities as society at large is accustomed to medical staff examining patients of the opposite sex and seeing them in a state of undress.

(3) Where the nature of the establishment makes it impracticable for the job holder to live elsewhere than in premises provided by the employer (*e.g.* lighthouse keepers, oil rig workers) and (i) there are sleeping or sanitary facilities for only one sex, and (ii) it is not reasonable to expect an employer to provide separate or alternative facilities for the opposite sex.

Hermolle v GCHQ

(unreported, EAT)

Ms Hermolle applied for a transfer to Ascension Island but was turned down because the only accommodation was in an all-male accommodation block. Suitable accommodation could have been provided but at a cost of £3,500. The Tribunal held that in light of the employer's resources it was not unreasonable to require suitable accommodation to be provided. Accordingly the employer was not able to rely on the GOQ.

(4) Where the work is to be done in an establishment (or part of one) like a hospital or prison for persons (who are all men (or women)) requiring special care or supervision and that its reasonable that the job should not be held by a woman (or man).

Fanders v St Mary's Convent Preparatory School

(unreported, EAT)

The school refused to appoint a male teacher at a school for infants in a girls' school. The children were perfectly normal and did not require any special care, supervision or attention. Held the school could not plead GOQ.

(5) Where the job holder provides persons with personal services promoting their welfare or education or similar personal services which can most effectively be provided by a member of a particular sex, for example rape crisis centre workers or even relationship counsellors.

London Lambeth Borough Council v Commission for Racial Equality

[1990] I.C.R. 768

Although this case concerns racial discrimination it is relevant for sex discrimination too. The Council wanted to fill two posts in its housing department and because most tenants were either Afro-Caribbean or Asian, applications were invited only from people in those groups. The work was managerial, involved minimal contact with members of the public and did not provide personal services but the Council argued that provided they provided "personal services promoting welfare" it did not matter that they were not provided by the job applicant.

Held that "personal" envisaged face-to-face, direct contact between the job-holder and the recipient of the services. Accordingly the Council could not rely on the GOQ.

(6) Where the job is likely to involve performance of duties in a country (e.g. certain Middle East countries) whose laws or customs would mean that a woman could not effectively perform the duties.

(7) The job is one of two to be held by a married couple, or a couple who are civil partners.

A GOQ may not be pleaded where the employer has sufficient employees of the appropriate sex who are capable of doing the GOQ part of a job and it would be reasonable to employ them on these duties (SDA s.7(4)).

Etam Plc v Rowan

[1989] I.R.L.R. 150, EAT

Mr Rowan was rejected for a job in a women's clothing store on the grounds that about 25 per cent of his time would be spent in or near the ladies changing rooms.

Held a GOQ could not be pleaded because only a small part of the duties required the presence of a female and those duties could be adequately done by other female staff.

INDIRECT DISCRIMINATION

Indirect sex discrimination occurs where an employer imposes a policy or criterion or adopts a practice across the board (i.e. what looks like a gender neutral criterion) but the effect in practice is that more women are disadvantaged by it than men (or vice versa), e.g. a minimum height of 6ft being imposed on both sexes in order to be selected for a job. On the surface it appears that it is a fair and neutral criterion but in practice it would exclude more women than men and it would be unlawful unless the employer could show it was a justifiable criterion having regard to the duties of the job. **6–5**

While the principle of indirect discrimination remains, the precise definition has been the subject of amendment. Section 1(2)(b) of the SDA contains the elements of indirect discrimination in relation to employment and training applicable since October 1, 2005:

- applying to a woman a provision, criterion or practice which is also applied to a man;
- the provision, criterion or practice puts women at a disadvantage compared to men;
- the woman claiming discrimination is in fact put at a disadvantage; and
- the employer cannot show that it is a proportionate means of achieving a legitimate aim.

The new wording replaces the need to show that the provision, criteria or practice is to the detriment of "a considerably larger proportion" of women than men and that the employer is unable to objectively justify the provision, criteria or practice. The new wording means that statistical calculations will no longer be required in every case to show disadvantage to a particular group. They may still be useful to establish that disadvantage in fact occurs but the new wording gives scope for this evidence to be provided by experts or other witnesses.

Examples of requirements or criteria having a potentially disproportionate impact are:

- full time hours only;
- age limits;
- qualifications;
- length of service before rights benefits acquired obtained; and
- benefits to permanent employees only.

The indirect discrimination provisions have been interpreted according to the reality of women's situations rather than any theoretical notion of what was physiologically possible for them to do. In *Price v Civil Service Commission* [1978] I.C.R. 27 an age range of 17–28 for applicants for certain posts in the Civil Service was one which considerably fewer women than men could comply with. This is because far more women than men in that age group were in practice not able to comply because of their child rearing and family responsibilities, even though when the population as a whole was considered the numbers of men and women in the age group were not significantly different. Similarly in race discrimination, in *Mandla v Dowell Lee* [1983] I.C.R. 385 the House of Lords in a relevant race relations case held that a school uniform rule that forbade wearing turbans meant that a Sikh pupil was not able to comply with the "no turbans" rule.

6–6 In assessing the disadvantage of one sex, it is not usually appropriate to look at the entire population but to consider the "pool" of people who are in fact affected by the policy or practice. For example, this may require consideration of those who have the required qualifications and to an extent therefore the employer is in a position to influence the parameters of the pool. Also it depends on the nature of the alleged discrimination. Thus if what is being challenged is the employer's criterion for selection for redundancy, the pool will be those who are employed in the types of work for which the employer no longer has a need. Similarly if a university or a large national company is proposing to recruit a Chief Executive or Principal the pool is likely to be all potential applicants, nationwide. On the other hand if the job is for clerical, technical or administrative work and is advertised only locally it could be argued that the pool would be those who live locally and are qualified for the position. There is no hard and fast rule as to the selection of the appropriate pool and much depends on the nature of the alleged discriminatory act and whether it is a case of recruitment or the treatment (including dismissal) of existing employees. In the case of treatment of existing employees, disadvantage may have to be judged in terms of only a part of the workforce. Thus in *London Underground v Edwards (No.2)* [1998] I.R.L.R. 364 it was proposed to introduce new flexible work rostering of train operators employed by London Underground. Ms Edwards argued that a considerably smaller proportion of women could comply with the new requirement. She was only one of 21 women employed as train operators and only she could not comply. All the other operators (2,023) were men and all of them could comply. When dealing with the identification of the pool Potter L J stated:

> "The identity of the appropriate pool will depend on identifying that sector of the relevant workforce which is affected or potentially affected by the application of the particular requirement or condition in question and the context or the circumstances in which it is sought to be applied. In this case the pool was all the members of the workforce of the Underground, namely train operators to whom the new rostering requirements were to be applied. ... [I]t did not include all employees of the London Underground. Nor did the pool extend to include the wider field of potential new applicants for

> the job of train operator ... because the discrimination complained of was the requirement for existing employees to enter a new contract embodying the new rostering arrangement; it was not a complaint brought by an applicant from outside complaining about the terms of the job applied for."

Under the amended definition, the claimant must also be able to show that she was in fact disadvantaged by the provision. This replaces the need to show a "detriment" under the old provisions but is unlikely to make a practical difference. Under the old provisions, the existence of a detriment was a question of fact but it was not a high standard and it was sufficient to show that the claimant was placed at some disadvantage. In *Ministry of Defence v Jeremiah* [1980] I.C.R. 13 men who volunteered for overtime were allocated to unpleasant, dirty work while women were not. The men were regarded as being subjected to a detriment even though they received extra pay for the dirty work.

The original provisions allowed an employer to defend a claim of indirect discrimination by showing that it was "justified". There was much debate in case law as to what this meant but generally it was accepted that this meant objective justification, balancing the reasonable needs of the business against the discriminatory effect of the condition (*Hampson v Dept of Education and Science* [1989] I.C.R. 179). This reflected the ECJ's view that the employer must show that the means chosen correspond to a real need on the part of the business and are appropriate and necessary to achieve that end (*Bilka-Kaufhaus v Hartz* [1987] I.C.R. 110). So, for example, there was no justification for the flexible rostering system introduced by London Underground which required employees to start early in the day as the employers could have made alternative arrangements which would not have damaged their business plans but could have accommodated the reasonable needs of the employees. Under the amended definition, employers have to show that policy or practice is a proportionate means of achieving a legitimate aim. However it is not anticipated that this will give rise to any difference in practice to the previous test of justification.

VICTIMISATION

The SDA protects those who have made complaints of unlawful **6–7**
discrimination under the Act, threatened to do so, or assisted another to do so by providing that less favourable treatment of someone for that reason will be victimisation and a separate type of unlawful discrimination. This could relate to conduct after the employment has ended (such as refusal to give a reference) provided that there is a substantial connection between the conduct and the employment relationship (SDA s.20A).

EMPLOYMENT DISCRIMINATION

6–8 The SDA definition of employment is "employment under a contract of service or of apprenticeship or a contract personally to execute any work or labour, and related expressions shall be construed accordingly" (s.82(1)). Clearly this definition embraces, but is also wider than, a contract of employment and can include some self-employed workers.

In *Hugh-Jones v St John's College, Cambridge* [1979] I.C.R. 848 although a research fellow was not employed under a contract of employment, she was engaged in the execution of work or labour in terms of s.82(1) and her treatment thus fell within the provisions of the SDA. In *Perceval-Price v Department of Economic Development* [2000] I.R.L.R. 380. Tribunal chairmen were held to be in "employment" for the purposes of EC law. In *Gillick v BP Chemicals Ltd* [1993] I.R.L.R. 437 an agency worker was held to be in the employment of the employment agency but not the host company at which she carried out her duties because there was no contract between the worker and the host company although such a worker may be protected under the SDA s.9 relating to contract workers. In order to fall within the definition of employment it is not necessary for the individual to carry out all of the tasks under the contract but personal performance must be the dominant purpose of the contract. In special circumstances a partnership may enter a contract to personally execute work (*Loughran & Kelly v N I Housing Executive* [1998] I.R.L.R. 593) but because a limited company has a separate and artificial legal personality it may not enter into such a contract.

The effect of the Equal Treatment Directive (to eliminate discrimination between men and women) is that an employee whose contract of employment is illegal may nevertheless lodge a complaint of sexual discrimination because the Directive is not dependent on a lawful contract but merely an employment relationship and the Directive does not permit derogation from the principle of equal treatment for reasons of public policy (*Hall v Woolston Hall Leisure Ltd* [2000] I.R.L.R. 578).

Section 6 makes it unlawful for an employer to discriminate against a person in relation to the following:

(a) the arrangements he makes for determining who should be offered employment, for example the recruitment and selection process;
(b) the terms on which he offers employment, for example requiring that the job holder works full time;
(c) by refusing to offer employment, for example rejecting a job applicant;
(d) in the way he affords access to promotion, training, transfer, benefits, facilities or services; or

(e) by dismissing or subjecting a person to some other detriment.

Dress Codes and Sexual Harassment

Dress codes may amount to a disadvantage; requiring women but not men to wear uniforms has been held to be a detriment (under the old definition) where it was uncomfortable and suggested a lower status than that of male employees of a lower rank. However, provided an employer's dress code does not discriminate against one sex it is permissible for an employer to prescribe different dress standards for men and women. Thus in *Smith v Safeway Stores* [1996] I.R.L.R. 456 the Court of Appeal held that a dress code that applies a standard of what is conventional in an even handed way between men and women is not discriminatory. The principle to be applied is that a dress or appearance code will not be discriminatory because it is different for men and for women provided it enforces a common principle of smartness or conventionality and if, taken as a whole and not garment by garment or item by item (e.g. hairstyle, jewellery), neither gender is treated less favourably in enforcing the principle, for example because of the impact of the code on health or comfort. The EAT in *Department for Work and Pensions v Thompson* [2004] I.R.L.R. 348 confirmed this approach. All staff were required to dress in a "professional and businesslike way". For men this meant a collar and tie and for women to dress "appropriately and to a similar standard". A male employee was not discriminated against simply by being required to wear a collar and tie when women had more flexibility. He would need to establish that overall, in the context of the dress requirement, men were being less favourably treated. The case was remitted to a new tribunal to consider if it was possible to have similar flexibility for male attire while still achieving the overriding standard of "professional and businesslike" dress. **6–9**

Sexual harassment has been considered to be direct discrimination under the SDA. In *Porcelli v Strathclyde Regional Council* [1986] I.C.R. 564, a female laboratory technician was subjected to suggestive remarks by two male technicians to make her leave. The question to be asked is: "was the applicant less favourably treated on the grounds of her sex than a man would have been treated?" The decision in *Porcelli* was interpreted in some subsequent cases to the effect that where the treatment suffered was "gender specific" that was sufficient to constitute discrimination with no need to consider how someone of the opposite sex would have been treated. So, for example calling someone a "bitch" or greeting a colleague with "Hiya big tits!" in front of clients could not be defended by an employer even if he would similarly insult male employees. While in most cases, such conduct will be discriminatory, the House of Lords in *Macdonald v Ministry of Defence* [2003] I.R.L.R. 512 made it clear that it is always necessary to consider whether someone of the opposite sex would have been treated more favourably. Ms Pearce had been verbally abused by pupils at the school in which she taught including being called "dyke" and "lezzie". She argued that while a male homosexual might have been similarly abused the words used would have been different and therefore she had been discriminated against on grounds of sex. The House of Lords considered that she had been discriminated against on grounds of her sexual orientation and not her sex. In order to establish sex discrimination she would have to show that she had been less favourably treated than a man in similar circumstances (i.e. a male homosexual). It was not sufficient to show that the treatment was different.

To constitute direct sex discrimination, it is not necessary that an act of harassment betrays a sexual motivation on the part of the person concerned; it may well be that the behaviour is motivated by bullying for example. An act of sexual harassment may be committed by a member of the same sex as the victim and a single act of harassment, if sufficiently serious, is enough. The key factor is that it amounts to less favourable treatment than a man would have received. While in certain environments there will be banter and humour, a woman is entitled to draw the line so that certain kinds of behaviour are acceptable while others are not and a woman is entitled to find certain behaviour acceptable from male A but not from male B.

6–10 From October 1, 2005, harassment has been set out as a specific ground of discrimination, unlawful under the SDA. A new s.4A was inserted into the SDA which specifies that a person subjects a woman to harassment when:

(a) on the ground of sex, he engages in unwanted conduct that has the purpose or effect—

(i) of violating her dignity, or
(ii) of creating an intimidating, hostile, degrading, humiliating or offensive environment for her;

(b) he engages in any form of unwanted verbal, non-verbal or physical conduct of a sexual nature that has the purpose or effect—

(i) of violating her dignity, or
(ii) of creating an intimidating, hostile, degrading, humiliating or offensive environment for her.

Where the harassment is not intended to have the effect that it in fact does have, then the tribunal will have to consider whether in all the circumstances it ought reasonably to be considered as having that effect. The intention of this provision is to exclude claims by overly sensitive claimants. In light of the existing case law it seems clear that even if the claimant is considered to be overly sensitive, once she has made it clear that she finds the conduct offensive, continuing with that conduct will usually constitute harassment. The combination of the two provisions makes it clear that both harassment that is on grounds of sex (where a man would not have been subjected to the conduct) and harassment that is sexually motivated will be unlawful sex discrimination. In the latter case there will be no need for a comparator of the opposite sex. The EOC has successfully challenged the wording of s.4A(a) on the grounds that the Directive does not require a comparison to be made with how a man would have been treated (*EOC v Secretary of State for Trade and Industry* [2007] IDS Brief 826). The Government has undertaken to amend the definition. At the time of writing no draft amendments have been issued.

GENDER RE-ASSIGNMENT

In its original form, the SDA did not confer protection against discrimination on the grounds of gender re-assignment. However in *P v S & Cornwall County Council* [1996] I.R.L.R. 447 the ECJ concluded that it is contrary to the Equal Treatment Directive to dismiss a person on the ground that he or she was intending to undergo or had undergone gender re-assignment; that was to treat him or her less favourably in comparison with persons of the sex to which he or she was deemed to belong before undergoing gender re-assignment. The Sex Discrimination (Gender Reassignment) Regulations 1999 (SI 1999/1102) (which apply to pay and non-pay discrimination) made it unlawful to discriminate against a person on the grounds of gender re-assignment and a person discriminates against another person (B) if he treats him less favourably than he would treat other persons and does so on the grounds that the person (B) intends to undergo, is undergoing or has undergone, gender re-assignment. The Department of Employment and Education has issued a guide to the Regulations (amended to take into account the Gender Recognition Act 2004, see below) which, although of no statutory authority, contain useful information and guidance regarding how gender re-assignment cases should be dealt with and suggests that the protection will begin as soon as an individual indicates an intention to commence gender re-assignment. **6–11**

In addition to the usual Genuine Occupational Qualifications (GOQ) (see para.6–4, above) the Regulations introduced new "supplementary" GOQs which apply only to gender re-assignment cases. These are: (a) the job entails intimate physical searches pursuant to statutory powers; (b) the job entails living in a private home and objection might reasonably be taken to allowing a transsexual physical or social contact with, or knowledge of intimate details of, the person living there; (c) it is impractical for the holder of the job to live elsewhere than in premises provided by the employer and it would offend decency or privacy if he or she was undergoing gender re-assignment and it is not reasonable to expect the employer to equip those premises with suitable accommodation; and (d) the holder of the job provides vulnerable individuals with personal services promoting their welfare. The existence of any such supplementary GOQ will be a defence for an employer who is charged with treating someone less favourably on grounds of gender re-assignment. The exceptions in (c) and (d) are temporary in that they only apply while a person is undergoing gender re-assignment. It is not entirely clear when that process "finishes" however the completion of surgery is likely to be key.

In *Croft v Consignia* [2003] I.R.L.R. 851, a pre-operative male-to-female transsexual claimed discrimination where the employer refused to allow her to use the female toilet, instead requiring that the gender-neutral disabled toilets be used. The employer successfully argued that health and safety regulations required separate toilets for each sex and that this overrides the 1999 Regulations. The Court of Appeal, however, warned that this could only be a temporary measure and that permanent refusal would be discrimination. The police have argued that they could not employ someone who had undergone male-to-female surgery as a police constable as, by law, statutory searches can only be carried out by someone of the same sex as the person being searched (*A v Chief Constable of West Yorkshire Police* [2003] I.R.L.R. 32). The House of Lords held that a post-operative transgender person is entitled to be recognised in the new sex and therefore the employer could not rely on the GOQ in these circumstances. The amendments by the 1999 Regulations specifically provide that where a job entails the carrying out of intimate physical searches, an employer will not be able to rely on the GOQ where the employer already has employees capable of carrying out such searches and it would be reasonable, and not unduly inconvenient to the employer, to have those staff carry out the searches (reg.9, inserting a new s.2A into the SDA s.7B(2)). In *KB v National Health Service Pensions Agency* [2004] I.R.L.R. 240 the ECJ found that a national law restricting benefits under a pension scheme to "surviving spouses" and therefore precluding a partner who was a transsexual and therefore unable to marry in the new sex was contrary to Art.141.

6–12 Since the Regulations were passed, the European Court of Human Rights has held that the United Kingdom's refusal to recognise an individual's change of sex following gender re-assignment surgery was in breach of the European Convention on Human Rights (*Goodwin v United Kingdom* [2002] I.R.L.R. 664). This has necessitated changes in UK law to recognise a person's desire to change sex. The Gender Recognition Act 2004 provides a system where an individual can apply for recognition of a change of gender. This will not necessarily need to involve surgery although the panel set up to approve such requests may take this into account in considering whether the person still has some uncertainty about the change of gender. If successful, the individual will be fully recognised in the new sex and will be able to obtain an amended birth certificate and to marry. While the gender re-assignment provisions in the SDA will continue to protect someone who has obtained recognition from less favourable treatment, the GOQs will no longer be available to an employer (Gender Recognition Act Sch.6).

The SDA now specifically prohibits harassment where, on grounds of gender re-assignment, a person engages in unwanted conduct which has the purpose or effect of violating the dignity of the victim or creating an intimidating, hostile, degrading, humiliating or offensive environment for him or her (SDA s.4A(3)). As with the other strands, where the effect of the treatment is unintended, the tribunal will consider whether in all the circumstances it should reasonably be considered as having that effect.

The Gender Directive 2004/113 will require that protection against discrimination on grounds of gender re-assignment is extended to the provision of goods and services.

RACE DISCRIMINATION

The Race Relations Act 1976 (RRA) is modelled on the Sex Dis- **6–13**
crimination Act 1975 (SDA) and it is dealt with here only insofar as it contains significant differences. Until 2003 there was no European involvement in racial discrimination although where the UK Government made changes to the SDA (usually in order to comply with European law) a similar amendment would be made to the Race Relations Act. However, the Race Directive 2000/43 was adopted and implemented in the United Kingdom by the Race Relations Act 1976 (Amendment) Regulations 2003 (SI2003/1626). Confusingly the Directive (and therefore the 2003 Regulations) relate to discrimination on grounds of race or ethnic or national origins. This is narrower than the RRA which also includes colour or nationality. Therefore the amendments in the 2003 Regulations do not apply where the discrimination is solely on the grounds of colour or nationality. In the majority of cases such discrimination will also be on the grounds of race or ethnic or national origins.

Under the terms of s.1(1)(a) of the 1976 Act a person commits an act of direct discrimination if "on racial grounds he treats a person less favourably than he treats or would treat other persons". This includes treating someone (A) less favourably because of another person's (B) race as where Mr Owens, who was white, was dismissed from his job as the manager of an amusement centre for failing to comply with an instruction to exclude young black people from the centre; the words "on racial grounds" in s.1(1)(a) are perfectly capable of covering any reason for an action based on race, whether it be the race of the person affected by the action or of others (*Showboat Entertainment Centre Ltd v Owens* [1984] I.C.R. 65).

Weathersfield Ltd v Sargent

[1999] I.R.L.R. 94

Weathersfield resigned form her job with a car rental company after she had been told to tell people from ethnic backgrounds that no cars were available. The Court of Appeal held that it was not appropriate to protect only those who were discriminated against because of their own race. The phrase "on racial grounds" had to be construed in the context of the statute which permitted a broad meaning.

The width of this provision has recently caused the courts some difficulty.

Redfearn v Serco

[2006] I.R.L.R. 623

R was a bus driver who stood as a candidate for the British National Party (BNP) in the local council elections. The BNP has a number of racially discriminatory policies against non-white people. The majority of passengers were of Asian origin. Following representations from trade unions and fellow employees, the driver was dismissed on health and safety grounds. The driver claimed direct and indirect racial discrimination. The Court of Appeal found that although racial considerations were relevant to the decision, the treatment was not "on racial grounds". To find otherwise would run contrary to the policy behind the legislation which is, Mummery L.J. stated, to promote an anti-discrimination policy. "Taken to its logical conclusion, R's interpretation of the 1976 Act would mean that it could be an act of direct race discrimination for an employer, who was trying to improve race relations in the workplace, to dismiss an employee, whom he discovered had committed an act of race discrimination, such as racist abuse, against a fellow employee or against a customer of the employer. I am confident that that is not the kind of case for which the anti-discrimination legislation was designed."

The Court of Appeal also dismissed R's argument that he had been discriminated against because he was a member of a party that only allowed white members. It held that R was treated less favourably not on the ground that he was white, but "on the ground of a particular non-racial characteristic shared by him with a tiny proportion of the white population, that is membership of and standing for election for a political party like the BNP".

> "The dividing line of colour or race was not made by Serco, but by the BNP which defines its own composition by colour or race."

Racial Grounds

"Racial grounds" under the 1976 Act covers colour, race, nationality, ethnic or national origins and "racial group" means a group of persons defined by reference to these characteristics (RRA s.3). Nationality covers nationality or citizenship of a State, whether acquired at birth or subsequently (s.78(1)). **6–14**

In *Mandla v Lee* [1983] I.C.R. 385—a case concerning whether Sikhs (Sikhism is undoubtedly a religion) were also an ethnic group—it was held that the term "ethnic origins" should be construed widely in a broad cultural and historic sense. An ethnic group had to regard itself as a distinct community by virtue of certain characteristics, two of which were essential. These were:

(1) a long shared history, of which the group was conscious as distinguishing it from other groups; and
(2) a cultural tradition of its own, including family and social customs and manners—often, but not necessarily, associated with religious observance.

Certain other characteristics were also held to be relevant to the assessment of whether an ethnic group existed. These were:

(3) a common geographical origin or descent from a small number of common ancestors;
(4) a common language, although this did not necessarily have to be peculiar to the group;
(5) a common literature peculiar to the group;
(6) a common religion different from that of neighbouring groups; and
(7) the characteristic of being a minority or being oppressed by a dominant group within a larger community.

The House of Lords held that Sikhs were a distinct ethnic group and therefore protected by the Act.

Similarly, Jews (*Seide v Gillette Industries Ltd* [1980] I.R.L.R. 427) and Romanies form ethnic groups (*CRE v Dutton* [1989] I.R.L.R. 8) but Rastafarians (*Crown Suppliers (PSA) v Dawkins* [1993] I.C.R. 517) and Muslims (*CRE v Precision Manufacturing Services Ltd* (ET Case No. 4106/91, unreported)) do not. However, often discrimination against individuals who are Muslims may be found to be indirect racial discrimination. For example, where an employer refused all employees the right to take holidays in June, the month of the Muslim festival of Eid, such a requirement is likely to be one with which a significantly smaller proportion of Asians (of whom many would be Muslims) could not comply.

6–15 While ethnic groups will not include Scots or English persons (*British Airways Plc v Boyce* [2001] I.R.L.R. 157), the RRA applies to racial groups within the United Kingdom as well as those outside the United Kingdom (*BBC Scotland v Souster* [2001] I.R.L.R. 150) and "national origins" means more than nationality, in the legal sense, acquired by an individual at birth.

Northern Joint Police Board v Power

[1997] I.R.L.R. 610

Power, who was English, claimed racial discrimination when he was not selected for interview for the post of Chief Constable of a Scottish police force. The employment tribunal held that the English and Scots are separate racial groups by reference to their national origins, on the grounds that Scotland and England are both nations in the non-legal sense and until the Act of Union 1707 they were both separate countries with their own status and identity. In *BBC Scotland v Souster* the Court of Session held that the racial group described as "Scots" did not meet the two essential conditions for an ethnic group set out in *Mandla* and where a person claims discrimination on the grounds of his national origins, Lord Cameron stated "it will be for him to prove that he is English, whether that be because his national origins are English or because he has acquired English nationality or that he is perceived to be English".

The result is that a Scot or an English person who believes he or she has been discriminated against on racial grounds may bring a claim under the Race Relations Act provided he or she can prove he or she is of Scots or English national origin.

Like sexual harassment, racial harassment has been similarly treated as direct racial discrimination under the RRA where the victim is treated less favourably than someone of a different racial group would be. The 2003 Regulations provided that harassment on grounds of race or ethnic or national origin would be a separate type of racial discrimination where the victim was exposed to unwanted conduct which had the purpose or effect of violating his dignity or creating an intimidating, hostile, degrading, humiliating or offensive environment for him (RRA s.3A). Where the effect of the treatment is unintended, the tribunal will consider whether in all the circumstances it should reasonably be considered as having that effect.

INDIRECT DISCRIMINATION

In relation to indirect discrimination, the provision, criteria or practice applied by the employer must put persons of a particular race or ethnic or national origin at a particular disadvantage compared with other persons unless it is a proportionate way of achieving a legitimate aim. This definition was introduced in by the 2003 Regulations. As discussed above, these Regulations do not apply to discrimination on grounds of colour or nationality. In these cases the original definition of indirect discrimination will remain, namely that the employer imposes a requirement or condition which is such that the proportion of persons of the same racial group as the claimant who can comply is considerably smaller than the proportion of persons not of that racial group who can comply and the employer cannot show that the condition or requirement is justifiable on objective grounds. With regard to indirect racial discrimination as originally defined, the following requirements or conditions have been held to be justifiable in particular circumstances (under the original definition): **6–16**

- forbidding a beard on the grounds of hygiene: *Singh v Rowntree Mackintosh Ltd* [1979] I.C.R. 199;
- requiring that a Muslim female nurse conform with the uniform prescribed by regulations by not wearing trousers: *Kingston and Richmond Area Health Authority v Kaur* [1981] I.C.R. 631); but in *Malik v Bertram Personnel Group Ltd* (1979, unreported, ET), the tribunal held that requiring Muslim women sales assistants to wear a skirt was not justified;
- requiring employees (Sikhs) to wear protective head gear may be justified on safety grounds but by s.12 of the Employment Act 1989 a requirement that a Sikh on a construction site wear a safety helmet instead of a turban is not justifiable;
- requiring previous managerial experience: *Ojutiku v Manpower Services Commission* [1982] I.C.R. 661;
- requiring highly qualified and skilled employees to produce written reports in English promptly.

The following have been held not to be justifiable:

- a requirement that labourers complete application forms in English in their own handwriting;
- a requirement that pupils attending a Christian school do not wear a turban (*Mandla v Lee* [1983] I.C.R. 385);
- a requirement that students who have not been ordinarily resident in the European Community for three years pay higher fees (*Orphanos v Queen Mary College* [1985] I.R.L.R. 349).

GENUINE OCCUPATIONAL QUALIFICATIONS AND POSITIVE DISCRIMINATION

6–17 Like the SDA, the RRA contains only limited opportunities for positive discrimination. Although a charity which confers benefits on racial grounds other than colour is outside the provisions of the RRA this does not permit employment discrimination by the charity (s.34). Thus a charity can lawfully confer its benefits only on Scots but it could not refuse to employ a person on the grounds that he or she was non-Scots. Other limited opportunities for positive action relate to making provision for the special needs (education, training or welfare) of a racial group or for employees not ordinarily resident in Great Britain (RRA ss.35, 36). Like the SDA, the RRA permits an employer to discriminate positively only in relation to providing existing employees with training where employees of that race are not well represented in a work group. However, while an employer may encourage the participation of under-represented racial groups he may not positively discriminate by employing a candidate of one racial group who is worse than a candidate of another racial group who has been rejected (RRA ss.37, 38).

The GOQ provisions have been amended by the 2003 Regulations, in respect of race or ethnic or national origins. In these cases the employer has to show that being of a particular race or ethnic or national origins is a "genuine and determining requirement" having regard to the nature of the job and the context in which it is carried out and it has been applied in a proportionate manner. Where the discrimination is on grounds of colour or nationality the original GOQs apply. These are similar to those under the SDA although there are fewer under the RRA s.5 than under the SDA. They operate where:

- the job involves participation in a dramatic performance or entertainment which requires a person of a particular racial group for authenticity, for example refusing to engage a black person to play the part of William Wallace;
- the job involves work as a model in the production of a work of art which requires a person of a particular racial group for authenticity, for example an artists or photographer's model;
- the job involves working in place where food or drink is provided to the public in a particular setting which requires a person of particular racial group for authenticity, for example, refusing to employ a native Scot as waiter in a Chinese restaurant; and
- the job holder provides members of a particular racial group with personal services which can most effectively be provided by one of the same racial group, for example not appointing an English person to work as a social worker for the Afro-Caribbean community.

SEXUAL ORIENTATION

6–18 Following the decision of the ECJ in *P v S and Cornwall County Council* [1996] I.R.L.R. 347, it was anticipated by some that the Equal Treatment Directive would similarly be interpreted to cover discrimination on grounds of sexual orientation. However, in *Grant v South West Trains* [1998] I.R.L.R. 206, this was rejected by the ECJ. The case concerned the restriction of cheap rail fares to the spouses or opposite sex partners of employees. The ECJ held that a lesbian employee who had been denied the travel concession could not rely on the Equal Treatment Directive if a male with a same sex partner would also have been denied the benefit. This approach has been followed in the United Kingdom (*Macdonald v Advocate General for Scotland* [2003] I.R.L.R. 512, HL). If, however, there has been differential treatment of male and female homosexuals this would be a breach of the SDA and the Equal Treatment Directive (*Smith v Gardner Merchant* [1999] I.C.R. 134).

Taking a different approach, the European Court of Human Rights found that the policy of the United Kingdom's armed forces of conducting investigations into the sexuality of its service men and women and subsequently discharging any found to be homosexual was contrary to Art.8 of the European Convention on Human Rights (*Smith and Grady v United Kingdom* [1999] I.R.L.R. 734). This does not mean that any less favourable treatment of homosexuals would automatically breach the Convention. In the *Smith and Grady* case it was the right to respect of an individual's private life that was breached (Art.8). The Human Rights Act 1998 requires that Convention rights be respected by all public authorities but enforcement of that right is by action in the appropriate court and not through the employment tribunals and such action would not be relevant where the employer was in the private sector. Although courts are required to interpret legislation where possible to give effect to Convention rights, the House of Lords has held that the SDA cannot be interpreted to cover discrimination on grounds of sexual orientation (*Macdonald v Advocate General for Scotland* [2003] I.R.L.R. 512, HL).

This debate, so far as it relates to employment and training, has effectively been superseded by measures to implement the EC Framework Employment Directive. The Employment Equality (Sexual Orientation) Regulations 2003 (SI 2003/1661) came into force on December 1, 2003. These Regulations mirror the concepts in sex and race discrimination and prohibit direct and indirect discrimination, victimisation and harassment "on grounds of" sexual orientation. As with racial discrimination this wording means that the discrimination may be because of the sexual orientation of someone other than the employee and will also cover discrimination based on perceived sexual orientation, whether or not the person is in fact of that orientation. "Sexual orientation" includes heterosexual, homosexual and bisexual orientation but no other preferences. As with other discrimination, the employer is vicariously liable for discrimination carried out in the course of employment. If a benefit is restricted to heterosexual couples this is unlawful. However where the benefit is aimed at married couples this is allowed by the Regulations. Amendments have been made to the 2003 Regulations to take account of the Civil Partnership Act 2004 which allows the registration of same sex relationships with effect from December 5, 2005. The amendment provides that the status of a civil partner is comparable to the status of a spouse for the purposes of these Regulations only. This enables a civil partner who is treated less favourably than a married person in similar circumstances to bring a claim for sexual orientation discrimination under the 2003 Regulations. There is a GOR for very limited circumstances where it can be shown that the requirement is for a heterosexual spouse rather than a civil partner. An example might be for a religious post. These amendments have no effect on events before December 5, 2005 and do not prevent the restriction of benefits to spouses and civil partners to the exclusion of other partners.

Genuine Occupational Requirements and Positive Action

6–19 Employers may require that the employee be of a particular orientation when, having regard to the nature of the employment or the context in which it is carried out, being of a particular sexual orientation is a "genuine and determining requirement" and where that requirement is applied in a proportionate manner. It will be very rare that someone's sexual orientation will be genuine and determining requirement. A possible example might be working for a lesbian and gay counselling service or being the public face of a gay rights organisation. However, just working for such an organisation would not usually require someone to be gay.

There is a further exception which allows employers to apply a requirement relating to sexual orientation where the employment is for the purposes of organised religion. This could include a requirement not to associate with gay people or to express certain views as well as being of a particular orientation. The requirement must be applied to comply with the doctrines of religion or to avoid conflicting with the strongly held religious convictions of a significant number of the religion's followers. In the latter case the tribunal will consider the nature and context of the work itself. This exception is intended for ministers of religion or other members of the clergy. It is possible that other people employed by an organised religion could be covered in appropriate circumstances but certainly is not a blanket exception for all employees of organised religions. The sexual orientation of the cleaner of a church is unlikely to be specified by religious doctrine and although some members of the church might not approve, the nature of the work and the context in which it is carried out would not seem to require such restriction.

Positive action is allowed for training and encouraging people of a particular sexual orientation to take advantage of opportunities at work. Due to the lack of available statistics, there is no need, as under the similar provisions of the SDA and the RRA, to show under-representation of the group which is receiving positive action.

RELIGION OR BELIEF

As has been discussed above, the Race Relations Act 1976 does not **6–20** expressly prohibit discrimination on grounds of religion. Some ethnic groups such as Sikhs and Jews have been able to establish that they constitute an "ethnic group" and are therefore protected by the RRA, while for other groups, as we have seen, less favourable treatment may constitute indirect discrimination on racial grounds. Although Art.9 of the European Convention on Human Rights protects freedom of thought, conscience and religion, there is a distinction between the right to hold a religion or belief, which is absolute, and the right to manifest that belief which may be restricted.

Ahmad v United Kingdom

(1981) 4 E.H.R.R. 126

Mr Ahmad was refused permission to attend weekly prayers. This was found not to breach the Convention as the employee had accepted the terms of the contract when taking up employment and the employer had made number of attempts to accommodate the employee's needs in other ways.

Coopsey v WWB Devon Clays Ltd

[2003] I.D.S. Brief 767

Employee was dismissed for failing to agree new terms which would have required him to work different shifts including some Sundays. He sought to rely on Art.9 as the working patterns would prevent him attending church service. However, the EAT considered he was free to resign if his religious commitments were incompatible with the hours of work that his employer wanted him to do. This freedom of choice, they considered, meant that there was no infringement of Art 9.

The Employment Equality (Religion or Belief) Regulations 2003 (SI 2003/1660) which implement the Framework Directive, for the first time give a general right not to be discriminated against on grounds of religion or belief. The Regulations mirror those for sexual orientation and prohibit direct and indirect discrimination, victimisation and harassment.

What constitutes a "religion or belief" is a question of fact for the tribunal. A "belief" is defined by the Regulations (as amended by The Equality Act 2006 with effect from April 6, 2007) as "any religious or philosophical belief". All well-recognised religions such as Christianity, Islam, Hinduism, Sikhism and Judaism will be covered as well as any branches such as Protestantism and Catholicism. However less common religions are also likely to be included and there is no value judgment built into the definition so what might be seen by the public as a "cult" may well be considered a "religion" by a tribunal. What is a "philosophical belief" will also need to be determined by the tribunals. The previous wording of the Regulations required that to be protected a philosophical belief needed to be "similar" to a religious belief. The word "similar" has now been removed by the amendments made by the Equality Act 2006, so it would appear that the scope of protection is now wider and could include political beliefs that were previously thought to be excluded. A claim by a US national who was instructed to remove a US flag was rejected by a tribunal. His loyalty to his native country did not amount to a religious belief (*Williams v South Central* (Case No. 2306989/03, unreported)).

The Regulations were amended by the Equality Act 2006 to make it clear that absence of belief is covered by the Regulations. The protection where the discrimination is on grounds of a perceived religion or belief has been removed. For example where an employee is thought to be Muslim but in fact is not. A claim can be made where the treatment relates to someone else's religion such as the religion of a spouse. There are provisions for limited positive action as for sexual orientation.

6–21 The majority of cases brought so far have involved claims by Christian or Muslim employees.

Williams-Drabble v Pathway Care Solutions Ltd

[2005] I.D.A. Brief 776

The employee worked as a residential social worker. The employee advised the employer at the interview that she could not work on Sundays as she was a practicing Christian and attended church on Sunday mornings. She agreed to work a Saturday "sleepover" once every three weeks. This finished at 10am and allowed her to rest and attend evening service. After about five months, her employer changed the rota which meant that the employee would have to work on Sundays from 3pm until 10am on Monday on a regular basis. When she complained she was told it was up to her to arrange a swap if she could and if she didn't want to work the new rota she would have to resign. She resigned and claimed that she had been both directly and indirectly discriminated against on grounds of religion or belief.

The tribunal considered that there was insufficient evidence to establish direct discrimination but that she had been indirectly discriminated against.

Khan v G and J Spencer Group plc v NIC Hygiene Ltd

(Case No. 1893250/04, unreported)

A Muslim employee had worked as a bus cleaner since 1996. In 2004 he asked if he could use his 25 day holiday entitlement and another week's unpaid leave to make a pilgrimage to Mecca. Although the employer did not respond his manager said he should assume he could go. When he returned to work he was suspended and subsequently dismissed for gross misconduct. He successfully claimed both unfair dismissal and religious discrimination.

Monaghan v Leicester Young Men's Christian Association

(Case No. 1901830/04, unreported)

M was a Christian and head of department in charge of running two hostels for asylum seekers. He claimed he was discriminated against on grounds of religion because his chief executive told him he should not try to convert people to the Christian faith. The chief executive believed that although the YMCA has a Christian ethos it is a multi-cultural organisation and it was wrong to try to convert asylum seekers to Christianity. The tribunal held that the action was taken not on grounds of M's religion but his action in trying to convert people to that religion and therefore dismissed the claim.

A high profile case was brought by a Muslim teaching assistant who was dismissed for refusing to remove her veil.

Azmi v Kirklees Borough Council

[2007] I.R.L.R 484

A, a devout Muslim, informed her employer that she had to have her head and face covered, apart from her eyes, when teaching with male colleagues. Her employers, having observed her teaching, concluded that the veil hindered her interaction with the pupils and their understanding of her. She was dismissed when she refused to remove the veil when teaching (although it could be worn at other times). Her claims of direct and indirect discrimination were unsuccessful. In relation to the claim of direct discrimination, the EAT found that the correct comparator was someone who covered their face for a reason other than religion. The tribunal had correctly found that such a person would also have been dismissed. The employer's policy that faces could not be covered did place persons of A's religion at a disadvantage but that the policy was justified.

This case should not be taken to mean that employers will be able to insist on employees not wearing veils or other religious dress. The key issue here was that the veil could be shown to be interfering with the employee's performance and that the employer had applied the requirement proportionately. Health and safety reasons might also be relevant in certain cases.

Genuine Occupational Requirements and Positive Action

6–22 Discrimination on grounds of religion and belief will be permitted where, having regard to the nature of the employment or the context in which it is carried out, there is a genuine determining requirement and where that requirement is carried out in a proportionate manner. There are few jobs where a person's religion or belief would be sufficiently important. An example might be where a hospital requires a Christian chaplin because nearly all the patients are Christian or the public representative of a religion.

There is an additional exception for organisations that have an ethos based on a particular religion or belief. These might include faith schools, nursing homes or charities run by religious groups or based on religious beliefs. These organisations will not have to show that having a particular religion or belief is a determining requirement, only that it is a genuine requirement. This is a less strict test but the employer will still have to show that the application is proportionate in the circumstances of the individual case. While it might be a requirement that a teacher in a faith school who is involved with the pupils moral development would require to be of that faith, it would not apply to a laboratory assistant, janitor or cleaner.

Positive action is allowed for training and encouraging people of a particular religion or belief to take advantage of opportunities at work.

DISABILITY

The first attempt to protect against discrimination on the grounds of disability were the Disabled Persons (Employment) Acts 1944 and 1958 (which required an employer to employ a quota of disabled people) which were largely ineffective. Exemption from the quota system was commonplace and although the Acts created criminal offences there have been only three prosecutions since 1966 and an individual who had been the victim of discrimination had no individual remedy. However, between 1982 and 1995 there were 15 private members Bills. Eventually a government Bill was passed to become the Disability Discrimination Act 1995 (DDA). The National Disability Council created by this Act has since been replaced by the Disability Rights Commission (DRC) with powers similar to the Equal Opportunities Commission and the Commission for Racial Equality (Disability Rights Commission Act 1999). This body will shortly be subsumed by the new Commission of Equality and Human Rights. **6–23**

The DDA has had a number of amendments, including some to implement the Framework Employment Directive, resulting in substantial renumbering in 2004. The DDA is to be read along with any Codes of Practice and Statutory Guidance issued. These Codes of Practice and Guidance do not have the force of law but tribunals are required to take them into account.

The approach of the DDA is to adopt a medical model as opposed to a social model of disability by concentrating on the inability to perform mental or physical functions because of impairment. The DDA renders unlawful discrimination against disabled persons and victimisation of those who have brought complaints or have helped other to do so (s.55). Unlike other strands of discrimination legislation, "positive" discrimination in favour of a disabled person is not unlawful . In fact in some cases it is required as an employer has to take reasonable steps to remove a disadvantage suffered by a disabled person employee or applicant (s.4A). At present it is not possible for a claim to be brought by someone who has been discriminated against because of the disability of another such as an employee with a disabled child or a disabled partner. In *Attridge Law v Coleman* [2007] I.R.L.R.88, this issue has been referred to the European Court of Justice to decide whether the DDA complies with the Employment Framework Directive 2000/78 in not extending to such claims.

Definition of Disability

6–24 To be eligible to claim under the DDA, a person must first show that he is "disabled" within the specific terms of the Act. A disability is "a physical or mental impairment which has a substantial and long term adverse effect on a person's ability to carry out normal day to day activities" (DDA s.1). This definition is further refined by provisions to the effect that: (1) mental impairment includes an impairment resulting from a mental illness; (2) long term effect means an impairment has lasted or is likely to last 12 months or life; (3) an impairment which has ceased to have substantial adverse effect is treated as continuing if its effect is likely to recur; (4) severe disfigurement has substantial adverse effect; (5) progressive conditions which are likely to impair day-to-day activities are to be regarded as impairments with substantial adverse effect as soon as they have any effect on day-to-day activities even though they are not yet in an advanced stage; and (6) one must judge the adverse effect of an impairment by ignoring medical treatment or prosthesis (except spectacles) (DDA Sch.1).

Certain addictions which would be regarded as impairments are excluded. Thus addiction to alcohol, nicotine or other substance, unless the result of medical treatment, is not a disability. However, the physical effects of alcoholism may amount to a disability. Certain disorders and conditions are not impairments (tendency to set fires, steal, physical or sexual abuse of other persons, exhibitionism, voyeurism and seasonal rhinitis (hayfever)). Similarly severe disfigurement may be an impairment but deliberately acquired disfigurements like tattoos and body piercing are deemed to have no substantial adverse effect on day-to-day activities (Disability Discrimination (Meaning of Disability) Regulations 1996 (SI 1996/1455)). The Disability Discrimination Act 2005 amended the definition of disability in two key areas. It removed the need for mental illness to be "clinically well-recognised" and provided that a person suffering from cancer, HIV and multiple sclerosis is deemed to be "disabled" for the purposes of the DDA even if there are not yet any symptoms. An impairment will be of long term effect if it has lasted or is expected to last 12 months or for life and if an impairment has ceased to have a substantial effect on normal day-to-day activities it is to be treated as having that effect if it is likely to recur (e.g. epilepsy, rheumatoid arthritis) (DDA Sch.1).

6–25 An impairment is measured in terms of normal day-to-day activities under one of the following prescribed headings, with examples (taken from Statutory Guidance) of when an impairment will have a substantial or insubstantial effect. Thus a person's day-to-day activity of mobility will be substantially affected if he or she is unable to use public transport. However, a person's day-to-day activity of physical co-ordination will not be substantially affected if he or she is merely unable catch a tennis ball. The day-to-day activity of continence would be substantially affected by infrequent loss of control of bowels unless asleep at the times.

SUBSTANTIAL	**NOT SUBSTANTIAL**
Mobility	
Inability to use public transport	Inability to travel by car for more than two hours without discomfort
Difficulty going up/down steps	Difficulty walking 1.5km without discomfort or having to stop
Manual Dexterity	
Unable to handle knife and fork at same time	Unable to thread small needle
Able to press buttons/keys but very slowly	Unable to reach standard typing speeds for secretarial
Physical Co-ordination	
Pouring liquid with unusual slowness	Clumsiness
Placing food into mouth only with concentration	Inability to catch tennis ball
Continence	
Infrequent loss of control of bowels	Infrequent loss of control while asleep
Frequent minor bladder leakage	Infrequent minor leakage
Memory, Powers of Concentration, Learning and Understanding	
Inability to adapt to change in work routine	Unable to concentrate for several hours
Persistent inability to remember names	Occasionally forgetting name of colleague
Considerable difficulty in following list of domestic tasks	Minor spelling/reading problems
Perception of Risk of Physical Danger	
Inability to nourish	Fear of height

Feel heat or cold by touch	Underestimate risk of dangerous hobbies
Unable to cross road	Underestimate risk of unfamiliar workplaces
Other Headings of Day-to-Day Activities Include:	
Ability to lift/carry everyday things; speech, hearing, sight	

The correct approach is to concentrate on what a person cannot do rather than what he can do.

In *Leonard v Southern Derbyshire Chamber of Commerce* [2001] I.R.L.R. 19, the applicant suffered from clinical depression. Although she could walk and drive the impairment caused her to tire easily and when this happened her physical co-ordination, vision and concentration were affected. The tribunal had considered examples of what she could do, such as eat and drink and catch a ball against what she could not do, such as negotiating the edge of a pavement. The EAT held that this approach was inappropriate as her ability to catch a ball did not alleviate her inability to negotiate the pavement!

EMPLOYMENT DISCRIMINATION

6–26 An employer may discriminate against a disabled person in several ways. It is discrimination if, for a reason which relates to a person's disability, he treats (or would treat) that person less favourably than a person to whom that reason does not apply and he (the employer) cannot show that the treatment is justified (s.3A(1)). Such treatment may only be justified if the reason for it is both material and substantial. If the treatment is "direct" discrimination it cannot be justified. This means that the disabled person is treated less favourably solely on grounds of the disability and not because of any effect the disability may have on the person's ability to perform the job. So where the treatment is a result of ignorance or prejudice that can never be justified. It is unlikely that such treatment would ever be considered justified but s.3A(4) now makes it clear. One of the unique features of the Disability Discrimination Act is the obligation on an employer to take steps to remove any disadvantage to a disabled employee or job applicant. So, where a physical feature of an employer's premises or any provision, criteria or practice applied by the employer puts a disabled person at a substantial disadvantage and the employer fails to make a reasonable adjustment to such physical feature, provision, criteria or practice in order to prevent it having that effect that is also discrimination by the employer (ss.3A(2) and 4A). This type of discrimination only arises if the employer knows, or ought to have known, of the person's disability (s.4A(3)) so that an employer (by failing to make an adjustment) did not discriminate against a person who had epilepsy when that person gave the employer an assurance that his epilepsy was under control.

Reasonable adjustment will require consideration of the practicability of an adjustment, the financial cost and disruption to the employer's business, the employer's resources and the availability of help from public or other funds but may require any of the following:

- altering premises;
- providing or modifying equipment;
- providing training;
- allocation of duties to another person;
- transferring to a vacancy;
- assigning to a different place of work;
- providing a reader or interpreter or supervision;
- altering working hours; or
- permitting absence for treatment.

It is no longer possible to justify a failure to make a reasonable adjustment (2003 Regulations). In practice it was always difficult to envisage a situation where an employer would need to use this defence as any "justifying" circumstances (such as expense or inconvenience) would usually prevent the adjustment being "reasonable" in the first place.

When considering whether an employer has treated a disabled person less favourably for a reason related to a person's disability it is vital to note that the comparison is not between how an employer treats a disabled person and how he treats a person who is not disabled, as seen in the case below. **6–27**

Clark v TDG Ltd (Trading as Novacold)

[1999] I.R.L.R. 318, CA

The applicant had suffered an injury at work and did not work again until his dismissal. At the date of dismissal the employers did not believe he would be able to perform his duties for another year. The applicant presented a complaint to an employment tribunal alleging unlawful disability discrimination. The employers accepted that the applicant had a disability falling within the Act but contended that if one compared the applicant's position with that of a person not suffering from a disability, then they would have acted no differently, and that he had not been treated less favourably because of his disability.

The Court of Appeal held that the employment tribunal

erred in holding that the applicant had not been treated less favourably when he was dismissed on the grounds of his absence due to disability, on the reasoning that the applicant was treated no differently than a person who was off work for the same amount of time but for a reason other than disability. For the Disability Discrimination Act it is simply a case of identifying others to whom the reason for the treatment does not, or would not, apply. The test of less favourable treatment is based on the reason for the treatment of the disabled person and not the fact of his disability. It does not turn on a like-for-like comparison of the treatment of the disabled person and of others in similar circumstances and it is therefore not appropriate to make a comparison of the cases in the same way as in the Sex Discrimination and Race Relations Acts.

Crucially, of course, an employer has an opportunity to justify such disability-related discrimination.

The following case illustrates the difference between "direct" discrimination (which cannot be justified) and discrimination for a reason related to a disability which can.

High Quality Lifestyles Ltd v Watts

[2006] I.R.L.R. 859

W worked as a support worker in a residential home for people with learning disabilities, autism and severely challenging behaviour. On occasion, support workers were bitten or scratched, sometimes drawing blood. W was HIV positive. When he informed his employers, he was disciplined for not disclosing his condition and subsequently dismissed after his employer carried out a risk assessment and concluded that his continued employment was "untenable". W claimed disability discrimination under s.3A(1) and (5) of the DDA (disability-related and direct discrimination). The tribunal found that he had been directly discriminated against on ground of his disability (s.3A(5)) and also for a reason related to his disability (s.3A(1)) that was not justified. The EAT considered that the tribunal erred in finding there had been direct discrimination. The fact that the disability was the reason for the dismissal was not sufficient. It had to be established that the treatment was less favourable than a comparator would have received in circumstances that "were not materially different" from that of the disabled person including his abilities. In this case the comparator should have been someone who had an attribute (but not HIV) that carried the same risk of causing others illness or injury of the same gravity. The tribunal's conclusion that the reason for the treatment was his condition rather than the risk of transmission of that condition was perverse. The tribunal's finding of disability-related discrimination was upheld. The tribunal's approach (quasi-unfair dismissal) of deciding that the employer had not acted reasonably because it had not carried out a proper investigation or adequate risk assessment and therefore had not justified the discrimination was sound. The tribunal was also entitled to find that the employer had not carried out reasonable adjustments.

The following are examples of when treatment of a disabled person may or may not be justified: the rejection of blind applicant to operate computer/keyboard would not be justified but the rejection of an applicant with psoriasis for a modelling job could be; rejection of applicant with severe facial disfigurement because other employees or a customer would object, would not be justified. Also justification is to be considered after a reasonable adjustment is made, so that whether it is justified to refuse an applicant with arthritis for a typing job whose speed would improve by provision of an adapted keyboard, should be considered in light of that provision.

DISABILITY DISCRIMINATION ACT IN ACTION

H J Heinz Ltd v Kenrick **6–28**

[2000] I.R.L.R. 144

Kenrick had been off sick for some months when his employers told him that if there was no likelihood of him being able to return to work he would be at risk of dismissal. Kenrick believed he had Chronic Fatigue Syndrome (CFS) and was dismissed before his condition had been confirmed by medical tests. When he was dismissed Kenrick complained of disability discrimination. The Employment Tribunal held that Kenrick had been treated less favourably for a reason that related to his disability. The employers appealed on the grounds that, as they did not know that he suffered from CFS until after they dismissed him, they could not be held to have treated him less favourably in relation to his disability. However, the EAT held that the Disability Discrimination Act did not require that the relationship between the less favourable treatment and the disability should be judged subjectively through the eyes of the employer so that it was not necessary to show that the employer knew of the disability in order to show there was less favourable treatment for a reason relating to the disability.

Kent County Council v Mingo

[2000] I.R.L.R. 90

After injuring his back Mingo, an assistant cook, was certified as fit for work provided it did not involve heavy lifting and after a period of working as a supernumerary helper it was recommended that he be redeployed. The Council's redeployment policy was to match internal vacancies with employees requiring to be redeployed. Category "A" deployees were those at the risk of redundancy and Category "B" deployees those to be deployed on health grounds. Category "A" deployees were given priority for suitable alternative employment. A Category "A" deployee had more than twice the chance of obtaining redeployment than a Category "B" deployee and although Mingo applied for internal vacancies he was not found to be suitable—on the ground that the job would involve heavy lifting—and was eventually dismissed. The employment tribunal held Mingo had been subjected to disability discrimination as he had been treated less favourably than staff in Category "A" to whom the reason for his treatment did not apply, namely his disability, and the Council had not shown that their treatment of him was justified. Also it was held that the Council had failed to make a reasonable adjustment to a vacancy for which Mingo had been rejected because it might involve heavy lifting; the Council should have considered whether there were reasonable adjustments that could have been made to the job to accommodate Mingo.

London Borough of Hillingdon v Morgan

(1998, unreported, EAT)

Morgan, a service information officer, suffered from Myalgic Encephalomyelitis (ME) and was off work for about eight months after which it was suggested by doctors that she should ease herself back into work gradually as her symptoms permitted, preferably by starting off on a part-time basis. However, when Morgan returned to work, arrangements had been made for her care or support and as she could not cope with the stress of the job she resigned and claimed that her employers had discriminated against her on grounds of her disability. Morgan had asked to work part-time at home but this had been refused even though it had been allowed for other employees who were on long-term sick leave, although she was placed on the employer's redeployment scheme by which she could be considered for jobs before they were advertised. The employment tribunal held that by placing Morgan on the redeployment scheme but not permitting her to work part-time at home the employers had treated her less favourably for a reason that related to her disability. The tribunal also held that the employers had not made a reasonable adjustment by ignoring the advice of their own occupational health adviser and allowing Morgan to return to work on a part-time basis. The tribunal's decision was upheld by the EAT which emphasised that the Code of Practice (para.6.20) makes it clear that reasonable adjustments are required to enable an employee to be retained in his or her job and had the recommendations of the occupational health adviser been followed, Morgan could have returned to her full-time job in a few months.

Archibald v Fife Council

[2004] I.R.L.R. 651, HL

Archibald was employed as a road sweeper. Surgery resulted in complications which meant she could hardly walk and could not continue in her previous job. She retrained with a view to getting a desk job with the council but despite applying for over 100 jobs (all of which were at a higher grade than her previous job) she was unsuccessful. She was subsequently dismissed. She claimed the Council had discriminated against her on grounds of disability by failing to make a reasonable adjustment to their policy, requiring all staff applying for a higher-rated job to undergo an interview.

The House of Lords held that where an employee becomes incapable of performing the duties of his or her job, an employer will be under a duty to make reasonable adjustments. They pointed to para.4.20 of the Code of Practice which states: "If an employee becomes disabled, or has a disability which worsens so she cannot work in the same place or under the same arrangements and there is no reasonable adjustment which would enable the employee to continue doing the current job, then she might have to be considered for any suitable alternative posts which are available".

The House of Lords considered that this was not restricted to transferring an employee to the same or a lower rated job could include transferring a disabled employee to an existing post at a slightly higher grade without requiring him or her to undergo competitive interviewing.

O'Hanlon v Commissioners for HM Revenue and Customs

[2007] EWCA Civ 283

Employee had clinical depression and it was accepted that she was "disabled". Her employer's sick pay provisions stated that she was entitled to full pay for six months, then half pay for a further six months after which the employee was on pension rate or half pay, whichever was less. There was an overriding maximum of 12 months paid sick absence in any four year period. The claimant argued that this policy put her at a disadvantage because of her disability and that periods of absence that were related to her disability should be discounted when calculating sick pay. Applying the test in *Clark v Novacold* 1999 I.R.L.R. 318, the EAT concluded that the claimant had been less favourably treated for a reason related to her disability. However they upheld the decision of the tribunal that it was not a reasonable adjustment to expect the employers to pay full salary when the claimant was absent for a disability-related reason having exhausted her rights under the policy and further that the treatment was justified. "If a tribunal finds that no reasonable adjustments are required, it will be a relatively rare case for any disability-related discrimination not to be justified ... If the objective test for imposing the duty of adjustment did not bite, there was never any real possibility that the more subjective test of justification would not be satisfied." The decision of the EAT was upheld by the Court of Appeal.

ENFORCEMENT AND REMEDIES

6–29 The method by which discrimination by employers may be challenged is similar whatever the ground of discrimination. Complaints may be made by affected individuals or, in the case of sex discrimination, enforcement of the obligations of employers may be by the Equal Opportunities Commission (EOC), in the case of racial discrimination this enforcement may be by the Commission for Racial Equality (CRE) and in the case of disability by the Disability Rights Commission (DRC). The Commission for Equality and Human Rights will take over the duties of the existing three organisations and will also be responsible for promoting equality and combating discrimination in relation to the three new strands of sexual orientation, religion or belief and age. It will also, as the name suggests, play a role in supporting human rights.

The EOC, CRE or the DRC may enforce the obligations on employers (and others) by way of conducting formal investigations, issuing of non-discrimination notices, taking action where there is persistent discrimination and in respect of discriminatory advertisements and instructions or pressure to discriminate. The Commissions have power to take preliminary action in employment cases by presenting a complaint to an employment tribunal and if the case is well founded may result in the Tribunal making a declaration of rights and recommending action to be taken by the employer to reduce the effect of an act of discrimination. Also the Commissions are empowered to give assistance to prospective claimants where a case raises an issue of principle and is complex and some important employment tribunal cases have been supported in this way. The Commissions also have powers to draw up and issue Codes of Practice containing practical guidance to employers on how to avoid discrimination and any such Code is admissible in employment tribunal proceedings.

The remedy for an individual who believes he or she was the victim of unlawful discrimination is to apply to an employment tribunal within three months of the act complained of, although this may be extended if the tribunal considers it just and equitable to do so, and in the event of the complaint being upheld the tribunal may grant any or all of the following remedies:

(1) a declaration of the rights of the parties;
(2) an award of compensation which may include a sum in respect of injury to feelings and interest;
(3) a recommendation that the employer takes action for the purpose of obviating the effect on the complainant of any act of discrimination.

Claimants must ensure that they comply with any relevant statutory procedure (see Ch.7, below). Failure to have commenced a grievance procedure (if appropriate) and waited 28 days will lead to the claim being rejected by the tribunal and where failure to complete any applicable statutory procedure is due to the fault of the claimant, compensation will usually be reduced by between 10 and 50 per cent. Conversely, where the failure is the employer's compensation will be increased by the same amount.

Initially compensation was limited and could not be awarded at **6–30** all in cases of indirect sex or race discrimination unless it was intentional (SDA s.65; RRA s.56). However, following a challenge to the arbitrary limit set by statute in the European Court of Justice (*Marshall v Southampton and South West Area Health Authority* [1986] I.R.L.R. 140) there is now no limit to the amount of compensation that may be awarded for an act of direct discrimination (Sex Discrimination and Equal Pay (Remedies) Regulations 1993 (SI 1993/2798); Race Relations (Remedies) Act 1994) and since the

Sex Discrimination (Miscellaneous Amendments) Regulations 1996 (SI 1996/438) even an unintentional act of indirect sex or marital status discrimination may attract compensation, but only if the employment tribunal considers it equitable to do so in addition to one or both of the remedies under (1) or (3) above. Similar provisions operate in relation to indirect discrimination on grounds of sexual orientation and religion or belief. As yet no compensation may be awarded in respect of indirect discrimination on racial grounds unless the requirement which leads to the indirect discrimination is applied with the intention of discriminating on the relevant ground; the onus of proof is on the employer to prove that it was not applied with that intention. "Intentional" has been given a wide interpretation to mean that if the employer is aware of the discriminatory effect then the discrimination is intentional even though it is not the motive for the conduct.

Claims can be brought under any of the discrimination statutes by workers even when the discrimination takes place after their contracts have ended provided that the discrimination arises out of or is closely connected to the employment relationship. So, for example, failure to provide a reference or harassment that takes place after the employment has ended could give rise to a claim.

Onus of Proof

6–31 Proving discrimination can be difficult and it may be that circumstantial evidence is all that is available. All the strands of discrimination now provide that, while the initial onus of proof remains with the claimant, once the claimant has proved facts that suggest discrimination has occurred, then unless the employer can provide an adequate explanation, the tribunal must find in favour of the claimant. The only exception is where the discrimination is on grounds of colour or nationality where the tribunal *may* make such an inference. An important tool for a person who believes that he or she has been the victim of unlawful discrimination is the questionnaire procedure. This allows such a person to serve on the employer a statutory questionnaire in which certain questions may be addressed to an employer (or prospective employer). While there is no obligation on the employer to respond to the questionnaire, any response is admissible in tribunal proceedings and if an employer's responses are absent, evasive or delayed, a tribunal may infer that an act of discrimination has been committed.

VICARIOUS LIABILITY

6–32 Liability for an act of discrimination committed by an employee in the course of his employment falls on the employer. Thus all of the three Acts provide that anything done by a person in the course of his employment shall be treated for the purposes of that Act as done by his employers as well as by him, whether or not the act is done with the employer's approval or knowledge, although it is a defence if an employer can show that he took reasonably practicable steps to prevent the employee doing such an act, for example by drawing up and applying a policy to eliminate discriminatory acts and behaviour and by disciplining those who contravene it. However, the approach of tribunals to what is or is not in the course of employment has been generous.

Jones v Tower Boot Company Ltd

[1997] I.C.R. 254

The Court of Appeal held that the phrase "in the course of employment" should be interpreted broadly and in accordance with a layman's understanding of these words. The applicant was referred to as "chimp", "monkey" and "baboon" by a fellow employee but the court held that it would be wholly inappropriate to apply a common law principle devised to deal with an entirely different area of vicarious liability (viz. the law of delict or torts) in such a way as to permit racial discrimination to "slip through the net of employer responsibility" and whether or not an act was committed in the course of employment was a simple question of fact "unclouded by any parallels drawn from the law of vicarious liability for acts of negligence". It was wrong to consider whether the fellow employees in this case were performing their duties in an unauthorised way or performing unauthorised acts for which the employer would not normally be liable.

Chief Constable of the Lincolnshire Police v (1) Stubbs, (2) Taylor and (3) The Chief Constable Of The North Yorkshire Police

[1999] I.R.L.R. 81

Constable Deborah Stubbs and Sergeant Walker were police officers and while working together incidents occurred which resulted in Stubbs complaining that she was being sexually harassed by Walker. One of these incidents occurred when Stubbs went for a drink at a pub after work with several fellow officers including Walker and a subsequent incident with Walker which also took place in a pub after an office leaving party. She complained that acts of sexual discrimination (harassment) alleged to have been committed by Walker were in the course of his employment for which the Chief Constable would be vicariously liable. The Chief

Constable argued that as the incidents had occurred in pubs in the context of social occasions when Stubbs and Walker were both off duty, they could not have occurred in the course of Walker's employment. The EAT rejected that argument as the employment tribunal has to consider whether what happened between Stubbs and Walker occurred in circumstances that were "an extension of their employment". Whilst there would be difficult borderline cases, two important factors would be whether or not the person was on duty and whether or not the conduct occurred on the employer's premises. In this particular case, although the incidents did not occur at the employer's premises, they were nevertheless social gatherings involving officers from work either immediately after work or for an organised leaving party. The incidents therefore came within the concept of course of employment as explained by the Court of Appeal in *Jones v Tower Boot Company*. It would have been different if the acts had taken place during a chance meeting.

PART-TIME WORKERS

6–33 Prior to the passing of the Part-time Workers (Prevention of Less Favourable Treatment) Regulations 2000 (SI 2000/1551) it had been possible for women and married persons to argue that treating part-time employees less favourably than full-time employees constituted either indirect sex or marital status discrimination. Thus by excluding part-time employees from promotion or training opportunities an employer could commit an act of sex discrimination on the grounds that fewer women than men or fewer married persons than unmarried persons would work full-time so as to be able to apply for promotion or a training opportunity. Unless an employer could justify his policy or rule that only full-time employees could apply for promotion or training he would commit an act of indirect discrimination against a woman or a married person who could not work full-time and therefore was not entitled to apply for promotion or training. Similarly, an employer who operated a pay scheme which treated part-time employees less favourably than full-time employees would commit an act of unlawful sex discrimination unless the differential could be justified.

These rights, which are found in Art.141 of the European Treaty, the Sex Discrimination Act 1975 and the Equal Pay Act 1970 have undoubtedly contributed towards the elimination of many differences between part-time and full-time employees. Nevertheless the problem remained that different treatment of part-time employees could only be challenged on the grounds that it was indirect sex discrimination. Particularly men who worked part-time were unable in many cases to argue that the employer's differential treatment had a disproportionate impact on men. However, if a woman was able show that the employer's policy or rule operated to discriminate against her indirectly and as a result the employer changed the policy then of course part-time male workers would benefit as well.

The Part-time Workers (Prevention of Less Favourable Treatment) Regulations 2000 have, since July 2000, enabled less favourable treatment of part-time workers to be challenged without the need for indirect sex discrimination to be established. It must be established that the sole reason for the less favourable treatment was the employee's part-time status not some other reason, such as geographical location as in *Gibson v Scottish Ambulance Service* [2005] IDS Brief 776. Note that this is different from other areas such as race discrimination where race must play a substantial part but need not be the only reason for the treatment.

The Regulations give effect to the Part-time Work Directive and **6–34** where possible have to be interpreted in line with the purpose of the Directive. Accompanying the regulations are guidance notes; these are non-statutory and do not have the same legal effect as a Code of Practice. Nevertheless the guidance is divided into two sections, one of which indicates what has to be done to "comply with the law" and another which deals merely with "best practice".

The essential principle is that a part-time worker has the right not to be treated by his employer less favourably than a comparable full-time worker as regards the terms of his contract or by being subjected to any other detriment by his employer (reg.5). Whether or not a worker is full-time or part-time depends on whether he is identifiable as such having regard to the custom and practice of the employer in relation to workers employed by him under the same type of contract; similarly a worker is a part-time worker if he is not identifiable as a full-time worker under the same type of contract. Regulation 2 makes clear that workers are employed under different types of contract if they fall into any of the following different categories:

(a) employees who are not employed on fixed term contract;
(b) employees who are employed on fixed term contracts;
(c) employees under contracts of apprenticeship;
(d) workers who are neither employees nor employed under fixed term contracts;
(e) workers who are not employees but are employed under a contract for a fixed term; and
(f) any other description of worker that it is reasonable for the employer to treat differently from other workers on the grounds that workers of that description have a different type of contract.

These different categories are important because a part-time worker is entitled to be treated not less favourably than a comparable full-time worker only if they are both employed under the same type of contract and are engaged in the same or broadly similar work.

> *Matthews v Kent and Medway Town Fire Authority*
>
> [2006] I.C.R. 365
>
> The EAT, and subsequently the Court of Appeal, refused a claim by part-time fire-fighters on the grounds that the full-time fire-fighters were not engaged on the "same or broadly similar work" even though the fundamental work to be carried out (fighting fires) was the same. However, the House of Lords allowed the part-time fire-fighters' appeal. Baroness Hale said there were two important issues to take into account: first the extent of similarity between the posts (rather than concentrating on any differences) and secondly the importance of the part-time posts to the organisation. The case was remitted to another tribunal.

The employer's defence is to show that the treatment is justified on objective grounds and the guidance suggests that less favourable treatment will be justified only if it is to achieve a legitimate objective, for example a genuine business objective, that it is necessary to achieve that objective and it is an appropriate way of achieving the objective.

Special provision is made for workers who have been full-time and become part-time and workers who return to work on a part-time basis after a period of absence (regs 3 and 4). In effect the terms upon which the worker is allowed to return to work on a part-time basis must not be less favourable, pro rata, than those enjoyed in the full-time capacity.

6–35 In all cases it is necessary for the worker to identify a comparable worker employed by the same employer and in determining whether a part-time worker has been treated less favourably the pro rata principle shall be applied unless inappropriate. Thus if an employer requires a full-time employee to work for a year before being considered for promotion a part-time worker who works 50 per cent of the hours done by the full-time worker could be required to wait two years before being considered for promotion.

Overtime rates of pay are frequently paid by employers only for hours worked in excess of the normal full-time working week for that employer and the Regulations expressly provide that where a part-time worker does overtime he or she will not be entitled to the overtime rate until he or she has performed for the number of hours which a full-time worker is required to work before becoming entitled to overtime payments (reg.5(4)). Accordingly, if a full-time worker becomes entitled to an overtime rate after 36 hours per week, a part-time worker who normally only works 20 hours in a week will not be entitled to overtime until he or she has worked at least 36 hours in the week. The EAT has made it clear that this provision applies only to overtime and not to any other arrangements.

James v Great North-Eastern Railways

[2005] IDS Brief 780

Both full-time workers and part-time workers had a set number of contractual hours. Full-time workers had an average 40-hour week calculated over eight weeks. Hours worked in excess of 35 hours attracted an "additional hours allowance" of one and a quarter times the basic rate and any hours in excess of the 40 contractual hours were similarly paid at one and a quarter times basic rate. Part-time workers also had a set number of contractual hours but they received the basic rate until they reached 35 hours, when they were paid one and a quarter times basic rate. The part-time workers claimed this was in breach of the 2000 Regulations, the employers relied on the exception under reg.5(4). The EAT held that the pro rata principle should be applied to the wages as a whole and therefore the part-time workers had been discriminated against as their hourly rate was less than the full-time workers for their contractual hours. They pointed out that it was open to the employers to justify the different treatment.

The issue of entitlement to public holidays has also been considered by the courts.

McMenemy v Capita Business Services

[2006] IDS Brief 806 (June)

M worked for a call centre that operated 7 days a week. Employees, whether full-time or part-time, were only entitled to public holidays if they fell on days that they would otherwise work and there was no time off or payment in lieu. M worked Wednesdays, Thursdays and Fridays and therefore did not benefit from public holidays that fell on Mondays. The EAT accepted the tribunal's decision that M did not receive holidays because he did not work on a Monday and not because of his part-time status. A full-time worker who did not work on a Monday would similarly have lost out.

Note that the situation may be different if a case relates to a workforce that is Monday to Friday where all the full-time workers will be entitled to the public holidays as they all work on Mondays. It would, of course, still be an opportunity for an employer to justify such a practice.

A worker who considers that he or she has been treated less favourably than the Regulations permit is entitled to request a statement from his employer giving reasons for his treatment and both workers and employees are permitted to apply to an employment tribunal in the event of their being dismissed or subjected to a detriment for seeking to enforce rights under the Regulations (reg.7) and a worker who considers that his rights under the Regulations have been infringed is entitled to make a complaint to an employment tribunal, in which case the onus is on the employer to identify the grounds for the less favourable treatment or detriment. If the complaint is upheld by the employment tribunal it may make a declaration of rights, order compensation or recommend that the employer take action to reduce the adverse effect on the complainant of any matter to which the complaint relates. The compensation shall be such as is just and equitable having regard to loss which is sustained by the worker and, although compensation may not include compensation for injury to feelings, where an employer fails to comply with a recommendation made by the tribunal the tribunal may increase the amount of compensation.

FIXED TERM CONTRACTS

6–36 The Fixed-term Employees (Prevention of Less Favourable Treatment) Regulations 2002 (SI 2002/2034) make it unlawful to treat an employee on a fixed-term contract less favourably in respect of any term of his contract (including pay and pensions) than a comparable employee who is not on a fixed term contract or to subject him to any detriment unless that less favourable or detrimental treatment can be objectively justified. The comparator must be engaged on similar work and generally at the same establishment.

The Regulations also tackle the practice of keeping employees on fixed term contracts for many years. After four years continuous employment on fixed term contracts, it will be unlawful to continue to employ the employee on another fixed term contract unless the employer can show it is objectively justified. (The four-year period can only start to run from July 10, 2002.) The employee will then be deemed to be a permanent employee.

In *Department of Work and Pensions v Webley* [2004] EWCA Civ 1745, the Court of Appeal held that the non-renewal of a fixed term contract was not, of itself, a breach of the Regulations. It might of course lead to a claim of unfair dismissal.

AGE DISCRIMINATION

Until 2006, there was no specific legislation prohibiting discrimination on grounds of age. Some cases were successfully brought where an age limit indirectly discriminates on other grounds. For example in *Price v Civil Service Commission* [1978] I.C.R. 27 an upper age limit was found to indirectly discriminate against women who would be more likely to have spent time away from the workplace because of family responsibilities and therefore be unable to acquire the other qualifications by that age. The Employment Framework Directive required that Member States implement age discrimination legislation in employment and training by December 2006. The Employment Equality (Age) Regulations 2006 (SI 2006/2408) came into force on October 1, 2006. However the provisions relating to occupational pension schemes were delayed for further consultation until December 1, 2006. **6–37**

> Regulation 3(1)
>
> For the purpose of these Regulations, a person ("A") discriminates against another person ("B") if—
>
> (a) on grounds of B's age, A treats B less favourably than he treats or would treat other persons, or
>
> (b) A applies to B a provision, criterion or practice which he applies or would apply equally to persons not of the same age group as B, but-
>
> (i) which puts or would put persons of the same age group as B at a particular disadvantage when compared with other persons, and
>
> (ii) which puts B at that disadvantage,
>
> And A cannot show the treatment or, as the case may be, provision, criterion or practice to be a proportionate means of achieving a legitimate aim.
>
> (2) A comparison of B's case with that of another person under paragraph (1) must be such that the relevant circumstances in one case are the same or not materially different, in the other.

This Regulation therefore covers both "direct" and "indirect" discrimination but note that unlike other strands of legislation, it is possible to justify not only indirect discrimination but also direct discrimination. An "age group" can mean either a particular age or a range of ages. For example a person may be discriminated against because he is "over 50" or "under 30" or "between 18 and 25". It is also made clear that discrimination because someone is thought to be of a particular age is covered by the Regulations.

6–38 Regulation 6 makes it clear that subjecting someone to harassment "*on grounds of age*" will amount to discrimination if it has the purpose or effect of violating that person's dignity or creating an intimidating, hostile, humiliating or offensive environment for the victim. There is a similar provision to other strands that where the conduct is not intended to have that effect, it will only be deemed to have the effect if it should "*reasonably be considered as having that effect*" having regard to all the circumstances, including in particular the perception of the victim.

Discrimination in Employment and Vocational Training

6–39 Regulation 7 makes it unlawful to discriminate on grounds of age in relation to:

- recruitment arrangements/offers of employment;
- terms of employment offered or afforded;
- transfer, promotion, training, other benefits offered;
- dismissal (defined by reg.7(6) to include constructive dismissal and expiry of a limited term contract which is not renewed on the same terms).

According to reg.7(4) it not be unlawful to discriminate against someone:

- in relation to the arrangements made for the purposes of determining to whom employment should be offered;
- by refusing to offer, or deliberately not offering someone employment;

if that person has attained the age of 65 (or an objectively justified lower normal retirement age) or would attain that age within six months of the date of the application. In other words there is a complete exclusion from protection so far as recruitment into employment is concerned for those who are over 65 or a lower justified retirement age. However if someone in this position is employed or offered a job, he must not be discriminated against on grounds of age in respect of his terms and conditions, opportunities for transfer, promotion, etc.

Genuine occupational requirements

6–40 Regulation 8 states that it will not be discrimination to use age as a criteria if

> "having regard to the nature of the employment or the context in which it is carried out—
>
> (a) possessing a characteristic related to age is a genuine and determining occupational requirement;
> (b) it is proportionate to apply that requirement in the particular case..."

Contrast the width of this provision with, for example, the wording in the Employment Equality (Sexual Orientation) Regulations which refers to an exception where "being of a particular sexual orientation is a genuine and. . ..etc". Does this mean, for example, in a shop which sells teenage fashion the employer could say that s/he wanted someone of youthful appearance? It is likely that despite the relatively broad wording, tribunals will interpret this provision in a narrow way.

Length of service benefits exception

Regulation 32 contains an exception where a benefit is awarded which varies depending on the length of service of the workers. The provision can be challenged by the disadvantaged worker but only if his length of service is more than five years. Even then the employer is allowed to justify the practice if it "reasonably appears" to him that "the way in which he uses the criterion of length of service. . . . . .fulfils a business need of his undertaking (for example, by encouraging the loyalty or motivation, or rewarding the experience of some, or all of his workers)". **6–41**

Although this appears to place a very low onus on the employer, it must be remembered that this exception needs to be read in light of the Directive and it is suggested that this still requires objective justification of the policy. Such policies may be challenged as discrimination on grounds of sex (see *Cadman v HSE* [2006] I.R.L.R. 969 recently before the ECJ). Note also reg.32(7), which states that the exemption in reg.32 does not apply where the benefit is awarded by virtue of ceasing to work for the employer.

Retirement

There is a specific exception for retirement dismissals. Regulation 30 states that it will not be unlawful age discrimination to dismiss an employee at or over the age of 65 where the reason for the dismissal is retirement. Where an employee is dismissed on grounds of age before 65, the employer will be required to justify the policy in the usual way for the purposes of a claim under the 2006 Regulations. It is likely to be difficult for employers to justify a blanket retirement policy below 65. Usually this will be found by the tribunal to be disproportionate. Even if there is a legitimate aim, such as health and safety, some form of individual assessment will usually be a more proportionate means of achieving the aim. Note that this provision only applies to "employees" and not other workers. **6–42**

Regulation 30 states that whether or not a dismissal is for retirement, it will be determined by the new ss.98ZA to 98ZF of the Employment Rights Act 1996 contained in Sch.8 to the 2006 Regulations. Briefly, the reason will be taken to be "retirement" where the dismissal takes place on a planned retirement date and the employee has been given between 6 and 12 months' notice both of the retirement date and of the reason for dismissal. If the dismissal takes place before the planned date it will NOT be retirement. Otherwise it will be for the tribunal to decide what the reason is, taking into account issues such as how much notice has been given and whether the employer complied with the rest of the procedure in Sch.6. (For the interaction with unfair dismissal provisions see para.4.21, above.)

Miscellaneous other Exceptions

6–43
- complying with a requirement of a statutory provision (reg.27);
- minimum wage (reg.31);
- national security (reg.28);
- most age-related criteria relating to occupational pension schemes (Sch.2);
- positive action to "prevent or compensate for disadvantages linked to age" (reg.29);
- enhanced redundancy payments mirroring statutory provisions (reg.33);
- life assurance cover to retired workers ceasing at 65/NRA (reg.34).

The Regulations require significant changes to common employment practices. In the majority of cases using age as a criteria for applicants will be unlawful and certain common practices may be challenged as indirectly discriminatory. For example, requiring that applicants be graduates may indirectly discriminate against older employees and specifying minimum levels of experience may discriminate against younger applicants. Of course it may be possible for employers to justify such requirements. Allowing employers to set a retirement age has been a very controversial issue and the lawfulness of the provisions have been referred to the European Court of Justice to determine whether they comply with the Employment Directive.

EQUAL PAY

6–44 The Equal Pay Act 1970 (EPA), as amended, seeks to ensure equal pay for men and women doing work of equal value. The short title states that it is "An Act to prevent discrimination, as regards terms and conditions of employment between men and women" and is concerned with contractual terms of employment including, but not limited to, those concerning pay. Every contract of employment contains an equality clause (s.1(1)). The Act only gives equality of pay between men and women in the same employment and only as a result of that does it have an impact on pay differentials generally.

The Three Entitlements

A woman (or a man) is entitled to equal pay with a man (or a woman) in the following three situations: **6–45**

(1) where the man and the woman are engaged on "like work" (s.1(2)(a));
(2) where the man and the woman are engaged on "work rated equivalent" viz. where a job evaluation study has been carried out in respect of the work (s.1(2)(b)); and
(3) where the man and the woman are engaged on in "work of equal value" (s.1(2)).

However, when comparison is being made between the pay of a woman and the pay of a man, in order to ensure transparency in the pay scheme each individual item of the contract has to be compared. Thus pay is compared with pay and sick pay with sick pay and on-call allowances with on-call allowances. The result is a woman who does like work with a man, but receives no sick pay while the man receives sick pay, is entitled to have her contract modified so that she receives sick pay (*Hayward v Camell Laird Shipbuilders Ltd* [1988] I.R.L.R. 257) and this may result in the man then having a claim (for a payment he does not receive but the woman does) using the woman as his comparator. The overall value of a pay package may be used as a defence against such "leap-frogging": *Leverton v Clwyd County Council* [1989] I.R.L.R. 28, HL. Thus if in the case of the woman claiming sick pay the employer could show that the overall value of her pay package was equivalent to the pay package of the man her claim would fail provided always that the difference between the man's contractual terms and the woman's was not due to sex.

Degnan v Redcar and Cleveland

[2005] I.R.L.R. 615

The Court of Appeal held that an attendance allowance and a bonus payment were all part of the "subject matter" of pay and should be aggregated with the basic pay rate to produce an hourly rate of pay for comparison purposes.

Like Work

This occurs where a woman and a man do work which is of the same, or a broadly similar nature and if there are any differences in the things that the man and the woman do they must not be of practical importance in relation to terms and conditions of employment. This means that the differences are not enough to be **6–46** reflected in collective bargaining in respect of the two jobs. For example, a man may be employed as a clerical assistant who types correspondence while a female clerical assistant types accounts and reports. They would be employed on work of the same nature even though occasionally one, but not the other, attends the annual board meeting to take minutes or occasionally one, but not the other, does photocopying work.

Work Rated Equivalent

6–47 This occurs when a woman's job, and that of the man, have been given an equal value in terms of the demands made on the worker under several headings like effort, skill, decision-making, etc. in a job evaluation study, or if the jobs would have been given such a rating but for the fact that the study itself was made using discriminatory criteria which favoured men or women. To be valid for this purpose, a job evaluation study must be thorough in its analysis and capable of impartial application. A job evaluation study which requires a subjective judgment to be made by management before an employee can be properly placed within the grading system is probably not a valid job evaluation study at all. Thus a female kitchen assistant and a male gardener could not be said to be employed on like work but it would be quite likely that their jobs would be given an equal rating on a scheme which measured the value of the job to the employer under different headings. If a job evaluation study has been properly carried out it will prevent a woman bringing a claim under the third entitlement, namely work of equal value.

Equal Value

6–48 This is a flexible route to equal pay and may be used where men and women are not engaged on like work and where there has been no proper job evaluation study undertaken. This permits a woman who is employed, for example, as a cook or a kitchen assistant to compare her pay and other contractual conditions with those of male workers employed as, for example, joiners, plumbers, engineers or accountants. The procedure is long and complicated even though since 1996 an employment tribunal has been able to determine the question of equal value without reference to an independent expert (Sex Discrimination and Equal Pay (Miscellaneous Amendments) Regulations 1996 (SI 1996/438)). Whether the Tribunal calls for an expert's report or decides the matter itself, it is the decision of the employment tribunal that will determine whether or not the man and the woman are employed on work of equal value. Amendments and new procedures introduced in 1994 are intended to streamline the equal value process so that these claims can be resolved quicker and more effectively (Equal Pay Act 1970 (Amendment) Regulations 2004 (SI 2004/2352) and Employment

Tribunals (Constitution and Rules of Procedure) (Amendment) Regulations 2004 (SI 2004/000)).

Genuine Material Factor

An employer faced with an equal pay claim may defend it by showing that the difference in pay is genuinely due to a material difference (or factor) between the woman's case and the man's (s.1(3)). At one time it was thought that in order to rely on such a defence the difference would have to be objectively justified, rather similar to the test of justification required in a case of indirect discrimination. However, it is now clear that provided the difference is genuine and is due to a factor other than sex the defence will be effective. **6–49**

Rainey v Greater Glasgow Health Board

[1987] A.C. 224, HL

Mrs Rainey received about £2,500 per annum less than a male employee who did the same kind of work—the fitting of artificial limbs. The male employee had previously been employed in the private sector and in order to attract him (and others) to the public sector the employer, the Health Board, had to offer the same salary that he was receiving while in the private sector; the Board was required to have the prosthetic service available within a particular timetable. Mrs Rainey together with some men was recruited directly into the public National Health Service as a prosthetist but at a lower salary than the males who had been brought in from the private sector.

It was held that the employers had shown the difference between the case of Mrs Rainey and those of the males employed from the private sector was genuinely due to material difference between the man's case and the woman's. Section 1(3) involved the consideration of a person's "case" and that necessarily involved the circumstances of that case and those might well go beyond the "personal equation" namely the employees' qualifications, experience, length of service, etc. and could include a difference that was connected with economic factors affecting the efficient carrying on of the business or other activity. It followed that a relevant difference for s.1(3) might relate to circumstances other than the personal qualifications or merits of the male or female workers who were the subject of comparison. In this case the employment tribunal had made it clear that the new National Health Service prosthetic service could never have been established within a reasonable period of time if the males (previously in the private sector) had not been offered a scale of remuneration not less than what they were previously enjoying. That was a good and objectively justified reason for offering them that scale of remuneration. From an administrative point of view it would have been highly anomalous if prosthetists alone—for the whole future—were to have a different salary scale which would have been the result if the females like Mrs Rainey, and the men employed directly into the National Health Service prosthetic service, had been paid the same as the men brought in from the private sector. Accordingly the grounds founded on by the Health Board were capable of constituting a relevant difference for the purpose of s.1(3).

Wallace v Strathclyde Regional Council

[1998] I.R.L.R. 146

Wallace and others were female teachers who did the same work as male principal teachers but were paid at a lower rate and not given the opportunity of promotion. The Council could not create new promoted posts because of restraints imposed by government. As a result, the appellants were doing the work of principal teachers without having been promoted to that grade and without receiving the salary commensurate with it. Relying on the Equal Pay Act these unpromoted female teachers sought equal pay with male principal teachers. An employment tribunal held that the Council had not shown that the difference was genuinely due to a material difference which was not the difference of sex.

It was held that the employment tribunal had misdirected itself by requiring that the respondents, in order to rely upon s.1(3), had to show that they had no reasonable alternative but to require the appellants to do the work of a principal teacher for less pay because, provided that there is no element of sexual discrimination, an employer establishes a s.1(3) defence by identifying the factors which he alleges have caused the disparity, proving that those factors are genuine and proving further that they were causally relevant to the disparity in pay complained of.

Glasgow City Council v Marshall

[2000] I.R.L.R. 272

The applicants in this case, seven women and a man, were instructors employed in special schools in Scotland for children with severe learning disabilities. Staff included both teachers and instructors, with teachers being paid in accordance with the collective agreement for teaching staff, on the other hand instructors, whether qualified as teachers or not, were paid according to the Local Authority's Scale.

The instructors brought an equal pay case, comparing their work with that of teachers of the opposite sex, and an employment tribunal found they were employed on like work and that the employers had failed to establish a defence under s.1(3), in that all they had done was to point to an historical basis for the disparity in pay.

The House of Lords held that the employment tribunal erred in finding that the employers had failed to prove that the variation in pay between the applicant instructors and the teachers was genuinely due to a material factor other than sex within the meaning of s.1(3) of the Equal Pay Act.

The House of Lords held the employer must satisfy the tribunal on several matters. First, that the proffered explanation or reason is genuine and not a mere sham or pretence. Secondly, that the less favourable treatment is due to this reason. The factor relied upon must be the cause of the disparity. In this regard and in this sense, the factor must be "material", that is, a significant and relevant factor. The factor must be material in a causative sense rather than in a justificatory sense. Thirdly, that the reason is not "the difference of sex", which is apt to embrace any form of sex discrimination, whether direct or indirect. Fourthly, that the factor relied upon is a material difference, that is, a significant and relevant difference, between the woman's case and the man's case.

An employer who proves the absence of sex discrimination, direct or indirect, is under no obligation to prove a "good" reason for the pay disparity and if the employer proves the absence of sex discrimination he is not obliged to justify the pay disparity. In this case, the employment tribunal erred in holding that a purely historical explanation of the pay difference between the sexes is insufficient. Since the genuineness of the employer's explanation had not been questioned and it had not been suggested that the pay disparity was tainted by sex discrimination, the employers had made good their defence under s.1(3).

The position has been confused by a decision of the ECJ in *Brunhoffer* [2001] I.R.L.R. 571 which appeared to suggest that even where the alleged discrimination was direct, then the employer required not just to explain the difference (as suggested by *Wallace* and *Marshall*) but to provide objective justification. In other words **6–50** the employer had to show that there was a reasonable business need for the treatment and that it was proportionate. There have been conflicting decisions of the EAT since the *Brunhoffer* decision. In *Sharp v Caledonia Group Services* [2006] I.R.L.R 4, the EAT held that objective justification was now required in every equal pay case. However in *Villalba v Merrill Lynch* [2006] I.R.L.R. 437, the EAT said that this was not required where there was no evidence that the difference in pay was part of a wider policy that disadvantaged one sex (indirect discrimination). To further confuse matters, the Court of Appeal in *Armstrong v Newcastle-upon-tyne NHS Trust* [2006] I.R.L.R. 124 followed *Marshall* without any reference to the ECJ decision in *Brunhoffer*! It is suggested that the approach in *Villalba* is the correct one but it is hoped that this matter will be clarified by an appeal soon.

Circumstances which may provide a defence under s.1(3) include:

- *market forces* (a requirement to pay an employee (male) more than another employee (female) because the male will not work for less);
- *personal factors* (qualifications, experience and length of service); and
- *red-circling* (where a group of employees have had their salaries conserved in order to agree to a change in duties which might occur where highly paid male employees have been persuaded to perform lower status and lower paid jobs as part of a re-structuring exercise and in order to persuade the men to take these lower status jobs, the employer has agreed to conserve their salary at the higher rate for a period of time).

Time Limits

6–51 Section 2(4) of the EPA requires a claim for equal pay to be brought in the employment tribunal within six months of the termination of the employment contract to which the claim relates and such a limit is not contrary to European Community law (*Preston v Wolverhampton Healthcare NHS Trust* [2000] I.R.L.R. 506, ECJ; *(No.2)* [2001] I.R.L.R. 237, HL). However, as every contract of employment is deemed to include an equality clause it follows that a claim for equal pay may be brought in the ordinary court founded on breach of contract and such a claim may be brought any time within five years (or six years in England) of the claim having arisen. It is not relevant that the claim for equal pay relates to a period more than six months before the claim is presented to the employment tribunal; the six-month period runs from the date the employment ended and not the date to which the claim relates (*Young v National Power Plc* [2001] I.C.R. 328, CA). Thus if a woman is paid unequally in a job that she stopped doing more than six months before her employment came to an end she can still bring her equal pay claim against her employer provided she does so within six months of her employment with that employer ending.

SAME EMPLOYMENT

In order to bring an equal pay claim a woman must be employed at an establishment in Great Britain and compare herself with a man in the "same employment" as herself (s.1(2), (6)). Her chosen comparator must be employed by her employer or an associated employer and if her comparator is employed at a different establishment there must be common terms and conditions at the two establishments either generally or in respect of the classes of employees to which the woman and the chosen male comparator belong (s.1(6)). However, s.1(6) must be interpreted in light of European Community law which applies equality of pay to those employed in the same establishment or service so that a female employee employed by one local authority may be able to claim equal pay with a male employed by another authority (*Scullard v (1) Knowles (2) Southern Regional Council for Education & Training* [1996] I.R.L.R. 344). **6–52**

South Ayrshire Council v Morton

[2002] I.R.L.R. 256

School teachers in State schools in Scotland are employed by local authorities and Morton, a female primary school teacher employed by South Ayrshire Council, claimed equal pay with a male primary school teacher employed by the Highland Council. Although the two employers were not associated employers within s.1(6) of the EPA there was sufficient community of interest for the whole of the structure of education in Scotland to be regarded as a service so that Mrs Morton's claim could proceed.

Allonby v Accrington and Rossendale College

[2004] I.R.L.R. 224

A part-time lecturer was forced to leave direct employment with the college and register with an employment agency in order to continue working with the college. The rates of pay were lower and she sought to compare herself with a male full-time lecturer still employed by the college. Following their earlier decision in *Lawrence v Regent Care Ltd* [2002] I.R.L.R. 822, ECJ, the ECJ held there was no single common source for the terms and conditions of the applicant and her chosen comparator.

Robertson v Department for the Environment, Food and Rural Affairs

[2005] I.R.L.R. 363, CA

The Court of Appeal upheld the EAT's decision that civil servants in one government department could not use comparators in another department. Although there is a common employer, authority to set terms and conditions is delegated to each department. There was therefore no "common source" from which the two sets of terms and conditions originated.

REMEDIES

6–53 The majority of equal pay claims are raised in the employment tribunal but, as indicated above, such claims may also be raised in the form of breach of contract actions in the ordinary courts although a court may transfer the proceedings to an employment tribunal which might be better suited to deal with the issues involved (s.2(3)).

Lest women be unwilling to raise equal complaints themselves the Secretary of State may make an application to a tribunal on behalf of women (or men) and an employer may ask a tribunal to declare the rights of employees and the employer in relation to an equal pay question (s.2(1A) and (2)).

Where a woman's claim to equal pay is upheld her contract is modified with regard to the future so that where in the past she received, say, £7 per hour when her male comparator received say £8per hour her contract after the decision of the tribunal will be performed as if it contained a term entitling her to £8 per hour (s.1(2)). With regard to the period before the claim is upheld the tribunal may award arrears of remuneration or damages (s.2(1)). By s.2(5) of the Equal Pay Act such arrears or damages was limited to a period of two years before the date the claim was presented to the tribunal. However, this limitation has been declared to be unlawful as contrary to European Community (*Preston v Wolverhampton Healthcare NHS Trust* [2000] I.R.L.R. 506, ECJ; [2001] I.R.L.R. 237, HL; *Levez v T. H. Jennings (Harlow Pools) Ltd* [1999] I.R.L.R. 36, ECJ) and has been replaced by the limitation period applicable to breach of contract claims, being five years in Scotland and six in England.

EUROPEAN COMMUNITY LAW

The role of European Community law has already been explained but it is necessary to emphasise that in the field of discrimination European Community law has had a significant impact on the law's development. In the field of sex discrimination Art.141 of the Treaty of Rome states, inter alia, that "each member of state shall ... ensure and subsequently maintain the application of the principle that men and women should receive equal pay for equal work". This obligation is amplified by the Equal Pay Directive (75/117) and the Equal Treatment Directive (76/207) prohibits discrimination in conditions of employment including dismissal. Article 141 creates rights which can be enforced by individuals against employers and overrides any contrary domestic law. **6–54**

Scope of Art.141

Equal pay without discrimination based on sex means that: (1) pay for the same work at piece rates shall be calculated on the basis of the same unit of measurement; and (2) pay for work at time rates shall be the same for the same job. The concept of pay is very broad and means the "ordinary basic or minimum wage or salary and any other consideration, whether in cash or in kind, which the worker receives directly or indirectly, in respect of his employment, from his employer". It has been held to include statutory maternity and redundancy pay (*Gillespie v Northern Health and Social Securities Board* [1996] I.R.L.R. 214; *Rankin v British Coal Corporation* [1993] I.R.L.R. 69), occupational pensions (*Barber v Guardian Royal Exchange* [1990] I.R.L.R. 240), employer's contributions to such pensions (*Worringham v Lloyds Bank* [1981] I.R.L.R. 178), concessionary travel entitlements (*Garland v British Rail Engineering* [1982] I.R.L.R. 111) and even compensation for unfair dismissal (*R. v Secretary of State for Employment Ex p. Seymour-Smith* [1999] I.R.L.R. 253). **6–55**

Unlike the Sex Discrimination Act the Equal Pay Act 1970 does not deal expressly with indirect pay discrimination. However, Art.141 is applied to eliminate all discrimination on the grounds of sex and must be given effect to through the medium of the EPA. Accordingly if different rates of pay affect a far greater number of women than men they will infringe Art.141 unless the employer can show there is an objective reason for the difference. An example of the effect of Art.141 (previously numbered Art.119) is seen in the following case.

R v Secretary of State for Employment Ex p. EOC

[1994] I.R.L.R. 176

The 1978 Employment Protection (Consolidation) Act required that an employee must work a specified number of hours a week to become entitled to a redundancy payment. Employees who worked for fewer than eight hours a week did not qualify for a payment but those who worked more than 16 hours a week did.

Lord Keith stated:

> "It was common ground that the great majority of employees who worked for more than sixteen hours a week were men and the great majority of those who worked for fewer were women so that the provisions in question resulted in indirect discrimination against women.

The important . . . issue in the appeal was whether the indirect discrimination against women involved in the threshold provisions of the 1978 Act had been shown to be based on objectively justified grounds.

It was claimed that the thresholds had the effect that more part time employment was available than would be the case if employers were liable for redundancy pay. It was contended that if employers were under that liability they would be inclined to employ fewer part time workers to the disadvantage of [women]. The bringing about of an increase in the availability of part time work was properly to be regarded as a beneficial social policy but . . . the question was whether the threshold provisions of the 1978 Act had been shown by reference to objective factors to be suitable and requisite for achieving that aim.

While in certain circumstances an employer might be justified in paying full time workers a higher rate than part time workers to secure the more efficient use of his machinery . . . that would be a special and limited state of affairs. Legislation that permitted a differential of that kind nation-wide would present a very different aspect and considering that the great majority of part time workers were women would surely constitute a gross breach of the principle of equal pay and could not possibly be regarded as a suitable means of achieving an increase in part time employment.

The next question was whether the thresholds were requisite and whether on the evidence before the . . . Court they had been proved actually to result in greater availability in part time work than would be the case without them."

> In Lord Keith's opinion that question had to be answered in the negative. The conclusion had to be that no objective justification for the threshold had been established and the thresholds were incompatible with Art.141.

Article 141 has had direct effect since April 8, 1976 with the result that female employees who were not entitled to participate in occupational pension schemes because they were part-time have been able to require that employers recognise their service as far back as 1976 and make the appropriate contributions to the pension fund trustees; provided the employees pay into the fund their contributions they will be entitled to a pension based on their entire period of service from 1976 (*Preston v Wolverhampton Healthcare NHS Trust* [2001] I.R.L.R. 237). However, the right to participate in the scheme must be distinguished from the right to receive equal benefits under the scheme. In respect of the latter, Art.141 only requires equality in respect of benefits due in respect of service after May 17, 1990 (the date of the European Court of Justice decision in *Barber v Guardian Royal Exchange Assurance Group* [1990] I.R.L.R. 240); subsequently there was added to the EC Treaty the "*Barber* Protocol" which provides that "for the purposes of Art.141 benefits under Occupational Social Security schemes shall not be considered as remuneration if and in so far as they are attributable to periods prior to May 17, 1990".

In order to enforce any right conferred by Art.141 an employee should still raise the case by way of a complaint to an employment tribunal which must then hear the complaint under the EPA by ignoring or "disapplying" any provision of that Act which is contrary to Art.141 (*Biggs and Barber v Staffordshire County Council* [1996] I.R.L.R. 209).

STATUTORY RIGHTS FOR WORKING PARENTS

Pregnant Workers

When making a risk assessment of the risks to health and safety of **6–56**
employees, as required by the Management of Health and Safety at Work Regulations 1999 (SI 1999/3242), an employer must include any particular risks to new or expectant mothers and their babies (reg.16). If the assessment reveals a risk, the employer must take any reasonable measures to avoid it which could include altering the worker's hours or conditions. If the risk cannot be avoided the employer must suspend the employee for as long as necessary and she is entitled to be paid during the suspension.

Leave rights

6–57 There are a number of leave rights available to employees with children. Employees are protected against detriment for exercising any of these leave rights and dismissal for these reasons will be automatically unfair. Details of most of the rights are contained in the Employment Rights Act ss.71–80 and s.99, the Maternity and Parental Leave etc. Regulations 1999 (SI 1999/3312) and the Paternity and Adoption Leave Regulations 2002 (SI 2002/2788). By the Work and Families Act 2006 the Government has indicated that it will extend these rights during the current Parliament. The period of paid maternity leave has been extended to 39 weeks with effect from April 2007, and the Government has indicated that it intends subsequently to increase this to 52 weeks; it is intended to bring in measures that will allow transfer of leave if desired from mother to father and the right to request flexible working has been extended to carers.

Maternity leave

6–58 Employees are entitled to 26 weeks ordinary maternity leave regardless of their length of service. This will be followed by a further 26 weeks of additional maternity leave for those employees who have 26 weeks continuous service with their employer by the 15th week before the week that the child is expected to be born. Every employee must take at least two weeks leave after childbirth.

While on maternity leave the woman's contract of employment continues and she is entitled to be treated for all purposes (apart from remuneration) as if she was not absent. A woman returning from ordinary maternity leave is entitled to return to her previous job with all rights of seniority, pension rights, etc. the same as if she had not been absent. If she is returning after additional maternity leave she may be asked to return to a suitable alternative job if it is not reasonably practicable for her to return to her previous job. While on maternity leave, the woman may, if her employer agrees, work up to 10 "keeping in touch" days without this interrupting her maternity leave. She must not be penalised if she refuses an opportunity to work such days but must be paid the normal rate of pay if she does so.

Maternity pay

6–59 Entitlement to leave does not necessarily mean a woman is entitled to maternity pay. To qualify for statutory maternity pay (SMP) a woman must have 26 weeks service by the 15th week before the child is expected to be born and be earning at least the lower earnings limit for national insurance. SMP is paid for six weeks at 90 per cent of earnings and then 33 weeks at a flat rate (or 90 per cent of earnings if that is less than the prevailing rate of SMP).

Paternity leave and pay

Two weeks paternity leave is available on the birth of a child or the placement of a child for adoption and can be claimed by the biological father or the partner of the mother in the case of a birth and by one of an adopting couple where the other is claiming adoption leave or by the partner or spouse of the adopter. The purpose of the leave must be to care for the child or to support the mother or adopter. The rate of pay is the same as the flat rate of SMP. **6–60**

Adoption leave and pay

This right is available to individuals who adopt or one member of an adopting couple when a child is newly placed for adoption. To be eligible the employee must have 26 weeks service. The right is to 26 weeks ordinary adoption leave followed by 26 weeks additional adoption leave. Adoption pay is at the same rate as for maternity pay, being six weeks at 90 per cent of earnings and 33 weeks at the flat rate of SMP. Eligibility for adoption pay is on the same basis as for SMP and there is the same option for "keeping in touch" days. **6–61**

Parental leave

The right to parental leave is available to all employees with one year's service who have the responsibility for caring for a child. The right is to take up to 13 weeks for each child (18 weeks if the child is disabled). No more than four weeks may be taken at one time and the leave must be taken in blocks of at least one week. The right applies during the first five years of a child's life (up to 18 if the child is disabled). The leave is unpaid and can be taken in addition to any of the other leave rights. **6–62**

Emergency time off

This is a right for employees to take a reasonable amount of unpaid time off to deal with incidents involving a "dependant" (ERA s.57A). A dependant includes a spouse, child or parent but would also include anyone who reasonably relies on the employee for assistance in emergencies such as an elderly relative or neighbour. The right is to provide assistance when a dependant falls ill, gives birth, is injured or assaulted; to make arrangements for the care of an ill or injured dependant; when a dependant dies, where care arrangements are unexpectedly terminated or to deal with an incident involving a child of the employee which occurs unexpectedly during school hours or other time when the school is responsible. **6–63**

The employee must tell the employer the reason for absence as soon as practicable and indicate when he expects to return. This right is not for protracted incidents and would not allow the employee to take indefinite time off to look after a dependant who is ill. The intention is that it covers the immediate emergency and the employee would be expected to put other arrangements in place or get the employer's consent for a longer absence.

Right to request flexible working

6–64 This is not a right to demand flexible working but a framework for requesting changes and setting out the reasons an employer may give for refusing. Details are contained in the Flexible Working (Procedural Requirements) Regulations 2002 (SI 2002/3207) and the Flexible Working (Eligibility, Complaints and Remedies) Regulations 2002 (SI 2002/3236). Eligible employees are those with 26 weeks continuous employment who are parents of children under six (or if the child is disabled 18). Also eligible are adopters, guardians, foster-parents and partners of any of these if they have responsibility for the upbringing of the child. From April 6, 2007 the Government has announced that the right will be extended to carers who care for, or expect to care for, a husband, wife or partner, another close relative or someone who is not a close relative but lives at the same address as the carer.

The right is to request changes in contractual conditions relating to hours of work, times of work and place of work as between home and the employer's premises. Examples might be flexi-time, home-working, term-time working, part-time working, staggered hours or shift working. The purpose of the change must be to enable the employee to care for the child. Once the contract is varied there is no entitlement to change back to the original terms at a later date.

Requests must be in writing and set out the date the variation would start, the pattern desired, the effect on the employer and how it could be made to work. The employer must consider the request and arrange a meeting within four weeks to consider the request. The employer must then write to the employer within two weeks with a decision. If he is refusing the request he must set out the "business reasons" for rejecting which must include one or more of the following: business costs; effect on ability to meet customer demand; inability to reorganise existing staff or find extra staff; impact on quality or performance; not enough work in the periods when it is proposed that the employee work; or planned structural changes. The employee should be given a chance to appeal, if the request is declined, the employee cannot make another request for a year. The employee can complain to an employment tribunal but only in respect of incorrect procedures or factual issues relating to the business reason given by the employer. The maximum compensation is eight weeks' pay. There is the usual protection against detriment or dismissal for exercising this right.

SAMPLE QUESTIONS

1. Betty applies for a job as an assistant at the local Sports Centre; one of her duties would involve locking up the premises at the end of the working day and she is required to check that all the customers have left the premises. This involves her checking the male shower room and changing facilities. She has previously worked in a sports club and has never before experienced any difficulty in performing this kind of work and when she attends for an interview she is surprised to be asked if she would be able to cope with having to check the changing rooms and did she think it was appropriate for a woman to check male changing rooms. Betty explained her previous experience and produced a letter of recommendation from her previous employer but was annoyed to be told the next day that her application was unsuccessful. She later learned that the job had been given to a male applicant who had never worked in a sports environment before. Betty seeks your advice about the possibility of raising a claim against the Sports Centre.

2. Bigbus Ltd, an employer which operates a fleet of buses, advertises for cleaners. They will be paid at the rate of the National Minimum Wage. The advertisements states that application is by letter in "your own handwriting". Mr Ahmed has only recently arrived in the United Kingdom to settle down with his family who arrived from India some years ago. He can speak English fairly well and can understand some written English but has never learned to write in English. When his son points out the advertisement Mr Ahmed telephones Bigbus Ltd to say that he is interested in the cleaner's job but is told that he must apply in writing. He further explains that he cannot write in English and could write in Urdu–his own language–but he is told that he must write in English and if he does not do so his application will not be considered.

He asks you if he might be able to claim racial discrimination. How would you advise Mr Ahmed?

3. Bob applies for a job with Oddit & Co, a firm of city centre accountants. He is extremely well qualified and his application shows that his experience is far better than that of any other applicants. At his interview he creates a very good impression and the interviewing panel has no difficulty in deciding that Bob is the best applicant by a long way. Indeed the next day Bob receives a letter offering him the position stating the terms and conditions generally, including the hours of work which are stated to be 9am to 5pm, Monday to Friday. Bob has just recently recovered from a depressive illness which lasted for just over a year—brought on by work overload in a previous job—and is still prone to panic attacks which make it difficult for him to travel on crowded public transport, he could start work at 10am and finish at 4.30pm saying that he would expect his salary to be reduced accordingly. He receives a letter in reply withdrawing the offer of employment and complaining that Bob made no mention of his panic attacks and transport problems at the interview. Bob wonders if he has any claim against Oddit & Co.

4. St Agatha's is a residential care home run by the Roman Catholic church and Jack is the medical director. When Jack was appointed in 2000, he had to sign a declaration that he was a practising Roman Catholic. In June 2007, Jack informs his employer's that he has lost his faith and no longer considers himself a Catholic. His employers have also discovered that he is gay. A number of the elderly residents are uncomfortable with Jack's sexuality. After a number of discussions with Jack and the local priest, the Board of St Agatha's decide to dismiss Jack and he asks you if he has any legal remedy.

SUGGESTED ANSWERS FOR CHAPTER SIX

1. Betty would seem to have a claim based on sex discrimination under the Sex Discrimination Act 1975 in that a man with less experience than her has been appointed. However, Betty will have the onus of proving that the Sports Centre have discriminated against her and to do so she will require to have evidence which would allow the employment tribunal to decide in her favour. To gather such evidence Betty should consider serving on the Sports Centre a s.74 questionnaire in which she is permitted to pose certain questions. Any answers the Sports Centre might give would be admissible in evidence in the employment tribunal and if the Sports Centre gives answers which are evasive or does not reply at all the employment tribunal may draw an appropriate inference.

No doubt, the Sports Centre will try to argue that the job Betty applied for was covered by one of the Genuine Occupational Qualifications. The most obvious one is that applying where the job requires to be done by a man because the job-holder is likely to work in circumstances where members of one sex might reasonably object to the presence of a member of the opposite sex because they are in a state of undress or are using sanitary facilities. However while men using showers or in a state of undress might reasonably object to the presence of a woman, the employer is not able to plead this as a defence if there are already employees of the required sex (in this case male) who could carry out that part of the assistant's job requiring to be done by a man, if it would be reasonable to require such men to check the changing and shower rooms and there were sufficient males employed to do this. If the Sports Centre was able to show that at the times the showers and changing rooms had to be checked there was always a female on duty (although not employed as an assistant) but that there was not always a male on duty they would be able to rely on the GOQ. However if that were the case it is arguable that checking that no users were in the changing rooms and showers would not need to be done by a male. It is feasible that ensuring that all male users had left the premises could be done without the job holder being present when they are undressed.

In the event that the Sports Centre could not rely on the GOQ Betty will have a good claim which she will have to present to the employment tribunal within three months of her being refused the job. She will be entitled to compensation which might include a sum for any injury to her feelings caused by the unlawful act of discrimination.

2. Mr Ahmed will be able to claim that he has been the victim of indirect racial discrimination in that Bigbus in its selection method has adopted a provision, criteria or practice that puts individuals of Indian origin at a disadvantage. Mr Ahmed may require to produce evidence to show disproportionate impact but it is essentially a question of fact for the employment tribunal. Detailed statistical evidence will not be essential. Mr Ahmed also has to show that he suffers a detriment by not being able to do so. This would not be difficult, as clearly he has suffered the detriment of not having his application considered. If Mr Ahmed can prove these matters Bigbus must, in order to show there has been no unlawful discrimination, prove that it was justified in requiring the applications to be handwritten in English. They must show that they were trying to achieve a legitimate aim and that the method they selected was proportionate. Clearly there will be many jobs in which an ability to write in English will be an essential qualification for performing the job. However, it would be unusual for bus cleaners employed at the minimum wage to require to be able to write in English and unless Bigbus could show that there was some requirement to write in English in order to perform the job it would not be able to show its selection practice was not discriminatory. It is insufficient for Bigbus merely to say that that was its policy or practice. There has to be some objective reasoning for the requirement in order for it to be regarded as justified. A tribunal has already held that a requirement that labourers completed applications forms in their own handwriting was not justified having regard to the nature of the work. Mr Ahmed would seem to have a very strong case and would be entitled to a declaration of rights and the Tribunal could recommend that Bigbus change its selection policy. He would not be entitled to compensation because, unlike in the case of sex discrimination law, according to the Race Relations Act (s.57(3)) the right to compensation for indirect racial discrimination only arises if the employer proves that the requirement in question was not applied with the intention of treating the applicant less favourably on racial grounds. If Bigbus cannot do so Mr Ahmed will be entitled to such compensation as is just and equitable.

3. Bob would be able to argue that he is disabled and protected by the Disability Discrimination Act. Clinical depression is regarded as a mental illness and Bob would be able to contend that he suffers from a mental impairment which has a substantial and long term adverse effect on his ability to carry out normal day-to-day activities.

However this requires further investigation. An impairment in order to be long term must have lasted or be expected to last for at least one year. In Bob's case he has suffered from depression for over a year. Then it is necessary to consider whether his mental impairment has a substantial adverse effect on his day–to-day activities. Day-to-day activities are set out in the Disability Discrimination Act and include the activity of mobility which the Guidance says has to be given a wide meaning. The Guidance also gives examples of when an impairment in mobility will be seen to be substantial; being unable to use public transport would generally be of substantial effect. In Bob's case, however, he merely finds it difficult to use public transport at certain times of the day. He does not appear to be unable to use it but even assuming that his difficulties are such that he is unable to use it he is still able to use at times when it is not crowded. It would be surprising if Bob's impairment of his mobility would be regarded as substantial. If that were so he would be regarded as having a disability and would not be able to derive any protection from the Disability Discrimination Act.

Assuming that he is disabled, however, Oddit & Co would not merely be able to say that the hours of work were 9am–5pm. Oddit & Co, once it became aware of Bob's disability, would be required to consider whether it might be able to prevent the terms and conditions offered placing Bob at a disadvantage. If it could remove such a disadvantage by making reasonable adjustment to the terms on which the employment was offered but fails or refuses without justification to do so Oddit & Co will be committing an act of unlawful discrimination. The Disability Discrimination Act gives examples of the kind of adjustments an employer might be required to make and includes altering the hours of work. Much would depend on the circumstances, including the number of other employees employed and whether the presence of Bob in the office between 9am and 10am and after 4.30pm was essential. The fact that Bob is prepared to take a reduction in salary would make it quite difficult for Oddit & Co show that it was not reasonable for them to adjust Bob's working hours in the way he suggests.

4. St Agatha's need to take careful heed of the Employment Equality (Sexual Orientation) Regulations 2003 and the Employment Equality (Religion or Belief) Regulations 2003. In respect of the religion (or lack of) held by the Director, it is now clear that discriminating against someone because of his absence of belief is subject to the Regulations. St Agatha's will need to convince a tribunal that the job falls within the allowed exception where holding a belief is a genuine occupational requirement. St Agatha's is likely to be classed as an organisation with a moral ethos and therefore they would only need to convince a tribunal that it was a genuine, and not a determining, need that the person holding the post be a practicing Roman Catholic. This provision is likely to be narrowly interpreted and it is unlikely that this post would fulfil the requirement. Therefore it is likely that to dismiss him because he is not a practicing Catholic would contravene the Regulations. As far as his homosexuality is concerned, the general exception covers the situations where being of a particular sexual orientation is a genuine and determining requirement. This would not seem to be the case for a medical director. Where the employment is for the purposes of an organised religion, there is a wider exception, however this employment would not seem to come into this category. Jack would also, of course, be able to claim unfair dismissal when the decision of the Board would be subject to the usual considerations of reasonableness.

CHAPTER SEVEN

INSTITUTIONS OF EMPLOYMENT LAW

INTRODUCTION

7–1 Disputes about the employment relationship may be about the contractual relationship or they may be about statutory rights and, occasionally, the same event may be pursued as a contractual dispute or one concerning statutory rights. An example would be where an employer withholds wages from an employee for poor timekeeping. Unless there is a term in the contract which allows the withholding of wages for poor timekeeping the employer will be in breach of contract and the employee would be entitled to sue for damages which would be the amount of wages withheld. Such an action would have to be brought in the ordinary courts and would probably require the assistance of a professional lawyer. However, by withholding wages the employer may contravene the provisions in the Employment Rights Act 1996 which prohibit an employer making deductions from wages unless the employee has agreed in writing or has had a written notice about the employer's right to make the deduction (see Ch.2, para.2.6, above). A claim that the employer has made an unlawful deduction from wages is a statutory claim and may only be brought in the employment tribunal whose proceedings are more informal than those of the ordinary courts and can be conducted perfectly well by an employee without professional representation.

The general principle of UK employment law is to give employment tribunals an exclusive jurisdiction to deal with statutory employment rights (like claims for unfair dismissal, redundancy pay, discrimination, maternity and parental rights, time off and rest breaks) and to reserve to the ordinary courts all other employment claims based on contract or delict and tort. The result is that employment tribunals, with one exception (see para.7–02, below), may not deal with claims based on breach of the contract of employment or claims for injuries sustained by employees in the course of their work—they are dealt with by the ordinary courts—and the ordinary courts may not deal with statutory claims for unfair dismissal, redundancy pay, discrimination, maternity and parental rights, time off and rest breaks, etc.—they are dealt with by the employment tribunals. However, the volume of claims dealt with by employment tribunals far exceeds the employment law cases dealt with by the ordinary courts. In the year 2001–2002, employment tribunals received 103,935 complaints, of which almost one half were of unfair dismissal although since then the number of claims has dropped. In 2006–2007, 105,177 claims were lodged compared with 109,712 for the previous year and undoubtedly part of the reason for the drop is due to the introduction of the Dispute Resolution Procedures introduced with effect from October 2004, discussed below.

EMPLOYMENT TRIBUNALS

7–2 Employment tribunals (until 1998 referred to as industrial tribunals) have dealt with employment disputes since 1965, until then their jurisdiction was limited to redundancy payments and the issuing of written terms of employment to employees. Since then with the expansion of employment law rights their jurisdiction has continually increased. Employment tribunals may hear complaints of breach of contract brought by employees against their employer but such complaints must be outstanding or arise on the termination of employment and may not be in respect of damages for personal injuries, intellectual property, duty of confidence or restraint of trade. Accordingly, complaints of breach of contract during the currency of the contract or contract actions about personal injuries, intellectual property or restrictive covenants must be raised in the ordinary courts, whether arising during or after the contract's termination (Employment Tribunals (Extension of Jurisdiction) (Scotland) Order 1994 (SSI 1994/000) and the equivalent English Order). In addition to its jurisdiction to hear complaints brought by workers an employment tribunal may hear employers' appeals against an Improvement or Prohibition Notices issued by the Health and Safety Executive (Health and Safety at Work Act 1974 s.24).

Procedure

7–3 The jurisdictions and powers of employment tribunals are set out in the Employment Tribunals Act 1996 and the Employment Tribunals (Constitution and Rules of Procedure) Regulations 2004 (SI 2004/1861). Tribunals are more informal than courts. Chairmen and Tribunal members do not wear robes or wigs and are referred to as "Members of the Tribunal" or "Mr Chairman" or "Madam Chairman" and everyone remains seated except when the Tribunal is entering or leaving the room or a witness is taking the oath or affirming, prior to giving evidence.

Generally Tribunals deal with complaints in a relatively short period of time and must conduct proceedings and apply the rules of procedure to deal with cases justly which means: (a) ensuring that the parties are on an equal footing; (b) saving expense; (c) reflecting the complexity of the case in the way it is handled; and (d) ensuring the case is dealt with expeditiously and fairly (Employment Tribunals (Constitution and Rules of Procedure) Regulations 2004 reg.10). It is not unusual for a tribunal to dispose of a case within a three-month period, beginning with the presenting of the employee's claim, which consists of filling in a simple form—the ET1 Form—and the employer's response—ET3 Form (specimen forms are in the Appendices)—and ending with the Tribunal's decision. In 2005–2206, 82 per cent of cases were heard within 26 weeks of an ET1 being lodged. However because of the increasing complexity of the law, particularly in areas of discrimination, other cases can extend for many months. Many employees and employers conduct their own cases without professional lawyers and, although employment law can be complicated, the absence of professional representation is compensated by the Tribunal's own knowledge and its ability to be interventionist and inquisitorial although the extent to which a Tribunal should adopt such an approach has been questioned by the Employment Appeal Tribunal: (see for example *Beales v Secretary of State for Work and Pensions* (EAT No.0602/05)). Perhaps the most important rule of tribunal procedure is r.14 to the effect that (i) the Tribunal shall make such enquiries of witnesses and persons appearing before it as appropriate and shall conduct the hearing in the most appropriate way for the clarification of the issues and the just handling of the proceedings; and (ii) the Tribunal shall seek to avoid formality in its proceedings and shall not be bound by any rule of law relating to the admissibility of evidence in proceedings in Court.

However in some cases striking the right balance between clarification and investigation can be difficult. In *Edinburgh Pharmaceutical Process Ltd v Lothian* (EAT No.0085/05) the EAT (Lady Smith) has stated

> "We do not intend to suggest that it is inappropriate for tribunals to ask questions of witnesses; such questioning ought however to be contained within the bounds of what is required fro clarification. Our tribunal system is an adversarial one and it is important not to confuse the extent to which a more relaxed approach may be adopted than in a court with any notion that a tribunal's function is investigatory. A tribunal should not be seen to be taking over the questioning of witnesses to the extent that appears to have happened in this case. The desire to make progress is understandable bearing in mind the need to make efficient use of tribunal resources and the principle that justice delayed may be justice denied. There are, though, times when the failure to take time will appear as justice rushed, and equally, justice denied".

Since 2001 in Scotland legal aid has been available in certain employment tribunal cases. This part of the legal aid system is called ABWOR (Advice By Way Of Representation) and was introduced by the Advice and Assistance (Assistance by Way of Representation) (Scotland) Amendment Regulations 2001 (SSI 2001/2).

Occasionally in Scotland, and frequently in England, the Tribunal will give an oral judgment at the end of the Hearing and within a few days of the Hearing the parties will often receive an Advance Notice of Decision letter which merely indicates whether the claim has been successful or not. About four weeks after the Hearing in most cases the parties will receive the Tribunal's judgment with reasons.

However, the form in which a judgment or decision is given, and **7–4** whether reasons are required to be given in writing, is now the subject of detailed provisions in the Employment Tribunals (Constitution and Rules of Procedure) Regulations 2004 (SI 2004/1861). It is not possible here to deal with these provisions at length but they may be summarised as follows.

Default judgment: where a party has not entered a response, or a response has not been accepted, a Chairman may issue a default judgment which may determine both liability (i.e. whether the claim succeeds) and remedy (i.e. how much should be awarded); in such a case while the decision must be recorded in writing no reasons are required (r.8).

Judgments and orders: a judgment is the *final* determination of the proceedings (e.g. an entire unfair dismissal claim including whether the claimant was dismissed, whether the dismissal was unfair and how much compensation should be awarded) or any issue in the proceedings (e.g. in an unfair dismissal claim whether the claimant was an employee or in a disability discrimination case whether the claimant had a disability as defined in the Disability Discrimination Act 1995) and it may include an order for expenses or costs to be paid by one of the parties (r.28).

An order requires a person to do or not do something but it relates to *interim* matters (e.g. an order that a person disclose certain documents; provide answers to questions; provide additional information; or an order that a hearing be postponed) (rr.28, 10). At the end of any hearing the Tribunal shall either issue an oral judgment or order or give it in writing later. All judgments shall be recorded in writing and shall be signed by the Chairman. Reasons must be given for all judgments (whether oral or written) but reasons for orders are only required if a request for reasons is made by the time of the hearing at which an order is made. Reasons are not required to be in writing if given at the time of issuing the judgment or order and where reasons are given orally they are not required to be produced in writing unless one of the parties has requested written reasons within 14 days of the judgment being sent to the parties or where the EAT requests reasons either regarding a judgment or an order (rr.29, 30). Although the giving of oral judgments and reasons is common practice in England and Wales the practice is not so widespread in Scotland, although the new Rules of Procedure may gradually change Scottish practice.

Composition of Tribunal

7–5 In most cases the Tribunal will consist of three members with equal voting rights—the Chairman (who must be legally qualified) and two other members, one from a panel which is representative of employees, and one from a panel which is representative of employers (Employment Tribunals (Constitution and Rules of Procedure) Regulations 2004 (SI 2004/1861), reg.8). With the agreement of the parties a case may be heard by a Tribunal consisting of a Chairman and one member in which case the Chairman has a casting vote; in certain cases the Tribunal may consist of a Chairman sitting alone, mainly in: (1) breach of contract cases; (2) unlawful deductions from wages; (3) where the parties have agreed in writing; and (4) withdrawn applications and cases no longer being contested but a Chairman may decide that because of the nature of the issues a complaint should be heard by a Tribunal of three (Employment Tribunals Act 1996 s.4). Where the complaint is one of discrimination, the nature of the complaint should be reflected in the Tribunal's membership (*Habib v Elkington & Co* [1981] I.R.L.R. 344).

Tribunal powers, procedures and hearings

7–6 Following an extensive review of employment tribunals the procedures for handling and disposing of claims were altered in 2004 to ensure greater efficiency and speed. The current rules are now contained in the Employment Tribunals (Constitution and Rules of Procedure) Regulations 2004 (SI 2004/1861) which apply to England and Wales and Scotland. The principal rules are contained in Sch.1 and these apply to all claims made to employment tribunals unless the claim involves national security issues (Sch.2); appeals against certain levies (Sch.3); appeals against health and safety notices (Sch.4); appeals against non discrimination notices (Sch.5); and equal pay claims based on equal value (Sch.6), the latter Schedule being added by the Employment Tribunals (Constitution and Rules of Procedure) (Amendment) Regulations 2004 (SI 2004/2351).

Until the 2004 Regulations there was no clear jurisdictional divide between tribunals in Scotland and in England and Wales. However, now the jurisdictions of tribunals in England and Wales on the one hand and Scotland on the other hand are clearly defined (Employment Tribunals (Constitution and Rules of Procedure) Regulations 2004 (SI 2004/1861) reg.19 r.1). Thus a Tribunal sitting in England and Wales only has jurisdiction to deal with proceedings where: (a) one of the respondents resides or carries on business in England or Wales; (b) for County Court purposes the cause of action would have arisen in England or Wales; (c) the proceedings have been referred to it by a Court in England or Wales; or (d) in the case of proceedings under Schs 3, 4 or 5, they relate to matters arising in England or Wales; similarly a Tribunal in Scotland only has jurisdiction to deal with proceedings where (a) one of the respondents resides or carries on business in Scotland; (b) the proceedings relate to a contract of employment the place of execution or performance of which is in Scotland; (c) the proceedings have been referred to it by a court in Scotland; or (d) in the case of proceedings under Schs 3, 4 or 5 they relate to matters arising in Scotland. In order for a Tribunal in Scotland to have jurisdiction under (b), above, the place of the performance of the contract must be "at least substantially in Scotland" (*Prescription Pricing Authority v Ferguson* [2005] I.R.L.R. 464, IH).

Tribunals now have express rules to case manage proceedings **7–7** and while r.10 provides particular examples of orders a Tribunal Chairman may—on his own initiative or on request—make in order to manage the proceedings it expressly permits the orders listed in r.10(2) as well as such other orders as the Chairman thinks fit. The Rules now also make distinctions between different types of hearing:

Case management discussion hearings: this is the most informal type of hearing and is held by a Chairman sitting alone and may be held in private, frequently by telephone conference. They may result in orders being made to assist the management of the proceedings but they cannot determine civil rights and none of the orders listed in r.18(7) may be made. These orders include the draconian measure of striking out a claim or response or making a restricted reporting order.

Pre-hearing reviews: these are generally interim hearings but may deal with issues of critical importance like the entitlement of a party to bring or contest the proceedings whether the Tribunal has jurisdiction, employment status, or whether a claim has been lodged timeously. In that respect therefore they are not interim in that the determination of such preliminary matters may in practice dispose of the claim and for this reason these hearings are in public and they are conducted by a Chairman sitting alone unless a party has requested in advance of the hearing that the hearing be conducted by a full Tribunal and the Chairman considers that one or more issues of fact are likely to be determined and that it would be desirable for the hearing to be before a full Tribunal. Unlike the earlier rules a Chairman may only order the hearing be by a full Tribunal where one of the parties has made a request to that effect (r.18).

The hearing: when the Rules refer to a "Hearing" with a capital "H" it is a reference to a Hearing under r.26 namely for the purpose of determining any outstanding procedural or substantive issues or for disposing of the proceedings and there may be more than one Hearing. For example, a Hearing may have determined that an employee was unfairly dismissed or the victim of discrimination but has not determined the amount of an award or whether an award of expenses or costs should be made. In such a case a further Hearing may be held at which evidence and submissions regarding the amount of any loss suffered and how much should be awarded. Hearings are in public and may be held by a full Tribunal or a Chairman sitting alone and those who are to give evidence may be excluded until their own evidence is to be given (rr.26, 27).

Review hearing: certain judgments and decisions may be reviewed. For example where a default judgment has been given or a judgment has been taken at a Hearing when a party was not present or the party did not receive notice of the hearing (rr.33, 34). In such a case a Tribunal may vary, revoke or confirm its earlier judgment.

Dispute Resolution Procedure

7–8 In order to reduce the number of claims being made to employment tribunals, which had reached a peak of 130,400 by 2002, the Government published the consultation document "Routes to Resolution: improving dispute resolution in Great Britain" which contended that the number of claims could be reduced by greater use of conciliation and internal/workplace machinery for resolving disputes between employees and workers and their employers. Legislation is now contained in Pt 3 of the Employment Act 2002 and the Employment Act 2002 (Dispute Resolution) Regulations 2004 (SI 2004/752) (hereafter referred to as the dispute resolution legislation) which became effective on October 1, 2004. The ACAS has also updated its Code of Practice on Disciplinary and Grievance Procedures.

As indicated in Ch.4, above (para.4.12) the dispute procedure legislation has had a significant effect on the law of unfair dismissal whereby a failure to follow the statutory disciplinary procedure results in the dismissal being automatically unfair, entitlement to a minimum basic award and the possible 50 per cent increase in the compensatory award. However, the dispute resolution legislation has effects outside the law of unfair dismissal and they may be summarised as follows.

Written particulars

7–9 As indicated in Ch.2, above employers are required to provide employees with written statements of particulars of their terms of employment and to update these statements when changes occur. One of the benefits of issuing and updating these statements is that employees and employers should know where they stand and there should be fewer disputes which might ultimately lead to claims in employment tribunals. Until the passage of the dispute resolution legislation there was no penalty if an employer failed to provide or update statements. Section 38 of the Employment Act 2002 now provides that where a claim is made to an employment tribunal under any of the jurisdictions listed in Sch.5 to the Act the Tribunal must either make a minimum award of compensation where the claim is upheld but no award of compensation is made or increase in any compensation awarded by between two and four weeks' pay unless there are exceptional circumstances in which it would not be just and equitable to do so. Thus if an employee's claim that his employer has made an unlawful deduction from wages of, say £50, is upheld if the employer at the time the claim is made has not provided or updated the employee's written statement the Tribunal may award the employee £50 and increase it by four weeks' wages which may be as much as £1,120. The intention is that the ability to increase awards in this way should lead employers to ensure that written statements are issued and updated in accordance with the provisions of ss.1 and 4 of the Employment Rights Act 1996.

Grievance procedures

The dispute resolution legislation introduces statutory grievance **7–10** procedures for employees. These are set out in Sch.2 to the 2004 Act and, like the Dismissal and Disciplinary Procedures, contain a Standard Procedure and a Modified Procedure, the latter applying where the employment has ended. Under the Standard Procedure the employee is required to set out his grievance in writing and send it to the employer who in turn must invite the employee to a meeting to discuss the grievance and inform the employee of the outcome and his right to appeal. However, the real significance of the statutory grievance procedure is that a failure to make use of it may prevent an employee being entitled to present a claim to the employment tribunal. This is the result of s.32 of the 2004 Act which applies where an employee (but not a worker (see Ch.1, above) makes any Sch.4 claim and (a) he has not set out his grievance in writing to his employer; (b) has set out his grievance in writing to his employer but has not allowed 28 days to elapse (which should allow the employer the opportunity of resolving the grievance) before lodging his Tribunal claim; or (c) he has set out his grievance in writing but more than one month after the date on which his Tribunal claim should have been lodged. Thus, even though the employee may have a legitimate claim against his employer his case will not be heard by the employment tribunal until he has at least attempted to resolve the dispute internally through the employer's grievance procedures. This may also be significant for constructive dismissal cases (see Ch.4, para.4.9, above).

A failure to complete a grievance procedure or a statutory dismissal procedure may also have an effect on the amount of compensation a Tribunal awards. This is the result of s.31 of the 2002 Act which provides that a Tribunal may reduce or increase any award where one of the statutory procedures (either the Statutory Dismissal or Disciplinary Procedure or the Statutory Grievance Procedure) has not been completed and the non-completion is due to the failure of the employee to comply with a requirement of the procedure or exercise an appeal right under it (in which case the award would be reduced) or a failure of the employer to comply with a requirement of the procedure (in which the award would be increased). However, an adjustment, which may be between 10 and 50 per cent, may only be made if it would be just and equitable to do so and if there are exceptional circumstance a Tribunal may decide not to increase or reduce the award at all.

By way of an example of how the dispute resolution legislation might operate as an incentive to encourage employers to provide up-to-date written particulars of employment and to follow appropriate pre-dismissal procedures consider the following scenario. An employee thinks that his wages are not being properly calculated. When he refers to his written statement he discovers that it says nothing about wages. When he asks his employer for clarification he is told that the employer has not has time to update the statement and in any event his wages are properly calculated. The employee lodges a formal grievance by writing to his employer but receives no response to his letter and as a result he lodges an employment tribunal claim under Pt II of the Employment Rights Act 1996 (unlawful deduction from wages). Assume that his claim is upheld and the Tribunal finds there to have been unlawful deductions of £200. Prior to the coming into effect of the dispute resolution legislation the Tribunal would not have been able to award any more that £200. However, as a result of the provisions discussed above, the Tribunal would be able to increase the award by between 10 per cent and 50 per cent under s.31 of the 2002 Act on the grounds that the employer had not complied with the statutory grievance procedure by not responding to the employee's letter and also by making an award of up to four weeks' pay under s.38 on the grounds that the employer had not complied with his obligation to provide the employee with a written statement setting out the required information about wages.

By way of example of how the dispute resolution legislation might operate as an incentive to encourage employees to use internal grievance procedure consider the following scenario. An employee believes his employer is making an unlawful deduction from his wages and raises his grievance in writing with his employer. However, he fails—for no good reason—to attend the meeting arranged by his employer to discuss the grievance but simply lodges a claim in the employment tribunal after 28 days. Assume the Tribunal upholds his claim and awards the amount unlawfully deducted (£200). Prior to the dispute resolution legislation becoming effective the Tribunal would have had no alternative but to award the full amount. However, as a result of the provisions discussed above, the Tribunal would be able to reduce the award by up to 50 per cent under s.31 of the 2002 Act on the grounds that the employee had not complied with the statutory grievance procedure by not attending the meeting.

Review of statutory procedures

Instead of making the resolution of disputes capable of resolution without the need for resort to employment tribunals the legislation had in some respects prompted much litigation as to just what an employee had to set out in his letter of grievance, whether a grievance letter was necessary at all and what or how much detail the employer had to set out in his letter inviting the employee to a meeting. **7–11**

In 2007 the Government announced a review of the operation of the statutory disciplinary and grievance procedures, "Success at Work: Resolving Disputes in the Workplace" which followed on the Gibbons Review which recommended that the statutory dispute resolution procedures be repealed. Consultation ended in June and at the time of writing no clear indication has been given regarding whether any of the Gibbons recommendations might be adopted. However as an indication of the problems produced by the statutory procedures the following cases are instructive. A failure to state a grievance in writing to his employer prevents an employee being able to present a claim of contractive dismissal. This may seem a draconian measure but in a series of cases the EAT has relaxed the statutory requirements. In *Shergold v Fieldway Medical Centre* [2006] I.C.R. 304 the EAT held that it is not necessary for the employee to state that he is raising a grievance or invoking a grievance procedure or that every detail of the employee's complaint is set out in the grievance letter. All the letter must do is ensure the employer can understand the general nature of the complaint and there is no requirement that the employee comply with any (more demanding or detailed) contractual grievance procedure. Similarly in *Commotion Ltd v Rutty* [2006] I.C.R. 290 the EAT held that where an employee had made a request to be allowed to have more flexible working hours her application, under s.80F of the Employment Rights Act, even although it did not state it was to be treated as grievance, her formal application for flexible working hours was to be treated as her raising a grievance so that when her request was rejected she was entitled to present a complaint of constructive dismissal. On the other hand it is specially provided (Dispute Resolution Regulation 2005 reg.14) that serving a statutory questionnaire under discrimination legislation is not to be regarded as the statement of a grievance (*Holc-Gale v Makers UK Ltd* [2006] I.C.R. 462, EAT). Difficulties have also arisen regarding whether an employee is required to comply with the grievance procedures where the claim is against not the employer but against another employee, for example, in a discrimination case: compare *Bisset v Martins* (EAT Case No. 0022-3/06) with *London Borough of Lambeth v Corlett* (EAT Case No. 0369/06).

The apparent rigidity of the statutory procedures was mollified by the EAT insistence that documents, be they grievance letters or letters inviting an employee to a disciplinary meeting, had to be considered in their context, thereby allowing the admission of evidence of the factual background against which the required documents had to be construed. In *Draper v Mears* [2006] I.R.L.R. 869 the EAT held that where an employee was alleged to have breached the "No alcohol" policy it was sufficient for the employer's letter to refer to "conduct which fails to ensure the health and safety of the employee and others" where there was evidence that the employee had already been told orally of the specifics of the allegation. The letter might have been ambiguous but the context left the employee with a clear understanding of the allegation. On the other hand if the letter is not ambiguous it has to be considered on its own without regard to the circumstances. Where an employee reasonably believes that an internal disciplinary or dismissal procedure was being followed the time for presenting a claim to the employment tribunal is extended by three months (Dispute Resolution Regulations 2005 reg.15) in order to avoid prejudicing the outcome of such a procedure by requiring the employee to present a claim within the normal time limit. In *Harris v Towergate London Market Ltd* (EAT Case No. 0090/07) an employee dismissed on grounds of redundancy mistakenly raised a grievance about the selection procedure rather than appealing to his employer against his dismissal. The EAT held that the time for his presenting his unfair dismissal claim was extended because he had reasonable grounds for believing a disciplinary or dismissal procedure was being followed.

APPEAL AGAINST TRIBUNAL DECISIONS

7–12 The decision of an employment tribunal may be appealed (within 42 days of receipt of the Extended Reasons for the employment tribunal's decision) on a point of law to the Employment Appeal Tribunal (Employment Tribunals Act 1996 s.21) which consists of a High Court judge and two members, one being from a panel representative of employers and the other from a panel being representative of workers (Employment Tribunals Act 1996 s.22) and where the employment tribunal has consisted of only the Chairman, the Appeal Tribunal may consist of the judge sitting alone. Further appeals lie to the Court of Session in Scotland and the Court of Appeal in England, and ultimately to the House of Lords.

ADVISORY CONCILIATION AND ARBITRATION SERVICE (ACAS)

ACAS plays an important role in the resolution of collective and individual employment disputes. ACAS is a publicly funded yet independent organisation whose statutory duties include the provision of conciliation services in individual employment disputes. Section 18 of the Employment Rights Act 1996 provides that an ACAS Conciliation Officer shall endeavour to promote the settlement of a complaint to an employment tribunal and the Secretary of the employment tribunal must send copies of complaints and other relevant documents to ACAS and advise the parties of the availability of ACAS services. Where a settlement is arrived at through an ACAS Conciliation Officer, the need for a Tribunal hearing is dispensed with and any such settlement prevents a subsequent application about the same matter to the employment tribunal, this being an exception to the normal rule that any agreement which prevents or restricts an employee's right to take proceedings in the employment tribunal shall be void (Employment Rights Act 1996 s.203). In order to facilitate settlements, anything communicated to a Conciliation Officer is confidential and may not be admitted in evidence in any Tribunal hearing which may subsequently take place (Employment Tribunals Act 1996 s.18(2)). **7–13**

ACAS is now empowered to arbitrate in cases of unfair dismissal and enforcement of the flexible working right. Where parties agree to submit their dispute to ACAS a single arbiter (an arbitrator is appointed) whose decision is final with no further right to lodge a similar claim in the Employment tribunal. However, the number of cases dealt with in this way is very small.

SAMPLE QUESTIONS

Jim is employed by Riccarton University as a gardener. His contract of employment provides that he will receive new boots and overalls on January 1 each year. In January 2007 the University refuses to provide the boots and overalls. Mary is also employed by the University and is dismissed for not wearing the uniform provided. The University dismisses Bill who presents a complaint of unfair dismissal but before it is heard he signs a statement prepared by a Conciliation Officer to accept £500 in settlement. Jean is a lecturer and after being frequently humiliated by he Head of Department in Departmental meetings she decides she cannot take any more and on Friday July 13, 2007 she decides not to go to work but instead writes a letter saying she has no alternative but the leave the University's employment.

Answer the following questions stating your reasons.
Can Jim sue the University for breach of contract in the employment tribunal?
Can Mary present a complaint of unfair dismissal in the ordinary court?
Does Bill's settlement prevent him proceeding with his unfair dismissal complaint?
Can Jean's claim for constructive unfair dismissal be accepted by the employment tribunal? If not what can Jean do to ensure her claim is accepted.

SUGGESTED ANSWERS FOR CHAPTER SEVEN

(a) Jim cannot sue the University in the employment tribunal because he is still employed by the University. employment tribunals can only hear actions for breach of the contract of employment once the employment has come to an end. As Jim is still employed by the University he cannot sue for breach of contract in the employment tribunal. However, if he wishes he can raise a breach of contract action in the ordinary court. The reason for this rule is that it would not be good for employment relations if an employee could raise a complaint in the Tribunal every time he believed his employer broke the contract; it would result in many aspects of the employment relationship being the subject of adjudication by Tribunals when such disputes are best resolved internally through employer's grievance procedures. If it is a serious matter the employee always has the option of raising an action in the ordinary court at any time—during or after his employment has ended.
(b) No, Mary cannot present a complaint of unfair dismissal in the ordinary court because by law only employment tribunals are permitted to hear unfair dismissal and other statutory complaints—they have an exclusive jurisdiction for these complaints. Tribunals are better able to deal with unfair dismissal because of their composition and the knowledge and experience of their members. Unlike the ordinary courts in which the decision is made by a single judge,

Tribunals consist of a legally qualified Chairman and two other members who have experience of employment relations. Mary can of course present her complaint to an employment tribunal which can dispose of her case without the need for her to employ professional lawyers who would normally be required for court proceedings.

(c) Yes, although the normal rule is that an agreement or settlement may not and does not prevent an employee from subsequently presenting a complaint to an employment tribunal, one of the exceptions to this rule is where the settlement has been arrived after the intervention of an ACAS Conciliation Office. In Bill's case the settlement has been arrived at after action by a Conciliation Officer and he will not be able to proceed with his unfair dismissal complaint. Had it merely been a settlement arrived between Bill and the University (without a Conciliation Officer being involved) Bill would have been able to have his case heard by a Tribunal even if he had expressly agreed not to proceed with his complaint. However if the tribunal upheld his complaint and awarded compensation it would reduce the compensation by any payment Bill had already received from the University.

(d) No. Before Jean can have her claim accepted she must send her employer a written statement of her grievance as her claim is one of those in Sch.4 to the Employment Act 2002 applies namely a complaint under s.111 of the Employment Rights Act 1996 and although normally complaints about dismissal do not require to be preceded by a written grievance as required by paras 6 or 9 of Sch.2 to the 2002 Act this rule does not apply to constructive dismissal claims like Jean's. Accordinglys,32 of the Employment Act 2002 prevents Jean's claim from being accepted s until she has set out her grievance in writing and sent to her employer. On receipt of her claim she will be advised of the need to do this by the employment tribunal and provided she does so and then waits 28 days for a reply her claim will be accepted. Her time for presenting her claim to the Tribunal will be extended by a period of three months from the expiry of the normal time limit for making her unfair dismissal claim. However if she fails to send her written grievance to her employer within one month of the expiry of the normal time limit for making her unfair dismissal complaint she will lose the right to make her unfair dismissal complaint for ever. See Employment Act 2002 s.32 and Schs 2,4 and reg.15 of the Employment Act 2002 (Dispute Resolution) Regulations 2004.

APPENDIX A

CLAIM FORM (ET1)

Claim to an Employment Tribunal

Please read the guidance notes and the notes on this page carefully before filling in this form.

By law, you must provide the information marked with * and, if it is relevant, the information marked with • (see guidance on Pre-acceptance procedure).

You may find it helpful to take advice **before** filling in the form, particularly if your claim involves discrimination.

How to fill in this form

All claimants **must** fill in **sections 1, 2 and 3**. You then only need to fill in those sections of the form that apply to your case. For example:

For **unpaid wages**, fill in **sections 4 and 8**.

For **unfair dismissal**, fill in **sections 4 and 5**.

For **discrimination**, fill in **sections 4 and 6**.

For a **redundancy payment**, fill in **sections 4 and 7**.

For **unfair dismissal** and **discrimination**, fill in **sections 4, 5 and 6**.

For **unfair dismissal** and **unpaid wages**, fill in **sections 4, 5 and 8**.

Fill in **section 10** only if there is some information you wish to draw to the tribunal's attention and **section 11** only if you have appointed a representative to act on your behalf in dealing with your claim.

If this form sets out a claim by more than one claimant arising from the same set of facts, please give the names and addresses of additional claimants on a separate sheet or sheets of paper.

Please make sure that all the information you give is as accurate as possible.

Where there are tick boxes, please tick the one that applies.

If you fax the form, do not send a copy in the post.

1 Your details

1.1	Title:	Mr ☐ Mrs ☐ Miss ☐ Ms ☐ Other
1.2*	First name (or names):	
1.3*	Surname or family name:	
1.4	Date of birth (date/month/year):	Are you: male? ☐ female? ☐
1.5*	Address:	Postcode

You do not need to answer 1.6 and 1.7 if you have appointed a representative (see section 11).

1.6	Phone number **(where we can contact you during normal working hours)**:	
1.7	How would you prefer us to communicate with you?	Post ☐ Fax ☐ E-mail ☐ Fax: E-mail address:

2 Respondent's details

2.1*	Give the name of your employer or the organisation or person you are complaining about (the respondent).	
2.2*	Address:	Postcode
2.3	If you worked at an address different from the one you have given at 2.2, please give the full address.	Postcode

2.4* If your complaint is against more than one respondent please give the names, addresses and postcodes of additional respondents.

3 Action before making a claim

3.1* Are you, or were you, an employee of the respondent? Yes ☐ No ☐
If 'Yes', please now go straight to section 3.3.

3.2 Are you, or were you, a worker providing services to the respondent? Yes ☐ No ☐
If 'Yes', please now go straight to section 4.
If 'No', please now go straight to section 6.

3.3• Is your claim, or part of it, about a dismissal by the respondent? Yes ☐ No ☐
If 'No', please now go straight to section 3.5.

3.4• Is your claim about anything else, in addition to the dismissal? Yes ☐ No ☐
If 'No', please now go straight to section 4.
If 'Yes', please answer questions 3.5 to 3.7 about the non-dismissal aspects of your claim.

3.5• Have you put your complaint in writing to the respondent?

Yes ☐ Please give the date you put it to them in writing.
No ☐

If 'No', please now go straight to section 3.7.

3.6• Did you allow at least 28 days between the date you put your complaint to the respondent and the date you sent us this claim? Yes ☐ No ☐
If 'Yes', please now go straight to section 4.

3.7• Please explain why you did not put your complaint in writing to the respondent or, if you did, why you did not allow at least 28 days before sending us your claim.
(In most cases, it is a legal requirement to take these procedural steps. Your claim will not be accepted unless you give a valid reason why you did not have to meet the requirement in your case. If you are not sure, you may want to get legal advice.)

4 Employment details making a claim

4.1 Please give the following dates if possible.

When your employment started

When your employment ended or will end

Is your employment continuing? Yes ☐ No ☐

4.2 Please say what job you do or did.

4.3 How many hours do or did you work each week? ....hours each week

4.4 How much are or were you paid?

Pay before tax £ each

Normal take-home pay (including overtime, commission, bonuses and so on) £ each

4.5 If your employment has ended, did you work (or were you paid for) a period of notice? Yes ☐ No ☐

If 'Yes', how many weeks or months did you work or were you paid for? weeks months

5 Unfair dismissal or constructive dismissal

Please fill in this section only if you believe you have been unfairly or constructively dismissed.

5.1• If you were dismissed by your employer, you should explain why you think your dismissal was unfair. If you resigned because of something your employer did or failed to do which made you feel you could no longer continue to work for them (constructive dismissal) you should explain what happened.

5 Unfair dismissal or constructive dismissal continued

5.1 continued

5.2 Were you in your employer's pension scheme? Yes ☐ No ☐

5.3 If you received any other benefits from your employer, please give details.

5.4 Since leaving your employment have you got another job? Yes ☐ No ☐
If 'No', please now go straight to section 5.7.

5.5 Please say when you started (or will start) work.

5.6 Please say how much you are now earning (or will earn). £ each

5.7 Please tick the box to say what you want if your case is successful:

a To get your old job back and compensation (reinstatement) ☐
b To get another job with the same employer and compensation (re-engagement) ☐
c Compensation only ☐

6 Discrimination

Please fill in this section only if you believe you have been discriminated against.

6.1• Please tick the box or boxes to indicate what discrimination (including victimisation) you are complaining about:

Sex (including equal pay)	☐	Race	☐
Disability	☐	Religion or belief	☐
Sexual orientation	☐		

6.2• Please describe the incidents which you believe amounted to discrimination, the dates of these incidents and the people involved.

7 Redundancy payments

Please fill in this section only if you believe you are owed a redundancy payment.

7.1• Please explain why you believe you are entitled to this payment and set out the steps you have taken to get it.

8 Other payments you are owed

Please fill in this section only if you believe you are owed other payments.

8.1• Please tick the box or boxes to indicate that money is owed to you for:

unpaid wages? ☐
holiday pay? ☐
notice pay? ☐
other unpaid amounts? ☐

8.2 How much are you claiming?

Is this: before tax? ☐ after tax? ☐

8.3• Please explain why you believe you are entitled to this payment. If you have specified an amount, please set out how you have worked this out.

9 Other complaints

Please fill in this section only if you believe you have a complaint that is not covered elsewhere.

9.1* Please explain what you are complaining about and why.
Please include any relevant dates.

10 Other information

10.1 Please do not send a covering letter with this form.
You should add any extra information you want us to know here.

11 Your representative

Please fill in this section only if you have appointed a representative. If you do fill this section in, we will in future only send correspondence to your representative and not to you.

11.1 Representative's name:

11.2 Name of the representative's organisation:

11.3 Address:

Postcode

11.4 Phone number:

11.5 Reference:

11.6 How would they prefer us to communicate with them?

Post ☐ Fax ☐ E-mail ☐

Fax:

E-mail address:

Please sign and date here

Signature: Date:

Data Protection Act 1998. We will send a copy of this form to the respondent(s) and Acas. We will put some of the information you give us on this form onto a computer. This helps us to monitor progress and produce statistics.

APPENDIX B

RESPONSE FORM (ET3)

Response to an Employment Tribunal claim

IN THE CLAIM OF: **Case number:** **(please quote this in all correspondence)**

This requires your immediate attention. If you want to resist the claim made against you, your completed form must reach the tribunal office within 28 days of the date of the attached letter. If you do not return the form by __/__/__ you may not be able to take part in the proceedings and a default judgment may be entered against you.
Please read the guidance notes and the notes on this page carefully before filling in this form.
By law, you must provide the information marked with * and, if it is relevant, the information marked with • (see guidance on Pre-acceptance procedure).

Please make sure that all the information you give is as accurate as possible.

Where there are tick boxes, please tick the one that applies.

If you fax the form, do not send a copy in the post.

1 Your details

1.1* Name of your organisation:

Contact name:

1.2* Address:

Postcode

You do not need to answer 1.3 and 1.4 if you have appointed a representative (see section 7).

1.3 Phone number:

1.4 How would you prefer us to communicate with you?

Post ☐ Fax ☐ E-mail ☐

Fax:

E-mail address:

2 Action before a claim

2.1 Is, or was, the claimant an employee?
If 'Yes', please now go straight to section 2.3.

Yes ☐ No ☐

2.2 Is, or was, the claimant a worker providing services to you?
If 'Yes', please now go straight to section 3.
If 'No', please now go straight to section 5.

Yes ☐ No ☐

2.3 If the claim, or part of it, is about a dismissal, do you agree that the claimant was dismissed?
If 'Yes', please now go straight to section 2.6.

Yes ☐ No ☐

2.4 If the claim includes something **other than** dismissal, does it relate to an action you took on grounds of the claimant's conduct or capability?
If 'Yes', please now go straight to section 2.6.

Yes ☐ No ☐

2.5 Has the substance of this claim been raised by the claimant in writing under a grievance procedure?

Yes ☐ No ☐

2.6 If 'Yes', please explain below what stage you have reached in the dismissal and disciplinary procedure or grievance procedure (whichever is applicable).
If 'No' and the claimant says they have raised a grievance with you in writing, please say whether you received it and explain why you did not accept this as a grievance.

3 Employment details

3.1 Are the dates of employment given by the claimant correct? Yes ☐ No ☐
If 'Yes', please now go straight to section 3.3.

3.2 If 'No', please give dates and say why you disagree with the dates given by the claimant.

When their employment started / /

When their employment ended or will end / /

Is their employment continuing? Yes ☐ No ☐

I disagree with the dates for the following reasons.

3.3 Is the claimant's description of their job or job title correct? Yes ☐ No ☐
If 'Yes', please now go straight to section 3.5.

3.4 If 'No', please give the details you believe to be correct below.

3.5 Is the information given by the claimant correct about being paid for, or working, a period of notice? Yes ☐ No ☐
If 'Yes', please now go straight to section 3.7.

3.6 If 'No', please give the details you believe to be correct below. If you gave them no notice or didn't pay them instead of letting them work their notice, please explain what happened and why.

3.7 Are the claimant's hours of work correct? **If 'Yes', please now go straight to section 3.9.**	Yes ☐ No ☐
3.8 If 'No', please enter the details you believe to be correct.	Hours per week
3.9 Are the earnings details given by the claimant correct? **If 'Yes', please now go straight to section 4.**	Yes ☐ No ☐
3.10 If 'No', please give the details you believe to be correct below. Pay before tax Normal take-home pay (including overtime,	£ each
commission, bonuses and so on)	£ each

4 Unfair dismissal or constructive dismissal

4.1 Are the details about pension and other benefits given by the claimant correct?
If 'Yes', please now go straight to section 5.

Yes ☐ No ☐

4.2 If 'No', please give the details you believe to be correct below.

5 Response

5.1* Do you resist the claim?
If 'No', please now go straight to section 6.

Yes ☐ No ☐

5.2* If 'Yes', please set out in full the grounds on which you resist the claim.

6 Other information

6.1 Please do not send a covering letter with this form. You should add any extra information you want us to know here.

7 Your representative

If you have a representative, please fill in the following

7.1 Representative's name:

7.2 Name of the representative's organisation:

7.3 Address:

Postcode

7.4 Phone number:

7.5 Reference:

7.6 How would they prefer us to communicate with them?

Post ☐ Fax ☐ E-mail ☐

Fax:

E-mail address:

Please sign and date here

Signature: Date:

Data Protection Act 1998. We will send a copy of this form to the respondent(s) and Acas. We will put some of the information you give us on this form onto a computer. This helps us to monitor progress and produce statistics.

INDEX

ABWOR (Advice by Way of Representation),
Employment Tribunals, 7–03
ACAS,
Code of Practice on Disciplinary and Grievance Procedures,
unfair dismissal, 4–02
Conciliation Officers, 7–13
powers, 7–13
role, 7–13
Administration orders,
termination of contract, 3–04
Adoption,
leave, 6–61
pay, 6–61
Advice by Way of Representation (ABWOR),
Employment Tribunals, 7–03
Advisory Conciliation and Arbitration Service,
See **ACAS**
Age discrimination,
agency workers, 1–18
background, 6–37
contract workers, 1–18
direct discrimination, 6–37
employment discrimination, 6–39
exceptions, 6–43
genuine occupational requirement, 6–40
harassment, 6–38
indirect discrimination, 6–37
length of service benefits exception, 6–41
redundancy, 5–02
retirement dismissals, 6–42
vocational training, 6–39
Agency,
See also **Agency workers**
trade unions, 1–44
Agency workers,
advantages, 1–18
age discrimination, 1–18
contract of employment, 1–17, 1–18, 1–19
definition, 1–18
disability discrimination, 1–18
discrimination, 1–18
employees, as, 1–18, 1–19
race discrimination, 1–18
Agency workers—*cont.*
religious discrimination, 1–18
sex discrimination, 1–18
sexual orientation discrimination, 1–18
tripartite cases, 1–19
Working Time Regulations, 1–18
Annual leave,
terms and conditions of employment, 2–20
Working Time Regulations, 2–20
Ante natal leave,
time off rights, 2–26
Appeals,
dismissal and disciplinary procedures (DDPs), 4–30
Employment Tribunals, 7–12
Apprenticeship contracts,
contract of employment, 1–22
Armed forces,
unfair dismissal, 4–04
Working Time Regulations, 2–15
Asserting statutory right,
unfair dismissal, 4–41
Atypical workers,
contract of employment, 1–13
mutuality of obligation, 1–13, 1–14

Bumping,
redundancy, 5–08

Capability,
fair reasons for dismissal, 4–15, 4–27
Care workers,
working time, 2–16
Careful performance,
implied terms of contract, 2–37
Case management discussion hearings,
Employment Tribunals, 7–07
Casual workers,
contract of employment, 1–13
mutuality of obligation, 1–13, 1–14
Civil servants,
contract of employment, 1–27
unfair dismissal, 4–04
Collective agreements,
advantages, 1–36
arrangements, 1–37
definition, 1–37
duration, 1–42

Collective agreements—*cont.*
exclusion, express, 1–42
formation of contract of employment, 1–29, 1–36
handbooks, 1–43
incorporation,
duration, 1–42
express, 1–40
formation of contract, 1–29, 1–36
implied, 1–40
legal effect of agreement, 1–38, 1–39
mechanics, 1–40
principles, 1–40
union membership, 1–41
legal effect, 1–38
redundancy, 1–40
rules, 1–43
subject matter, 1–42
union membership, 1–41
voluntarist approach, 1–38
written, 1–37
Commission for Racial Equality (CRE),
enforcement by, 6–29
Common law,
sources of law, 1–02
Competition,
terms and conditions of employment, 2–39
trade secrets, 2–40
Conciliation Officers,
ACAS, 7–13
Conduct,
appeals, 4–30
unfair dismissal, 4–16, 4–28
Confidential information,
terms and conditions of employment, 2–40
Constructive dismissal,
meaning, 4–09
Continuous employment,
redundancy, 5–02
unfair dismissal, 4–03, 4–05
***Contra proferentum* rule,**
terms and conditions of employment, 2–02
Contract of employment,
agency workers, 1–17, 1–18, 1–19
apprenticeship contracts, 1–22
atypical workers, 1–13
casual workers, 1–13
changes to, 1–32
civil servants, 1–27
construction of documents, 1–20
contract for services distinguished, 1–09
control test, 1–11
Crown employees, 1–27
delegation of performance, 1–15
development,
Contract of employment—*cont.*
development—*cont.*
common law, 1–02
European law, 1–03
legal absentionism, 1–07
statute, 1–02
directors, company, 1–24
disputes,
court, dealt withy by, 1–05
Employment Tribunals,
See **Employment Tribunals**
European law, 1–26, 1–27
formation,
See **Formation of contract of employment**
implied contracts, 1–30
importance, 1–06
integration test, 1–11
law or fact, question of, 1–20
legal absentionism, 1–07
multiple and variable test, 1–12
mutuality of obligation, 1–13, 1–14
name, 1–16
office holders, 1–27
organisation test, 1–11
personal service, 1–15
prison officers, 1–27
pro hac vice, employment, 1–21
public employment, 1–25
rationale for identification, 1–09, 1–10
regulation of, 1–01
social policy, 1–07
terms and conditions,
See **Terms and conditions of employment**
tests,
agency workers, 1–17—1–19
atypical workers, 1–13
casual workers, 1–13
control test, 1–11
generally, 1–11
integration test, 1–11
law or fact, question of, 1–20
multiple and variable test, 1–12
mutuality of obligation, 1–13, 1–14
name of contract, 1–16
organisation test, 1–11
personal service, 1–15
summary, 1–12
understanding employment law, 1–01
written statement of particulars of employment *See* **Written statement of particulars of employment**
Contract of service,
meaning, 1–09
Contract for services,
contract of employment distinguished, 1–09

Contract for services—*cont.*
exclusion from employment protection regime, 1–09
Control test,
contract of employment, 1–11
disadvantages, 1–11
example, 1–11
meaning, 1–11
Courts,
employment disputes dealt with by, 1–05, 4–02, 7–01
jurisdiction,
general rule, 1–05, 7–01
wrongful dismissal, 4–02
Covenants,
restrictive, 2–41, 2–42
Criminal law,
regulation of employment law, 1–01
Crown employees,
contract of employment, 1–27
unfair dismissal, 4–04
Customs,
wages, 2–03

Damages,
injury to feelings, 3–14
psychiatric injury, 3–14
reputation, loss of, 3–14
stigma, 3–14
wrongful dismissal, 3–13—3–15
DDPs,
See **Dismissal and disciplinary procedures (DDPs)**
Default judgment,
Employment Tribunals, 7–04
Delegation,
contract of employment, performance of, 1–15
Demotion,
dismissal, alternative to, 4–01
Directives,
acquired rights, 1–04, 5–16
domestic law, interpretation of, 1–04
emanation of the state, 1–03, 1–26
implementation, 1–03, 1–04, 1–26
sufficiently precise and clear, 1–26
transfer of undertakings, 1–04
wording, 1–03, 1–26
working time, 1–03, 1–26
Directors, company,
contract of employment, 1–24
insolvency, 1–24
Disability discrimination,
See also Discrimination
addictions, 6–24
background, 6–23
comparator, 6–27
direct discrimination, 6–26
disability, definition of, 6–24

Disability discrimination—*cont.*
Disability Rights Commission (DRC), 6–23, 6–29
employment discrimination, 6–26
justification for less favourable treatment, 6–26, 6–27
less favourable treatment, 6–27
long-term effect, 6–24
medical model, 6–23
normal day-to-day activities, 6–24, 6–25
positive discrimination, 6–23
practical application of provisions, 6–28
quotas, 6–23
reasonable adjustments, 6–26
severe disfigurements, 6–24
substantial effect, 6–24, 6–25
symptoms, disability without, 6–24
Disability Rights Commission (DRC),
creation, 6–23
enforcement by, 6–29
Disciplinary proceedings,
See also Dismissal and disciplinary procedures (DDPs)
review, 7–11
wages, 2–08
Discrimination,
See also **Age discrimination; Disability discrimination; Equal Pay; Race discrimination; Religious discrimination; Sex Discrimination; Sexual orientation discrimination**
agency workers, 1–18
background to legislation, 6–01
direct,
age discrimination, 6–37
disability discrimination, 6–26
race discrimination, 6–13
religious discrimination, 6–20
sex discrimination, 6–03
sexual orientation discrimination, 6–18
dress codes, 6–09
employee, concept of, 1–10
employment discrimination,
sex discrimination, 6–08
enforcement,
Commission for Racial Equality (CRE), 6–29
compensation, 6–30
Disability Rights Commission (DRC), 6–29
Equal Opportunities Commission (EOC), 6–29
mechanisms, 6–29
onus of proof, 6–31
European Convention on Human Rights, 6–01
fixed term contracts, 6–36

Discrimination—*cont.*
gender re-assignment, 6–11, 6–12
genuine occupational qualifications,
race discrimination, 6–17
religious discrimination, 6–22
sex discrimination, 6–04
sexual orientation, 6–18, 6–19
harassment,
racial, 6–15
sexual, 6–09, 6–10
indirect,
age discrimination, 6–37
race discrimination, 6–16
religious discrimination, 6–20
sex discrimination, 6–05, 6–06
onus of proof, 6–31
part-time workers, 6–33—6–35
positive,
disability discrimination, 6–23
race discrimination, 6–17
religious discrimination, 6–22
sex discrimination, 6–04, 6–17
questionnaires, 6–31
transsexuals, 6–11, 6–12
vicarious liability, 6–32
worker, concept of, 1–10
Dismissal,
alternatives, 4–01
constructive, 4–09
expiry of limited term contract without renewal, 4–08
frustration, 4–11
generally, 4–01
injury to feelings, 3–14
meaning, 4–06—4–11
minimum wage, 2–14
operation of law, 4–11
pay in lieu of notice, 3–16
procedures,
See Dismissal and disciplinary procedures (DDPs)
redundancy, 5–03
resignation which is genuine and intended, 4–10
Scotland,
pay in lieu of notice, 3–16
remedies, 3–12
summary, 4–02
termination of contract by employer, 4–07
unfair,
See **Unfair dismissal**
wrongful,
damages, 3–13—3–15
jurisdiction, 4–02
meaning, 3–10, 3–11, 4–02
office holders, 4–02
remedies, 3–11—3–15
Scotland, 3–12
unfair dismissal distinguished, 4–02
Dismissal and disciplinary procedures (DDPs),
appeals, 4–30
collective dismissals, 4–13
exceptions, 4–13
failure to use, 4–12
gross misconduct, 4–12
introduction, 4–12
requirement, 4–12
review, 7–11
Dispute resolution procedure,
Employment Tribunals, 7–08
grievance procedures, 7–10
introduction, 7–08
statutory procedures, review of, 7–11
written particulars, 7–09
Doctors,
Working Time Regulations, 2–15, 2–16
Domestic incidents,
parental leave, 2–27
Dress codes,
sex discrimination, 6–09

Emanation of the state,
directives, 1–03, 1–26
Emergency time off,
right, 6–63
Employee,
definition, 1–10, 1–17
Employee representatives,
time off rights, 2–28
Employment Appeal Tribunal,
appeals, 7–12
Employment law,
importance, 1–06
institutions,
See Employment Tribunals
management, 1–08
practical results for employers and workers, 1–08
Employment Tribunals,
admissibility of evidence, 7–03
advantages, 4–02
Advice by Way of Representation (ABWOR), 7–03
appeals, 7–12
case load, 7–01
case management discussion hearings, 7–07
claim form, 1–05
commencement of claim, 1–05
composition, 1–05, 7–03, 7–05
conduct of proceedings, 7–03
default judgment, 7–04
disposal of case, 7–03
dispute resolution procedure,
grievance procedures, 7–10
introduction, 7–08
statutory procedures, review of, 7–11

Employment Tribunals—*cont.*
dispute resolution procedure—*cont.*
written particulars, 7–09
evidence, 7–03
exclusive jurisdiction, 1–05, 7–01
generally, 7–01
health and safety, 7–02
Hearings, 7–06, 7–07
historical development, 7–02
informality, 7–03
judgment, 7–03, 7–04
jurisdiction,
exclusive, 1–05, 7–01
extension, 4–02, 7–02
general rule, 1–05
Scotland, 7–06
wrongful dismissal, 4–02
legal aid, 1–05
orders, 7–04
powers, 7–06
pre-hearing reviews, 7–07
procedure, 7–03, 7–04
representation, 1–05
review hearing, 7–07
Scotland, 1–05, 7–02, 7–03, 7–06
time limit for claims, 1–05
written statement of particulars of employment, 7–09
Equal Opportunities Commission (EOC),
enforcement by, 6–29
Equal pay,
background, 6–44
comparators, 6–45
entitlements, 6–45
equal value, 6–45, 6–48
equivalent, work rated, 6–45, 6–47
European law,
development, 1–03, 6–54
role, 6–54
scope of Art.141, 6–55
genuine material factor, 6–49, 6–50
job evaluation studies, 6–47
leapfrogging, 6–45
like work, 6–45, 6–46
market forces, 6–50
personal factors, 6–50
red-circling, 6–50
remedies, 6–53
same employment, 6–52
terms and conditions of employment, 2–01
time limits, 6–51
work rated equivalent, 6–45, 6–47
Equipment,
pro hac vice, employment, 1–21
Equivalent, work rated,
equal pay, 6–45, 6–47
European Convention on Human Rights,
discrimination, 6–01
European law,
contract of employment, 1–26, 1–27
directive,
contract of employment, 1–26, 1–27
domestic law, interpretation of, 1–04
emanation of the state, 1–03, 1–26
implementation, 1–03, 1–04, 1–26
sufficiently precise and clear, 1–03, 1–26
wording, 1–03, 1–26
working time, 1–03, 1–26
emanation of the state, 1–03, 1–26
equal pay,
development, 1–03, 6–54
scope of Art.141, 6–55
impact of EC membership, 1–07
implementation, 1–03
importance, 1–03
influence, 1–07

Fair reasons for dismissal,
See also Unfair dismissal
admissible evidence, 4–24
capability, 4–15, 4–27
conduct, 4–16, 4–28
reasonableness,
Polkey rules, 4–25—4–29
procedural issues, 4–25
substantive issues, 4–23
redundancy, 4–18, 4–31
retirement, 4–17, 4–21, 4–22
some other substantial reason (SOSR), 4–20
statutory enactment, contravention of, 4–19
Family leave,
unfair dismissal, 4–42
Fidelity,
implied terms of contract, 2–38, 2–40
Fixed term contracts,
discrimination, 6–36
frustration of contract, 3–06
termination of contract, 3–08
unfair dismissal, 4–04
Flexible working,
right to request, 6–64
Formation of contract of employment,
collective agreements,
See Collective agreements
exceptions, 1–29
general rule, 1–29
generally, 1–28
implied contracts, 1–30
intention, 1–29
negotiations, 1–29
Scotland, 1–29
special cases, 1–29
written contract, 1–30, 1–35

Formation of contract of employment— *cont.*
written statement of particulars of employment,
See Written statement of particulars of employment
Frustration of contract,
dismissal, 4–11
evidence, 4–11
examples, 4–11
factors relevant to, 3–05
fixed term contracts, 3–06
illegality, 3–06
meaning, 3–02
notice, 3–02
sickness, 4–11
termination of contract, 3–05

Gender re-assignment,
sex discrimination, 6–11, 6–12
Genuine occupational requirement,
age discrimination, 6–40
race discrimination, 6–17
religious discrimination, 6–22
sex discrimination, 6–04
sexual orientation discrimination, 6–18, 6–19
GPs,
See Grievance procedures (GPs)
Grievance procedures (GPs),
dispute resolution, 7–10
failure to complete, 7–10
introduction, 4–12
Modified Procedure, 7–10
requirements, 4–12
review, 7–11
Standard Procedure, 7–10
Gross misconduct,
dismissal and disciplinary procedures (DDPs), 4–12

Handbooks,
collective agreements, 1–43
Harassment,
age discrimination, 6–38
race discrimination, 6–15
sex discrimination, 6–09, 6–10
Health and safety,
Employment Tribunals, 7–02
pregnancy, 6–56
unfair dismissal, 4–40
Hearing,
Employment Tribunals, 7–07
Holidays,
annual leave entitlement, 2–20
Hours of work,
redundancy, 5–07
See Working time

Illegality,
frustration of contract, 3–06
Implied contracts,
formation of contract of employment, 1–30
Implied terms of contract,
careful performance, 2–37
categories, 2–32
confidential information, 2–40
examples, 2–31, 2–32
fidelity, 2–38, 2–40
generally, 2–31
hours of work, 2–34
obedience, 2–33
place of work, 2–34
safety, employer's duty of, 2–36
scope of contract, 2–35
trade secrets, 2–40
trust and confidence, 2–32
underlying obligation, 2–32
Industrial action,
redundancy, 5–10
unfair dismissal,
generally, 4–33
official, 4–35
protected, 4–34
unofficial, 4–36
Injury to feelings,
damages, 3–14
Insolvency,
directors, company, 1–24
redundancy, 5–15
Institutions of employment law,
Employment Tribunals,
See Employment Tribunals
generally, 7–01
Integration test,
meaning, 1–11
Intention,
formation of contract of employment, 1–29
Interim relief,
unfair dismissal, 4–51

Job evaluation studies,
equal pay, 6–47
Jury service,
unfair dismissal, 4–44

Law or fact, question of,
contract of employment, 1–20
Leave,
adoption, 6–61
annual,
terms and conditions of employment, 2–20
Working Time Regulations, 2–20
ante natal, 2–26
domestic incidents, 2–27, 4–42
emergency time off, 6–63

Leave—*cont.*
parental, 2–27, 4–42, 6–60, 6–63
paternity, 6–60
pregnancy, 2–26, 6–57, 6–58
Legal absentionism,
period of, 1–07
Legal aid,
Advice by Way of Representation (ABWOR), 7–03
Employment Tribunals, 1–05
Like work,
equal pay, 6–45, 6–46

Management,
employment law, 1–08
strategy, 1–08
Marital status,
sex discrimination, 6–03
Maternity rights,
See also **Pregnancy**
leave, 6–57, 6–58
pay, 6–59
Minimum wage,
calculations, 2–13
development rate, 2–13
dismissal, 2–14
enforcement, 2–14
introduction, 2–13
output work, 2–13
pay reference period, 2–13
piecework, 2–03
rate, 2–13
record keeping, 2–14
terms and conditions of employment, 2–01, 2–13.2.14
unmeasured work, 2–13
Mobile road transport workers,
Working Time Regulations, 2–15
Multiple and variable test,
meaning, 1–12
National Insurance fund,
redundancy payment out of, 5–15
National minimum wage,
See Minimum wage
Negotiations,
formation of contract of employment, 1–29
Night work,
Working Time Regulations, 2–18
Notice,
frustration of contract, 3–02
length, 3–01
minimum periods, 3–02
pay in lieu of, 2–10, 3–16
reasonable, 3–01
resignation, 3–01
statutory minimum periods, 3–02
termination of contract by, 3–01
verbal, 3–01
Notice—*cont.*
waiver of entitlement, 3–02
withdrawal, 3–01

Office holders,
contract of employment, 1–27
sex discrimination, 1–27
wrongful dismissal, 4–02
Offshore oil work,
Working Time Regulations, 2–15
Organisation test,
meaning, 1–11
Output work,
minimum wage, 2–13
Overseas employees,
unfair dismissal, 4–04

Parental leave,
domestic incidents, 2–27
emergency time off, 6–63
rights, 6–57, 6–62
Part-time workers,
discrimination, 6–33—6–35
less favourable treatment, 6–33, 6–34
sex discrimination, 6–33
Partnerships,
dissolution, 3–03
Paternity,
leave, 6–60
pay, 6–60
Pay,
See Wages
Pensions,
transfer of undertakings, 5–26
Performance of employment contract,
careful, 2–37
delegation, 1–15
termination of contract, 3–08
Personal service,
contract of employment, 1–15
Piecework,
minimum wage, 2–03
wages, 2–03
Place of work,
implied terms of contract, 2–34
terms and conditions of employment, 2–34, 2–35
Police,
unfair dismissal, 4–04
Working Time Regulations, 2–15
Positive discrimination,
disability discrimination, 6–23
meaning, 6–04
race discrimination, 6–17
religious discrimination, 6–22
sex discrimination, 6–17
Pre-hearing reviews,
Employment Tribunals, 7–07
Pregnancy,
See also Sex discrimination

Pregnancy—*cont.*
ante natal leave, 2–26
health and safety, 6–56
leave rights, 6–57, 6–58
maternity pay, 6–59
unfair dismissal, 4–42
Prison officers,
contract of employment, 1–27
***Pro hac vice*, employment,**
contract of employment, 1–21
Psychiatric injury,
damages, 3–14
Public employment,
contract of employment, 1–25
public law, regulation by, 1–25
Public interest disclosure,
unfair dismissal, 4–43
Public law,
public employment, regulation of, 1–25

Questionnaires,
discrimination, 6–31

Race discrimination,
See also Discrimination
background, 6–13
Commission for Racial Equality (CRE), 6–29
direct discrimination, 6–13
ethnic origins, 6–14
genuine occupational qualifications, 6–17
harassment, 6–15
indirect discrimination, 6–16
less favourable treatment, 6–13
positive discrimination, 6–17
Race Directive, 6–13
racial grounds, 6–14
Re-engagement,
redundancy, 5–09
transfer of undertakings, 5–25
unfair dismissal, 4–47
Reasonableness,
Polkey rules, 4–25—4–29
unfair dismissal, 4–23
Polkey rules, 4–25—4–29
procedural issues, 4–25
Receivership,
termination of contract, 3–04
Red-circling,
equal pay, 6–50
Redundancy,
age discrimination, 5–02
background to provisions, 5–01
bumping, 5–08
cessation of business, 5–05
claim for payment, 5–12
collective agreements, 1–40
continuous employment, 5–02
Redundancy—*cont.*
contractual approach, 5–05, 5–06
definition, 5–05
discrimination, 5–02
dismissal, 5–03
entitlement to payment, 5–02
example, 5–05
exclusions, 5–13
fair reasons for dismissal, 4–18, 4–31
general principles, 5–02
hours of work, 5–07
industrial action, 5–10
insolvency, 5–15
making claim, 5–12
maximum length of employment, 5–01
misconduct, 5–10
National Insurance fund, payment out of, 5–15
onus of proof, 5–11
payments,
calculation, 5–14
claim, 5–12
economic and social policy issues, 1–07
entitlement, 5–02
insolvency, 5–15
pay, as, 5–02
place of employment, 5–05
preservation of entitlement, 5–12
proof, 5–11
provisions relevant to, 5–01, 5–02
re-engagement, 5–09
renewal, 5–09
strikes, 5–10
time off work to find work, 2–25
unfair dismissal, 4–18, 4–31, 5–01
volunteers, 5–04
Reinstatement,
unfair dismissal, 4–47
Religious discrimination,
absence of belief, 6–20
agency workers, 1–18
another, religion of, 6–20
direct discrimination, 6–20
ethnic groups, 6–20
examples, 6–21
genuine occupational requirement, 6–22
indirect race discrimination, 6–20
philosophical beliefs, 6–20
positive discrimination, 6–22
provisions covering, 6–20
religion or belief, 6–20
spouses, 6–20
Remedies,
damages,
wrongful dismissal, 3–13, 3–14
equal pay, 6–53

Remedies—*cont.*
unfair dismissal,
compensation, 4–48—4–50
general rule, 4–46
re, engagement, 4–47
reinstatement, 4–47
wages, 2–04
Working Time Regulations, 2–21
wrongful dismissal, 3–11—3–15
Representation,
Employment Tribunals, 1–05
Reputation, loss of,
damages, 3–14
Rescission of contract,
communication, 3–07
termination of contract, 3–07
wages, 2–03, 3–07
Resignation,
genuine and intended, 4–10
notice, 3–01
Rest periods,
Working Time Regulations, 2–19
Restrictive covenants,
terms and conditions of employment, 2–41, 2–42
Retail workers,
wages, 2–07
Retirement,
age discrimination, 6–42
fair reasons for dismissal, 4–17, 4–21, 4–22
right to request to continue working beyond retirement date, 4–22
Review hearing,
Employment Tribunals, 7–07

Safety,
See also Health and Safety
employer's duty of, 2–36
Safety representatives,
time off rights, 2–29
Scotland,
dismissal,
pay in lieu of notice, 3–16
remedies, 3–12
Employment Tribunals, 1–05, 7–02, 7–03, 7–06
formation of contract of employment, 1–29
wages,
entitlement, 2–03
late payment, 2–04
written contract, 1–35
wrongful dismissal, 3–12
Seafarers,
Working Time Regulations, 2–15
Self-employment,
meaning, 1–10
Servants,
meaning, 1–09
Service personnel,
unfair dismissal, 4–04
Sex discrimination,
See also Discrimination
agency workers, 1–18
background, 6–02
"but for" test, 6–03
defence, 6–04, 6–06
detriment, 6–06
direct discrimination, 6–03
dress codes, 6–09
employment discrimination, 6–08—6–10
Equal Opportunities Commission (EOC), 6–29
gender re-assignment, 6–11, 6–12
genuine occupational requirement, 6–04, 6–19
harassment, sexual, 6–09, 6–10
indirect discrimination, 6–05
justification, 6–06
marital status, 6–03
motive of employer, 6–03
office holders, 1–27
part-time workers, 6–33
positive discrimination, 6–04
pregnancy, 6–02
transsexuals, 6–11, 6–12
victimisation, 6–07
Sexual orientiation discrimination,
See also Discrimination
agency workers, 1–18
Equal Treatment Directive, 6–18
genuine occupational requirement, 6–18
human rights, 6–18
meaning of sexual orientation, 6–18
statutory provisions, 6–18
Sickness,
frustration of contract, 4–11
Statutory Sick Pay, 2–05
wages, 2–05
Social policy,
collective agreements, 1–07
contract of employment, 1–07
EC membership, impact of, 1–07
legal abstentionism, 1–07
redundancy payments, 1–07
Some other substantial reason (SOSR),
fair reasons for dismissal, 4–20
Sources of law,
common law, 1–02
generally, 1–01
statute, 1–02
SSP (Statutory Sick Pay),
wages, 2–05
Statute,
sources of law, 1–02
Statutory Sick Pay (SSP),
wages, 2–05

Strikes,
redundancy, 5–10
Study and training,
time off rights, 2–30
Summary dismissal,
meaning, 4–02
Suspension,
dismissal, alternative to, 4–01

Teachers,
Working Time Regulations, 2–16
Termination of contract,
administration orders, 3–04
agreement, 3–09
fixed term contracts, 3–08
frustration of contract, 3–05
notice,
See Notice
partnership dissolution, 3–03
performance, 3–08
receivership, 3–04
rescission of contract, 3–07
resignation, 3–01
winding up, 3–04
wrongful dismissal,
meaning, 3–10, 3–11
remedies, 3–10—3–13
Scotland, 3–12
Terms and conditions of employment,
annual leave, 2–20
careful performance by employee, 2–37
competition, 2–39
confidential information, 2–40
contra proferentum rule, 2–02
contract or statute, 2–01
equal pay, 2–01
express terms, 2–02
fidelity, 2–38, 2–40
hours of work,
See Working time
implied terms,
See Implied terms of contract
interpretation, 2–02
minimum statutory rights, 2–01
minimum wage, 2–01, 2–13.2.14
parental leave, 2–27
place of work, 2–34, 2–35
restrictive covenants, 2–41, 2–42
safety, employer's duty of, 2–36
Scotland,
wages, 2–03
source, 2–01
time off rights,
domestic incidents, 2–27
employee representatives, 2–28
finding work upon redundancy, 2–25
parental leave, 2–27
provision, 2–22
Terms and conditions of employment— *cont.*
time off rights—*cont.*
safety representatives, 2–29
study and training, 2–30
trade union duties and activities, 2–23
trade secrets, 2–40
wages,
See Wages
Time limits,
Employment Tribunal, claim to, 1–05
equal pay, 6–51
finding work upon redundancy, 2–25
public duties, 2–24
trade union duties and activities, 2–23
written statement of particulars of employment, 1–32
Time off rights,
ante natal leave, 2–26
employee representatives, 2–28
finding work upon redundancy, 2–25
provision, 2–22
safety representatives, 2–29
study and training, 2–30
trade union duties and activities, 2–23
Trade Boards,
introduction, 2–01
Trade secrets,
competition, 2–40
Trade unions,
agency, 1–44
collective agreements,
See Collective agreements
membership,
collective agreements, 1–41
unfair dismissal, 4–37—4–39
subscriptions, 2–08, 2–12
time off rights, 2–23
Transfer of undertakings,
Acquired Rights Directive, 1–04, 5–16
background, 5–16
changing terms of employment, 5–24
defence, 5021
dismissal and re-engagement, 5–25
economic, technical or organisational reasons, 5–21
effect of Regulations, 5–20
pensions, 5–26
re-engagement, 5–25
relevant transfer, 5–17
transfer, 5–19
undertakings, 5–18
unfair dismissal, 5–22, 5–23
Transsexuals,
sex discrimination, 6–11, 6–12

Tribunals,
See Employment Tribunals
Truck shops,
meaning, 2–06
Trust and confidence,
implied terms of contract, 2–32

Unfair dismissal,
ACAS Code of Practice on Disciplinary and Grievance Procedures, 4–02
admissible evidence, 4–24
age limit, 4–03
appeals, 4–30
armed forces, 4–04
asserting statutory right, 4–41
automatically unfair dismissal,
dismissal and disciplinary procedures (DDPs) , failure to use, 4–12
pregnancy, 4–42
redundancy, 4–31
trade unions, 4–37—4–39
capability, 4–15, 4–27
civil servants, 4–04
compensation,
basic award, 4–49
compensatory award, 4–50
elements, 4–48
conditions for protection, 4–03
conduct, 4–16, 4–28
continuous employment, 4–03, 4–05
contracting out, 4–04
Crown employees, 4–04
dismissal,
constructive dismissal, 4–09
frustration, 4–11
limited term contract expiry without renewal, 4–08
meaning, 4–06—4–11
operation of law, 4–11
termination of contract by employer, 4–07
dismissal and disciplinary procedures (DDPs),
appeals, 4–30
collective dismissals, 4–13
exceptions, 4–13
failure to use, 4–12
gross misconduct, 4–12
introduction, 4–12
requirement, 4–12
fair reasons,
admissible evidence, 4–24
capability, 4–15, 4–27
conduct, 4–16, 4–28
Polkey rules, 4–25—4–29
reasonableness, 4–23, 4–25
redundancy, 4–18, 4–31
retirement, 4–17, 4–21, 4–22

Unfair dismissal—*cont.*
fair reasons—*cont.*
some other substantial reason (SOSR), 4–20
statutory enactment, contravention of, 4–19
family leave, 4–42
fixed term contracts, 4–04
grievance procedures (GPs),
introduction, 4–12
requirements, 4–12
gross misconduct,
dismissal and disciplinary procedures (DDPs), 4–12
health and safety, 4–40
industrial action,
generally, 4–33
official, 4–35
protected, 4–34
unofficial, 4–36
interim relief, 4–51
jury service, 4–44
meaning, 4–02
motive, 4–02
overseas employees, 4–04
parental leave, 4–42
persons protected, 4–03
police, 4–04
pregnancy, 4–42
public interest disclosure, 4–43
qualifying conditions, 4–03
re-engagement, 4–47
reason for dismissal,
admissible evidence, 4–24
capability, 4–15, 4–27
conduct, 4–16, 4–28
fair reasons, 4–15—4–20
See also **Fair reasons for dismissal**
Polkey rules, 4–25—4–29
reasonableness, 4–23, 4–25
redundancy, 4–18, 4–31
requirement to show, 4–14
retirement, 4–17, 4–21
statutory enactment, contravention of, 4–19
reasonableness,
Polkey rules, 4–25—4–29
procedural issues, 4–25
substantive issues, 4–23
redundancy, 4–18, 4–31, 5–01
reinstatement, 4–47
remedies,
basic award, 4–49
compensation, 4–48—4–50
compensatory award, 4–540
general rule, 4–46
re-engagement, 4–47
reinstatement, 4–47
retirement, 4–17, 4–21, 4–22
service personnel, 4–04

Unfair dismissal—*cont.*
some other substantial reason (SOSR), 4–20
special cases, 4–45
statutory enactment, contravention of, 4–19
statutory provisions, 4–02
trade union,
activities, 4–37, 4–38
membership, 4–37, 4–38
recognition, 4–39
transfer of undertakings, 5–22, 5–23
whistle-blowing, 4–43
wrongful dismissal distinguished, 4–02
Unmeasured work,
minimum wage, 2–13

Vicarious liability,
discrimination, 6–32
Victimisation,
sex discrimination, 6–07
Vocational training,
age discrimination, 6–39

Wages,
agreed deductions, 2–08
calculations, 2–12
customary payment, 2–03
deductions, 2–01, 2–06, 2–07—2–09, 2–11, 2–12
definition, 2–09
disciplinary proceedings, 2–08
entitlement, 2–03
equal pay,
See Equal pay
express terms of contract, 2–03
failure to pay, 2–04
itemised pay statement, 2–12
late payment, 2–04
method of payment, 2–06
minimum, 2–01, 2–13, 2–14
national minimum, 2–01, 2–13, 2–14
non-payment, 2–04
notice , pay in lieu of, 2–10
overpayment, 2–08
payment, 2–06, 2–07
piecework, 2–03
recovery of unlawful deductions from, 2–11
remedies, 2–04
repudiation of contract, 2–04
rescission of contract, 2–03, 3–07
retail workers, 2–07
Scotland,
entitlement, 2–03
late payment, 2–04
sickness, 2–05
statutory regulation, 2–03
Statutory Sick Pay, 2–05

Wages—*cont.*
terms and conditions of employment, 2–03
trade union subscriptions, 2–08, 2–12
unlawful deductions, 2–03
Wages Councils,
introduction, 2–01
Warnings,
dismissal, alternative to, 4–01
Whistle-blowing,
unfair dismissal, 4–43
Winding up,
termination of contract, 3–04
Worker,
agency, 1–17, 1–18
business on own account, 1–10
definition, 1–10, 1–17
dominant purpose of contract test, 1–10
Working Time Regulations, 1–17
Working time,
care workers, 2–16
directives, 1–03, 1–26
doctors, 2–15, 2–16
Regulations,
See Working Time Regulations
teachers, 2–16
Working Time Regulations,
agency workers, 1–18
annual leave, 2–20
armed services, 2–15
average working time, 2–17
doctors, 2–15, 2–16
enforcement, 2–21
exclusions, 2–15
extending, 2–15
maximum working week, 2–17
meaning, 2–16
mobile road transport workers, 2–15
modifications, 2–15
night work, 2–18
offshore oil work, 2–15
police, 2–15
provisions, 2–15
reduced protection, 2–15
remedies, 2–21
rest periods, 2–19
scope, 2–15
seafarers, 2–15
teachers, 2–16
time off rights,
provision, 2–22
worker, 1–17
Written contract,
evidential use, 1–35
formation of contract of employment, 1–30
legal status, 1–35
Scotland, 1–35

Written statement of particulars of employment,
alternatives, 1–32
changes to terms of contract, 1–32
content, 1–32
Employment Tribunals, 7–09
evidential use, 1–34
formation of contract of employment, 1–31
instalments, 1–32
legal status, 1–34
remedy, employee's, 1–33
status, 1–34

Written statement of particulars of employment—*cont.*
terms of statement, 1–32
time limit, 1–32

Wrongful dismissal,
damages, 3–13—3–15
jurisdiction, 4–02
meaning, 3–10, 3–11, 4–02
office holders, 4–02
pay in lieu of notice, 3–16
remedies, 3–11—3–14
Scotland, 3–12